D0025329

teful acknowledgment is made to the copyright
nade part of this copyright page.

n Data

/ by Hans Ostrom, Wendy Bishop [and]

and index.

roblems, exercises, etc. 2. Creative writing—Problems,
Haake, Katharine. III. Title.

99-086070

esley Educational Publishers Inc.

p://www.awl.com

S—03 02

Chief: Jo
ociate Editor: Liza K
Marketing Manager: Melanie
Production Manager: Denise Phillip
Project Coordination, Text Design, and Ele
Cover Design Manager: John Callahan
Cover Designer: Kay Petronio
Cover Image: Dene Croft, *Meeting the Train*, Cour
Senior Manufacturing Buyer: Dennis J. Para
Printer and Binder: Courier Corp.
Cover Printer: Phoenix Color Corp.

For permission to use copyrighted material, gra
holders on pages 428–429, which are hereby

Library of Congress Cataloging-in-Publicatio

Ostrom, Hans A.
    Metro : journeys in writing creatively
Katharine Haake.
    p. cm.
    Includes bibliographical references
    ISBN 0-321-01132-5
    1. English language—Rhetoric—
exercises, etc. I. Bishop, Wendy. II.
    PE1413.O78 2000
    808'.042—dc21

Copyright © 2001 by Addison-W

Please visit our website at ht

ISBN 0-321-01132-5

3 4 5 6 7 8 9 10—CR

New York San F
London Toronto Sydney T
Mexico City Munich Paris Cape

Contents

Chapter Three
RIDING THE ORANGE LINE—DEVELOPMENT AND IMPROVISATION 118

Chapter Four
RIDING THE RED LINE—REVISION AND EDITING   165

PART II
MINI-ANTHOLOGY 279

Alternate Contents
By Genre

Note: Some of the exercises listed under each category explicitly concern the genre in question. Others do not but may be easily adapted to help produce work in that genre.

Poetry

RIDING THE ORANGE LINE—DEVELOPMENT AND IMPROVISATION   118

RIDING THE RED LINE—REVISION AND EDITING   165

UNION STATION—ALTERNATIVE GUIDED-WRITING SCENARIOS   194

Fiction

RIDING THE RED LINE—REVISION AND EDITING   165

UNION STATION—ALTERNATIVE GUIDED-WRITING SCENARIOS   194

Essay, Creative Nonfiction, Autobiography, Journal

Drama

Alternative Forms, Experimental Modes, Mixed Genres

Introduction
With Mainly Teachers in Mind

Colleagues:

Metro: Journeys in Writing Creatively has at least three characteristics that, in the way they are combined, distinguish it from other textbooks. It is a multi-genre book. It is a book composed chiefly of writing exercises that have been "class-tested"—that spring from our collective teaching experiences. And, conceptually, the book is based on the notion that "guided" or "directed" writing is one effective, reliable, and flexible way to teach writing.

Multi-genre: Although *Metro*'s first level of organization is not by genre, for reasons we shall explain in a moment, the book features exercises applicable to work in poetry, fiction (especially short fiction), drama, and what's come to be known widely as "creative nonfiction." The alternate table of contents (organized by genre), the headings of exercises, and often the opening paragraph of exercises identify genres for which each exercise is appropriate. *Metro*, then, may be used either in classes that focus on one genre or in ones that cover several genres.

Class-tested writing exercises: For many years and in different undergraduate and graduate programs, each of us has had students explore elements *of* writing *by* writing, and nationwide this inductive approach is widespread, grounded in contemporary pedagogy and composition theory but also connected in spirit to the notion of imitation, which dates back at least to Quintillian's educational program. We have used *Metro*'s exercises in our courses, refining and revising them based on such field testing. Sometimes we have adapted exercises other teachers or writers have used, in which case we do our best to identify the original source of the idea. Just as we believe that students often learn about writing best by means of writing, we also believe teachers learn best not just from experience in general but also from experimenting with very particular classroom practices. You might say *Metro* collects such particular, tested practices but presents them so as to invite further experimentation, to incite improvisation.

Guided or directed writing: Although each exercise has evolved as it has been used in courses and revised for the book, the whole of *Metro* springs from a general rationale underlying the use of directed writing, for which precise guidelines, options, and/or purposes are established beforehand. Whereas many textbooks provide a chapter-length discussion of an element—*plot*, let's say—and may or may not include at chapter's end specific ideas for writing or revision, *Metro*'s approach is to ground all discussion in a specific idea for writing or revision; the writer then approaches an element, a term, a concept, a convention, or a genre characteristic through the avenue of writing. The avenue becomes as crucial as the destination, hence the emphasis on "writing creatively," a subtle shift from "creative writing" but one that stresses the pleasure and discipline of the process.

As noted, we are hardly alone in seeing directed writing as one useful approach to instruction, but we do not see it as excluding a more deductive one. Indeed, one may easily use guided writing in conjunction with other teaching methods, traditional or otherwise. Our view is not "either/or" but "both/and."

Unique organization: This inductive approach influenced the way we organized the book. We structured *Metro* not according to isolated techniques (such as rhyming or character development, to name but two) but to broad areas of **the writing process,** *within* which questions of form and technique often arise. The broad areas are as follows: **reading,** as an inevitable context of writing, a source of inspiration, and a trigger of improvisation; **invention,** or ways of "getting started" that are not necessarily linked to reading; **development,** or working with and improvising upon drafts; **revision** and **editing,** or more focused, structured, precise ways of revisiting texts; overt **experimentation**—including multimedia work; and finally manipulating **grammar, usage, and style,** or homing in on linguistic particulars.

We recognize that although these categories of the writing process are fairly orthodox, **the** writing process is a Platonic ideal, and therefore any mode of categorizing cannot always avoid seeming arbitrary. As with most aspects of *Metro,* however, the **chapter-divisions** and placement of exercises within chapters can be traced back to our teaching. Virtually all textbooks use reading inasmuch as they refer to specific texts, allude more implicitly to traditions of literature or criticism, and point to more-or-less canonized texts and authors as models. **Chapter One** by no means abandons these uses of reading, but it also takes a different tack insofar as it uses texts and the process itself of reading to generate specific writing tasks. Moreover, it acknowledges that students have been reading (and absorbing language and narrative art) for quite some time already. And in many instances, it makes use of "reading" in the broader sense of interpreting not just texts but language in general and experiences. Exercises in this chapter fuse students' reading and writing more explicitly and inject more improvisation into imitation than may be the case in other textbooks.

With regard to **Chapters Two** (invention) and **Three** (development), here's our approach: Essentially, we have used **"invention"** exercises in our own classes when students are starting from scratch, are truly just beginning to move toward a story, poem, or nonfiction piece—or maybe even don't know yet what genre toward which they're gravitating. In this sense Chapter Two continues the work of Chapter One but with less emphasis on literal and figurative uses of reading. Indeed we assume many teachers using the book might choose to reverse the order of these chapters or draw on them simultaneously; as noted, we invite such improvisation. The invention chapter is the largest one in the book because students seem especially to respond well to variety where invention is concerned.

In our own teaching, we've used **"development"** exercises (Chapter Three) when students have substantial drafts underway. A given exercise in Chapters One or Two may indeed seem closely related to exercises in Chapter Three; nonetheless, *"no draft yet"* vs. *"assume* some *kind of draft exists"* is the classroom-based way we contrast invention with development.

Chapter Four moves beyond general admonitions, strategies, and practices concerning revising and editing; it provides particular tasks, kinds of which are not found often in other textbooks, many of which deliberately move beyond mainstream notions of "revising for clarity," for example. Teachers tend to mark students' writing assertively, even aggressively, but they tend to be less assertive about providing tactics and tasks of **revision** and **editing** that might come into play *before* the student turns in a poem or a story. And especially with regard to revision and editing, teachers are more accustomed to telling students what *not* to do or what to avoid ("avoid the passive voice") than what *to* do or what to explore. In general, teachers are more likely to come up with ideas about invention and development than with ones about late-process elements. So in Chapter Four we've included some unusual revising and editing exercises that turn students into more adventurous (re)writers and that give them a range of ways to use the criticism they receive in workshops and other classroom settings.

A spirit of adventurousness also informs **Chapter Five**, which includes exercises drawing students toward overtly experimental kinds of writing, toward combinations of media, toward new models of authorship, audience, publication, and genre.

Chapter Six is unusual because it includes exercises based on those elements of writing that, certainly at first glance, seem most resistant to the notion of guided writing—grammar, punctuation, style, and precision. One premise here is that writers can, do, and should bring as much inventiveness, imagination, and improvisation to such allegedly "basic" areas of writing as they bring to generating ideas for stories or drafting a poem.

Mini-anthology: Part II of this book is a brief **anthology**, the main purpose of which is to gather texts to which we refer in some of the exercises; another purpose is to have at least a handful of texts available between the covers of *Metro*, even if, as we fully expect, students will encounter a significant amount of other assigned reading in a given course. The main goal of Part II, as an anthology, is modest but focused and practical: to provide some concrete points of reference.

Briefly, a few other matters: Following the main table of contents is an **alternate table of contents**, organized according to the following genre-categories: poetry; fiction; essay, autobiography, creative nonfiction, and journal; drama; and alternative forms, experimental modes, and mixed genres. After each category heading, we list the chapters in order but identify only those exercises in each chapter that pertain to the genre in question. Many exercises work well with two or more genres, in which case they appear in multiple categories. In addition, each exercise has a **boxed summary** that identifies genres being targeted, ideas and concepts explored, and a list of authors and works mentioned.

A listing of **"Ideas and Concepts to Explore"** in each boxed summary lets you know what specific issues the exercise will address or at least raise, thereby allowing you to select some for emphasis, link them to ongoing discussions, bring in related material you've found to be successful, and so on. Here is an example of a boxed summary:

Writing from Expertise, Not Just from Experience

Use to Write:	Reportage; Short Fiction; Longer Fiction; Poetry; Autobiography; Creative Nonfiction; Essay; Journal
Ideas and Concepts to Explore:	expertise; specialized language; "unpoetic" and "unliterary."
Authors/Works Mentioned:	Amiri Baraka; Frederick Busch, *Closing Arguments;* Emily Dickinson; Ernest Hemingway; Herman Melville; V. S. Pritichett, "The Camberwell Beauty" and *Collected Stories;* John Steinbeck.

A **glossary** at the back of the book defines literary, critical, and creative terms used throughout *Metro*.

When an exercise depends upon another text, we have reprinted a significant excerpt or the whole text, either in the exercise itself or in the anthology (Part II). In some exercises we briefly discuss our own educations and writing and—in rare instances—even our own poems, stories, or essays. In both textbooks and class-rooms, such self-reference must occur rarely, but it's appropriate if it keeps teachers and textbook writers honest or helps frame a particular point.

The structure of *Metro* and the format of exercises, refined through revisions in response to numerous manuscript reviews, are—obviously—intended to be useful, sensible. Aiming for usefulness in this case, however, for us meant composing a book that could be easily dismantled, that could be deployed in a true variety of classrooms, and that could contribute to a course taught by a first-year graduate instructor as well as one taught by a seasoned, crafty teacher.

Indeed, the sheer number of exercises—and options within exercises—is not supposed to look like the route of a forced march. They are supposed to resemble a storehouse, a compendium, a smorgasbord—or whatever synonymous expression you'd prefer. Quantity in this case should be interpreted as an invitation—to mix and match exercises, to sample, to experiment, to supplement methods and material that have served you well. Most of the exercises in *Metro* invite students to improvise, and one basic purpose of the book is to invite teachers to improvise as well.

Three lives of learning, teaching, and writing are no doubt better than one, meaning we believe the collaboration has drawn strength from diversity and reflected the reality that all writing comes out of one kind of community or another. And speaking of community, we hope a certain professional empathy with you, the other workers in our field, comes through clearly. Circumstances make you invisible to us at the moment, but that hasn't stopped us from trying to envisage you as we worked on *Metro*.

Acknowledgments: Also invisible to us were numerous colleagues who read and commented on several drafts of the book: Alan Ainsworth, Houston Community College, Central College; Robin Becker, Pennsylvania State University; Patrick Bizzaro, East Carolina University; Jennifer Brantley, University of Wisconsin—River Falls; Scott Cairns, Old Dominion University; François Camoin, University of Utah; Michelle Carter, San Francisco State University; James Cervantes, Mesa Community College; Julie Checkoway, University of Georgia; Marvin Diogenes, University of Arizona; Faulkner Fox, University of Texas—Austin; John Gallaher, Ohio University; Paul K. Haeder, University of Texas—El Paso; Michael Heffernan, University of Arkansas; Jack Hicks, University of California—Davis; Nancy McLelland, Mendocino College; Anna Monardo, University of Nebraska—Omaha; Stephanie Mood, Grossmont College; Hilda Raz, University of Nebraska—Lincoln; and Sue Standing, Wheaton College. We thank them for their time, ideas, thoroughness, and honesty. More visible were the steadfast, patient editors at Longman: Lisa Moore, who knew the book when it was merely an idea; Lynn Huddon, who worked on early drafts; Natalie Hart, Ruth Halikman, and Liza Rudneva, whose fresh eyes and refreshing ideas helped this particular *Metro* run much more smoothly than before; and Laura McKenna. Thanks to Jim Moore and Sandra Alcosser for ideas in the first exercise of Chapter Two. We also gratefully acknowledge the work of Pat McCutcheon and C. R. Batten in helping to prepare the manuscript for printing.

Morgan Bishop, Bill Haltom, Nancy Krusoe, Holly Jones, Rod Moore, Dean Newman, Jacquelyn Bacon Ostrom, Spencer Ostrom, Jeff, Sam, and Joey Tanzer, and Tait Pollard deserve warm thanks for their ideas, good conversation, and sustaining wit.

Hans Ostrom, *Tacoma, Washington*
Wendy Bishop, *Tallahassee, Florida*
Katharine Haake, *Northridge, California*

Introduction
With Mainly Students in Mind

1. What Is *Metro*?

Metro is a collection of short, informal pieces with different specific purposes but one general one: to get you writing, productively and pleasurably. Every piece invites you to write—to write something specific, and to write it now.

If you would learn to write, write—that's *Metro*'s method in a nutshell. But also: Write beyond your comfort zone; stretch; experiment; improvise; play seriously— think of a jazz musician—with language and literary forms. *Metro* is designed to help with this latter part, too.

There are other ways to learn to write. Just talking about writing with other writers helps a lot, sometimes. Reading—systematically, indiscriminately, carefully, impulsively—is a vast resource, naturally. So is having one's writing scrutinized by generous but straightforward, critical but fair readers. *Metro* is only one of many resources on which you'll draw, but because it's based on your writing (on you, writing), it's different from many other textbooks.

Metro, therefore, is a book of "exercises." Some are linked specifically to a *genre*—such as *poetry* or *the short story*. Others are more versatile or wide open. Some conclude by giving you one or two options of something to write. Others conclude by giving you dozens from which to choose. Sometimes we use other terms in place of "exercise," such as *trigger*, *prompt*, or *freewrite*, mainly to relieve monotony but also because they bring shadings of meaning with them.

Our intent in all the exercises is about as far away from the notion of "busy work" as we can make it. The pieces in *Metro* make demands of you, offer possibilities, create "spaces" in which to improvise, explore, experiment. True, you will find lots of terminology in the book, references to other authors and works, some theoretical concepts, some advice, but in the end the intent of the exercises can be expressed in just two words: "Try this."

We might toss out a premise, present you with a challenge, have you try on a technique for size (or remodel one to your liking), have you look at one of your drafts from a surprising angle, define a form in which you might write. As we do these things, and others, we're mainly giving you some boundaries of one sort or another; you bring the ideas into this loosely demarcated space, and if your ideas redefine or even wreck the boundaries, think of us as celebrating with you if you're creating something powerful, authentic, satisfying. . . .

All writers are inevitably connected to other people, other writers, other readers; to histories and cultures. Nobody truly writes alone. Still, you might legitimately ask, "Why would I need 'exercises' to get me writing?" You don't need them, necessarily. But being given a premise, a challenge, a variation, or a new direction is not necessarily unhelpful, either, nor does it mean you've relinquished creativity or given up control over what you write. These exercises are one more stimulus for *your* writing.

2. *"Metro" the Metaphor*

The act of writing is often full of contradictions; sometimes it's even paradoxical; even on good days it can be mysterious. Using the metaphor of a metro or subway system as an organizing factor for the book reflects some of these qualities. At first glance, what could be simpler than riding the metro? If you haven't ridden one yourself, think of books you've read or films you've seen with subways represented in them. You pay a fare, the train comes up and stops, you get on, you ride, you get off at one of the stops. A similar simplicity can apply to writing. You've been writing since you were five or six, speaking complex sentences since you were about two. From grocery lists to postcards, messages to job applications, e-mail to history papers, you write frequently, speak language constantly. So what's the big deal? That's a useful rhetorical question to keep handy because it will help you remember that you can, in fact, write.

But. But there can be something bewildering, alienating, even frightening about a metro system—potentially, at the very least. After all, those books and movies usually have bad things happen in the subway. Similarly, there can be something difficult, frustrating, unmanageable, slippery, even frightening about writing. So "metro" expresses the strange tension between the straightforward, pleasant side of writing and the difficult, bewildering side.

The metro metaphor works in another way: You can think of writing as a kind of transportation. It transports the past to the present—in such forms as autobiography and creative nonfiction. It transports far-flung images toward a coherent poem. It hauls in impressions, opinions, intuitive notions of "story," the childhood notion of "pretend," adult concerns with love, money, desire, power, right, wrong, etc., and brings them together into something we call a narrative, a "fiction." So for us, and we hope for you, this book is a Writer's Transit Authority.

The notion of going underground contains another relevant connection between writing and the metro. Part of the danger sometimes associated with metro systems is literal: a person can get mugged. But another part of it is purely associative; we associate "underground" with the unknown, the mysterious. With writing, a lot of the digging-in is straightforward: recording what you see and hear, assembling sentences and paragraphs in a way that works, mining your memory. But some of the underground work in writing is far less predictable. As you write, the writing takes an unexpected turn, *appears* at least to shape itself. Or you'll stop writing, go to a job, take a nap, see some friends—and suddenly a problem with a poem or a story seems to have solved itself; out of nowhere comes a good idea, as if your subconscious mind had been working on the piece of writing all along and gradually brought the results from underground to the surface.

And finally, just as no one truly masters travel, nobody ever stops learning how to write or overpowers all the difficulties writing can throw at us. After all, oft-published, much-rewarded, very famous novelists have been known just to get flat-out stuck—stuck like a beginner.

Metro springs from the experiences of students who probably aren't so different from you. It springs from specific courses and particular class sessions. It's grounded in real lives, real writing—in real and therefore really imperfect circumstances. We think it's a book that will work for you because it's based on material that's worked for students and us. That's what *Metro* is.

Hans Ostrom
Wendy Bishop
Katharine Haake

Prologue
Concerning Writing Exercises
and Ways to Approach Them

Confession: I cannot remember ever having seen a writing exercise until I started inventing them for class. Partly this is a function of when I (and Wendy and Hans) went to school because to some degree writing instruction went through a revolutionary period just as we were finishing our undergraduate work. At any rate, I do remember being told at some point or another to "write a character sketch" or "describe a setting." And I rolled a little camera through my head and started beating my brains out for just the right words to describe the scene I was seeing. This is what I call "writing backwards," and because I don't think it is very good for writing, when I started teaching, like many writing teachers, I preferred to set my students loose with a blank page, ever curious to see what they could to.

But the true thing is, my own son, from the age of five, turned stricken-faced and panicky when confronted with the blank page, and I understood this. Because while a blank page can sometimes be a generous invitation, it can just as often be a burden. You know what I mean. You've been there yourself. You stare at the blank page and you want to weep. Then, when you are done weeping, you do what you already know how to do. You fill up the space with the comforting sounds of what is already familiar.

I like to tell students writing a story is a lot like solving a math problem. You know the parameters of the equation, but you have to figure where, exactly, to go with them, and how, and why. And when the math gets really hard, the logic gets pretty intuitive; you keep trying things out until, finally, they fall into place, but it's never exactly what you thought when you began.

For me, teaching is a lot the same, and I suspect that the whole idea of guided writing came to me as an unexpected way to open up for students some new writing spaces. When I started using guided writing, I made up the exercises, more or less, as I went along, sometimes alone, and sometimes in collaboration with other teachers/writers. *Metro* brings together some of what we all made up, and it is a kind of invitation to join in the conversation.

My own process in developing an exercise is to work backwards from a writing problem that engages me. Maybe I wonder what would happen if I were to reverse things in a story, maybe just some things, maybe everything. Maybe I wonder what a story would look like where the main story is the unwritten story between two parallel stories. Maybe I'm curious about how to push the envelope of the sentence, or experiment with nonlinear form, or just get started on a blank-minded day. So I write an exercise to see.

Alternatively, I'll work from a theory or another writer's observation. My dissertation advisor, François Camoin, used to insist that if you want to build a funhouse, a set of blueprints will prove more useful than what we think a funhouse is supposed to be like. Structuralist theory can provide a kind of blueprint for writing, as long as we read it like writers. So I may take a concept like focalization, or temporality, and wonder how to turn it into a writing problem.

This is not magic, or some complex rubric, or a trick. It is a little bit like thinking from the outside of your writing toward its inside—and discovering in the process not just what "makes it tick," as the cliche goes, but also what makes your writing compelling to you.

If I am going to ask students what interests them in their writing (and I always do), I ought to be able to answer the question myself. Both the questions and the answers provide the basic material for guided writing. But because what interests us is fluid and will change, not just slowly over time, but from moment to moment, we must learn to be flexible as well with what we've written, to add to, to change, to move on.

My colleague, Jan Ramjerdi, tells me that in Paris, in the fifties, a group of artists and writers known as the Situationalists developed an art form they called a *Des Rives*. Jan says it means "a wandering," but for the longest time I also had it mixed up with my high school French and the concept of dreaming—*des reves*. Change the "a" to an "o" and you also get "a wondering." The original idea was literally to wander around Paris, stopping wherever the feeling might strike the wandering artists, to write or to draw or to record observations. It was a form of "mapping" the city, as it had never before been mapped, impressionistic and revealing, maybe not of how to use the metro, but of what it is like above the surface when you are underground.

I like to think of writing exercises as being a little like that. You map the way your own writing might have seemed to unfold, and then you let your students in on that.

An exercise can be elaborate, or it can be as simple as the following: write yourself into the blank space of this text, translate a story you've written, replace each word in a model story with its opposite, write something in a borrowed discourse or a stolen language, design a system for randomly generating words and weave them into a story, experiment with gaps and disruptions, cross genres, collaborate, make a hybrid text fusing creative and critical discourse, imagine a new scene of writing, and so on. It can be spontaneous, or carefully developed. For the most part, a good exercise will not only direct a student in a process but also describe the theory that informs the directions, where it comes from and why students are being asked to explore it. The goal for me is not just to lead student writers into new experiences in language and form, but also to train them to invent other guided writings with which they can further explore their own strongest interests in writing, moving ever forward to the next set of problems and questions.

"No surprise for the writer," Robert Frost says,"—no surprise for the reader."

So much about teaching is about providing the material and space in which students can learn to surprise themselves, and then moving aside. The pay-off, as you step away, is that you get to be part of the process as well, and you never can know ahead of time exactly what is going to happen. So much about learning is about being willing to surprise yourself.

The other guiding principle of any exercise I write is that it should be fun, provocative and, in its own way, demanding. Writing is hard enough work as it is. We ought not to add to the burden of the blank page. At least we should find pleasurable ways in which to work with existing burdens. "Fun," that is, need not mean "effortless," just as "demanding" need not mean "painful" or "dull."

And anyway, isn't writing, finally a little bit about dreaming, a little bit about wandering, and a little bit about wonder? *Metro* maps a little of all three. Where you go with it is up to you.

Katharine Haake

PART
I

Writing
Prompts
and Activities

Riding the Blue Line

Reading

Getting Started

1 ▸ **Of Reading**

Use to Write:	Short Fiction; Poetry; Journal; Essay; Autobiography
Ideas and Concepts to Explore:	reading—memories of; —political significance of; —stereotypes connected with.
Authors/Works Mentioned:	Hans Ostrom, "Of Reading"; Richard Wright, "Library Card," from *Black Boy;* World Wide Web.

Unlike writing, reading leaves few visible traces. The following sequences are designed to make the invisible visible, to help you remember how reading aids your writing. To start, read the poem, "Of Reading," by Hans Ostrom, in the anthology.

A. Respond to the poem in a short, general "freewrite".

B. Respond by writing your memory of each member of your family: What did they/do they read, when, why, how, and so on?

C. Write about your relationships to words, sentences, books, tales, computer screens, electronic mail, letters, articles, etc.

D. Write some of your beliefs about reading by using metaphors or statements of belief. Example: "For me, reading is like . . ." or "I believe that books . . . ."

E. Review what you've written in response to A through D. Continue a piece already begun or start another piece—poem, essay, story, or something else.

To come at the writing from slightly different angles, read and then respond to Richard Wright's essay, "The Library Card." This work may take you in different directions because it may prompt you to ask more questions, such as . . .

- Who is encouraged to read in our culture? Who is kept from reading?
- What is your relationship to books, poetry, authors? What stereotypes, beliefs, and understandings do you have about different genres of writing? Have you been trained to think of "genre" fiction (mystery, romance, science fiction) as of equal or of less value than "literary" forms, such as poetry and "mainstream" novels?
- Do you believe in clichés about librarians? Are they all women? Are all readers nerds? Do you go to libraries willingly, eagerly, or with great reluctance? What is the future of the book as artifact, object? What is the future of libraries?
- How has on-line information-access changed your attitudes about and relationships to reading and libraries? How would living in the age of the World Wide Web change Richard Wright's story—if at all?

(W.B.)

2 ▸ **Fitting Yourself into the Conversation of Writing You Love**

Use to Write:	n/a [the exercise may lead to work in virtually any genre]
Ideas and Concepts to Explore:	formal dimension; hypercriticism; motives for writing; resonance.
Authors/Works Mentioned:	n/a

Do you remember when you started writing? Do you remember why or how, or once you started, why you kept at it? Maybe, like us, you can remember learning to read, but memories of writing somehow pale by comparison.

And anyway, most of us start out thinking we write the way we do because it's somehow "natural," but the more we think so, the more "unnatural" our writing starts to sound. In part this is because we neglect to ask ourselves broad questions about writing in the first place: Why do we do it? What guides us through it? How would we have it judged, and by whom? Where and how do we want it to move through the world?

These are important questions, for they can frame our writing beyond the plain desire that it be "good." Think of a shelf in the library or a bookstore. An award-winning juvenile mystery misplaced among adult thrillers will not seem so successful in its unintended context. If you want to write popular science fiction you ought not to feel discouraged by the hypercriticism of more literary types (and vice versa). When we start out writing, we assume the standards by which our work is judged will lie outside ourselves—in our teachers, our workshops, our readers, those library shelves. On occasion, it is useful to look inward.

In this exercise, think first about what might constitute your "ideal story." Of course, this notion will be mutable and fleeting. A story or month or two later, and it may all change. But for now, for the purposes of this exercise, ask yourself what in particular interests *you* in the possibilities of language, form, and expression. Where would you locate your work in this culture? Who would you have read it, how and why?

That's the first thing.

The second is to imagine that writing takes place in a conversation with the rest of writing. How you hear that conversation, where you enter it, and why are critical to your understanding and the subsequent development of your work

This exercise is something like a cross between a treasure hunt and a scavenger hunt.

The rules of the hunt are simple: closely consider the writing you love.

The aims of the hunt also are simple: find two pieces of writing—two poems, two stories, two essays, two autobiographical sketches, or (somewhat more challenging) one each of two different genres. Choose one by a living author, the other by a dead one.

Important note.

If you don't already know what you would choose, you must begin to hunt for it. Browse the library or a favorite bookstore. Imagine a shelf in the store you'd like to see your work on, and look there. Anthologies are good; cruise through them. One student used her own mother's journals she'd found in their living-room bookcase. The hunt is an important part of this exercise.

Then listen closely to the "conversation" between your two texts. What holds them together—a quality of language or expression, a certain formal dimension, a recurring theme or narrative, some emotional power?

We once knew a wild-haired painter who'd hunker down for hours at his water colors, working furiously, with intense passion. At the end of each day, he'd thumb-tack his work to the wall beside a reproduction of a beloved masterpiece, looking, he said, for a kind of resonance, or thrumming, between them. If he didn't hear it, he'd throw all his work away, just crumple it up and toss it in the trash.

Imagine that kind of thrumming.

Now, listen for something like that between the two texts you have chosen. Where does it come from? What is it like? Is it anything you've ever noticed before?

It is important to remember that such a thrum does not mean your texts should sound alike (this is not about imitation), but rather that they share a particular affinity, one for the other, which you may only recognize at first by instinct.

Now imagine a space between your two texts, an empty space, silent, but surrounded by this other thrum that draws you.

The rest of the exercise is simple: write yourself into that space.

Afterward.

Now your conversation consists of three texts. What can you say about them? What holds what you have written to what you read around it?

(K.H.)

Reading Yourself

③ ▶ And How About Your Reading Habits?

Use to Write: Essay; Literacy-Narrative; Journal; Creative Nonfiction; Performance Piece

Ideas and Concepts to Explore: reader's life story; truism.

Authors/Works Mentioned: Charles Dickens; Groucho Marx; Rick Moody, "Primary Sources"; Leo Tolstoy; *Time; National Geographic; Rolling Stone; Fear Street; Pogo; The Princeton Encyclopedia of Poetry and Poetics; The World's Greatest Love Letters; TV Guide; How To Survive On a Desert Island* (apocryphal text).

Outside of a dog, there's nothing I love more than a good book. Inside of a dog, it's too dark to read.

—Groucho Marx

Writer's truism: Writers should read. We should subscribe to literary journals and support arts communities. Young writers should read old writers, any writers, lots of writers. "Eat" books, poems, texts of any sort. Read the world. Travel. Sketch in words in your journals.

Don't stay inside of a dog. Get out and read.

But, you might say, as some writers we know say, *I never read much. I came (early or) late to writing but I prefer to write. I read only mystery novels but like to write poems. I want my future children to read but I didn't much. I only read the TV guide and menus. I don't have much time—what time I have, I'd rather write. I don't know what to read. I don't know how to read like a writer.*

We think you can find out an enormous amount about yourself by reading but also by acknowledging that you are, more than you suppose, *a reader.* You will find out that even if you've been living inside a dog, you've probably been influenced by books, or texts of some kind. You might have completed this chapter's first exercise and realized your bookless home was filled nonetheless with texts. As a kid, you may have read cereal boxes and seen your father, a coach, reading coaching manuals and your mother reading Bible Psalms and your little sister endlessly reading comic books. Or you may have grown up in a book-lined house but preferred to run outside and play ball. But every once in a while you may have leafed through your father's Pogo books, or your mother's *Time Magazine* and *National Geographic* or your brother's collection of Fear Street books or even the classics—Dickens and Tolstoy—that your grandfather left your aunt who left them with her sister, your mother, who left them in the garage where you found them and. . . .

Equally, you may not have collected books until forced to buy them in college and some you saved (and some you sold back). Perhaps, some magazines and newspapers and a stray *Rolling Stone* still clutter your shelves. You decide to be a writer and even if you're not a life-long reader (or even if you are), you find yourself drinking coffee in bookstores and looking at sale racks of odds and ends books (odd books all) with some interest.

To see who you are today, at this point as a reader—inside or outside your imaginary dog—walk around the house and pick up ten to twenty texts: CD liner notes to Visa bill fine print to books and magazines. Collect texts: nonliterary and literary. Set each one down before you at the computer. Type out a bibliography of these items. (This will exercise you in MLA or Chicago style. Use your college handbook to help you out. Essentially you want author, title, place of publication, and date). Then use your nifty footnote capability on your computer or use your pen and number each entry.

Now, for each footnote number, write a memory piece for each text you are footnoting. Eventually, you can reorder those memories to tell a story about you as a writer. For instance, one of us might collect her *Encyclopedia of Poetry and Poetics*—a new edition replacing the one she bought for a class in graduate school in poetry twenty years ago. And then she might tell a story about learning to be a poet, using this handbook. She might also pick the old used-book-store-volume of *The World's Greatest Love Letters,* given to her by a friend. She doesn't really read this book—she carries it ritualistically from house to house. And so on. Still, she can construct one version of herself as a reader outside the dog, in the light of day, as she annotates these texts.

This wasn't our idea, by the way. We borrowed it from Rick Moody, whose essay, (structured the same way), "Primary Sources," appears in the anthology. Compare your reading "life story" to his. You can vary this exercise by writing an "ideal reading life story"—all the books you'd like to read but never got around to reading. Or undertake the classic: compile a list of texts you'd take to a desert island (one possible title choice would be *How to Survive On a Desert Island*) and annotate these items in a way that lets readers see why you chose them.

(W.B.)

4 ▶ Your Own Canon

Use to Write:	Autobiography; Literacy narrative; Essay; Journal
Ideas and Concepts to Explore:	canon; freewrite.
Authors/Works Mentioned:	Randall Jarrell, poetry drawing on fairy tales; John Keats, "On First Looking Into Chapman's *Homer.*"

A "canon" can be said to be an agreed-upon list, catalogue, or body of material. It can also be said to be an *unagreed*-upon list, catalogue, or body of material;

that is, such things are always under debate, cause for argument, and in flux because they are, after all, products of people—of communities, cultures, moments in history: all three of which produce, among other things, enormous disagreements. Etymologically, "canon" is rooted in Old French and Latin and originally meant something like "measuring line" or "rule." How should one, how should we, measure a text or a collection of texts? It all depends. . . . Hence, all the arguments.

Chances are you've taken part in or at least observed "canon debates" ("What *should*, what *must*, students read?") that have taken place nationally and locally. So you probably have some idea of how easily the topic of "a canon" can start squabbles.

For the moment, however, let's leave the big debates to fend for themselves. For the moment, create your own provisional canon of reading by listing your favorite books, poems, stories, or plays from preschool to the present. If the word "canon" makes you nervous, then think in terms of a history of your reading—or, even more loosely, a "record of stuff I've read." Let the list evolve over several days. You could go at it randomly, or you could list the reading by age: preschool, kindergarten, grades 1–3, grades 4–6; or develop your own scheme. Next:

Write about the list. **You might . . .**

. . . freewrite about any single work—what you **remember** about first reading it or having it read to you; why the work has stuck with you, how your response to it has changed or not changed, how it made you see the world differently, what it looked like, physically, maybe even what it smelled like or felt like to the touch.

. . . freewrite and then construct an **autobiographical essay** about the whole list. What connects this reading? What does this list reveal about you? What changes in your life does it reflect? Are there "milestone" works, and if so, why are they milestones and what parts of your life do they mark? How much of this canon is accidental? How much of it reflects the values of your family, your social class, your nationality, or other aspects of your background? How much of "you," your **self,** is in the list—and what does that mean, for goodness sake?

. . . track down a book on the list that you haven't read for a long time. **Reread** the book. What do you think of it now? What had you forgotten about the book? What had you remembered correctly? Will you keep the book in your canon? Why or why not? Write about these and other questions that come to mind. This writing might point toward an **essay,** a **story** in which the book figures significantly, or a **poem** that makes use of the book. (You might look at American poet Randall Jarrell's several poems that draw on fairy tales, and at John Keats's rather famous poem, often anthologized, "On First Looking Into Chapman's *Homer.*")

(H.O.)

5 Reading Your Times: When You Came to Be

Use to Write:	n/a [the exercise may lead to work in virtually any genre]
Ideas and Concepts to Explore:	to "fictionalize"; list poem.
Authors/Works Mentioned:	almanacs, facts-on-file, yearbooks (two kinds).

Spend some time reading about the year, month, and day you were born. Range widely in this reading: histories, yearbooks (both the high-school kind and the encyclopedia kind), popular magazines, newspapers, almanacs, lists (Top–40 hits, bestsellers), facts-on-file.

In what ways do you see yourself as a product of the times evoked by this reading? Is there one big historical event that's somehow shaped your life or that resonates with you? Has the apparent absence of such an event shaped your life in any way? What are you surprised you didn't know about that year, month, or day—until you did the reading? Are there any events, historical figures, trends, fads, political crises, etc., that serve to comment uncannily or ironically on how your life has developed since Day One? In what ways do you feel distant or unaffected by the specific era into which you were born? How were your parents' lives shaped by such things, in your opinion?

Such material can be a rich source of imagery, conflict, raw information, and historical perspective—all of which can lead directly or feed indirectly into ideas for poems, stories, and autobiographical pieces. You could, for example, . . .

1. Write a list poem that catalogues events that happened on your birthday or in your birth year; play with different organizational schemes.

2. Write a fictionalized account—in short-story form—about your parents, or a couple like your parents, and what they were doing and thinking the day of your birth.

3. Write a poem based on one especially potent photographic image you discover in your research.

4. Write an autobiographical essay that explains why you do or do not (or both) feel particularly connected to the world evoked by your reading.

5. Turn #4 into a piece of creative nonfiction or a performance piece.

6. Set a short play in the "era" in which you were born.

Work with this exercise could dovetail with parts of the exercise, "History as a Collaboration of Fact and Imagination" in this chapter (#12).

(H.O.)

Reading Home:
Organizing and Developing Memories

⑥

Use to Write:	Autobiography; Creative Nonfiction; Poetry; Journal
Ideas and Concepts to Explore:	"house" vs. "home"; reading/interpreting "home"; literacy-biography.
Authors/Works Mentioned:	Lynda Barry, "The Teenage Room", Wendy Bishop, "Propositions On the Lost Name of a Street"; Sandra Cisneros, *The House on Mango Street*; Joan Didion; Nancy Mairs, *Remembering the Bone House*; Malcolm X, *The Autobiography of Malcolm X*; Sheila Ortiz-Taylor, "Re/Collection"; Sharon Sloan Fiffer and Steven Fiffer, *Home: American Writers Remember Rooms of Their Own*; Virginia Woolf; [the architect Frank Lloyd Wright is mentioned as well].

I don't remember the brick bungalow on Bourbonnais Avenue, although I must have taken my first steps, spoken my first words there. I couldn't tell you much about the three-bedroom tract house on Western Hills Drive or the small brick ranch on Hawkins Street, where my mother still lives. I can, however, conjure up the floor plan, the fleur-de-lis wallpaper, and the maple early American furniture of the Cape Cod on Cobb Boulevard—the only house I ever called home.

—Sharon Sloan Fiffer

This passage comes from the introduction to *Home: American Writers Remember Rooms of Their Own*. Editors Sharon Sloan Fiffer and Steven Fiffer create a single, composite "home" through their arrangement of essays in this volume; each essay, composed by a different author, is set in a different room.

Nancy Mairs, in her book *Remembering the Bone House*, takes readers from house to house, home to home. This technique allows her to render her complicated and compelling life journey—presenting disorderly memories in a (semblance of) orderly progression and logical compartments.

Sheila Ortiz-Taylor in "Re/Collection" (see anthology) places characters in different rooms of a house in order to juxtapose their stories.

In her novel, *The House on Mango Street*, Sandra Cisneros uses "house and home" as a kind of center-of-gravity in a coming-of-age story.

Primary Exercise.

We want you to read your home (metaphorically) by remembering how you read (literally) in your home. Here's how this works: Think of a house, apartment, trailer, or other living space from your earliest years, years when you were learning to read and write. For most of us, this would be preschool through elementary school years.

From memory, draw a floor-plan of that living space. Then, number each room in the living space, including, if it applies, outdoor areas. For each number, in a list at the bottom of the page, remember a literacy story—an episode, an event, a recurring practice involving learning to read or write. Examples: Reading "forbidden magazines" in the bathroom; parents reading to you in the bedroom; someone telling you a story in the living room; hiding outside with a book; playing with a parent's computer; trying to type a story for Mother's Day; "reading" (interpreting) family fights; doing your first homework assignments; "reading" (interpreting) how your older sister or brother got dressed for a date.

In a journal, write enough notes for each numbered location to remind you of this story later. Finally, choose the most memorable reading memory and cluster or write a bit of this experience on a separate sheet of paper. To cluster, you place the word for the room in the center of your paper and then free associate around the word, listing words, circling them, connecting them to the next cluster of thought, word, impression. Or, you may simply choose to place the room name at the top of your paper and write an uncensored paragraph, prompted by memory.

To continue, you might choose to write a literacy autobiography. Samples of these are found in essays by Joan Didion and Virginia Woolf on how they write or in the often anthologized section of the *Autobiography of Malcolm X* where Malcolm X describes learning to read in jail by copying out the dictionary longhand. Your literacy autobiography can start at any age and consider reading and writing in the broadest sense—reading texts, reading home, reading family, reading neighborhood, culture, religion, and so on.

Alternate Exercises.

A. In the collection *Home* (mentioned above), read Lynda Barry's description/story of a teenager's room. Read/remember your own teenager's room. If you're a parent and if you dare, enter your child/teenager's room and read it into prose. Finally, if you're not (yet) a parent, predict a teenager's room. Read the future for your imagined child.

B. How do you distinguish between a house and a home? Is there a difference? Create a poem/essay/story/screenplay that illustrates your view (without stating your belief that house and home are similar or different—show us). This is a little like trying to define the words "traveler" and "tourist." You might want to undertake a classic essay—defining home, defining house, and then wandering through associational/definitional connections to take us, your readers, into a deeper understanding of whichever remains for you the primary term. That is, in prose wander through this idea.

C. Interview others—classmates, friends, family—concerning what their (your) ideal house would look like. What would their (your) ideal home consist of? See where such primary research and thinking takes you. For instance, Frank Lloyd Wright's architectural compound—Taliesen West—in Phoenix, Arizona, embodies an entire vision of how to live, in the way the house is sited on the land and constructed to function in the arid environment. It embodies his architectural principles large and small, all the way down to the furniture he designed to go into the house he designed. Thinking like Frank Lloyd Wright and embodying a "life/living" vision in prose might take you into the realms of science fiction or utopian writing.

D. Like Nancy Mairs in *Remembering the Bone House,* take readers on a tour of every house you've lived in (or home you've inhabited—this again gets down to house/home distinctions). You might use family photographs to prompt your memory. I used the "Listing and Memory" invention exercise on the Green Line to help me compose the prose poem "Propositions on the Lost Name of a Street" found in the anthology. I could remember living on Christman Avenue and Breaker Drive, but I couldn't remember the name of the street I describe emotionally in this poem until I went to visit my stepbrothers last summer. "Wakeforest Drive," they told me promptly. "Oh," I said. "Oh yes." I realized then that the house had less compelling connections to "home" for them than it did for me. Anyway, as I did, you may want to tap into the memories of other members of your (biological or adopted or chosen) families.

(W.B.)

Correspondences: Imitation and Inspiration

7 ▶ Collecting Epigraphs for a Textual Mosaic

Use to Write:	n/a [the exercise can apply to virtually any genre]
Ideas and Concepts to Explore:	epigraph; excerpt-quilt; text-mosaic; text-collage.
Authors/Works Mentioned:	Elizabeth Bishop, "Man Moth"; William Shakespeare, *Romeo and Juliet*; Karl Shapiro, "Drugstore."

An *epigraph* is a sample of a published text—some quoted lines of poetry, for example—that usually appears after the title but before the body of a poem, an essay, a story, or a novel. Sometimes it's used as a kind of prelude, sometimes as an acknowledged source of inspiration, sometimes as a sincere or ironic comment on or counterpoint to the text that follows it. For instance, when Karl Shapiro published a poem about 1950s drugstores, he chose a couple of lines from Shakespeare's *Romeo and Juliet* (lines concerning "an apothecary," or druggist) as an epigraph. The epigraph, from perhaps the most famous play about passionate youth, served as a kind of backdrop to Shapiro's own take on American youth some 350 years after Shakespeare's era. There's perhaps an ironic edge to it, too, because it hints at the suicide in the famous play, and it may also direct us to compare unfavorably the youth of "Drugstore" with the immortal, articulate imaginary heroes.

When you encounter passages in your reading that leap out at you, put them in a notebook or in a computer file. Record the source carefully. The reading can be *any* reading—textbooks, newspapers, advertisements, road signs, web-site material, poetry, novels, graffiti, essays, government regulations, Shakespeare, lyrics on CD packages. Even passages with typographical errors can be useful: Elizabeth Bishop composed a marvelous poem that she would not have written if she had not seen the word "mammoth" misprinted as "manmoth" in a newspaper; the poem essentially imagined this "Man Moth" creature. What a lovely, lucky accident—and Bishop knew what to do with it. With an epigraph, she paid tribute to the misprint.

Draw on the file you assemble; use it as a source of epigraphs for poems or stories you have written or are writing. Perhaps use the passages also as starting points for poems and stories.

Expand the project eventually, if you've a mind to do so, creating an Exerpt-Quilt or -Mosaic or -Collage from these quotations, arranging and rearranging them according to different schemes, principles, whims. Look for different combinations, different ways in which the selections comment on one another or contradict one another or in other ways begin to create a community of texts. Such a collage (quilt, mosaic, compendium) can be a startling way of mapping the reading you do, of tracing your interests and obsessions. And it can reveal hidden connections between texts in your reading life that may seem at first to be completely unrelated.

(H.O.)

8 ▶ Writing Provocations: Responding to Other Writing

Use to Write:	n/a [the exercise may lead to work in virtually any genre]
Ideas and Concepts to Explore:	epigraph; incubation; provocation.
Authors/Works Mentioned:	[The exercise contains short excerpts from the writing of numerous authors].

What makes anyone write? A feeling, a need, a desire to say, to be heard. But also there's the need to write not just from the self but in response to others— others' words, others' selves. Put another way: I often write to write back. I save quotations in my journal. I reread journals across time to see what once seemed significant to me. The words of others are puzzles, warnings, provocations. I share my gathering here to invite you to collect your own, to write from those which tease and provoke you. For fun, I've divided my list into two—those I've already used to start (mainly) poems (though these might well start you on an essay or story) and those I still plan to use.

Some days, I want to write but I don't know how to write—I don't know where to start. So I look at my provocation lists. I choose one, and, if I have the time, I let it incubate—while I go running, all morning as I sit in a meeting, in my dreams, sometimes for days. Then one day, when ready, I place the provocation at the top of a new file on my computer and respond to it—sometimes with a prose freewrite, sometimes by jumping in and shaping a poem or prose text from an idea hatched during my previous days' incubation period. Sometimes the provocation remains in the finished text as an introductory epigraph. Sometimes the need for the provocation is gone, and I let my text go out into the world without it.

Here are the lists, then, and naturally I'm implicitly encouraging you to start collecting your own lists of quotations, which will provoke you to "write back":

Those I've Used.

And there's something to be said for fucking up. In fact, fucking up, if you aspire to be an artist, may be the great creative principle: getting broken, broken wide open, and then delving among the shards.

—Breyten Breytenbach

". . . most computer users choose predictable passwords; among the most common are 'love' and 'sex' as well as 'car makes, movie stars, sports teams, and vacation sites.'"

—*Harpers*, November 1991

Every contact, for the lover, raises the question of an answer. . .

—Roland Barthes

All families build a Glass House, open to the world, and live inside it; these houses are our inheritance. My family's house has the burden of being real as well. It needs to be heated and have its taxes paid.

—Dominique Vellay

We die containing a richness of lovers and tribes, tastes we have swallowed, bodies we have plunged into and swum up as if rivers of wisdom, characters we have climbed into as if trees, fears we have hidden in as if caves. . . . We are communal histories, communal books. We are not owned or monogamous in our taste or experience.

—Michael Ondaatje, *The English Patient*

Huck just moves on. Alice just wakes up.

—Adam Gopnik

(. . . a thought unembodied in words remains a shadow. . . .

—Lev Vygotsky)

[she was] "exultant to make it to the point where a man is already blasé."
—Simone de Beauvoir, *Francis & Gontier*

"It's like anything, you can't see the possibilities until they engulf you."
—E-mail from Kate

There is an extravagance in the means my sanity took to rescue their madness that makes the one look uncommonly like the other.
—Rebecca West, "Parthenope"

[6] Movie-(Adventure)** "Angel on the Amazon" 1948 George Brent, Vera Ralston. Weird story of an old woman who looks like a young girl because of an accident on the Amazon. (105 mins.)
—Television Guide

In only one of Daguerre's pictures does a man appear, by chance a pedestrian on the boulevard held still during most of the image.
—B. Newhall

[She] never mellowed. As one temporary housekeeper noted, "Her life, even now, is black and white and crimson and purple and wild." Her last secretary. . . never thought of her before her final illness as an old lady: "she was just a lady who happened to be old."
— V. Glendinning, *Rebecca West: A Life*

"To reshape one's body into a male body is *not* to put on male power and privilege."
—Susan R. Bordo

My homicidal maniac is of a peculiar kind. . . what he desires is to absorb as many lives as he can and he has laid himself out to achieve it in a cumulative way. He gave many flies to one spider and many spiders to one bird, and then he wanted a cat to eat the many birds. What would have been his later steps? It would almost be worth while to complete the experiment.
—From Dr. Seward's Diary, *Dracula*

Justice Marshall McComb, 82, did not contest his wife's petition to be named conservator of his estate after she told the court her husband is "obsessed with the moon. He gets quite excited about it. . . . He enjoys it but it's not a normal enjoyment of the moon."
—UPI

Paul Valery speaks of the 'une ligne donnee' of a poem. One line is given to the poet by God or by nature, the rest he has to discover for himself.
—Stephen Spender

Tait asks—"How were questions invented?"

—Wendy Bishop

It is no less difficult to write a sentence in a recipe than sentences in *Moby Dick*. So you might as well write *Moby Dick*.

—Annie Dillard

At the beginning of each picture there is someone who works with me. Toward the end I have the impression of having worked without a collaborator.

—Christian Zervos, conversation with Picasso in *The Creative Process.*

Those I'm Still Incubating.

trichotillomania—compulsive hair pulling

It is easy to fly into a passion—anybody can do that. But to be angry with the right person to the right extent and at the right time and with the right object and in the right way—that is not easy, and it is not everyone who can do it.

—Aristotle

We travel into or away from our photographs.

—Don DeLillo

Poetry is addressing the world and fiction is getting the world to talk to you.

—Grace Paley

How odd it is, when remembering early days, that the weather seems constant in certain places. In my nursery at Torquay it is always an autumn or winter afternoon. . . . In the Ealing garden it is always summer—and a particularly hot summer.

—Agatha Christie, *An Autobiography*

My seventies were interesting, and fairly serene, but my eighties are passionate. I grow more intense as I age. To my own surprise I burst out with hot conviction.

—Florida Scott-Maxwell

Scientists occasionally amuse themselves by trying to figure out how much a human body might be worth. Chemists have painstakingly added up the market value of skin, flesh, bone, hair, and the various minerals and trace elements contained in it, and have come up with the paltry sum of a few dollars.

—Mihaly Cisikszentmihalyi

I believe, rather, that therapy transforms when it is the slow learning about connection and separation, the visceral study of painful lacunae and blue links. I believe in a place, somewhere in the air, where my self and your self might meet, merging in what we might learn to call, at least for a moment, love.

—Lauren Slater, *Welcome to My Country*

"Why do you fall in love? Nothing could be more complex: because it is winter, because it is summer; from overwork, from too much leisure; from weakness, from strength; a need for security, a taste for danger; from despair, from hope; because someone does not love you, because he does love you. . . ."

—Simone de Beauvoir, "What Love Is—and Isn't"

"He has heard that 9 out of 10 people die before the hours of 4AM and 5AM, so he tries to get up like clockwork at 3:30 and not fall back asleep until 6."

—*Tally Democrat*, Aug 29, 1993, "Room for the Doomed" AIDS patient John Santos

"What is the past? What is it all for? A mental sandwich."

—John Ashbery, "37 Haiku"

Like a stroke victim retraining new parts of the brain to grasp lost skills, I have taught myself joy, over and over again. It's not such a wide gulf to cross, then, from survival to poetry.

—Barbara Kingsolver, *High Tide in Tucson*

Margaret Atwood summed it up when she asked women what they most feared in the other sex and they answered: that a man would kill them. Men responding to the same quesiton said: that a woman might laugh at them.

—Dalma Heyn, *The Erotic Silence of the American Wife*

Lunatics are similar to designated hitters. Often an entire family is crazy, but since an entire family can't go into the hospital, one person is designated as crazy and goes inside. Then, depending on how the rest of the family is feeling, that person is kept inside or snatched out, to prove something about the family's mental health.

—Susanna Kayser, *Girl, Interrupted*

Life, of course, never gets anyone's complete attention. Death always remains interesting, pulls us, draws us.

—Janet Malcomb

Men are always asking, "What do women want?" I think women mainly want men to cook and to show up on time—you know, some of the basic stuff.

—Hans Ostrom, letter

And I have learned that the only way to enter another's life is to find the vector points where my self and another self meet. . . . There is no way, I believe, to do the work of therapy, which is, when all is said and done, the work of relationship, without finding yourself in the patient and the patient's self in you. In this way, rifts within and between might be sealed, and the language of our separate lives might come to share syllables, sentences, whole themes that bind us together.

—Lauren Slater, *Welcome to My Country*

(W.B.)

Eight Steps for Inhabiting and Transforming a Poem

9

Use to Write:	Poetry
Ideas and Concepts to Explore:	found poem; "inhabitation" as a strategy for reading and writing; syntax.
Authors/Works Mentioned:	Tasima Naslin, "Character"; Farida Sarkar; Carolyn Wright.

I've found that I can learn poetry better by using the following methods for taking over and inhabiting a poem, from the inside out. I call these willful inhabitations transformation: times I willfully experiment with the text the poet has given me. First, I copy the poem down myself. In a way, simple copying is a reverse transformation, for I bend my own sentences and syntax patterns to the poet's own, taking on the rhythms of the words as I find them, cutting lines as the poet cuts them, placing each word bead on the poem's string, just as the poet did. Then I do the following to explore the world of the poem inside out, transforming it by changing gender, point of view, genre, and so on. When you're done, I think you'll see how this exercise could be followed with a prose passage, too.

1. First copy the following poem (by hand or by typing). Then, immediately write down your first reaction to it (about one page).

Character
by Taslima Nasrin

You're a girl
and you'd better not forget
that when you step over the threshold of your house
men will look askance at you.
When you keep on walking down the lane
men will follow you and whistle.
When you cross the lane and step onto the main road
men will revile you and call you a loose woman.

If you've got no character
you'll turn back,
and if not
you'll keep on going
    as you're going now.

—Translated from the Bengali, by Carolyn Wright and Farida Sarkar.
The New Yorker August 22/29 (1994): 77.

2. Read the poem again and retell its story in four or five sentences.

3. Speculate about the narrator of the poem and the person to whom he/she is talking. In particular, try to decide what **isn't** being said.

4. Rewrite this poem as a reversal—start with "You're a boy . . ." and make any necessary changes to make a statement about the way men are socialized.

5. Find a prose passage in any collection of stories or a writing anthology and cut this passage into lines in the same way this poem is cut into lines:
    You...
    and...
    that...
    men...
    Try to make similar phrase–or sentence–breaks (be sure to indent the last phrase as this poem does). Now take the "found" passage and cut out any extra words you can to keep some meaning but make the "found poem" read more tightly.

6. Choose three words from "Character" and freewrite on each for two or three minutes. Then write your own small poem (on any subject) of no more than 13 lines. Try breaking it into two parts (stanzas), as this one is broken, but you don't need to break at the same spot.

7. Write your own poem—prompted by any aspect of transformation you've experienced so far.

8. Write a general, one–page response discussing the effects of all these transformations—what did you like, not like, what worked, didn't work, what, if anything, did you learn about poetry by inhabiting this poem in each of these different ways?

Finally, with this or other poems, here are some other transformations you might want to try:

A. Change the point of view—tell the poem, say, from the point of view of the girl's mother.

B. Change the person—tell the poem using a first person voice: "I'm a girl."

C. Change the time—"When I was a girl" or "When she was a girl."

D. Write the poem backwards, using the last line as the first, and so on. "You're going now. . . "

E. Write a poem or prose passage about what you've identified isn't being said (question 3 above): do this, though, by letting us see a scene, using images, actual people, telling a story, etc.

F. Make up your own ways to transform the poem.

I'll end here by taking you through these steps as I did them—not as a model, but as an encouragement. This type of close study of the work of others can enhance our own. First I rewrote the poem by hand; imagine it right here. And then I worked through the transformation prompts in order.

2. **Tell the poem's story:**

This poem catches my eye the way it did the first time I read it (I can't claim it's my first reading, first reaction)—certainly I get sucked in with the "You're a girl" and wonder how men will read this line, and I slow down on "threshold" and especially "askance"—they don't invoke particular places, but the words themselves are unusual enough to call the same type of reading attention to the lines as do images. Certainly I think of rural things and remember walking in the dust in Nigeria—I always felt more vulnerable there, and watched others walking—women having to walk behind men, sometimes chattering at them into the wind. I also like, of course, the powerful turn of the decision, both the taunting—"if you've got no character"— and the affirmation of "as you're going now" make me think of a fond older relative talking to a daughter or niece, hoping it will be different for her than it was for women in the past.

I like the simple lining and the way the last stanza falls down the page in fits and starts that mirror the twist of the message—decide now, character or no character.

3. **Speculate about the narrator—what isn't being said?**

The narrator is telling a younger woman, a relative, a lesson about "how things are"—that is, life is harder for women when they leave the security of their homes; men will judge them and call them names, upbraid them for their sexuality. The narrator is almost testing the listener to measure herself—go on and you've got character; turn back, you'll have none and you'll just be reabsorbed and mastered by these men (by culture). The narrator affirms that the listener, who must be walking out, is on the right path, the "main road."

Oh, I guess I've done some of this. I got caught up in the relationship between speaker and listener and I guess I identify with the listener, think, yes, I wish someone had told me these things. What might not be said is what has happened to the speaker—did she find her main road, or is she wishing better things for her listener? Is she speaking from "sad" experience or already more free and telling someone to follow after her? I'd say she's certainly speaking from experience in the way she says things so authoritatively—you're a girl, better not forget, when you step men will, when you cross men will. She's certainly been there. What's not said is whether *she* had the character to take the step(s) she's urging for the listener.

4. Write a reversal.

Character

You're a boy,
and you'd better not forget
when you leave the threshold of your house
women will look at how you hold your head, what you bring, who you are.
When you keep on walking down the lane
women's eyes will follow you, estimating, deciding.
When you cross the lane and step onto the main road
your woman will cry over you and call you a heartbreaker.

If you've got no character,
you'll keep on going
and if not
you'll turn
    as you're turning now.

5. Find a "poetic prose passage and rewrite as a poem—I chose a passage from Annie Dillard's *Pilgrim at Tinker's Creek.*
Dillard's original—

For a week last September migrating red-winged blackbirds were feeding heavily down by the creek at the back of the house. One day I went out to investigate the racket; I walked up to a tree, an Osage orange, and a hundred birds flew away. They simply materialized out of the tree. I saw a tree, then a whisk of color, then a tree again. I walked closer and another hundred blackbirds took flight. Not a branch, not a twig budged: the birds were apparently weightless as well as invisible.

    —transformed into this "found" poem:

Migration

Last September red-winged blackbirds
feeding by the creek
at the back of the house.
I walked up to a tree, an Osage orange,
and a hundred birds flew away,
materialized out of the tree.
I saw a tree, then a whisk of color
then a tree again.
I walked closer,

another hundred blackbirds took flight.
Not a branch, not a twig budged:
the birds were plainly weightless
    as well as invisible.

6. Choosing three words from the original poem, I freewrite on each: **threshold, whistle, character.**

   thresholds—easily suggests thresholds of pain, of expectations. There's
something about stages, jumping higher, the moongate in the Madame M
movie, the way empty cities open out in thresholds, the threshold of different horizons, are the stars thresholds? Is life a stair-step double-helix or W.
B. Yeats' gyres, way to turnings, thresholds are held onto, felt, thresholds are
boxes unfolding, origami paper unfolding, openings and closings, there are
two words—*thresh* and *hold*—does the word come from strike, to flail and
hold, encompass, circle around?

   whistle is the sound of air between lost baby teeth, it's the pucker of child-
fat, it's the shrill steamwhistle that doesn't exist anymore except in movies, yet
is so vivid like black and white night–train rides going into mystery, and yet
this country doesn't have a train system like that. Whistling wind along the
side of the car as my hands are held out in western air. Do these cicadas whistle, can a whistle rattle? Is any air that sounds or doesn't sound part of a whistle, between fingers, blades of grass, while you work, while you play, calling a
dog home, calling a child? Whistles that sing like birds fly, coming out and
finding the mockingbird shrilling at me and looping the loop. . .

   character—to have it, to be it, like personality Play Doh, lines in men's
faces have more than lines in women's faces, something about the way the
skeleton is held, something as ferocious as air hollowing down between
canyon ledges, when everything's the same it can't be said to be—it's set
apart, arty—it's having the character to do something impossible, character
that scrapes the body with denial. Is there generous character? Charity begins
in character and at home. How to know the character of a day, the character
you've become, when you're in or out of character? How to write a poem
about a concept, tell a character's story, characterize—*crouching*, sounds like
cracker and caretaker—that *ack ack* that has to be memorized for spelling,
the banana spider outside my window that made a second egg sac after I took
away the first—is that an instance of insect character or simple biology? Can
you see your own character or only be invested with by others?

7. **Compose a new poem.**

   Using all the feelings and insights generated from this excerpt, I composed my own poem (notice it can drift very far, as this one does, from the
original poem—only the title really remains—but I would have never
"found" this poem without experiencing the first poem).

Character

Banana spider weaves her second egg sac
the day after I clear out the first.
Slant fall light—color of her gold and black bars—
brands her captives, mosquito legs,
lovebugs wrapped each in the other, endlessly
on her perfected wires.
She plays the odds—the spheres—

Slung taut in airs by shapely double X legs.

Larger than a silver dollar,
relaxed, barters her complete attention
for the Braille of distant tremors,
the scared breath of everything
    tossing and turning.

8. **Write a page, exploring what was learned.**

It was interesting to reverse the gender and see how hard it is to move from "boy" to "man," yet it's easy to move from "girl" to "woman"—my sensing that boys don't like to be called boys very long but girls can stay girlish longer and merge into womanhood? Also, whose poem is it? By simply reversing it but using the same syntax patterns, do I make it mine yet? Bakhtin the theorist says the word is always half someone else's but here, and in the Anne Dillard prose–to–poem transformation, it still seems to belong to the other; the word is not yet half mine. In "Character," the borrowings are roughly form, the turn in thought after the stanza break and the title. But the poem feels like mine since I'm writing from my experience of watching this banana spider all summer out my writing–room window. Also, I think it hearkens back to Robert Frost's poem "Design" (a sonnet, actually) in that it's impossible for me to write about a spider without remembering Frost writing about it. I had trouble with interrupting explanation—how to place and punctuate "color of her gold and black bars" and "the spheres" and wondered if the archaic language of "spheres" and "airs" (Shakespearean breath) really works with the attempt to "draw" her with "shapely double X legs." Also wondered if "shapely" was too easy and somehow sexist. Oh well, it was fun to inhabit this box—interesting to paint a picture—this feels like a still life—instead of telling a story (more normal for me in my writing)—I got done and worried if this picture would matter to anyone else.

(W.B.)

Travels With the Essay

10

Use to Write:	Essay; Autobiography; Creative Nonfiction
Ideas and Concepts to Explore:	academic/nonacademic; associative; anecdote; contradiction; define/"definitional"; discursive; essay; digression; implicit argument; multiple truths.
Authors/Works Mentioned:	Diane Ackerman, "Mute Dancers"; Alys Culhane; Jill Carpenter, "Consanguinity"; Mary Paumer Jones, "Meander."

Aha. Paradoxically, an elucidation . . . contains more questions than answers.

—Jill Carpenter, "Consanguinity"

The essay (academic, nonacademic, personal, public, light or profound) is an ornery thing. There are lots of books about writing them, and lots of them written. Almost everyone agrees that they partake of their root word—they wander as the writer takes "a try," makes an "attempt." Lots of other adjectives concatenate—experimental, occasional, critical, mnemonic, inquiry, itinerant, unfolding, emerging, seeking, opening, insightful, stimulating, tentative, incomplete, wise, searching, feeling, toying, fluid, in progress, exploratory, celebratory, rambling, tentative, uncertain, ambiguous, contradictory, digressive, tolerant.

Most writers on writing the essay do as I have done in quoting Jill Carpenter; they offer a partial and tentative definition and then try to make "sense of what they sense" about this protean form—"protean" meaning in this case "bursting with possibilities" or "hard to pin down." For my part, I'd like to look at three things three of my favorite essays achieve (all three essays appear in the minianthology). In "Meander" Mary Paumer Jones does just that, wanderingly ponders explicit, tacit, and connective definitions—looks at a word, looks at it again, again, connects, backtracks, tries, retreats, continues on and composes a small gem of an essay on the meandering form of the essay.

Diane Ackerman in "Mute Dancers: How to Watch a Hummingbird" moves more assuredly—instead of tiptoeing through the essay form like Robinson, she strides along in hobnailed hiking boots offering detail and data, facts grounded in experience and interest (as the essay may do and often does, especially in its journalistic manifestation). The way Ackerman comments and compounds, the way she scatters and shares her research is especially intriguing. She defines, tells us how to define, but she also exhibits many of the moves of academic writers that my friend Alys Culhane, who specializes in reading, studying, and writing essays, has found to be foundational. In Culhane's experience, *academic* essays exhibit these characteristics:

- contradiction
- association
- the use of one or more voices
- multiple truths
- digression
- implicit argument
- open-endedness.

If you take these characteristics and apply them to Ackerman's essay, you'll see exactly what Alys is arguing. This essay appears firmer, more certain. It defines. Then it redefines—digresses, implies. It *performs* the way scholarly writing is thought to perform, only the performance takes place on a modified stage, one grounded in a personal voice and anecdote (some would argue a more human, engaging and appealing stage—but that's another issue).

Finally, I'd ask you to read "Consanguinity" by Jill Carpenter to see a writer plying the middle territory between Ackerman's and Jones's texts. Carpenter, a scientist, is also, I would argue, a poet. In "Consanguinity" she weaves a tapestry of theme and variation on the word, the idea of, the meaning of, blood. She meanders like Jones but also strikes as precisely as Ackerman.

None of these essays is the first or last word in essay–writing, of course. But they give you some footholds from which to launch yourself into writing essays.

1. Write a discursive, associational, definitional essay on a single word. Make yours as short and compact as "Meander" or as discursive as "Consanguinity." Write from some research perhaps, but also from a heavy portion of personal experience, investment, and/or interest in the word.

2. Reverse the proportions. Write a how-to essay about a topic which is of interest to you but relatively new to you—learn about an animal, a plant, a mineral, an activity, a culture. Research it, but in your reporting, meander through the information you've collected. Share your knowledge but keep us interested in that sharing by keeping us guessing where you're going.

3. Write an essay that defines essay–writing. Use the reference books I've listed below for triggering quotations. Here's one I almost used, for instance, before I chose Jill Carpenter's line. "Essays 'are experiments in making sense of things.'" (Scott Russell Sanders, "The Singular First Person" quoted in Heilker 89). Perhaps read what some people have written about earlier essayists such as Montaigne, Francis Bacon, Samuel Johnson, Addison and Steele, Mary Wolstonecraft, Thomas Paine, Edmund Burke, Thomas Jefferson, William Hazlitt, Leigh Hunt, Henry David Thoreau, Ralph Waldo Emerson, Dorothy Wordsworth (her journal), Matthew Arnold, George Orwell, Edmund Wilson, Dorothy Parker, E.B. White, James Baldwin.

4. After you've written your essay, draw it. Make an actual map of the essay's territory. Or give a reader directions for navigating your "experiment in making sense of things." Write a prologue to the essay—operating instructions.

5. Use some of the essay's own attributes as a structuring pattern—choose to start each paragraph with a rhetorical or a real question, choose to follow an essayist's shape that you foreground—starting small and opening ever outward—moving from a point of a triangle to a wide base or trekking a concentric spiral outward. Use titled subheadings, as Hans Ostrom does in "Anomalies In Relief: Notes of a California Expatriate." These can be added after a draft or two, when the essay suggests its sections; or you can use them as you begin to write, a tactic that allows you to write essays (essayettes?!) within an essay.

6. Read essays and analyze the authors' strategies (even open-ended forms are planned to be that way—open ended; and what does that term mean exactly?). Look for recurring patterns; make your own categories of types of essayist, then affiliate and imitate and improvise.

For further reading

Forman, Janis, ed. *What Do I Know? Reading, Writing, and Teaching the Essay.* Portsmouth, NH: Boynton/Cook Heinemann, 1996.

Heilker, Paul. *The Essay: Theory and Pedagogy for an Active Form*. Urbana, IL: National Council of Teachers of English, 1996.

[And consult a library's card catalogue or online catalogue regarding any of the essayists named in #3]

(W.B.)

Reading and Writing Out of Other Art

Use to Write:	Short Fiction; Longer Fiction; Poetry; Creative Nonfiction; Drama Performance Piece; Autobiography; Journal; Art Criticism
Ideas and Concepts to Explore:	elegy; homage; inspiration.
Authors/Works Mentioned:	[a checklist of poetry, fiction, and drama appears in the body of the exercise].

Other works of art—painting, sculpture, textiles, music, cinema—can be a rich source of inspiration to writing. We can write in reaction to or in sympathy with a specific work; we can write in homage (or opposition) to another artist's worldview; or, even less directly, we can use a work of art or an artist as a mere starting point, producing a piece of writing that has only a slight or even a subterranean connection to the point of departure.

If you'd first like to see how other writers have written "out of art," you might start with the following brief list (but seek out other writings and writers on your own, too):

Oscar Wilde, *The Portrait of Dorian Grey*

W.H. Auden, "Museé Des Beaux Arts"

Elizabeth Bishop, "Large Bad Picture"

Amiri Baraka, "Coltrane"

William Carlos Williams, "Danse Russe"

Don Maclean, "Vincent" (popular song); there is also an oft-produced play entitled *Vincent*; Leonard Nimoy was the original lead actor.

Robert Lowell, "For the Union Dead" (poem that responds, in part, to a statue)

Richard Wilbur, "Museum Piece"

John O'Hara, "The Day Lady Died" (elegy for/homage to jazz singer Billie Holiday)

Derek Walcott, "For the Altarpiece of the Roseau Valley Church, Santa Lucia"

Adrienne Rich, "The Ninth Symphony of Beethoven Understood at Last as a Sexual Message"

Langston Hughes, "Dream Boogie"; "The Dove"

Bernard Malamud, "Rembrandt's Hat" (short story)

You might also look at the work of American poets John Ashbery and Kenneth Patchen; Latin American fiction writers Carlos Fuentes, Gabriel Garcia Marquez, Jorge Luis Borges, and Clarice Lispector; British poet William Blake; British novelist John Fowles; and the comparatively recent film, *Basquiat.*

To write your own work "out of art," you might. . .

1. Write a poem "about" a work of art. The word is in quotation marks to emphasize that you should interpret it loosely. Your poem need not, for example, describe or interpret or report on the artwork. The "about" can be a lot more tangential than that. You decide.

2. Write a poem that reflects, responds to, or reacts to an era of art, one artist's "take" on the world, how you see the world differently because of certain art you've studied, and so forth. Sample titles: "How Georgia O'Keefe Would See My Back Yard" or "Why I Dislike Landscape Painting."

3. Write a story in which some kind of work of art plays a key role.

4. Write a story in which a figure in a painting "comes alive."

5. Write a collage of responses written as you go through a museum exhibit. The writing can be about guards, other visitors, plants, the lighting, etc., and not just about the exhibit, of course. This work could lead to a play, a piece of creative nonfiction, a performance piece, a story—what have you.

6. Use a film as an immediate or a distant backdrop to a short story.

7. Write a poem about a public statue.

8. Write a poem that argues with another poem that's about art. That is, you might write a poem that disagrees with or modifies Auden's interpretation of Breughel (in "Museé Des Beaux Arts") or that disagrees with or modifies Rich's interpretation of Beethoven (in her poem on the Ninth Symphony).

9. Write an elegy for a dead painter, rock star, reggae artist, rapper, jazz musician, sculptor, ceramicist, dancer, or some other artist.

10. Write a poem about some kind of art you have attempted—throwing pots, painting, drawing, dancing, composing, singing, what have you. You need not be or have been an expert at it, of course. The poem might even celebrate your limitations.

(H.O.)

12 ▶ History As A Collaboration of Fact and Imagination

Use to Write:	Short Fiction; Longer Fiction; Poetry; Journal; Creative Nonfiction
Ideas and Concepts to Explore:	historical fiction; historical poetry; "poetic license"; speculative fiction.
Authors/Works Mentioned:	[a checklist of historical fiction and poetry appears in the body of the exercise].

Historical fiction and poetry are difficult to write because they owe allegiance both to fact and imagination in particular ways other writing does not. But for the same reason, and for other reasons, they are extremely satisfying to read and definitely worth trying, at least, to write. Historical fiction and poetry position writers—and readers—in relation to the past in unusual ways, and they invite writers—and readers—to combine knowledge and speculation powerfully.

How much do you have to know about a person, an era, an event, and/or a culture in order to write historical fiction and poetry? This, perhaps, is the most daunting question. To give the most obvious and discouraging answers first: It's hard to imagine a situation in which you could know too much, and it's easy to imagine a situation in which your knowledge would be too thin.

However, historical fiction and poetry are not the same as history; there is an aspect of play to them—the play of improvising, combining, melding, speculating. Indeed, it's possible to be *too* loyal to fact—to be insufficiently playful with the past—even if it's unlikely that any of us will know too much about the subject about which we've chosen to write.

Moreover, it's almost impossible to know what you need to know before you start writing fiction or poetry situated in history. Therefore (here's a bit of logical judo), not knowing enough works to your advantage, for you are licensed to jump in and begin imagining your version of whatever "past" to which you're drawn, about which you are passionate.

It's also helpful to begin by reading historical fiction, poetry, and drama—to get a sense of just how various the options are, how different the uses and treatment of history are. In no particular order, here are some suggested works:

William Shakespeare, *Julius Caesar* and *Antony and Cleopatra*

Leo Tolstoy, *War and Peace* (concerning the Napoleonic Era and Napoleon himself)

Gore Vidal, the "American" series of novels: *Burr, 1812, Washington, D.C., Lincoln, Empire, Hollywood*

Charles Dickens, *A Tale of Two Cities*

Stephen Crane, *The Red Badge of Courage*

Irving Stone, *The Agony and the Ecstasy* (concerning Michelangelo)

Giuseppe De Lampedusa, *The Leopard* (a novel of 19th century Sicily)

Robert Penn Warren, *All the King's Men* (based mostly on the life and times of Louisiana demagogue Huey Long)

Herman Melville, "The March into Virginia" and "Shiloh" (American Civil War poems)

William Butler Yeats, "Easter 1916" (concerning Irish civil war)

Gwendolyn Brooks, "Medgar Evers" (concerning the slain Civil Rights leader)

Seamus Heaney, "The Tollund Man" (poem imagining so-called "prehistoric" human existence)

Jean Auel, *The Clan of the Cave Bear* (novel imagining so-called "prehistoric" human existence)

Bill Hotchkiss, *Medicine Calf* (concerning American frontiersman Jim Beckwourth)

Daniel Hoffmann, *Brotherly Love* (long poem concerning American colonist William Penn)

Lawson Fusao Inada, "Concentration Constellation" (poem concerning the internment of Japanese Americans during the Second World War)

Sir Walter Scott, *Waverly* (concerning the Jacobite Rebellion, 1745, in England and Scotland)

Lydia Maria Child, *Romance of the Republic* (concerning the Reconstruction period of American history)

Kurt Vonnegut, Jr., *Slaughterhouse-Five* (concerning, in part, World War II and the Allied bombing of the remarkable cultural center, Dresden)

Toni Morrison, *Beloved* (concerning, in part, African American slavery)

Elizabeth Keckley, *Behind the Scenes: Thirty Years a Slave and Four Years in The White House*

This and other reading will continue to show how wide the range of historical fiction and poetry is; the degree to which "facts" are used, ignored, or in dispute; reverent and irreverent attitudes toward history; the way some writers look at history through the eyes of common people (*The Red Badge of Courage,* for instance, is about one imagined common soldier, not about famous real generals); and most especially, what your interests in history and tastes for historical literature are. Also, there's a specialized and somewhat strange subset of historical fiction called "speculative fiction." In bookstores it's often shelved with science fiction and/or fantasy. Several books in this sub-genre have based stories on the premise that Adolph Hitler and the Germans prevailed in World War II. In a sense, then, speculative fiction situates itself against a backdrop of history, but then it assumes (or begins from the premise) that history took a different track, and it spins a story that answers the question, "What if. . . [Hitler and the Germans had won the war]?"

Yet another subgenre we should mention is "historical romance." Books in this category are enormously popular. Essentially, they set fairly standard, even formulaic, "romance" stories in a specific historical era. Literally thousands of historical romances have been set, for example, in the Regency Period—late 18th and early 19th century Britain. In historical romances, authors don't really try to imagine history so much as they use a vague, even inaccurate, but terribly appealing sense of a period's exotic "history" to reinforce the romantic or sentimental nature of the plot. An excellent cultural-studies question to explore would be why these books enjoy such enormous popularity among twenty-first-century readers, almost all of whom are women.

But now let's move on to writing: To embark on writing your own historical fiction or poetry, you might. . .

1. Write just one scene about a real historical personage in whom you're interested. Any personage, any culture, any era. The scene need not be based entirely on fact, and it need not be overtly dramatic—perhaps the person is merely having breakfast or taking a walk; nonetheless, you will be "imagining history."

2. Choose any era or "moment" in any culture—something which interests you. Now write one scene about an imagined common person: A merchant's wife in Venice in 1500; a child in a Shoshone village before the arrival of Europeans; a sailor on one of Columbus's ships; an old woman in a Viking village.

3. Write a scene that, in a way, combines 1 and 2: An imagined common person meets a famous person. For example, baseball star Babe Ruth used to "barnstorm" in the off season, playing in exhibition baseball games all across the nation. He visited Tacoma, Washington, once. So one could write a scene in which an imagined Tacoma resident from that era meets Babe Ruth—cooks his breakfast, cleans his room, plays in the game against him, drives him to the Union Station, whatever.

4. Draw on a family story and use it to dramatize or evoke an historical era. Perhaps, for example, your parents met during the Viet Nam War. You could write a story based partly on the story of their meeting but also try to imagine that era.

5. What was life like at the college you attend 20, 50, 100 years ago? Write a story or a poem that answers the question imaginatively. Write a science fiction story in which one character steps through time and two collegiate eras are thereby connected.

(H.O.)

13 ▶ Shadows, Doubles and Others

Use to Write:	Short Fiction; Longer Fiction; Poetry; Drama; Creative Nonfiction; Performance Piece; Literary Criticism
Ideas and Concepts to Explore:	doppelgänger; cloning; "closeting"; the collective unconscious; cross-dressing; the divided self; the double; duality/dualism; ego; id; the Jungian shadow; libido; the "other"; replication; repression; shape shifting; superego; the subconscious mind; suppression; the unconscious mind.
Authors/Works Mentioned:	Sigmund Freud; Carl Jung; Masao Miyoshi, *The Divided Self*; [also, a checklist of works appears in the body of the exercise; the motion pictures "Big" and "Jack" are also mentioned].

Duality—split personalities, rival siblings, "good" and "bad" twins, "good" and "bad" witches, mythic figures representing colliding forces, etc.—has always been a potent source for folklore and literature. In the 19th century, as interest in psychology grew—reaching a peak in Sigmund Freud's elaborate theories of psychology— literature exploring duality abounded, and some of it is so famous that we tend to be aware of it even without having read it. The literary term (and German word, in case it's not obvious) *doppelgänger* (the double) springs from this period. You might consider reading some or all of the following works you haven't already encountered (and if you're in a scholarly mood, you might look at a critical study called *The Divided Self*, by Masao Miyoshi, which came out about 15 years ago but remains useful):

Robert Louis Stevenson, *Dr. Jekyll and Mr. Hyde*

Mark Twain, *The Prince and the Pauper*

James Hogg, *Confessions of a Justified Sinner*

Joseph Conrad, "The Secret Sharer"

Mary Shelley, *Frankenstein*

Edgar Allan Poe, "William Wilson"

Folklore and mythic traditions from every part of the globe also abound in stories of duality, and cinema too has worked with ideas of shadows, doubles, and others. Hollywood seems especially interested in adults who become their childhood others again or who are "inhabited" by children: The films "Big" and "Jack" are but two examples. And the notions of biological cloning, replication, closeting, crossdressing, and shape-shifting have been exploited by fiction writers, science-fiction writers, television writers, and screenwriters to dramatize duality. The writings of Sigmund Freud and Carl Jung remain interesting lenses through which to view duality in its many forms, giving us psychological concepts of ego, id, superego, libido, shadow, the unconscious mind, the collective unconscious, and so forth.

Rummaging around in these works will give you some perspective on the wide spectrum of ideas, themes, narrative strategies, cultural obsessions, views of technology, and mythic precursors embodied in "the art of the double."

In your own writing, you might. . .

1. Write a monologue poem spoken by voice belonging to your "other," however you wish to define that entity. This could become a performance piece.

2. Write a story in which an adult and her/his earlier childhood self somehow coexist.

3. Write a story in which someone's psychological Other or Shadow exists only in Cyberspace—on e-mail, on the Internet, in a company's mainframe. Many narrative approaches are available: a serious psychological parable, a gothic tale, a parody of some of the works mentioned above, a comedy, and so forth.

4. Write a dialogue poem, spoken by voices representing competing elements of one person's identity.

5. Write an essay that looks at a group of books, stories, poems, or films and develops an interpretation of the group's use of the double and/or of the culture's fascination with this particular construction of the double, the other, or the shadow. That is, why might Americans be especially drawn to movies in which adults can magically become their childhood others for a while, as is the case in "Big" and similar films?

6. Write an essay that compares and contrasts selected writings by Freud and Jung, with regard to their concepts of divided, competing, or multiple personality elements. (The ongoing struggle between Freudians and Jungians is legendary, when it's not a tad comic.)

7. Read Jorge Luis Borges' short narrative, "Borges and I," from the book, *Labyrinths,* and then write a piece of your own that loosely imitates it.

(H.O.)

14 **Can You Name That Epiphany?**

Use to Write:	Short Fiction; Longer Fiction; Poetry; Autobiography; Creative Nonfiction; Literary Criticism
Ideas and Concepts to Explore:	epiphany; to make [something] "manifest," and "to manifest"; to realize/realization.
Authors/Works Mentioned:	Will Baker, "My Children Explain The Big Issues"; James Joyce, "Araby" and "The Dead"; Doris Lessing, "Martha Quest"; William Shakespeare, *King Lear;* Sheila Ortiz-Taylor; the story of "the Epiphany" in the Christian tradition.

Here's how Sheila Ortiz-Taylor explained it one day when we were talking. "A realization" she said, "happens in the mind. An epiphany connects to the body." Her distinction helped me to explore a crucial issue in narrative writing. I started to sketch it out on my notepad like this:

If—

Realization = gaining a puzzle piece in a continuing puzzle
= taking place mostly in the mind, as a verbal, thinking construct, *then*

Does—

Epiphany = understanding that goes from mind to body, and
= often wordless, change or insight beyond words (at least beyond them for a moment, since writers often try to capture epiphanies in words)?

Realizations—you realize or you don't. You say/claim, decide you get it—or you don't. You now see what you didn't see. In narrative, this happens when the next event occurs, the next scene unfolds. Realization after realization can happen, and can deaden. Realizations are important but don't necessarily take us to the heart of things where we often, as readers (and writers), want to be. Another character enters the chapter stage left. Another layer of memoir takes us to a new location, opens into a tale of another family member, a journey begun or ended. But we crave something more, perhaps.

Epiphanies—true or false. You think you have one but it turns out only to be another realization—a false epiphany?, true epiphany and you're changed?—you're small but now feel connected in a new way to a larger whole? There's this spiritual, beyond-the-mind-dimension to epiphany. That's why, perhaps, we say certain works of literature "changed" us—writers led us to more than understanding, more than realizing, "Gee, I'm like that character." In a way, we become that author, partake of his or her family emotion, understand our own family, let's say, in a starburst, a concussion of altered awareness.

Now I don't want to make this sound cut and dried—"Apply the epiphany/realization test and improve your narratives 100%!" It's not that easy or that certain. I'm not sure realization isn't just as important to human life as epiphany, and I'm pretty sure each resides as much in the reader as in the text. My epiphany may be your realization, and vice versa. For instance, I don't know if I had a realization or an epiphany when I listened to Sheila explore this distinction. For all I know, all epiphanies start as realizations and then run amok—as when I started writing notes for this chapter: I suddenly recognized in an ordinary conversation between writers the germ of an idea I needed/wanted/could use.

But nonetheless, thinking of these "insight-intensities" is important for us as writers because we do try to manipulate them in a text—as if we used a rheostat, like the one we can put on house-lights to dim or raise them. We all try at different points in a narrative to intensify the effects we're striving to create.

Epiphanies. James Joyce is famous for them and brought the term into the vocabulary of twentieth-century writing and criticism. The ending of his story "The Dead" is an example. (So is "Araby," a much more spare story than "The Dead," but nonetheless representing a shift in consciousness in the main character.) The narrator of "The Dead" takes a careful reader from a contemplation of the particular to the universal in a way that makes the hair rise on the back of the reader's neck. Many readers, at least, have found this to be so.

Sheila also mentioned to me Doris Lessing's "Martha Quest." And I can remember many personal, literature-related epiphany moments. Once I watched leaves fall in a campground in Europe and began to recall Gerard Manley Hopkin's poem "Summer and Fall," and I felt I shared, finally, his insights about loss, seasonal change, and the glory of words and God, and in so doing felt I understood more about my life and what I wanted from my life (more moments of insight, realization, and with luck—pure epiphany). One of my *Metro* coauthors remembers being affected in a similarly powerful way while reading the end of Shakespeare's *King Lear.*

To realize, says my dictionary—to make real; bring into being; achieve. To make appear real. To understand fully; apprehend.

There's something quite cognitive and cerebral and instrumental about that definition. And certainly a good story or essay often works on my brain this way, helping me to understand and to realize something about something.

Epiphany raises the stakes tremendously.

An epiphany, says the same dictionary—is something which "shows forth," which manifests. An appearance or manifestation of a god or other supernatural being. A sudden manifestation of the essence or meaning of something. A comprehension or perception of reality by means of a sudden intuitive realization. The word "epiphany" comes to us via Middle English and Old French from Greek, and one of its original references was to the Christ child being made manifest, as a supernatural presence, to the Magi. Obviously, this epiphany was almost unbounded in its effects, changing whole cultures, whole views of reality; and there are similar crucial moments of the supernatural revealed in other religious traditions as well. Contrasted with the Christian epiphany, our personal epiphanies or "epiphanic" moments in narratives may seem trivial, but context is everything: there's nothing trivial in a life being changed forever because of a moment of awareness. And this is one area in which literature and life seem to connect most powerfully, inasmuch as literature represents, shows forth a vision of reality, and inasmuch as the "narratives" or journeys of our lives can be redefined dramatically in moments of epiphany.

This connection, perhaps, goes to the heart of the difference between "I can explain" and "I can barely put my finger on it, but I'll try to by telling you this."

Many types of short-short fiction popular today and of contemporary lyric poetry rely on epiphany for the economy of expression we find in such intuitive leaps. But fiction and nonfiction writers aim to trade in sudden insight, too, because humans rely—still—on bodily connection with their intelligence. Look at the short piece by Will Baker, "My Children Explain the Big Issues," in the minianthology and you'll see a writer who knows he can't "explain" what lessons he's learning from his children. Instead, he uses four scenes with his three children to show how he learns from those children. The first three scenes end with his reporting a child's epiphany, and the last scene reports one of his own—or at least allows him to outline the perplexities he sees in learning to know who we are as humans, the contradictoriness that allowed him to watch and see, to gain "comprehension" when dealing with his children. See, he says this all so much better in his prose while I struggle to detail an intellectual explanation of what his text more ably provides via intuitive, snap-shot-like leaps of prose, if we let it. Epiphany.

So what might you, the writer, do with these definitions and these distinctions?

- First, explore them a bit for yourself. List moments of realization and epiphany from your life and test them—does one grow from the other, does one manifest differently, as Sheila Ortiz-Taylor claimed, in the head and in the body? Do those categories, in fact, make sense to you? Next, do the same with your own writing. List change/insight/realization/epiphany moments. Are they one or the other or both? Do you have texts without any such moments? (Do we like living life without these moments? Do we like reading literature without these moments?). How is the rheostat working? Would your text benefit from more intensity, building toward bodily insights? How is this done?

• Can you take a moment of insight and describe it in a paragraph? Can you retell this instance again and create a moment of epiphany for reader? Writer? Character? What did you do? What was at issue?

• As you read through the anthology for *Metro,* or as you read other literature, sometimes keep these terms in mind and highlight or otherwise annotate places in texts that seem to exemplify what we've discussed here. Did this moment feel like an insight? That one an epiphany? Why? What did the author do to achieve this effect in you? What was going on in your mind/experience that made you receptive to such triggering of awareness?

• Finally, you might in your journal keep track of daily insights and small epiphanies—for a week or so. Then, of course, you might transform those into texts and share them with interested readers. Sit down, name that epiphany.

(W.B.)

15 ▶ The Narrow Road to Mixing Genres

Use to Write:	n/a [the exercise explores ways of mixing many genres in one work]
Ideas and Concepts to Explore:	collage; found poem; guest writing; haiku; mixing genres; modern/ postmodern; montage; "quilting".
Authors/Works Mentioned:	Matsuo Basho, *The Narrow Road To The Deep North;* Bessie Head, *Autobiography.*

Matsuo Basho's chief work, the title of which is often translated as *The Narrow Road to the Deep North* (the Penguin edition is a good one), has maintained a readership for over 200 years. Usually its stature is attributed to Basho's having refined a Japanese form of poetry, *haiku,* in the book. But a deeper reason for the work's seeming immortality may lie not with the perfection of this single genre but with the way Basho actually mixes numerous genres—travel reporting, meditation, autobiography, tales, poetry, guest poems by people he runs into on his journey, and so forth. Well before its time, Basho's book used techniques of montage, collage, "quilting," and other sorts of purposeful fragmentation and genre mixing we myopically consider modern or postmodern.

Read *The Narrow Road to the Deep North* and get a feel for what Basho's up to—in the journeys he took and in the way he writes about them and out of them. (Another remarkable genre-mixing book deserving a recommendation is the autobiography of Bessie Head, a twentieth-century African writer; seek your own examples of genre-mixing works.)

Then begin your own mixed-genre work, a work made of other works, a work that defines its form and content as it goes. It can start as a journal and then absorb poems, tales, fragments, notes, guest pieces, collaborations, found poems—whatever. Later you can revise it, shape it more deliberately, "purify" it—or not. Obviously, no work of writing is completely egoless, but there is an egoless *aspect* to Basho's book, a sense in which he gives up the world (or the idea of controlling the world) to gain something more, gives up one version of himself to learn more about what may be a deeper self, and lets the world—and the world of words—come to him in all its jaggedness and unpredictability.

(H.O.)

Reading *Form* As a Product of Perspective

Use to Write:	Short Fiction; Longer Fiction; Poetry; Autobiography; Creative Nonfiction; Literary Criticism
Ideas and Concepts to Explore:	accented syllables; blues poem; British Romantic poets; macrocosmic; organic form; form; rhyme; sestina; stanza; triad of conflict/crisis/resolution; villanelle.
Authors/Works Mentioned:	W.H. Auden, "Museé des Beaux Arts"; Richard Brautigan; Wayne Booth, *The Rhetoric of Fiction;* Italo Calvino; Samuel Taylor Coleridge; William Faulkner, *As I Lay Dying;* Ernest Hemingway, "The End of Something," from *In Our Time;* John Keats; Herman Melville, "Bartleby the Scrivener"; Wallace Stevens, "13 Ways of Looking at a Blackbird"; Leo Tolstoy, "The Death of Ivan Ilych"; William Carlos Williams, "The Red Wheelbarrow."

There are numerous ways to discuss form in fiction and poetry, and each one is a kind of lens focusing on one element but blocking out others. If, for example, we tell ourselves that stories (perhaps poems, too) should have a beginning, a middle, and an end, then the "forming" we do as writers and the interpreting we do as readers will flow from that piece of self-advising. Or perhaps we think in terms of another venerable triad—conflict, crisis, resolution. In another part of the forest, some types of lyric poetry actually force us to think of ourselves as following an architectural blueprint with precise numbers of lines, accented syllables, stanzas, repeated sounds (rhyme; key words in a sestina...), repeated lines (blues poem; villanelle...), and so on.

To some extent, the examples above depict form as something imposed upon material. That is, you might have a vague idea for a story, but if "conflict, crisis, and resolution" are uppermost in mind, then the idea will *conform* to that way of looking at the world of fiction. But it's also possible to depict form as something that emerges from the inside out, something that springs from perspective. Some of the nineteenth-century, British Romantic poets—such as Wordsworth, Coleridge, and Keats—were exploring this second possibility when they wrote about "organic form," a term which these days we might associate with "organic food" (grown without pesticides) but which they used in this sense: The *real* shape or integrity of a poem (in their case), even if the poem is written using a conventional blueprint, will be determined by the ideas, emotions, and associations flowing from the poet into the poem. In this sense, form is something that *grows* from the inside out; hence the term "organic."

As you read stories, poems, and novels, ask what perspectives are being represented by narratives, by evocations of voice, by images, and so forth. For instance, in the little world evoked by a short story, who speaks? Who has *authority* in the narrative, and how does this presence of authority shape the tale? What "side" of the story is being told? Whose problem is considered central to the narrative—and peripheral? Who's represented as seeing things clearly—or not clearly? Whose way of seeing things is changed—and how, and why? As the story begins, what perspective, vantage point, worldview, set of values, or "voice" is the point of entry into the little world? After exploring such questions—and related ones you craft yourself—speculate about how the form of the story—the narrative structure, the order of things—is shaped by perspectives you've identified.

Reading a poem, be alert to the images the words create. In what ways do these images honor or degrade the people, places, or things they represent? For instance, one could argue that in William Carlos Williams' famous poem, "The Red Wheelbarrow," the wheelbarrow is honored—given value—by the image we're presented, how the wheelbarrow is *seen*. And this sense of honoring seems to shape the poem, a shape that might be described as restrained, reverent, self-effacing—placing all attention on the wheelbarrow. To explore this example further, write a few lines about a wheelbarrow from a perspective that dismisses, sees little value in, or hates wheelbarrows: "Nothing depends on the red wheelbarrow," in other words. And as you read poems, ask—as you might of a photograph or painting or music video, from what angle or distance are people, places, and things being depicted? Where is the seeing eye of the poem? Think of other perspectivist questions to ask and speculate about how perspective has shaped the poem. If you like, begin with two famous poems that overtly deal with perspective: Wallace Stevens' "13 Ways of Looking At a Blackbird" and W.H. Auden's "Museé De Beaux Arts." Both poems are widely anthologized, easy to find.

It's also helpful sometimes to think of perspective in a broad or macrocosmic sense. After you've read several poems or stories by an author, for instance, you might ponder the general worldview or set of values of which these works seem to be evidence. What implicit judgements do the works seem to make about. . . the natural world, work, sex, love, men, women, children, war, death, power, money, religion, God, memory, loyalty, friendship, family, and so on? How close to, or far away from, is your own worldview in comparison to the one represented in these works? If the form of these works seems hard, impenetrable, and confusing to you—or easy, accessible, understandable—how much of this springs from differences or similarities of worldview?

For example, many of my students resist the *form* of stories like Tolstoy's "The Death of Ivan Ilyich" or Melville's "Bartleby the Scrivener," but often as we pursue the resistance, conflicts of time and culture seem to be the deeper sources of dislocation. Naturally, the resistance is sometimes phrased as, "These stories are so long!" but this seems to be just an easy peg on which to hang the resistance. Moreover, many students resist the form of very short stories; some by Richard Brautigan and Italo Calvino come to mind. As wildly different as Tolstoy and Brautigan are as writers, we can still say that they're letting their fiction manifest the way they see the world, trying *to give form to perspective.* Therefore, often when we step back for a moment and ask in class, in a variety of ways, *How does this author see the world through the eyes of this work?* then the resistance becomes another tool with which to interpret the story. The resistance becomes a site from which to explore the collision of perspectives, and at that site, one may ask, "How does this Tolstoy person see his society, which segment of society is it, and why—in 'The Death of Ivan Ilyich'—does he place so much value on multiple perspectives, which in turn influence the structure (and length!) of the story?"

Some additional ideas, then, for reading form as a product of perspective:

1. When you encounter a poem or story and find yourself resisting its form, find yourself having to push to read the thing, then step back and contrast your perspective with that represented in the work. What are the major differences? Are there any points of similarity?

2. Rewrite part of a poem or story or novel with which you have difficulty connecting. The implicit point here is not to say, "Well, since I don't really like Faulkner's novel, I think I'll rewrite it MY way." Instead, the idea is to use so-called *creative* writing as a way of gaining a foothold, which will aid understanding and perhaps lead to more successful *interpretive* writing. Creating, of course, is one kind of interpretation. Another goal here is to explore different perspectives toward the text.

   For instance, I sometimes use *In Our Time,* Hemingway's first collection of fiction, in courses, in part because the book is uneven, showing Hemingway struggling sometimes with perspective and form, as all young writers (and some old ones) do. One particular class showed some resistance to the story, "The End of Something," in which *In Our Time*'s recurring protagonist, Nick, breaks up with his girlfriend, Marjorie. I had the students rewrite the end of the story from Marjorie's point of view—a little monologue—and we used these pieces as a stepping-stone to a discussion about what sort of character Hemingway was giving us in Nick, what sorts of gender conflict recurred in the book, why Nick often seemed "at home" with men and not women, and so forth. We didn't reach a uniform view on these issues, but we were able to explore them better after "rewriting" "The End of Something."

3. Referring to Wayne Booth's *The Rhetoric of Fiction,* map perspectives in stories or novels; actually sketch a little chart describing the author's perspective, characters' perspective, where the focal point of the narration is, where you would locate your own reader's perspective, and so forth. You can do the same with a draft of a story of your own.

4. Write a three-part story in which each part gives a different character's perspective on the same event. Instead of plot being a playing out of conflict, crisis, and resolution, plot will become a movement around a subject, almost like a satellite circling a globe. This is an extremely concrete example of how form is a dramatization of perspective. You might look at Faulkner's *As I Lay Dying* or Tolstoy's "The Death of Ivan Ilyich" for examples of the narrative effects such multiplicity of perspective creates.

5. After Wallace Stevens' "13 Ways of Looking at a Blackbird," write a poem that is a certain number of ways of looking at something—5 ways of looking at a freeway, for example, or 7 ways of looking at a foot.

(H.O.)

Reading and Writing in the Workshop

Responding to, Evaluating, and Grading Alternate Style

(17)

Use to Write:	short fiction; longer fiction; poetry; creative nonfiction; journal writing; autobiography
Ideas and Concepts to Explore:	alternate style; "formative" evaluation; "summative" evaluation.
Authors/Works Mentioned:	Robert Coover; James Joyce; Gertrude Stein.

Those of us who read literature in graduate school know that Joyce's later work and Stein's work of any period are difficult to read, no matter how rewarding. Experimental writing—writing that expressly establishes itself beyond the mainstream; ec-centric writing, writing that sets itself up outside the circle of convention—taxes our reading schemas. Instead of quick reliable matches, we get disjunctions: For example, "Once upon a time" means relax and listen to the fairy tale unfold, but the "Once upon a time" of a Robert Coover short story throws us into a topsy-turvey world of challenging textual stress. When I sat down with my first batch of radical revisions intentionally assigned to students, I wanted to cry. The first few were exciting AND depressing. One seemed to "work" and the next to "fail miserably" in relation to the one that had just "worked."

After I forced myself to read and then reread the revisions, I started to see that, although each was stylistically unique, text strategies could be identified. (In fact, it was by reading several classes' worth of writing over a few years that I developed my guidelines for attempting radical revisions, shared in Chapter Three). Some students wrote snapshots, others produced textual video clips, others created new amalgams, fragments sewn together into prose crazy quilts. I had to have patience and tenacity as a reader—perhaps to a greater degree than my students had to have—because I had to set aside my English teacher's hyper-literacy and stop judging alternate writing against an implicit canon of genres in my head while I investigated the convention-making-and-breaking in which my students were engaged. After assigning radical revisions, I had gotten what I asked for; now I had to ask myself to be a different kind of reader. As your own reading life (and writing life) proceeds, you will need to do the same. Many texts will come your way that you will want to resist, even reject. But resistance and rejection are not always the place to stop; often we need to find ways to stay with the text, to overcome resistance, to resist the powerful urge to reject.

I'd like to share some responding and evaluating advice for writers and readers, advice I've collected over time. These notions should prompt you to develop your own—course–specific and assignment–specific—variations.

Responding to Alternate Texts.

Questions a writer can ask him/herself about alternately styled writings.

1. Can I describe why this writing requires this style/format? *(for instance, can I assure a reader that this was an intentional choice not simply an easy way out?)*

2. Are there places in the writing where I covered up, patched, ignored problems I was having understanding my own writing goals or aims? *(did I find that I couldn't pull my two metaphors together in the middle so I simply left white space hoping no one would notice?)*

3. If I recast this as a traditionally styled writing, what would I lose and what would I gain? *(was this, perhaps, fun to write alternately—the surprise of drafting this way got me started, but actually the topic would lend itself better to a traditional format in the final draft; or, conversely, would casting this as a regular essay lose the power of talking in my own and my mother's voice—a core issue in the essay being the contrasted yet generational echoes between these two voices?)*

4. In my final draft, am I paying attention to the reader? Have I done everything I can to "teach" the reader how to read my piece while still maintaining the integrity of my writing goals and ideas? *(for instance, sometimes it's okay to just come out and label a piece as exploratory, experimental, collaged, etc. at the beginning and help the reader set his/her reading expectations; alternate and/or experimental doesn't mean "anything goes" it means intentional in a different manner—how can I usefully signal my intentions?)*

Questions a classmate (or teacher) can ask (one-to-one, in peer groups with the writer) about alternately styled writings.

1. Can you tell us what effects you were hoping for, where you achieved them and where you think you may have fallen short?

2. What pleases you most and/or worries you most about what you've attempted here?

3. What did you learn while going through the act of drafting this writing in this way? Particularly, tell us things that you learned that don't necessarily show up in the finished text.

4. Here's how I read your text. Here's where I had trouble reading your text and why.

5. In this section, did you do _____ on purpose and why?

6. It would help me read (understand, enjoy) your text if you did this _____. How would that effect your goals for creating an alternately styled text?

7. Your text reminds me most of _____ writing. I read it like I read _____.

8. What do you wish you had done (what would you still like to do) to push this text even farther? Why haven't you? How can you?

Grading Alternate Texts

With process cover–sheets. Use a process cover–sheet to ask a writer to tell you about how well he/she has accomplished his/her and class writing goals. These may include learning about drafting through changing a text from one style to another, taking risks, pushing boundaries and borders, attempting difficult tasks according to the writers' own strengths and weaknesses, and so on. I ask the writer to do several things in drafting a process cover–sheet which I characterize as the *story* of the writing of the text. I ask that these be cast as personal letters from the writer to me, the teacher (this could also be cast as a letter to a writing partner, to a response group, or to the writer's own self).

Sample

Directions—Choose six out of eight of the following questions and include your responses in a letter, from you to me, of 1 to 2 single spaced pages; of course, add anything else that you'd like to add to help me understand your writing process.

1. Tell me in some detail about the drafting particulars on this writing—where did it start (ideas to drafts on the page) and where did it go (through how many revisions, taking place where, for how long, under what conditions)?

2. What were your goals for this piece? Where were you challenged? What did you risk in writing the text this way?

3. Who is your ideal reader? What would she/he have to bring to the text to give it a best possible reading?

4. To have this piece published in a journal, magazine, newspaper (choose a particular one to talk about), what would you have to change? You may say

why this piece is perfect for a particular site or publication *or* what you'd do to make it fit better. In either case, go into some detail.

5. If you had three more weeks, what would you work on?

6. According to your own goals for the paper and the class assignment, estimate your success with this text. Be specific, perhaps quote from sections of the text.

7. What did you learn about yourself as a writer and/or writing in general while drafting this piece?

8. You've given this text to a friend. He or she says, I like it but. . . and gives you four ideas for making it stronger and/or more accessible to a general audience. What would those four things be and how would you feel about doing them: how would each change improve your paper or ruin what you've been attempting?

Grading options: (1) Grade the letter as a traditional persuasive essay for the insights discussed and explored and don't grade the project beyond done/not done. (2) Grade both the letter and the project as part of an entire course portfolio. This may mean allowing for more experimentation (even individually productive "failure") by evaluating this "slot" in the portfolio as done/not done (in good faith). (3) Grade the text on the basis of traditional criteria—a mixture of assignment goals and teacher's estimate of the degree to which those goals were met, using the process cover sheet to add depth to this subjective evaluation. (4) Another combination of these options.

As a Class or Small Group. Class members and small groups should outline the challenges of the project before the project begins and then again after drafting—grading could rest on checklists of these qualities, each member responding to and grading the project; classes reading a text for a workshop discussion followed by completion of the checklist, and so on.

	Yes	No

1. Explores a genre/style new to this writer:

2. Writer's choices seem appropriate and/or effective:

3. Uses language/style in an engaging manner:

4. Explains learning in a detailed process cover–sheet:

5. Explores topic of _____.

6. Even though unconventional, grammar and proofreading choices appear intentional and under writer's control.

7. Text is successful:

By teachers. Teachers will want to choose from the most appropriate procedures listed above in order to encourage exploration and to encourage control.

It's important that a writer stretch, but also that the writer know *how* he/she was stretching and that the writer become more and more *able to articulate what was learned.*

It is essential that writers make "good faith" efforts (and that writers and teachers try to describe what constitutes good faith in this classroom at this time).

Always allow for the inevitable failure that good–faith efforts may produce. Obviously, there is learning in the process as well as in the product and writers should have both valued in a classroom.

Teachers should make clear what they are valuing and should offer formative as well as summative response.

- Formative evaluation helps the writer improve along the way through initial discussion of projects, peer and/or teacher conferencing, review of drafts, and so on.
- Summative evaluation lets the writer know what he/she accomplished—a written evaluation and/or a written response and grade on the piece (or on its contribution to a writing portfolio). Summative evaluation can and should also make connections and suggest future directions.*

(W.B.)

---

*(From, Bishop, Wendy, ed. *Elements of Alternate Style: Essays on Writing and Revision,* Portsmouth, N.H.: Boynton/Cook, 1998.)

Riding The Green Line

Invention

Getting Started

Dislodge the Icon of "The Writer"

Use to Write:	n/a [the exercise may lead to work in virtually any genre]
Ideas and Concepts to Explore:	the image of "the writer"; Gothic; memory and "memory space"; Modernist/Modernism; the privilege of speaking; the scene of writing.
Authors/Works Mentioned:	Linda Brodkey; Herman Melville, *Moby Dick;* William Shakespeare, *King Lear.*

Working our way into memory, most of us are aware that our lives are not very like the stuff of great literature. Ahab has his Moby Dick, Lear his unfaithful daughters, but sometimes it seems as if we are lucky if our lives are dramatic enough to include a shoot-out soccer match or a hike where we take a wrong turn.

Write what you know, novice writers are told, but novice writers often feel as if what they know just isn't that interesting. Their lives, they may feel, are boring. Who'd want to hear about such boring lives?

Or, as one young woman recently put it, "The Chinese have their Mah-Jong, exotic silks and teas, the Latinos have their barrios and music. I grew up between cornfields, is all. Nobody cares about cornfields anymore."

How we conceive of our lives in relation to the monument of literature directly affects how we *feel* about our own writing acts, which begin with *who* we are in the writing moment. Imagine this scene: *Genius Male Writer Creating Literature Alone in His Attic Garret by the Light of a Thin Gray Candle.* If it seems familiar to you, it may be because this is what Linda Brodkey has described as the Modernist Scene of Writing, a picture of writing so universally inscribed in our collected consciousness as to be present every time we write.

Maybe the writer who haunts you when you write does not literally hunker down in an attic. Maybe he runs with the bulls; maybe she composes alone in a garden; maybe it's a set of electronic pulses somewhere out in cyberspace. The point is not in **how** you may construct the image, but in the fact **that** we all carry in us an image of the " the writer" against whom we do not often measure up very highly. So we feel inadequate, our writing charged with dissonance. How should we even dare? we sometimes think.

Add to that our "uneventful" lives.

And sometimes all of the above-mentioned leads us into silence. And sometimes we end up trying to sound like someone other than who we really are. And sometimes this makes us feel as if, since our own lives are uninteresting, we must make everything up.

If it is true that a person never simply speaks, that there has to be a context in which that person feels privileged to speak, then too often the writer who haunts us is connected with a scene that denies us the very privilege we seek. To claim it for ourselves, first we must look at all its parts. Then we must give ourselves permission to own what it is we know, to let our stories really count, to be present in our own writing scenes.

This exercise is a multipart activity designed to examine the various dimensions of what may count as permission in such a context. In Part 1, we explore the space of memory through which we may discover what we may not know we know. In Part 2, we look more closely at the writer who haunts our writing scene in an attempt to make more room for ourselves. In Part 3, we return, but with an important difference, to that space of memory where we started. As a whole, this exercise seeks to frame a process in which we come to know better not just our own stories, but ourselves as writers, and to claim our own space and the privilege to continue.

Part 1.

Take twenty minutes and write the autobiography of your writing life. In it, you should include something from the following categories. The categories themselves are broad and abstract, but you encounter them in your own life through actual events and experience. They are designed here to provide an organizing structure through which you should write yourself fluidly. Don't think too much; just let yourself go. Think of this writing as cruising your life.

The categories:

love

aging

travel

conflict

your body

knowledge

literature

coming of age

life as a wo/man

male/female awareness

child/parent awareness

public/private life

life in language

your education

spirituality

sexuality

childhood

politics

nature

dreams

loss

Example. "But dear, I heard my mother say to my father on the eve of the Good Friday I was to be allowed to shave my legs for the first time, Katharine's legs are so much hairier than her sister's were. I was twelve at the time, a full year younger than my sister had been when she started shaving. I lay in bed listening to them argue about my body and development, and imagined my legs, sleek beneath my Easter dress, glistening with promise at dawn in the house of God."

Categories. conflict, my body, coming of age, male/female awareness, child/parent awareness, public/private life, sexuality, childhood, loss, spirituality, nature, and dreams.

Time yourself and stick to twenty minutes.

Repeat, as desired.

Part 2.

A writing teacher once advised that if you want to be a writer, all you need to do is sit four hours at your desk every day. Whether you even wrote or not at first wouldn't really matter, because eventually you'd get bored enough to start producing.

Then he added, "Be sure to let your wife know not to disturb you."

Imagine, again, that garret where the genius (male) writer sits, authoring great literary works. Or replace him with that writer who haunts your own internal writing self, who may instead be a woman with children, feeling guilty over sometimes choosing writing first. It may be a mountain man in Montana, living on the edge of the wilderness using only paper and pen. It may even be your writing teacher, either your first one or your current one, or someone in between. It doesn't really matter who or what this writer is, the one who haunts you. What matters is the dissonance created between your ideal image of a writer writing and you yourself, fumbling for words. What matters is that sometimes this dissonance makes writing seem harder than it really is, creating unnecessary struggle.

For of course, when we try to force ourselves to fit this ideal image we begin to work at odds with our own purpose. When we try to sound like "the writer," we end up trying not to sound like ourselves. It's a form of disappearance on the page, and we all go through it sometime. I myself started out British and male, but with a Southern Gothic twist, and what I wrote was horrid. It took me years to discover I really only wrote well when I cleared my head of other writers and let my own self speak.

What about you? What do you think you are trying to sound like, and what is the difference between that and who you really are?

In Part 2 of this exercise, we examine more closely our own "writing scene"— that is, not the place where we write, but where it comes from, who informs it, and how it affects our writing. We do so to frame the question: how might our writing be affected if we gave ourselves permission to sound exactly like ourselves when we write?

The Directions. To begin, think about where you write.

Do you write in the kitchen, near the window facing east? Will the children soon wake up, and will they want a complicated breakfast? Who will be driving them to school?

Or do you write, instead, late at night in your local coffeehouse, buzzed on nicotine and caffeine and resolving, in the morning, to stop smoking?

Do you write in bed, letters to your great Aunt Willa, who lives in Nebraska and sends you corn crafts?

Do you write four hours undisturbed at your desk?

Now write for twenty minutes, and answer the following questions:

Where are you?

Who is with you?

What do you want?

What are you afraid of?

What are you writing?

When you are done, pause for a moment. Read over what you have written. Think about it. What "works" and what doesn't about where and how you write now?

If you could imagine an ideal scene of writing, where everything would be perfect for you as a writer, what would it be? Imagine it now. Think about it for a moment. Then begin again, writing for another twenty minutes and responding to the same questions above.

Compare the two versions of your writing scene.

Part 3.

Imagine yourself in your ideal scene of writing. Return to Part 1 of this exercise, and cruise your life again, writing it in your own voice.

Variation. Do this exercise in a group of three to five. Share what you write. Can you imagine an ideal scene of writing that would work for every member of your group? What would it be like? Write about it. Write "in it." Share what you write.

(K.H.)

▶ **2** Narrative Anxiety Cure-All (Not Sold In Stores)

Use to Write:	Short Fiction; Longer Fiction; Autobiography; Creative Nonfiction; Journal
Ideas and Concepts to Explore:	narrative anxiety; narrative as "secret".
Authors/Works Mentioned:	*Robinson Crusoe;* Samuel Richardson, *Clarissa.*

Writers sometimes have predilections, even instincts. Some forms make better sense to them than others. And for writers, the reverse is also true. If one form makes sense, another may not, leading, in some cases, to pronounced writerly anxieties.

Kate, for example, started out and kept on telling stories, with a single summer's failed foray into poetry, which still strikes her as confounding. Wendy wrote poetry for years before gradually adding both narrative and prose. But Hans, who has been writing stories for a long time now and published one novel, initially suffered from narrative anxiety.

As he puts it, back when he started out he enjoyed writing poems—and reading them. In general, they just sort of made sense to him; many seemed like little conversations; he enjoyed the way most of them used imagery and played with language to some degree. When he first tried to write stories, however, they seemed so big and heavy contrasted to poems. He felt as if he were moving furniture and grew impatient with the form, but, ironically, instead of writing quick fictions, he allowed his impatience to translate into sluggishness. He labored, and his stories were laborious. He'd get a new idea for a story but would dread writing the story itself because he was afraid (anxious) that the good idea would somehow get lost in this big heavy form, narrative. In the end, he did write his way out of and around the anxiety, but it took a while, and now that is where he is most comfortable.

Maybe you are like Hans, and you "get" poem writing right away, or maybe you're more like Kate, and you "get" story writing instead. Probably (though this is just a hunch) poetry anxiety is more common than its partner in narrative just because of the way poems move through the culture—in the more "difficult" classroom, coffee shops where the dress code is all black, quiet library corners drenched with aged air and dust motes. They say to the world *look at me, I am ART*. And ART, in this manner, is marked by its own exclusivity, which novice writers may experience like a KEEP OUT sign. (A good response to this is to kick the sign down.)

But if you are one of those for whom poems are easy, and stories, instead, seem big and cumbersome and scary, it may be useful to consider exactly why. Besides stories' sheer length, we believe there are two main factors that contribute to narrative anxiety, which may affect us without our even knowing. The first has to do with the overwhelming proliferation of stories in the culture. And the second, more elusive, is related to what we will call the problem of material.

In the first case, narrative really does suffuse, define, sometimes litter our culture. Stories inundate and bombard us. Count the stories, say, in a nightly news broadcast, your little sister's favorite commercial, the billboards you pass on your way to school, your local Little League team, the season's latest blockbuster movies. Never mind the stories you tell yourself about why you didn't do so well on your physics midterm, or why your boyfriend doesn't call, or why your sister (you suspect) is using drugs. Your mother's skin cancer, your father's disa/rea/ppearing act, your childhood tree fort: you have stories about these, too. What you tell the cop who stops you for speeding, your teacher when your paper is late.

In the midst of all these stories (especially the big movies and t.v.), you may wonder how you can possibly compete. You may also mix them up, the different modes of storytelling, big screen, or t.v., or *Oprah*, and write yourself into a hole.

The problem of material is more vexed and relates to what you think you are doing when you tell a story. If you think you are telling about what really happened, you may feel obliged to put it all in, just the way it was, or else people will think you are lying. If you think, instead, that writing stories is about pure invention, you may be reluctant to include anything "real" or "true," since that would make your story less "creative." Plus, your writing teacher tells you to "write what you know," when you may feel that what you know is not that interesting or too personal to put on the page. So if you don't already feel overwhelmed by the surfeit of stories in "competition" with your lonely voice, you may when you try to imagine what you can possibly write.

This exercise is designed to remind you that:

1. **British** fiction began in the 18th century with the narrative convention that a lie was the truth. Robinson Crusoe's story was "found in a bottle," and Samuel Richardson's novel, *Clarissa*, was composed of hundreds of letters "discovered in an attic." The convention itself was driven by a deep suspicion people harbored toward invention (lying) as immoral, so even when they did it (wrote novels), they had to make fiction "true."

2. If a lie can be true, just by saying it is, then so can the truth be a lie. Fiction is, by definition, made-up (a lie). So, whatever you put in it, true or not, becomes, inside the frame of a fictional story, just that, an invention. If your mother does or says something in a story your mother really did or said, it refers, not to your mother, but to the story it is in, and its own storiness, which is fiction, a made-up convention.

3. Sometimes you have to exaggerate, or add things, or change things, just to get closer to what your story really *felt* like. Maybe your family corrects you, "Oh no, you are exaggerating. It didn't happen like that at all." Maybe your mother warns, "Don't lie, your nose is growing." If so, you may have the instinct of a real story teller, who knows that, in the interests of authenticity, stories bend the "truth" all the time.

4. Writing stories is not the same as making movies or reporting news on the t.v.

5. Though stories inundate us in countless forms—comic strips, opera, e-mail, t.v., and so on—our medium is language and we must use it to its fullest potential.

While this exercise may not cure everything that ails you, it may work to loosen the things up, in particular the things that get stuck in your throat, which belong in your ear anyway. One sentence after another.

Here's what you do:

Begin by writing a secret, one you would never tell anyone. Write for ten minutes, as close to the bone of the secret as you can. This writing is only for you.

Next, write the same secret in second person, using "you," not "I" as your subject. This writing is still only for you.

Example.

> **First writing:** Sometimes I wish I did not have this to remember, like a tiny piece of sand or glass inside my skin. I never meant to say the words I said, never thought them out beforehand, never even believed them after I said them, or during, I think. It was just, she made me angry, my sister, and after everything I'd done for her since she left home.
>
> **Second writing:** Sometimes you wish you did not have this to remember, like a piece of grit in your eye, soot or aerosol spray. You never meant to say it like that, never thought things out, and didn't even believe them while you were flinging the words at your sister, and after everything you'd done for her, since she left home.

Next, write the same secret, only this time, do two things to change it: alter the facts in some significant way, and write it in the third person. (In the example above, you might change the sisters' roles: ". . . and after everything she'd done for me since I left home." Only in third person: ". . . and after everything she'd done for her . . .") This piece of writing you will share with others in the class, so you should change whatever you want to keep secret. But maybe, already, what you are writing is so far removed from where it started that you don't really recognize it as yours anymore. Maybe your secret has turned into "fiction."

In this next part of the exercise, share your work in a group with several others, ideally anonymously. Talk about what you have written. At home, try weaving several of the "secrets" you heard in class together in a single story. Then share these final stories, and listen to what has happened to your "secret" in other peoples' fiction.

One thing you may notice is what a great relief it is not to have things happen exactly as they happened. Another is that someone else's "elaboration" on your original "idea" may have made it more powerful. Or that weaving three "secrets" together may be possible because language is more plastic than other more linear media, like film, and more complex than the billboard you pass on your way to work. Or that it all sounds somehow different now, more like fiction, freed up.

Listen, especially, for what surprises you. Pay attention to the pleasure of it.

(K.H.)

Coming to Our Overlooked Senses

Taste: Writing About Food and Family

3

Use to Write:	n/a [the exercise may lead to work in virtually any genre]
Ideas and Concepts to Explore:	appetite, eating, hunger, nourishment: their symbolic, figurative meanings; cliché; aphorism; triggering topic; associational chain.
Authors/Works Mentioned:	Devan Cook, "Jazz, Fried Okra Afternoon"; Wendy Bishop, "Sudden Hunger"; Henry Fielding, *Tom Jones;* Chang-Rae Lee, "Coming Home Again"; Li Young Lee, "Eating Together"; Maxine Kumin, "Appetite"; Robert McCloskey, *Blueberries For Sal* (children's book); Christina Rossetti, *Goblin Market;* Ann Turkle,"Cheetos."

Along with the big topics—death, war, love, religion and sex—food and family memories are some of the great triggering topics for writers. We associate eating with nourishment and with abandonment, with power and control, and with loss of control or powerlessness. Many of our most notorious and prominent family memories, we'll find, center on hunger, satiety, deprivation, denial—feasts, (family) meals, holiday dinners that did or should not have taken place. The following invention activities are aimed at getting you started on writing about food, family, and memories of both. The genre, audience, directions you take as you revise your responses are up to you and will depend on your immediate writing needs and interests.

To begin—and before choosing from the writing prompts listed at the end of this chapter—listen to (or read) each poem, prose poem, and the prose passage, twice. After the second reading, write for three minutes, capturing any memory/response it elicits.

Appetite

I eat these
wild red raspberries
still warm from the sun
and smelling faintly of jewelweed
in memory of my father

tucking the napkin
under his chin and bending
over an ironstone bowl
of the bright droplets
awash in cream

my father
with the sigh of a man
who has seen all and been redeemed
said time after time
as he lifted his spoon

Men kill for this.

—Maxine Kumin

Sudden Hunger

I open two cans of new-style stewed tomatoes with basil & garlic and one of plain red tomato sauce. When the hamburger & pork has browned sharply with the large-cloved, persistent Peruvian garlic, I skim the meat fat for Lucy the dog & add the sauces to the wok & cinnamon & sugar from the kid's shaker, no separate spice & sweet left, Then Cuisinart the whole because my children won't eat tomatoes in lump-form, although I'm hopeful. Return this messily to the wok, wok to stove, add bay leaf—the last—two inches of Sebastiani Cabernet & stir this meaty-soup, the spices, reds, browns, fats, melding. Suck some off a spoon, needily, like marrow from bone, add more cinnamon, stir some more, carnivore-like: remember Italian heat, summer slipping into my bones in a rented room in Rome, louvered windows filtering too much sunlight, the shouts of men & women loud as the backfire from Vespas, exhaust & exhaustion until warm evening. Fill this pasta pan with already hot water—waste it from the faucet in hunger—the choice, linguine or angel's hair—grate Romano & place the colander in the sink. Spoil myself with more meat sauce as I lean over, steam, & wait.
—Wendy Bishop

Jazz, Fried Okra Afternoon

Fried okra, hot coffee, bacon grease melting in black iron skillet from the drippings can on the stove, jazz on the radio, mid-afternoon, sun behind the little live oak with three trunks that shades the trailer, windows open, dirty screens, two horses outside asleep beside the viburnum hedge, 85 degrees, breeze from the woods, okra from the woods garden. Flowers like cotton, like sticky fuzz. Okra comes from Africa. Cut the pods every day. Slice young and tender into rounds, 1/4 inch wide, roll in meal and egg and meal again. Salt and pepper, red pepper too. Fry in hot bacon grease and stand back: it spits. Eat with green beans, green onions, bacon, corn bread with lots of butter, coffee: strong, hot, black.

Black iron skillet. Jazz on the radio. Shoes off, air thickening in the kitchen, dark, heat from cooking lingers around the stove. Wash dishes. Windows face west: watermelon red sunset lights the stove, then fades, then the last green line before it's over. Sun sinks into the woods—vines cover it. Sun buries in old leaves. The trailer cracks and settles, letting the heat go, rise. Dogs wander off toward the woods. Swallows above the barn and garden, then sounds of the first whippoorwills and a hoot owl in the woods where a breeze rises. Birds. Children catch fireflies. We sit on the steps and listen.

Breezes rise. Open doors and windows, breathe, blow through the whole hot place, bacon smells, coffee, okra, corn meal, jelly smeared on the bedspread covering the couch, blow into the bedrooms in back. Cooler now. Stained curtains puff. Heat lightning, clouds stack toward the west, the Gulf, over the woods. Baths, clean white cotton pajamas folded flat under white cotton pillowcases, sheets stretched taut over still warm beds, spreads folded down to air bedding. Smell of sun, light, grass, bleach. Children eat cookies and drink kool-aid. Dark is thick and sweet, muscadines ripen behind the barn, woods move toward the road. Lights on in the house above the pasture. Dust settles on road, leaves. Another hoot owl answers the first, fireflies hover, doors close, lights out. Lightning closer now, leaves scratch screens, breeze over beds. Dogs under the trailer. Rain's coming.

—Devan Cook

Eating Together

In the steamer is the trout
seasoned with slivers of ginger,
two sprigs of green onion, and sesame oil.
We shall eat it with rice for lunch,
brothers, sisters, my mother who will
taste the sweetest meat of the head,
holding it between her fingers
deftly, the way my father did
weeks ago. Then he lay down
to sleep like a snow-covered road
winding through pines older than him,
without any travelers, and lonely for no one.

—Li Young Lee

Cheetos

Salty, fat, neon
orange, precisely what I don't
need. I savor them,
fingers pollinated by
cheese twigs. Timid rebellion.
See, Mother, I eat what I like!

—Ann Turkle

I would enter the kitchen quietly and stand beside her, my chin lodging upon the point of her hip. Peering through the crook of her arm, I beheld the movements of her hands. For *kalbi,* she would take up a butchered short rib in her narrow hand, the flinty bone shaped like a section of an airplane wing and deeply embedded in gristle and flesh, and with the point of her knife cut so that the bone fell away, though not completely, leaving it connected to the meat by the barest opaque layer of tendon. Then she methodically butterflied the flesh, cutting and unfolding, repeating the action until the meat lay out on her board, glistening and ready for seasoning. She scored it diagonally, then sifted sugar into the crevices with her pinched fingers, gently rubbing in the crystals. The sugar would tenderize as well as sweeten the meat. She did this with each rib, and then set them all aside in a large shallow bowl. She minced a half-dozen cloves of garlic, a stub of gingerroot, sliced up a few scallions, and spread it all over the meat. She wiped her hands and took out a bottle of sesame oil, and, after pausing for a moment, streamed the dark oil in two swift circles around the bowl. After adding a few splashes of soy sauce, she thrust her hands in and kneaded the flesh, careful not to dislodge the bones. I asked her why it mattered that they remain connected. "The meat needs the bone nearby," she said, "to borrow its richness." She wiped her hands clean of the marinade, except for her little finger, which she would flick with her tongue from time to time, because she knew that the flavor of a good dish developed not at once but in stages.

[Paragraph from "Coming Home Again"
by Chang-Rae Lee, *The New Yorker*]

Now, star the three most interesting prompts in the list that follows. Write toward each response for five minutes on each prompt. Read through everything you've written so far and choose one piece, or place, to continue on from—drafting a poem, essay, prose sketch, short story, or play.

Five-Minute Writing Choices:

- Write on six of the following words (in any order): appetite, hunger, food, milk, fat, sugar, spice, meat, mother, father, sister, brother, grandmother, grandfather, lover.

- In the manner of the poem "Appetite"—list the foods different members in your family like. Choose one, and have the person eating that food, with whatever emotion is appropriate, told as graphically as possible. As Kumin does, write your last line as something that relative might say.

- Write about a "scene" of eating in the third person—watch a family member, describe and interpret his/her actions.

- Share a recipe, but in doing so, like "Sudden Hunger" tell a story. Decide how detailed your recipe needs to be (should the reader actually be able to prepare what you prepare?) and equally, how closely—explicitly—you tie your narrative to the recipe.

- Write about eating in relation to times of day—morning, noon, night, late night, between meals, while traveling, while doing something else.

- Write about not eating, starving, and or avoiding eating. "Cheetos" touches on those themes. Or, as Ann Turkle does in "Cheetos," use a named food—a junk food, green onion, or sesame oil or red raspberries or chop suey, to let you say something about eating and those who eat.

- Describe in great detail, in the manner of "Coming Home Again," someone who means something to you cooking something that means something to that person and/or to you in particular. Don't tell us what anything means, though, unless you do in the last line or two, like Chang-Rae Lee.

- In her prose poem "Jazz, Fried Okra Afternoon," Devan Cook weaves two themes, food (fried okra and all it evokes) and jazz—the jazz of a regular day (or has she condensed many days, many memories?). Use her prose to start you on your own associational chain. You also might try to write yours in the imperative—do this, do that—how-to voice. ("Fry in hot bacon grease and stand back: it spits.")

- Like Ann Turkle in "Cheetos," talk back to someone or explain something you've never been able to explain about you, food, your memory of a food.

- Remember the great "food" scenes from literature and movies—eating peaches in *Tom Jones*, the dinners in *Eat Drink Man Woman*, the whole of the movie *The Big Night*, the eating that takes place in Christina Rossetti's long poem, *Goblin Market*, and so on. What scene from your past would lend itself to especially vivid, pungent fiction scenes or to filming? Film it in words.

- Write about a joyous moment with food, celebration, satiety, etc.

- Do the same with loss or absence as in "Eating Together" by Li Young Lee.

- Write about the humor of foods—the humor is often in the detail of the object (embarrassingly large and glossy purple eggplant) or the moment (a child eating more berries than she puts in the pail and then finding a bear as happens in the award–winning children's book *Blueberries for Sal* by Robert McCloskey).

- Explore your attitudes toward food in a series of propositions: "Never trust people who don't like to eat." "You are what you eat." "I will never eat an insect." "I fell in love with a man who ate guacamole for dinner." Write at least forty clichés, aphorisms, beliefs, propositions, blunt statements. Choose two to write about in more depth, as mini essays, sketches or a short-short story.

- List five foods you used to eat often in your childhood but don't any longer. Write the words on blank paper and explore why you did then but don't now.
- Free associate a list of twenty foods. Choose five and invent a story in paragraph form about each food—the stories are linked only in that you're the person stringing them together; they don't have to be in order or in the same style or voice.

(W.B.)

Sounds and Smells

Use to Write:	Short fiction; Longer fiction; Poetry; Creative nonfiction
Ideas and Concepts to Explore:	n/a
Authors/Works Mentioned:	Terry Wike; Gregorian chants; [composers Bela Bartok and Philip Glass are also mentioned.]

1. Starting with some ideas I got from Terry Wike, I've often brought "sounds" into creative-writing classes or had students write on their own in response to sounds. I've used tapes of environmental sounds (rain, jungle sounds, seashore sounds, etc.); of Gregorian Chants; of music by unusual composers (Bela Bartok, Phillip Glass); and of jazz. Often I play shorter samples of several tapes (sometimes dimming the lights) and have students make notes after I stop the tape each time. Then, after a session of sound-playing and note-taking, I have students start poems or stories or more extended nonfiction reaction-pieces. Obviously, a student listening to jungle sounds might first come up with a scene or a story set in the Amazon, but he or she might later come up with a less obvious narrative strategy, perhaps involving someone who only dreams of jungles, someone who has decided to live in a greenhouse, etc. I encourage students not to get locked in, necessarily, to one poem or story early on but explore different points of view, different images, different ways of "reading" the sounds. On the other hand, if a poem or story really seems to begin to take off, there's no reason to halt it arbitrarily. Nor is it necessary to stay tethered to the sounds, which may in fact lead to poems or stories that eventually have little or nothing to do with the tape-recorded starting point for this writing.

   In class, outside of class with a smaller group, or on your own, get some "sounds"; listen to them, make notes, and start to work toward poems, stories, or nonfiction pieces.

2. Apply similar inventive approaches to smells, odors, and aromas. Often we emphasize images so much in creative writing that we neglect the sense of

smell and how we might represent smells, odors, or aromas when we shape scenes, develop narrative suspense, construct poems, and so forth.

What smells, for instance, do you associate with your childhood? With adolescence? With different places you lived? With different relatives (a grandmother's certain perfume, a grandfather's aftershave)? What *particular* smells do you associate with different seasons in different places—that is, not just a cliché notion of "flowers in Spring" but an odor linked with a specific time and place, with spring rains in a medium-sized city, with harvest time in a particular farming region, etc. If you have worked in a family business, what smells do you associate with it: carpentry and lumber; a restaurant and cooking; an office and its smells; and so on?

After listing and briefly describing such smells, odors, and aromas, write about memories and scenes they call to mind, expand associations, invent or imagine other situations, work toward stories or essays. Write an "odiferous" poem. Challenge yourself to describe certain odors accurately and originally; for instance, without using the words "sour," "bad," or "onion," how might you describe the breath of a character who's just consumed onions?

(W.B. and H.O.)

Places and Things

The Familiar Place As Frontier:
Seeing the Rare in the Ordinary

5

Use to Write:	Short Fiction; Poetry; Creative Nonfiction; Essay; Drama
Ideas and Concepts to Explore:	found dialogue; set/setting.
Authors/Works Mentioned:	n/a

When we think of adventure, quest, exploration, or pioneering, we tend to think of people going into unknown or unfamiliar territory; this habit of mind may be especially common to Americans (and perhaps to many peoples in the Western Hemisphere), whose cultural mythologies are so wrapped up in people crossing oceans, in westward migration, conquering or taming so-called wild places, and starting so-called new lives. Ironically, however, when familiar surroundings become ultra familiar they become unknown again—because we think we know everything about them, because habitual responses require less energy from us, and because there is no apparent urgency to be alert, as there is—for example—when we arrive at a place new to us.

At some level, however, most writers make poems, stories, and other writing out of the familiar, out of everything that's nearby. Therefore, it follows that writers must rediscover the familiar, must see it again and notice what is, in fact, rare about it. So this exercise addresses the writer's work of rediscovery.

Select a place or a routine or a routine in a place; what you select should be so familiar that it has come full circle to become, in its "invisibility," a frontier. An abode, a cafe, a sports site, a part of a campus, a job site, a routine stroll across campus, the table you eat at (and the eating) every day: these are examples.

Then select a time when you are able to treat the familiar as a frontier—to look deliberately at it as if you were looking at it for the very first time. What do you notice that, because of familiarity and routine responses, you had ceased to notice? Become aware of as much of the "scene" as you can. Reacquaint yourself. Figuratively and literally, look in odd corners. Make the peripheral central to your observation. Take extensive notes, probably with no thought yet to where these recorded observations will lead.

Images you record might lead to a new poem or enhance an existing one. A poem or a story might be *set* in this place. Perhaps you'll record pieces of conversations that may seem like dialogue in a story or a play, that might suggest conflict, or that may just seem linguistically intriguing. (Playwrights sometimes refer to such recorded conversations as "found dialogue".) These and other possibilities lurk out there, but the main purpose of the exercise is to allow you to see again, to observe the familiar in a "writerly" way.

(H.O.)

6 ▸ Beginning With Nostalgia: Lost Childhood Places

Use to Write:	Autobiography; Fiction; Poetry; Creative Nonfiction; Journalism/Opinion Piece
Ideas and Concepts to Explore:	nostalgia; sense-of-place; sentiment/sentimentality.
Authors/Works Mentioned:	*Oxford Dictionary of the English Language;* William Wordsworth, *Tintern Abbey.*

Writers often find themselves being warned away from nostalgia as a source of inspiration or ideas for writing, or even as a starting place. Why? Mainly because teachers, other writers, and editors fear that nostalgia is just a trap, that if writers fall into it, their writing may suffer from self-indulgence, sentimentality (sentiment that's overdone), excessive sweetness, or boring, shapeless pining for what's lost. Sometimes it's good to pay attention to such warnings; sometimes it's not; in this particular instance, you are licensed to ignore the warnings and jump into the trap. To play a riff on the old pop song, "it's your (nostalgia) party, and you can cry if you want to."

In class once, students got on the subject of fields and other wild or "undeveloped" places where they had played when they were children. Almost everyone in the class had a story about a field, a wooded area, or a creek she or he played in or near; and almost everyone now reported that the place had disappeared, victim to further housing—or business—development, to the seemingly relentless American drive to fill up open spaces. A wave of nostalgia and loss washed over the classroom. Clearly these places, and the memories of them, had become complicated symbols. In a sense, they represented—were "signs" for—childhood itself. They also represented a measure of liberation and independence because the play that went on there was significantly *away* from the adult world. Thinking again about the places often sparked memories of something magical, or foreign, or secret—the sorts of memories that can lead to poems, stories, or autobiographical pieces. In a more public or political way, the fact that these places had disappeared seemed to intensify feelings of childhood lost because not only had everyone in the class grown up (or at least was working on it), but also a special place of that growing up had disappeared, literally could not be visited again. In this context, nostalgia was not so much a sweet, self-indulgent feeling as it was a symbol of independence lost, magic remembered, or geographical change regretted.

For this writing prompt, begin thinking about, writing about, and/or listing memories of such a childhood place—a place you often visited (alone or with friends), a special place of childhood play. Your locale may indeed have been a field or wooded area, but of course it might have been a different sort of place—an abandoned house, a schoolyard, a basketball court, a mall. There is no official list of such places; what matters is what the place meant to you and your childhood. And the first task is to record memories, images, recollections of what went on in that place, oddities of the place. Has a piece of playground equipment on the schoolyard endured, become a kind of monument? Who plays on the basketball court now? Does part of the mall architecture seem terribly out of date? Was there a special tree or rock in that field—and is it gone now? If it's still there, does it seem the same? At this stage, there is little pressure to filter or categorize the memories.

As you proceed, consider what emotions seem to be linked to particulars. Are there, for instance, good and bad memories? Uncertain or ambivalent feelings toward the place? When and why did the place cease to be special? What has happened to the place? To what extent was the distinctiveness of the place owing to just the place itself, and to what extent was it owing to what went on there, or to some particular person who went there with you, or to some legendary status conferred on the place by your family, friends, or community? To what extent was it *your* special place, and to what extent was it a generally known special place? (For example, a swimming hole in a small town might be special to both an individual and to the community, whereas the woods behind one family's house or an alley behind an apartment house is more private and localized.) You might also ask, "Was it such a great place after all?"

Don't worry about being overly sentimental. Honor whatever emotions come your way, even if they seem sappy or cheesy. It's your party. . . . One question to ask is why the emotions attached to the place *are* so powerful. Then begin to sort out the emotions and responses. Perhaps the emotions are contradictory; perhaps you love and hate the place both at once. Maybe the place appealed to you only when you were a certain age. Also, consider the possibility that you have *invented* certain "memories"; for example, supposedly huge fields may have been postage-stamp size, or maybe that old rusted-out husk of an abandoned car was actually in another place, but for some reason your memory has transported it to this place. Why?

Another option is to try to find photos of the place, or photos of yourself at the time you visited the place. Or talk to family members and childhood friends: What do they remember? What do they remember differently? In what sense does your history of the place conflict with theirs?

After some or all of this preliminary work, think about what sort of writing might now take shape. An autobiographical piece. A journalistic piece on such-and-such woods or this-or-that field and what's happened to it since. A piece of fiction set in such a place but involving an imagined story (license yourself to disregard "the facts" and invent, at will.) A lyric poem. A narrative poem. (In chapter seven we've included one of the most famous poems in our language, and it's essentially a nostalgia poem, William Wordsworth's *Tintern Abbey,* which combines narration and lyricism and examines complex relationships between person and place. See how well you think Wordsworth handled issues we've raised here, such as sentiment/sentimentality, memory and loss, and so forth.)

If and when this work leads to a separate piece of writing, go back and track your progress—from the first jotting down of memories to a finished essay, poem, or story. What did you discover about particular memories and the way memory operates? Based on this writing journey, how would you define "nostalgia"? (You might also look up the word and its origins in the *Oxford Dictionary of the English Language*). How would you describe the interplay between memory and reality, fact and fiction, childhood and maturity—based on this writing?

H.O.

⑦ Places, Memories, and Desires

Use to Write:	Poetry; Short Fiction; Longer Fiction; Drama; Autobiography; Creative Nonfiction; Journal
Ideas and Concepts to Explore:	the "geography of memory"; the logic of juxtaposition; negative space.
Authors/Works Mentioned:	[artist Lisa Bloomfield is mentioned].

To some extent, this exercise dovetails with the two previous exercises in this chapter, "The Familiar Place As Frontier" and "Beginning With Nostalgia: Lost Childhood Places"; however, the exercise can be used independently, too.

Artist/teacher Lisa Bloomfield directs students to photograph places that were important to them in the past: their childhood bedroom, the intersection where they wrecked their first car, a recital hall, soccer field, dormitory, movie theater, the beach. They record these places with their cameras exactly as they are, then scan the images into computers. The project is to change the images somehow—to fragment them, or jam several together, or erase whole parts into negative space.

Writers, too, return to places in their minds, a journey that may be charged as much, or more, by time as it is by geography. Maybe you went every summer to the same sleep-away camp that had a particular smell you learned, years later, to name sugar–pine sap. Maybe you went on a raft trip, on which you spent a full seven days drifting as far out of the world as you could conceive, and then you came back. The bedroom you grew up in, or the first hotel you stayed in—these are two different kinds of geographies, and writers map them differently in words.

One is a place you know like a worn pair of slippers, an habitual place, so familiar through long association that it may lose its sharp contours in your mind. The other is a place you knew only briefly, where something important happened. Despite the clarity with which you have remembered it over the years, little by little, you keep losing parts of it.

Imagine that raft trip, after which you made a practice of daily remembering, a vivid movie you ran through your head, each ochre crevice, each humped river rock, each swoop of swallow you could recall. Maybe you kept this up for years, but over time it has become a blur of ragged canyon wall and green water. When you want it back, you have to make it up.

But a back window view from your parents' house where you lived for eighteen years and to which you still return, this you imagine as permanently etched in your memory, how you will always know the way the river curves among the trees in which seasons, the arch of the black railway trestle. You want to believe this, but time passes.

This exercise has two parts, designed to reinvoke and supplement a geographic practice vital to writing. It proceeds from a logic not of description, but desire.

In the first, imagine a place of importance to you that you knew well, over time, in the past, and put it back together, on the page, in words. Don't try to organize your memory, or pan a camera around the room, or even finish sentences. Just let the words of the images accumulate around the sensation of your memory—what comes first? What is associated with that? What did you forget? Memory comes to us in fragments. Let it flood you, as you flood the page.

Now, look around you and take five objects, colors, sounds, impressions— something—from where you are now to the place you remember. Ten. Fifty. Imagine something that couldn't possibly belong there—a tiger, an opium pipe, underwater breathing equipment. Add this to your remembered place, describe, and go back again. What else have you just remembered? Add that too.

In the second, return to a place that was important to you but that you knew only briefly—your first rock concert, that alpine lake you hiked to, around which swarms of hummingbirds thrummed, a museum. Repeat the process described above, first jamming everything in you can remember, then adding to it anachronistic or disjunctive elements.

Fiction.

To develop further what you have written, you may want to imagine a character to move through these two places you have written. How does this character, returning from a visit to a museum exhibit of microminiature sculptures—all of Noah's Arc on the eye of a needle, the sculptor's self-portrait on a shaft of his hair—react to her mother's hushed announcement that there is a tiger in her bedroom? You are on your way to the Orioles game, in the car you have lovingly restored, when your uncle, drinking martinis from a thermos in the back seat, has a heart attack and dies.

Poetry.

Write a poem organized around the logic of juxtaposition, using the two places you have just imagined. Write two stanzas, one about each separate place. Write a poem in which each line shifts from one place to the other. Alternate places in multiple stanzas. Jam both places into the same poetic space.

Remember.

There are no pure lines in writing. Just because something happened, or was a real place, doesn't mean everything you write about it has to be "true." Just because you are making something up, doesn't mean everything you write about it has to be invented.

(K.H.)

The Text(ure) of Public Places

Use to Write:	Short Fiction; Longer Fiction; Poetry; Creative Nonfiction; Journal; Literary Criticism; Drama; Performance Piece
Ideas and Concepts to Explore:	mimesis/mimetic; symbols.
Authors/Works Mentioned:	Aristotle; T.S. Eliot, *The Waste Land*; Lincoln Kirstein, "Fall In"; Katherine Mansfield, "Germans At Meat"; Flannery O'Connor; Karl Shapiro, "Drugstore"; Gary Snyder, "All In The Family".

Is literature—stories, poems, etc.—made of language or of life or of both? Some would have it that literature is its own reality, "just words"—arrangements of signs and symbols that refer only to other signs and symbols, squiggles of ink on paper or, in the Computer Age, bits of light amongst other bits of light, all of it a world of its own, only just seeming to refer to what's commonly called "the real world." People who see literature this way think of it, perhaps, as a labyrinth of words. Others, Aristotle among them, would have it that literature does indeed mirror life—that words are not "just words" but representations adding up to a record of life observed, even if the record bears the stamp of the recorder, the one who observes and writes.

The following prompts may seem to spring from the second view because they ask writers to *observe* and then write down what they observe. A *mimetic* or mirroring process is therefore implied. However, these prompts are not necessarily rendered null and void by the first point of view, which is skeptical about the mirroring capacity of literature. The prompts can be said at least to energize different kinds of word arranging —to spice up and stir the stew of language.

Theoretical stands are good to take; maybe it's impossible not to take one, whether doing so is good or not. Debates about "What is literature?" are not without pleasure, and if you have not done so already, you will encounter many conflicting views of language and reality as you study literature, philosophy, anthropology, communication, even history and politics. Any deliberate observation you undertake—including the one toward which this exercise nudges you—will occur against the backdrop of these arguments.

For the moment, however, let's consider an observation attributed to writer Flannery O'Connor—"A writer should never be ashamed to stare": A refreshing bit of advice that cuts through theoretical debate, to some extent; at least it grounds us in what is, what seems to be, the work of writing: look, see, think, imagine, *write*—regardless of how one might conceptualize each of these elements. Unashamedly, then, let's stare; the language-and-reality debates will be waiting for us when we return; they're not going anywhere.

The following prompts send you to public places to look, see, think, imagine, *write,* with the idea that public places are rich, are thick with textures [text(ures)?] of images, sounds, encounters, conversations, commerce, webs of desire, intrigues, odors, moods, spaces . . . and so on. When we say "see," then, the word actually represents all sorts of observations involving any number of sensors.

1. Airports: What is the language of airports? (Conversations, signs, warnings, announcements, special lingo?) How do people wait there? How do they behave . . . on escalators, at security checks, toward strangers, toward friends and family arriving or departing? What conversations do you overhear? How do *you* feel at airports? What memories or emotions do airports seem to call up in you? Just how many different sounds can you hear (and list) at an aiport? What's in all those bags? What are the rhythms of an airport? Write; observe. Observe; write. Look for possible stories or poems—lurking there, seemingly ready to be seen, imagined, written. Bus stations will work, too, of course.

2. Eateries—cafeterias, coffee houses, taverns, fast-food places, restaurants, soup kitchens: What are the body languages at such places? Who sits where and why? What are the obvious but also the almost unheard sounds and sights? What are the explicit and implicit protocols (rules of behavior)? What do people do before the food arrives? As it arrives? Focus on chewing until it loses its familiarity and can be seen for the truly weird activity it is. After all, people in the most elegant eateries on the planet are doing exactly what hyenas and cougars are doing during their respective meals—grinding food with teeth. What do people do with their hands? What hidden power relationships do you see? Guess what the relationships are: Is that person on a job interview? Is that couple breaking up? And so on. People in love, people dating, people who are intimate but quarreling—how do they behave in "a food context"? Observe, write; write, observe. Perhaps a closely observed "thing poem" will take shape. Look at the poem, "Drugstore," by Karl Shapiro, written when drugstores were also eateries; it's in Chapter Seven. You might also look at the "pub" sections of T. S. Eliot's *The Waste Land* ("Hurry up, please. It's time.") Look also at Katherine Mansfield's story, "Germans At Meat."

3. Locker rooms: What is the real humor of locker rooms? That is, does it *really* consist only of dirty jokes? Is there indeed very much humor to be found there? If not, what do you find in its place? How do people behave when they have to dress and undress in such a public venue? What are the legendary and real, obvious and not-so-obvious aromas of locker rooms? To what extent is the conventional, perhaps cliché, notion of locker rooms chiefly a *masculine* one, chiefly a *mythical* one? Write, observe; observe, write. Look for the seeds of stories or poems. You might look at Lincoln Kirstein's poem, "Fall In" (much anthologized), or Gary Snyder's poem, "All In The Family," from his Pulitzer-Prize-winning volume, *Turtle Island*.

Other public places to write about: Motels, hotels, dormitories, camps, campsites, youth hostels, stadiums (*stadia*), malls, farmers' markets, bus stations, supermarkets, swapmeets, race tracks (auto and horse), parks. Any place where we humans form our human crowds, large and small.

After you've taken one of these writing expeditions and looked at your notes, go back and think for yourself about the extent to which language (literature) mirrors life. That is, if you feel like it, pay homage to the variety of debates about what language and literature *are,* really. In your view, for instance, how *mimetic* are your notes? Is there a way to prove or disprove that they represent the "life" of the place you visited? Did you, the observer, change, with your very presence, what was being observed? Think about your perspective on the issue of "language and reality." Perhaps ask a teacher to point you to some literary criticism, sociolinguistic work, or philosophy—an anthology, perhaps—that sketches the ongoing debates.

Public places tend to be so rich in material that, most likely, a specific piece of writing will suggest itself to you. Most likely, a poem, story, scene, or nonfiction sketch will announce itself. If this turns out not to be the case, then begin by writing about the one image, event, conversation, example of behavior, or what have you that remains most interesting to you. Describe it as vividly as you can. Then write why it remains so interesting. From this foundation of first-writing, you may then consider what writing should come next.

(H.O.)

9 Writing About or With Objects

Use to Write:	Poetry; Short Fiction; Longer Fiction; Autobiography; Creative Nonfiction (including travel writing); Journal
Ideas and Concepts to Explore:	"object writing"; thing poem; riddle/poem; talisman/talismanic.
Authors/Works Mentioned:	John Keats, "Ode on a Grecian Urn"; David Kirby; Peter Meinke, "Liquid Paper"; Tim O'Brien; Sylvia Plath, "Metaphors"; Theodore Roethke, "Dolor"; Scott Russell Sanders; Sheila Ortiz Taylor; Anne Waldman.

For many years I've used something called "object writing" in my creative-writing classes, aided in part by ideas from other writer-teachers, including David Kirby and Anne Waldman, and inspired in general by the notion of "thing poems," which are found in every culture. Well known thing poems range from anonymous Old English riddles to John Keats's famous "Ode on a Grecian Urn" to contemporary poems like some by Sylvia Plath and Charles Simic. "Thingness" translates also into strong prose writing as found in the nonfiction of Scott Russell Sanders and the fiction of Tim O'Brien or the imagined facts shared in Sheila Ortiz Taylor's recent autobiography, for example. No doubt you can call to mind your own examples of thing poems.

Essentially, object writing begins with my bringing or my students' bringing "stuff" to class. This sharable stuff might include (but is certainly not limited to) what I've listed here:

1. Objects I've collected in my travels, or that students have collected on theirs: small masks, coins, trinkets, hats, stones, carved dolls, post cards, etc.

2. Two objects or ideas, per writer, that are normally not related to one another can be joined. For example, a student of mine once united an object (an intricately carved fan) with a (person/occupation) woodsman and created a sketch developed from the imaginative joining of these two objects.

3. Objects produced on-the-spot—from pockets, purses, and bookbags—or stuff found in the room itself. Theodore Roethke's poem "Dolor" and Peter Meinke's poem "Liquid Paper" offer examples of the way import and significance can be extracted from the most commonplace things that we usually take for granted or view only instrumentally—paper, pens, paperclips, and liquid paper, for instance.

4. So-called "talismanic" objects—items that individuals have carried around for a long time. On the surface (literally and figuratively), they may seem like ordinary, even worthless, things, but they have acquired "layers" of significance, histories, or hold "sentimental value" for the owners. They can be anything, really: ticket stubs, combs, coins, dried flowers, toys, pens, cheap rings—also expensive rings. Provisionally, at least, a tattoo could be classified as a talismanic object. (Obviously, you don't have to work within the structure of a class to work with object writing—see the "Power of Things" prompts elsewhere in this chapter for more ideas.)

Some options for writing (once "the stuff" is collected):

1. Simply write in response to one or more objects. Place it before you, touch it, turn it, consider it in its actual physical substance. Write about what you see, what's obvious, not so obvious, or strange about the thing(s), what the thing(s) make(s) you feel, think, or remember, what stories, fictional people, or possible conflicts might be bubbling up in your imagination, and so on. Later, you can look at Scott Russell Sanders' essay "The Inheritance of Tools" in the anthology to see how deeply into a consideration of life the contemplation of one thing—his father's hammer—took Sanders. You can try to go similar or further distances.

2. Invent, in writing, possible reasons, stories, scenarios that account for the importance of someone else's talismanic object. Let's say you bring in a ticket stub and someone else brings in a comb. Before hearing any information about the objects, you would write a speculative piece about the comb, and your colleague would write one about the ticket stub. You've begun by granting the object "special powers," but you've also begun by "fictionalizing," using your imagination, writing *your* story about the thing. Whether you want to get the "real" story along the way is up to you; usually people can't help spilling the beans. But in your writing don't be swayed by "the facts" unless you think they're useful.

3. Write a poem or story that springs from the juxtaposition of two apparently unrelated objects or of an object and an idea/or person. The example above links the carved fan and the woodsman.

4. Write a poem "spoken" by an object. After you do this, you might want to try your hand at a riddle; examples include anonymous Old English riddles and a well-known modernized riddle-poem, "Metaphors," by Sylvia Plath. Check your library for these.

5. Write an autobiographical piece centered on an object, using it as a lens to view part of your life or changes in your life or important episodes; equally, you might use an inherited object to imagine the story of someone else's life. Sheila Ortiz-Taylor does this in "Polar Palace". Here, she considers shoes in her parents' closet, which leads her to the ice skates they wore, which opens into a story of their courtship. I thought of this selection from Sheila's book *Imaginary Parents* when I noticed my friend Libby Rankin had mounted her grandfather's ice skates on a wall of her North Dakota house. The lovingly cherished hand-forged skates from the 1890s certainly have more than one story to tell. That is, they are more than just things.

6. Have people tell stories about their objects and make notes on what's interesting about the stories.

7. Write a highly *associative* poem about an object, working not out of description so much as out of surrealism—what Robert Bly calls "leaping poetry." For example, Charles Simic's poem "Stone" begins, "Go inside a stone./That would be my way." And suddenly we're inside the stone, and lots of surreal, "impossible," dreamlike things happen. Leap, take risks of thought, imagination, and association. Make the poem a kind of waking dream.

8. On your own or with others, consider other possibilities for writing about objects. Consider categories and connections. Discuss, perhaps, how archeologists and anthropologists, architects and interior designers, archivists and librarians deal with objects and the past. Equally, you might want to consider (predict) things of the future or detail the objects you'd include in your personal time capsule.

(W.B.)

Writing from Expertise, Not Just from Experience

10

Use to Write:	Reportage; Short Fiction; Longer Fiction; Poetry; Autobiography; Creative Nonfiction; Essay; Journal
Ideas and Concepts to Explore:	expertise; specialized language; "unpoetic" and "unliterary."
Authors/Works Mentioned:	Amiri Baraka; Frederick Busch, *Closing Arguments;* Emily Dickinson; Ernest Hemingway; Herman Melville; V. S. Pritchett, "The Camberwell Beauty" and *Collected Stories;* John Steinbeck.

As you may already have discovered, everyone from your friends to your teachers to interviewed writers likes to advise, "Write what you know" or "Draw on your experience." There are a few problems with this well-meant, well-worn advice. First, do we really need to be told to draw on our experience? Second, if "what we know" includes what we've read, some of us might begin by writing science fiction, adventure tales, romances, or fairy tales—narratives whose situations have nothing to do with our (nonreading) personal experience, assuming we haven't traveled to the planet Zarcon, searched for treasure in the mountains of Paraguay, fallen in love with a member of King Arthur's Court, or been turned into a blue cat by an ill–tempered wizard. Third, there is the matter of fiction and imagination—concepts based in part not on writing what you know but on . . . *making up stuff,* to phrase the matter colloquially.

I once interviewed novelist Frederick Busch for a books column I was writing on his novel, *Closing Arguments,* which could be classified as a "legal thriller." I asked him how difficult it was to write courtroom scenes that were both dramatically satisfying to him and readers but also accurate. He said that having a brother who was a lawyer helped to some degree, but then he said—and I paraphrase here—"I'm a fiction writer. It's my job to invent things, so I *imagined* court-room scenes." His point was that while accuracy and experience shouldn't be undervalued, invention drives fiction, and the job of fiction writers includes making up what they don't know.

Elsewhere in **Metro** are writing prompts based on experience and others based on invention. This exercise explores a third way and is based neither on general experience nor on pure invention but on **expertise**. That is, the exercise assumes that there is some genuine potential and often underexploited power in writing about what you *really* know—even if you use expertise as a springboard to invention, "fictionalizing," making things up.

Without thinking about it too hard, I came up with a list of things about which my students over the years have had expertise:

fly-fishing

horse-back-riding as a form of therapy for the developmentally disabled rock climbing

baseball-card collecting

the history of jazz

swimming (competitively, that is)

skateboarding

the evolution of the Grunge Scene, a popular-music subculture based in Seattle (and now, alas, rather old-fashioned)

accounting

landscape gardening

rowing (crew, that is)

farming

ranching

suicide prevention

motorcycle repair

music recording

garbage collecting

I find out about such expertise chiefly in first-year composition courses, where I often point students toward a couple of so-called "personal" essays. It's surprising how infrequently, by comparison, such expertise informs my students' poetry and fiction. Sometimes I think my students contemplate writing about what they know only in a general sense: If they grew up in Colorado, they might write stories set there. Also, I think students may believe reflexively that their expert knowledge is too arcane or somehow too "unpoetic" or "unliterary" to serve as a springwell of ideas. Or maybe they just think of themselves as students, non-experts by default. They—and you—know better than I about this issue of expertise. But it's important for us to remember how much expertise finds its way into literature we read. For instance, John Steinbeck set some of his work in the California coast and coastal valleys because he lived there for a while, but more than that, he made fiction out of his expert knowledge of fishing and farming. Emily Dickinson was an expert observer of birds and other creatures, and this knowledge is everywhere in her poems. Technically she was an amateur naturalist, but she had the habits of a professional. Melville was an expert on ships and sailing. Amiri Baraka is an expert on jazz, John Ashbery on art.

When students *do* work their expertise into poems or stories, the results are often startlingly successful. And why shouldn't this be the case? Expertise inspires confidence, and confident writers automatically write with more power. They take on the "authority" that "authors" need. Expertise also brings with it a subtlety of knowledge—ready-made complexity, wit, depth, dimension. And not least of all, expertise brings expert language, which can indeed read as mere jargon, but which just as often can enliven, electrify, or add texture to the more ordinary language of literature. And after all, writers write words, just as painters paint paint; writers can't have too much language in the storehouse.

Begin by identifying your expertise, by remembering what you know, by collecting any documentation related to your expertise—books, pay-stubs, worksheets, photographs, news clippings—*anything*. Such documentation has a certain physical weight to it, a heft to remind you of what you know. Collecting it is a way of "reading" your expertise.

It's also possible to "finish off" what you know. Via an example, here's what I mean: I grew up in the High Sierra and therefore was always interested in birds. There are so many, and so many different kinds. In particular, I've been around cowbirds all my life—stout little birds that often perch on top of cows or horses, picking the bugs off. Such background doesn't qualify me as an expert on birds, but recently I've read more about cowbirds, learned how—for instance—they don't make their own nests but instead kick other birds out, lay their eggs, then have the other birds hatch them. The reading began to "finish off" my cowbird expertise. How might this knowledge find its way into my writing? Well, as a writer, you just never know— that's the first answer. Such knowledge always seems handy when writing fiction, especially novels, in which one is creating whole little worlds of one sort or another. Also, I know some people who behave like cowbirds; they are usurpers. Maybe I'll write something about that; that is, *metaphorical possibilities* arise from expertise. The point is, you may know quite a lot about . . . rock climbing, let's say, but you could also finish off your expertise by reading about earlier rock climbers, or about rock climbing in other cultures, or about the hidden environmental impact of rock climbing; and the expertise, the textured knowledge, will find a way to invite itself into your writing, even if you don't make the first overt move.

But now let's think about a possible first overt move: The most direct way to write about what you really know is to report on it—writing an article about it for a newspaper, like a college daily or weekly—or writing to a specialized audience via a newsletter, a magazine, or an Internet site. Such writing is not totally unrelated to poetry and fiction, by the way; authority breeds authority, and reporting on something can help incubate ideas for nonreportorial writing. One easy example to point to: before writing novels set against the backdrop of war, Hemingway reported on war for the *Toronto Star*. Both the journalistic style and the literal substance of his reports informed his fiction.

If you write poetry or fiction that springs from your expertise, you're more free to explore metaphorical possibilities, of course—more free to place the expertise in the background, to improvise upon or deconstruct the special language that may accompany your expertise, to explore imaginatively the psychological or social dimensions of the expertise. Example: what sorts of people collect Barbie dolls, and what desires or internal conflicts might get projected onto the collecting? A devil's advocate might appropriately ask, "Is the world of collectibles really the stuff of poetry and fiction?" One answer would be: Read V.S. Pritchett's unforgettable story, "The Camberwell Beauty," set in the world of London antique dealers, who might well seem at first to be eccentric at best, dull at worst. (The story is in his *Collected Stories*, New York: Random House, 1988). Pritchett sees through the surface of this world, exposing prime material for superb short fiction, ignoring the superficial assumption that antique collecting is too specialized, boring, and dry to turn into good fiction. And he *makes things up.* When we write about what we *really* know, we can be led by the material past superficial assumptions to such hidden potential. So—get on with it: acknowledge your expertise, add imagination, and write something: *now.*

(H.O.)

Language and Form

The Power of Names

Use to Write:	n/a [the exercise may lead to work in virtually any genre]
Ideas and Concepts to Explore:	the power inherent in the act of naming; "the double" and *doppelgänger;* folktales of "naming"; creation myths.
Authors/Works Mentioned:	*The Book of Genesis;* "How Coyote Got His Name" (Native American folktale); Hunt Hawkins; Margaret Mitchell, *Gone With The Wind;* Marianne Moore; Melanie A. Rawls; [the television series, *The Prisoner,* is also mentioned].

We know names matter. We like or don't like ours. We were named after someone or wish we had been. We rename ourselves, have secret friends whom we named. We scoff at others' suggestions for names, for only we know what to call a new kitten or pup. We pore over historical derivations for names in baby books before we name our own children. We don't believe in telling our real names and losing the power the name has, so we offer another. We name places for others, after others, in spite of others, after ourselves, after their shapes, to capture a site's power, to turn a place into a commodity, to control how we or others think about the thing named. We test names for cars and products. (When invited to help name a new brand of automobile, poet Marianne Moore suggested "Tyrolian Turtletop." Perhaps the most infamous car name in history was that of the inventor's son, "Edsel.") We connect names to failures and triumphs. We call names. We are called names. Names circulate in cycles and decades, go in and out of fashion, are modified by different spellings: Carrie becomes Kari. We fashion ourselves to suit our names, to live the name down or to live up to it. We choose pen names and e-mail names. We try on personae and names for size and suitability. We grow to accept our names. We make up stories about names. Our names are mispronounced. We hide a name.

After reading the following freewheeling associations about names by Melanie A. Rawls, try out some of the writing-prompts that follow it.

Naming

You're gonna be sorry you asked me about naming. . . .

My mother once told me that she gave me my first name because she liked the name of the character in *Gone With The Wind*. I never expected to like any heroine of a novel that extolled the Confederacy. Turns out I don't like Melanie Hamilton—I just dislike the character less than I thought I would.

Melanie, which means "black" in Greek (oh, felicitous naming!), is black damask. My middle name, Annette, is French, means "grace" (very nice, yes?), and is angular and the color of magnolia seeds.

Black grace.

We run to strange nicknames in my family. My family name is Ginny (pronounced with a hard "g"). My dear Aunt Essie used to call me "Ginny hen." My father used to call me "Mudzin." Nicknames bestowed in my family include Boochie, Donnie, Raytee, Fats-pedly-edly, boo-hoo-ca-howrie, Pouch, Bugs, Tootie, Scooterpoo, Scoot, Bal-Ball, Ari-belle, Kelli-bear, Pud, Pudman, Tammi-lamb, Nato-potato, Beady, Brown Sugar, and Boo (twice). I started the tradition of prenatal names—names which a child-to-come is called. My sons were called "Thumper" and "Toot." My niece Ariel was (dis)graced with the prenatal name of "Junior Fries." These names by no means exhaust the subject in my family.

If I ever write a romance novel, I'll write under the name of Melyssa Raynes or Melyssa Reyes. Or, perhaps, as Rian River McComb. If I'm going to write romance, I may as well indulge my taste for the mellifluous.

My family's names are mellifluous. My parents are Elijah Daniel and Senella Evangelyn, and their children are Danielle Evangelyn, Raytheon Michelle, Melanie Arnette, Maria Bachelda, and Carmen Bianca. Their grandchildren are Dana Angelyn, Nathaniel Hawthorne, Tamela Rose, Kellen Daniel Arthur, Ariel Senella, and Shelby Marla Delores (Bal-Ball). Reading off our family names is like eating five pounds of Death-by-Chocolate..

Here are some prompts for writing about names; they are *options* from which to choose:

1. Write about how you were named. If you don't know and can't ask, make up a story.

2. Try to find out about the actual derivation of your name. How do you respond emotionally to what you learn? Put another way, to what extent do you sense a connection between your view of yourself and the definition or derivation of your name?

3. What does your name sound like to you? What are some metaphors (use the five senses) for feelings/pictures evoked by your name or by the names of others?

4. Talk about nicknames—your own, others', how you feel about giving and receiving them. What nicknames have you given to inanimate objects, such as cars, stuffed animals, fishing gear, carpentry tools, pieces of furniture?

5. If you have children, tell stories of naming them. If you don't have children, write imaginary names for imaginary children. Or recall the names of children with whom you grew up.

6. Tell a story about when you took the power of naming and named something—a person, an animal, a place, a project, an object.

7. What names don't you like and why? Explore your past history that developed those likes and dislikes.

8. Tell about the most interesting place name of a place you've been. Does the place live up to its name or not? Do you know how it got its name?

9. If you were to write a novel about your life, what names would you give the major players? How would you rename people as you turn them into fictional characters? What associations led you to choose the new names?

10. Hunt Hawkins has a poem about names. (See anthology.) He asks where all the old names went—when, for example, did "Edna" get replaced in popularity by "Jenny," and so on? Think about names in such generational terms. What were the names of your parents' generation? Your own? What names abound right now? What do you make of this?

11. What would you be named or like to be named in another culture? For example, "John" turns into Ian or Hans or Juan or Jan—to what effect? If you're from another culture besides that of the U.S., what have you experienced sharing your name with people in the U.S.—or in other cultures? How do you feel when people pronounce your name wrong or insist on giving you a nickname or make fun of your name? What supposedly unremarkable names common in the U.S. seem odd to you—and why? If you've chosen a nickname, why—and how do you feel about it? If you live in more than one culture simultaneously, how do names work in each?

12. What does it matter who has the power of naming? Do you think we should all rename ourselves at puberty, perhaps? Why or why not? Why should parents have the power of naming their children?

13. In several of my classes over the last few years, older women students, returning to school, have renamed themselves, reverting to their "maiden" names and in a case or two, simply choosing a new name. What do you think of this phenomenon? What do you think about *patrilineal* or *matrilineal* naming?

14. On the computer, run your name or other names through a spell-check program, and see what alternate words the computer comes up with. Any uncanny surprises? Hilarities? Improvements?! Perhaps write a story of your "double" (as in Jeckyll/Hyde) who has one of these computer approximations for a name—and the personality to go with it. (One liter-

ary term for "the double" or a "split" personality comes from the German: *doppelgänger.*)

15. How do you feel if your real (or imaginary) child gives up his/her name? (And yes, some men are changing their names upon marrying, too.)

16. My children have a computer software game called "Conquest of the New World." If you were to name a world, a country, a region, or a city, what theory of naming would guide you?

17. If you were an explorer and had just discovered your favorite landscape, what might you rename some of the places there? What names would you retain and why?

18. My neighborhood was named by the developer after his relatives. We have Sally Lane and Uncle Glover Road. I'd rather live one street over—Moss View Way—but I ended up on Dwight Davis Drive—another relative, this one the Davis of the Davis Cup Tennis Award, I learned. If you were given the streets of a neighborhood to name, what would you call them?

19. If we were numbered instead of named, do you think numbers would take on nuances, resonances, coloration, feeling—the way most names do? Look at an episode of the now-legendary television series, *The Prisoner,* for one imaginary take on such a world. (I realize some of us feel "numbered" already because of Social Security numbers and the blizzard of other identification numbers we are assigned.) If you could create your own human ID system, what would you come up with—and why?

20. In almost all the British mystery novels I've read, houses are named, not streets. What would you name a house and why (or a ranch, a boat, etc.)?

21. Find some "naming" folktales and/or "creation" myths, from any culture. (For example, there are several versions of a Native American tale called "How Coyote Got His Name"; and the Book of Genesis in The Bible concerns naming). Probably you are familiar with some of these already. Then write a piece in which you retell and perhaps contemporize the tale or myth, or a piece in which you create a tale or a myth that "explains" how something or some animal got its name. You might even try a tongue-in-cheek piece, such as "How the Big Mac Got Its Name."

(W.B.)

Writing from Your Name: An Introductory Poem (an Acrostic)

12

Use to Write:	Poetry
Ideas and Concepts to Explore:	acrostic.
Authors/Works Mentioned:	Wendy Bishop; Melanie A. Rawls.

List all the letters of your name but in a mixed order except the last letter: (work your name/nicknames to be between 8 and 14 letters)
For the first letter—

- Write a sentence with six words and a color, describing you.
- Write a reoccurring dream you've had or have.
- List several things, beginning with the same initial letter, that can be found in your room.
- Include something you regularly say, spoken words.
- Describe yourself (use physical attributes).
- Describe yourself (use habits).
- Describe yourself (include eyes, hair, or facial features).

- List your five favorite possessions.
- Describe yourself in your favorite clothes.
- Include something you're often found eating.
- Use a sentence with two dashes.
- Include nicknames you've liked or disliked.
- Tell something people can't tell from looking at you.

- Write a sentence with three or less words.
- Include animals or plants you like.
- Choose the words "but I never"
    "but I always"
    "someday I'll"
    "in the meantime"
    or any transition that helps close the poem. Add them to the second to the last letter line of your name.
- End with a truth or insight.

Then, rearrange the lines so that your name, spelled in the right order, forms the initial letter of each line. Modify things to create movement between the lines. Here's the exercise again, with an example:

Introductory Poem

Wendy Bishop

List all the letters of your name but in a mixed order except the last letter:
    Y S H B W I N E O D P
    (work your name/nicknames to be between 8 and 14 letters)
For the first letter—

Write a sentence with six words and a color, describing you.

  Yellow, not my color, blue, yes.

Write a dream you've had or have.
Sliding past the angry ringing telephone in the long hall.
List several things, beginning with the same initial letter, that can be found in your room.
Hairbrush, white plastic hairclips, brown and blue hats, heavy books, no high heels
Include something you regularly say, spoken words.
"Be good," I call to Morgan and Tait, hurry them to the bus stop.
Describe yourself (use physical attributes).
Wide-shouldered, with sturdy peasant ankles.
Describe yourself (use habits).
I brush my teeth too many times a day, drink coffee, chew peppermint gum.
Describe yourself (include eyes, hair, or facial features).
Notice the steady gaze—blue curious eyes, refracted through glasses.
Tell a secret:
Eat chocolate at least once a month.
Write a sentence with three or less words:
Oh, mornings!
Include animals or plants you like and end the sentence with the words, "but I never"
"but I always"
"someday I'll"
"in the meantime"
or any transition that helps close the poem.
Devoted to two housecats, birds in the live oak trees, cactus, and daylilies, someday I'll
End with a truth or insight
Plant these words and the garden will spring up, talking.
Then, rearrange the lines so that your name, spelled in the right order, forms the initial letter of each line:

W

E

N

D

Y

B

I

S

H

O

P

Modify things to create movement between the lines.
Be ready to share your naming poem.

Introduction: Wendy Bishop

Wide-shouldered, with sturdy peasant ankles.
Eats chocolate at least once a month.
Notice the steady gaze—blue curious eyes, refracted through glasses.
Devoted to two housecats, jays in the live oak trees, cactus, and daylilies,
Yellow, no make me green, green.

"Be good," I call to Morgan and Tait, hurry them to the bus stop.
I brush my teeth, many times a day, drink coffee, chew peppermint gum.
Slide past the angry ringing telephone in the long hall.
Hairbrush, white plastic hairclips, brown and blue hats, heavy books
Oh, mornings!   Someday I'll
Plant these words and the garden will spring up, talking.

And here's what happened when Melanie Rawls went diving into a name poem, draft one, written in class:

Name Poem

Moss, oaks, roses. Mushrooms. Violets. Sweetpeas.
     Birds—sandpipers and tufted titmice.
easier to tell: Harry Belafonte's album "In My Quiet
     Room." A Silk dress. Rose quartz and citrine crystals.
     Lord of the Rings.
long fingers. long face. Short hair. Short waist.
articulate your thoughts! Answer! I always want to
     know but understand about not knowing.
not any color but blue, very cool and clear
I dream in color, Technicolor—violet and
     last night orange
eager, easygoing, reticent (continues to include last name)

And then the deeper dive of the final draft, completed out of class:

Name Poem

Morning glories. Roses, willows and oaks. I like. But I'm not showy—more
     like a forget-me-not, something small. If I were a bird, I'd be a
     sandpiper—something on the margins between two worlds, or a tufted tit-
     mouse—Quaker-plain but with an unusual ornament.
Easier to tell: I treasure Harry Belafonte's album *In My Quiet Room*. A blue-
     green silk dress. Rose quartz and citrine crystals. *The Lord of the Rings*. I
     have

Long fingers to touch these things.
Articulate your thoughts" I tell my students, I tell myself.
Not any color but blue for me, very cool, very clear. Water and air . . .

I dream in color—Technicolor, solid rainbows: violets of winter evenings, flaming summer orange sunflowers. Sometimes
Eager. Easygoing. Reticent. But not, I think, enough.
Also, shy. Sometimes.
Reading. I read and sleep and read and eat and read and listen to music and read. . . . Another treasure.
Attention. Always paying attention though often to the dreamworld, to the dreaming time, in a dream . . .
Why, I'm known for eating tupelo honey. Usually
Late—on other people's time, usually on time by my own time. I believe in time, taking time, living *in* time, not *by* time . . .
Someday I'll go to Japan and, standing in total stillness in Kyoto (under cherry blossoms? By a temple wall? On an earthen path steep-winding up a crooked hill?), I'll understand about silence.

—Melanie A. Rawls

Most simply, Melanie is doing what poets do, aligning art and the unconscious in her drafting—finding out what dreams mean, understanding what the relationship between sandpiper and titmouse—seemingly arbitrary choices—signifies to her, and then taking that rendering and sharing it with us to re-render into our own understandings. In the Introductory Acrostic Poem . . . you meet yourself as you read—and read through—your name.

(W.B.)

⑬ First Words of Stories: This Sentence, These Words

Use to Write:	Short Fiction; Longer Fiction; Journal; Creative Nonfiction; Poetry; Performance Piece; Writing/Reading Notebook
Ideas and Concepts to Explore:	alliteration; assonance; rhyme; "hypnagogic hallucination" (defined in the text).
Authors/Works Mentioned:	June Akers; Perle Besserman; Jane Bowles; Nicole Brossard; Anthony Burgess; Italo Calvino; Lan Samantha Chang; Anton Chekhov; Dennis Cooper; Julio Cortazar; Elizabeth Denton; Joan Didion; Frederick G. Dillen; Louise Erdrich; William Faulkner; Raymond Federman; William Gass; Nancy Krusoe; Ann Sexton; Eve Shelnutt; Osvaldo Soriano; Christa Wolf.

Whether beginning a story is the hard part or the easy part for you, it is always the part that comes first and very often constitutes a kind of writing logic. Maybe what you write in the beginning ends up in the middle of your text. Maybe you toss it. Maybe it turns into your ending. Maybe it stays where it is.

No two writers begin exactly the same way, but many describe the writing itself as a process of discovery, of finding the story embedded in an initial recognition of a sentence, an image, some words. Often almost audible in the writer's own head, this sentence, these words, contain the whole rest of the story that will emerge, if nothing stops it, out of the imperative and logic of the language itself. Think of it as a kind of treasure hunt, with your own words the only clues to where you will end up.

Then, listen:

All my books literally come to me in the form of a sentence, an original sentence which contains the entire book.

—Raymond Federman

I know very simply when I start what's going to happen. I just have a very general idea, and then the thing develops as I write.

—Aldous Huxley

I start at the beginning, go on to the end, then stop.

—Anthony Burgess

You think about what actually happened, you tell friends long stories about it, you mull it over in your mind, you connect it together at leisure, then when the time comes to pay the rent again you force yourself to sit at the typewriter, or at the writing notebook, and get it over with as fast as you can.

—Jack Kerouac

I always know the ending; that's where I start.

—Toni Morrison

With me, a story usually begins with a single idea or memory or mental picture. The writing of the story is simply a matter of working up to that moment, to explain why it happened or what caused it to follow.

—William Faulkner

Sometimes you get a line, a phrase, sometimes you're crying, or it's the curve of a chair that hurts you and you don't know why, or sometimes you just want to write a poem and you don't know what it's about. I will fool around on the typewriter. It might take me ten pages of nothing, of terrible writing, and then I'll get a line, and I'll think, "That's what I mean!" What you're doing is hunting for what you mean, what you're trying to say. You don't know when you start.

—Ann Sexton

William Gass says that the first paragraph of a story rewrites the first sentence, and that the rest of the story rewrites the first paragraph.

Italo Calvino begins in "combinatorial play," seeking the sparks between words that lead to the place where writing happens.

Joan Didion describes a "shimmering image," that starts the writing off, a lure at the edge of her consciousness that turns writing into a process of finding her way back to the image.

Eve Shelnutt talks about the manner in which she sifts through memory and language to carve out the beginning of a story that will show her the way to the end.

How do you begin?

Part 1.

This open-ended exercise asks you to explore your own process and instinct for beginning. Consider the following list of first lines. Read them, study them, worry them, listen to them, hold them, repeat them, learn them.

When you are ready, choose ten from among them and, for each, write the first paragraph of the story you would write if you were writing the story that begins with the sentence you chose. Here, what you write has more to do with listening to where you are than it does with imagining where you are going. What does each sentence tell you about the sentence that must come after it? It is all there, in the first words, if you listen.

Then again, you don't quite know how to proceed, try one of the following tricks:

1. Repeat one word from the first sentence in the second, from the second in the third, and so on.
2. Make the second sentence into a question which derives from the first, and then answer it.
3. Describe in detail a single word from the original sentence: predawn, dutiful, crazy.
4. Put a name in the second sentence.
5. Write the rest of the paragraph without using any words from the sentence you start with, not even "and," not even "the."
6. Write the rest of the paragraph in same-length sentences as the first, using principles of rhyme, assonance, and alliteration.
7. Add a color (blue), a sound (dogs barking), a smell (ammonia), a taste (bitter almond), a touch (something raspy brushing you).
8. Say your sentence out loud over and over until you slip into the next sentence.
9. Write the sentence over and over in different handwriting (Jane Bowles actually did this) until you slip into the next sentence.
10. Stay very still and quiet until, in the silence, you hear the next words.
    Now, begin:

On a day about which I cannot write in the present tense, the cherry trees will have been in blossom.

—Christa Wolf

Would I find La Maga?

—Julio Cortazar

The highest street in the blue Moslem town skirted the edge of a cliff.

—Jane Bowles

In the beginning, sometimes I left messages in the street.

—David Markson

The desert is indescribable.

—Nicole Brossard

. . . it doesn't depend on will.

—Julio Cortazar

Never in my life had I been on the road without a penny to my name.

—Osvaldo Soriano

A barn is a beautiful place where cows are milked together.

—Nancy Krusoe

I am now an American citizen and I live in Washington, capital of the world.

—V.S. Naipaul

In the neighborhood where I grew up, women didn't work.

—June Akers Seese

I guess you'd call him crazy.

—Elmer Kelton

For years I put off telling the tale of my voyage to W.

—Georges Perec

People in my family tend to die either during the tail end of a March blizzard or right in the middle of one of those premature May heat waves you get in New York City.

—Perle Besserman

Something has changed.

—Susan Volchok

My mother worked in charms.

—Lan Samantha Chan

Her Gart went round in circles.

—H.D.

When you draw the curtains in the morning you stand in front of the window like a black dog.

—Helen Simpson

I would like to tell you about a legendary witch who lives in the mountains.

—Ohba Minako

Awakening in the predawn darkness, I grope among the anguished remnants of dreams that linger in my consciousness, in search of some ardent sense of expectation.

—Kenzaburo Oe

Once more he breathed the air of freedom.

—Nabuid Mahfouz

When Mike saw a pretty face, he liked to mess it up, or give it drugs until it wore out by itself.

—Dennis Cooper

A calm August night.

—Anton Chekhov

The first time she drowned in the cold and glassy waters of Lake Turcot, Fleur Pillager was only a girl.

—Louise Erdrich

It is not true that Billy Renfro was killed during that trouble in Houston.

—James Alan McPherson

My father was a dutiful, orderly, straightforward man.

—Joao Guimaraea Rosa

She was glad he could not read.

—Ghita Orth

The true Hero was as unseen by everyone else as by himself.

—Frederick G. Dillen

Again and again, the snow interferes with my remembrance, its flurries commingle with my retrospective fantasy of Louise, with the moist almost of her name in my mouth, my ear.

—Jaques Roubaud

Not one of the four large-breasted, narrow-hipped young girls saw their mother put on her hiking boots and the dowdy Chinese coat that looked like a quilt and begin her trek up the mountain.

—Elizabeth Denton

There are three stories in Sergeant Grimshaw's life which, if I string them together, may approximate a single story.

—Rod Val Moore

Part 2.

Keep a notebook in which you maintain your own list of possible first sentences.

Things overheard in a parking lot.

What you read in the paper.

Your child's hair, and how it strikes you in a certain light.

A murmur.

The words of the sentence you suddenly hear.

Pay attention to what psychologists call "hypnogogic hallucinations," those images that come to you in the moments just prior to sleep. A pair of red high-heeled shoes, floating in the night sky beyond that fringe of mountains out your parents' car window when you are ten and dozing off. Your boyfriend's illuminated silhouette. The arc of your soccer ball, flying into the net. All the voices.

Form your own first sentences and write opening paragraphs for the ones you like best.

Part 3.

Write a story, or two, or more from among the first paragraphs you've written.

(K.H.)

The Perfect Grammar of Form: Finding Your Own Ideal Form

14

Use to Write:	Short Fiction; Poetry; Creative Nonfiction; Autobiography
Ideas and Concepts to Explore:	grammar—in reference to deep structures of language and narrative; action/crisis/denouement—in reference to story-structure; equilibrium and displacement—in reference to story-structure.
Authors/Works Mentioned:	Roland Barthes; Trinh Minh-Ha; Gertrude Stein, *How to Write;* [architect Frank Lloyd Wright and painter Wasily Kandinsky are also mentioned].

For health reasons late in his life, Frank Lloyd Wright moved his winter home from Wisconson to the Arizona desert, where he built a second school of architecture, *Talliesen West.* Wright derived many of his architectural concepts from nature, and the magnitude of such a move is impressive, from thick wet forests to the high Sonoran desert, superheated rocks, toxic plants, the utter absence of trees, a whole new geography and botany to learn. The arc of desert hills, a vast terrain of barren rocks, stretches low against high blue sky. The furry-looking spines of the cholla cactus contain the very acid that produces arthritis in our bodies. Touch one, and you will ache for days.

Wright's architecture was designed around three geometric shapes, which he considered to be above all others: the square, for integrity; the triangle, for aspiration; and the circle, for continuity.

"Learn these three," he said, "and you will learn the perfect grammar of form."

What, you may wonder, is the perfect grammar of a poem? A narrative? Where can you learn it, in what book?

From *How to Write,* by Gertrude Stein:

Grammar returns to need.
Grammar is in origin.
Grammar has had it and has not lost it.
Grammar may carry opportunities.
Grammar is not restless if there is sun at a distance.
A grammar without distress.
Hills a grammar.
Grammar, regain leaves.
A grammar consists in having more made maiden in eclipse. A tail of a comet
    is a memory. Grammar may be fortunately within a call. Consider
    grammar.
A place is very near there.

Once, when my first son was a baby, I found myself wandering in a museum, baby sleeping on my back with me wandering to keep him asleep. It was random, my wandering, and my baby was sleeping as I wandered. And then I turned an unexpected corner, not the one in front of me but the one to my left I noticed only at the last moment, caught by the corner of my eye, and then, like that, I stopped, which is true, stopped and stood and stared, my baby sleeping on my back, at this painting that had caught the corner of my eye and turned this unexpected corner to a painting all circles and triangles and squares. It was a painting by Kandinsky, all in muted colors, as if earth. It was circles and triangles and squares. My baby was sleeping on my back.

Now I stood and stared at this painting for a long time. Now I stood and stared. Now I knew that everything was changed. Now something opened up inside me. Now I wanted to climb inside the earth-colored geometry of painting. Now I recognized it in an instant. Now my baby slept. Now this whole story is true.

Wright says, *learn these three, and you will learn the perfect grammar of form.* Stein says, *grammar. Fills me with delight.*

What I was thinking: *Let me write this story. The perfect grammar of story,* I was thinking. It wasn't nonsense I was thinking, but I was thinking almost without words, only in shapes, because what I was really thinking was that this, Kandinsky's unexpected-out-the-corner-of-my-eye-corner painting was for me the perfect grammar of story.

Forget grammar and think about potatoes, Stein says.

But we know better.

Anyone can see nearly what I mean, Stein says.

The French theorist, Roland Barthes, once described a narrative as a long sentence. In later years he said there was no sentence.

A story, you may have learned in school, is a little triangle, consisting of a rising action, a climax and a denouement. This is classic narrative structure and the first sentence Barthes had in mind. It is familiar, and we can name its different parts.

But my painting, with its triangles and circles and its earthy-colored squares, what sentence was that?

Another way of thinking about story is as a sequence of events arranged according to a logic of placement, displacement, replacement, or equilibrium, disequilibrium, re-equilibrium.

But if "there is no sentence," does this mean there is no structure? Maybe it means what Trinh Minh-Ha calls the "coming into being of the structure of the moment." Of the moment. For of course it cannot be that there is no structure (no sentence), but rather that there is no structure (no sentence) that will never change, and that every structure (sentence) comes into being in its moment.

Or, a story may not seek to fill a preexisting structure, but rather to discover the *structure of the moment,* how it knows itself, its own rise and fall and cadence, and shape.

An unexpected painting by Kandinsky, for example. Your mother's mother's ancient bedroom quilt. A set of well-used tools your father took with him, to every house you moved to, all across the country, up to and including the place where he retired and putters still. A rock you carried back from the top of a volcano, or one you go to sit on at the beach, or one that glows otherworldly in black light. Dominoes. The netless basketball hoop in your old backyard. An elegant mathematical equation.

In this exercise I am thinking not about the literal shapes of things, but instead about the space they open up in you, and its form.

You think about that too. Your Little Leage baseball mitt. The olive tree you planted in your back yard. Magic.

Decide on something that opens something up inside you—an artifact, or view out a window, the course of a river, a painting, a symphony or song. Imagine the space as your ideal story structure or shape. Think about its different parts, its grammars of forms, how it is built and what connects to what. Maybe map it. Then write it, a story coming into being in this structure.

For example, the sleeve of a childhood sweater is your Aunt Ana, who knitted scratchy sweaters for all the children in the family no one ever wore, but they were beautiful. The buttons are each of your Aunt Ana's children, your remote cousins, hard and difficult to manage. The other sleeve, your mother, Aunt Ana's sister. The neckline, the last time you three were together. And that thread that is unraveling . . . ?

Frank Lloyd Wright built his house in the desert as a "lying-down house," the contours of which were meant to disappear into the contours of the hills, as if it were a desert hill itself. Write your story to disappear into the shape you've imagined for it. Get into it, what opens up inside you.

Lie down.

(K.H.)

Nonsense and Sound Poems: Demystifying Formal Verse

15

Use to Write:	Poetry; Experimental Fiction; Creative Nonfiction; Performance Piece
Ideas and Concepts to Explore:	formal verse; free verse; sonnet; villanelle; sestina; meter; rhyme; iambic pentameter; heroic couplets; "nonsense" poetry.
Authors/Works Mentioned:	Lewis Carroll; Robert Frost; Edward Lear; Dr. Seuss; Ron Padgett, *Handbook of Poetic Forms*.

Nearly all poets have had the experience of trying to write formal verse—sonnet, villanelle, sestina, what have you—only to feel as if the constraints of meter, rhyme, and other formal patterning obliterate any chance to have the poem say what they want it to say, mean what they want it to mean, do what they want it to do, and/or sound even vaguely *natural,* however one might want to define that word. In reaction, many poets abandon all attempts at formal verse and flee to the friendly unconfining confines of free verse. In some cases, poets may seek out free verse not so much for what it has to offer but for what it does *not* require.

Robert Frost, a poet who worked superbly in formal verse, cautioned against rushing automatically to free verse. He is alleged to have said, "Writing free verse is like playing tennis without a net." Let's improvise on his analogy for a moment. Tennis coaches have been known to have their pupils learn good serving form by encouraging them to forget about getting the ball over the net. That is, the coaches want the novice player just to hit a lot of balls properly, using the right stance, the right toss, the right extension, and so forth, and they want the player not to let a short-term concern with getting the ball over the net to intrude on getting comfortable with form. A pragmatic mind, or a mind like Frost's, might ask, "But isn't the whole point to get the ball over the net and in play?!" Yes, but there's short-term and there's long-term pragmatism. A player who concentrates only on getting the ball over the net may never progress far enough as a server, whereas a player who hits thousands of balls into the net may gradually grow into a fine server who does indeed get the ball over the net—with a vengeance. The apparent silliness of ignoring where the ball goes is actually the more sensible path of progress. Every sport has analagous training routines that ignore short-term ineffectiveness in favor of long-term control, if not mastery.

Granted, the analogy between sports and writing—between playing tennis and writing formal verse—has its problems, but it does get at the notion of needing to *demystify* form—patterns, boundaries, barriers—in order to *master* form. So for a moment, at least, let's apply the same training rationale to the writing of formal verse. Intead of worrying about the effectiveness of a poem in terms of what it's saying, what it's meaning, or how "natural" it sounds, let's surrender entirely to the form, devoting ourselves to sound evoked by printed words. Here are two lines of rhymed iambic pentameter that cheerfully hit the ball smack into the net, as it were, because while they satisfy the requirements of rhymed iambic pentameter, they give up trying to satisfy the form *and* make sense.

> The spring of books revered the red-clay songs.
> She studied fleas and bought a pair of tongs.

Nonsense, of course. Just a "sound" poem—although, ironically, one finds oneself struggling *not* to make sense: a rather abrupt reversal of the usual situation with writing formal verse, in which one struggles *to* make sense while satisfying the demands of form.

First, find a form you'd like to try—sonnet, villanelle, sestina, heroic couplets. Study what's required. Ron Padgett's *Handbook of Poetic Forms* is a good place to begin. You may also want to look at the "nonsense verse" of Lewis Carroll and Edward Lear—or dig out a Dr. Seuss book. And remember that, with glee, with an *attitude*, without fear, you may take on what you think is the most daunting form because . . . who cares if you don't make an ounce of sense? The main goal is to get comfortable with the form, to play with the nuances of meter and rhyme, to dissolve whatever discomfort or dread you may feel toward formal verse. Immerse yourself in the sound-itself of language. After writing several no-sense, nonsense, ball-into-the-net "sound poems," try your hand at working with formal verse *and* achieving what else you usually want to achieve in poems—making sense, making meaning, discovering meaning, projecting a voice you want to project, and so forth. Also, *within* these sound poems may exist lines, images, or ideas on which to build a so-called no-nonsense poem. That is, writing sound poems can be a surprisingly effective source of *invention*, a roundabout way of discovering subjects, images, ideas, lines, and phrases.

(H.O.)

16 ▶ Burrowing:
Writing That Springs from Language Itself

Use to Write:	Short Fiction; Longer Fiction; Autobiography; Creative Nonfiction; Essay; Journal
Ideas and Concepts to Explore:	burrowing, as a writing technique; signs, signifier, signified, supplement, surplus: all in the context of linguistics and literary theory.
Authors/Works Mentioned:	Jacques Derrida; Nancy Krusoe, "Lanscape and Dreams"; Robert Stone.

One is improvising when one writes, and you pick up in the same way a musician starts to improvise and detect the inner structure of what he's playing—that's the way I think it works in the writing of (fiction). You pick up the beat.

—Robert Stone

Imagine writing as a perpetual unfolding: you begin with a single sentence, to which you add, by the sheer force of language itself, just another sentence, which adds a little bit to the first. Now, in place of a single sentence, you have two, to which you add a third. Each time you supplement your text, you are adding on to the whole that precedes it, and each time the whole is transformed. You keep adding and keep adding, and the story grows.

There is a complex post-structural logic by which I have come to understand exactly how writing grows out of language, its own imperative carried in the weight of each sentence, by which the next sentence is always already determined. This logic suggests that the meaning-making impulse of language (itself a system of *signs*) is organized according to a process of substitution and replacement. In this process, we replace the idea-of-the-thing (*signified*) with the idea-of-the-sound-of-the-word-of-the-thing (*signifier*), and in this way agree to let a certain meaning stand. It is also, this logic, about such wondrous things as paradox and contradiction, presence and absence, desire and identity and writing, but for our purposes we will concentrate on writing.

Writing itself, for example, is ongoing, shifting, and fluid, and the meaning we agree on will not stand for long, but continue to be subject to the arbitrary play of the very process that produced it. For instance, let's say we're writing a story, and we add sentence three to sentences one and two. Not only do we have a third sentence, but the third sentence has changed what sentences one and two mean—maybe slightly, maybe enormously. This is one example of what Jaques Derrida calls a *supplement*. We are telling you this because the very same principle of shifting that inheres in how we make meaning in language repeats itself in writing, moving writing forward in an endlessly unfolding process that grows, paradoxically, not out of some preexisting idea in our heads, but the logic of writing itself.

For the most part, however, this is not how we learn how to write; we do not immerse ourselves in the mysterious logic of language itself, in which all these substitutions and supplements are occurring. Most of us learn, instead, to write "backwards," as if our ideas *did* exist somehow outside language. We turn writing into a struggle to find the right words to express the ideas. In this model of writing you can see how successful you are by working backwards from the text to your ideas, just the same way you can check an arithmetic problem by reversing its procedures. But it dulls the writing, turns it to translation, never mind what it does to your head and your heart, where writing also comes from.

Some writers say that this way of talking about writing is not useful; and certainly most writers simply aren't used to this lingo of "sign" and "supplement" and "substitution." Other writers claim it is transforming. Fiction writer Nancy Krusoe, for example, wrote the award-winning story, "Landscape and Dreams" (see anthology), by exploring this logic in a class exercise. As she described it herself:

> The idea (was) to take a word or sentence and burrow into it—to supplement it—following wherever it takes you until it stops or you lose the desire to continue. Then add another piece of language and repeat the process. I began with "A barn is a beautiful place . . ." and worked from one word to the next, each set of words calling for another set, and I discovered that words in stories, like poems, could touch in pleasurable ways that would bring up new material, a new situation, and more words. This process became compelling and exciting, each word charged by its own necessity and surplus, and the distance was reduced between me and the sound of the sentence.

Theory is as theory does.

It is just a way of writing. It is a way of writing that relieves us of the obligation to know what's coming next and gives us permission to play—to reduce, if you will, the distance between ourselves and the sound of the sentence, so to ignite pleasure. It's about how to "pick up the beat."

This exercise proceeds from the logic of what Derrida calls "supplementary" and what we call "burrowing." But here's good news: You may, if you wish, forget about Derrida and these terms we've been tossing around—because all you really need to do is write. In the following exercise, you play the mole of language, digging far and deep. It is one way of writing, which you should explore here without preconceptions, to see how it works for you—one sentence after another.

Begin, then, with a single sentence. Listen hard for the beat to see and hear where it touches, in what pleasurable ways, other words and sounds and sentences. Then add another sentence and repeat. Add another. Add another. Keep adding and adding. Burrow deep into the sentences you write, as if on an archaeological dig. Turn your words and their sounds and their sentences over and over. Pay close attention to sound and rhythm. Listen for sparks, for connections, to the force of your own desire.

When the initial impulse of your first sentence—its sense of play and what grows out of it—has exhausted itself, stop. Make a white space, begin again with a new sentence, and continue.

Repeat.

Continue.

Pick up the beat. (Story will take care of itself.)

(K.H.)

There's Something About a Sonnet: Easing into Writing a 10 × 14 Poem

17

Use to Write:	Poetry
Ideas and Concepts to Explore:	couplet; iambic; Italian sonnet; meter; octave (as a poetical term); pentameter; rhyme-scheme; sestet; Shakesperian (English) sonnet.
Authors/Works Mentioned:	Elizabeth Barrett Browning; Robert Frost, "Design"; Gerard Manley Hopkins; John Keats, "On The Sonnet"; George Meredith; Edgar Allan Poe, "Sonnet—To Science"; Richard Wilbur, "Praise in Summer"; William Butler Yeats.

Sonnets. We've all read them. Shakespeare's mostly. The form is strict, constrained. Fourteen lines of iambic pentameter verse: ta-DA taDA taDA taDA taDA times 14 lines. Rhyme schemes—for the English sonnet: abab cdcd efef gg. For the Italian: abbabba—in the octave and in the sestet—cdecde. Often about love. Often, an issue/theme is set up in the first stanzas or the octave and resolved in the sestet of the Italian or final couplet of the English sonnet. Often, poets play with the form—loosening the meter, shortening or lengthening lines, abandoning rhyme, changing the rhyme (making 7 rhymed couplets, for instance) and in general playing with this tight box of a shape.

So many loves and losses have been poured into the shape. The shape has endured so many years, centuries. It leads me to think we have, as humans, just the attention span of a sonnet—we like it the same way we like a perfect piece of chocolate, a jewel, a statement of affection, well-phrased. In a way, it's all those. And modern poets—like you and me—who weren't raised up on rhyme and meter can still have quite a bit of fun exploring this shape.

First, you might read a lot of sonnets. Chances are you've read some in high school or college, and you've been asked to or told to go over them with a magnifying glass. You've been invited to enjoy them—or else! But as you read this time, read fast. Gobble some sonnets. Read them out loud. Read them using different voices, some serious, some mocking. Set some to a Rap beat. Use a Clint Eastwood Voice, an Eddy Murphy voice, a Sandra Bullock voice, whatever. Eat the language of them. Don't belabor the interpreting. Suggested authors? Okay: His Obviousness, William Shakespeare; Gerard Manly Hopkins, William Butler Yeats, Elizabeth Barrett Browning, George Meredith, John Keats (especially "On the Sonnet," which is a meta-sonnet, a sonnet full of lots of opinions about sonnet-writing), Edgar Allan Poe ("Sonnet—To Science"), Robert Frost ("Design"), Richard Wilbur ("Praise in Summer").

Now, to ease into sonnet writing, I'll ask you to draft what I call a 10 × 14 poem. A poem of 14 lines with 10 syllables in each line. Not quite a sonnet, but partaking of some of the sonnet's demands and delivering on much of the sonnet's condensed power. Here's how to try the almost sonnet, the 10 × 14 poem.

The process goes like this—freewrite—then recast prose into a box-like shape—aiming for nearly 10 syllables a line. Then, as you tinker and make the poem say what you want it to say, get more ruthless about the shape. Before freewriting you might want to re-read several sonnets and then catch an image or scene and contemplate it, writing nonstop for 5 minutes. Or, you might want to do as I've done in the sample. Freewrite about something, anything: In this case, my class and I freewrote about postcards I collected and brought in to share. I wrote about a postcard from Canada showing three views of moose. The cards I have are often of landscapes and strange places, the Corn Palace, Lake Tahoe, Mt. Rushmore. More seriously, you could freewrite on an art print or photograph or just walk outside and observe a scene. I suggest first describing literally what you see—in the case of the postcard, describe its physicality. Then you might make up a story about what you see. Then describe all the colors, smells, textures, etc. Then make comparisons between what you see and other things. Each of these could be a separate freewrite. Then, shape into lines, then cut your lines to fit the 10 × 14 poem's demands. Then revise. Ask yourself, how does it feel to inhabit this box, this small space? Then, you might want to line the sonnet's rhyme pattern on your computer in the margin and try drafting a poem right into them, trying for a rhymed sonnet, but not worrying about line length and meter, just stop, of course, after fourteen lines.

Drafting and Revising a 10 × 14 Poem

1. Freewrite. 5 × 3 slightly bent and yellow Canadian postcard titled. Deer and moose. Place for stamp and address. Title: Lords of the Canadian Forest. Three photos—two moose, one deer in white out-lined photo box captions.

In the tall green grass with dry grass white fluffy pods, the moose front on square as a camel or horse but distinctive, his horns covered in a brown-green fur and alert S-shaped bird resting on one. The smell of tundra unfreezing for a summer moment mud black and sterile fertility—the heavy breath of an old athlete through those rime heated nostrils.

moss green

mud hot syrup brown, the green of celery veins. the horn color of dirty fingernails. the midday high sun feels like an oven that grows cold, as the earttips, clear day hazy at the edges, summer forest fires.

rank like lovers rolling in a meadow embrace. mud to the kneecap. thick scalp. the birds secret downfeathers

the whorls of tough hair around the antlers

the bitter grit of mud the joygrowth

too much too fast of summer grass

2. First Notebook Draft Moose Postcard

1. When the tundra unfreezes for a summer's
2. snapshot, day like the taste of mud, bitter
3. grit, knee-deep in the joy growth of grasses,
4. the heavy breath of this old athlete. The
5. nearsighted anvil head, large leaf-shaped
6. ears, horns covered by a softer velvet,
7. his bellows barrel chest frozen this mom-
8. ment. The moose is framed by his dignity—
9. that indifferent jaw movement, that sticky cud
10. he grows white-haired, moss green, he whisks head, tail,
11. except for the S-shaped white and gray
12. bird like a sentry pointing the wrong way
13. or a boutonniere for the celebrat-
14. tion, "Lord of the Canadian forest

3. Typing a Shaped Draft (about five drafts went into this draft)

In Another Moose Postcard

Slowly tundra unfreezes for summer's
snapshot, days like taste of fresh mud, bitter,
gritty. Knee-deep in joy-growth of grasses,
near-sighted, anvil-headed, large leaf-shaped
ears, spread-finger horns lapped by the softest
velvet, his bellows-barrel chest frozen
in the shutter's instant, then released, this
moose shifts hooves. Framed by a hot breath's dignity,
slow jaw moving across the stick-coarse cud,
he shows white-haired, moss green, whisks head, tail
misses, the S-shaped white and gray bird stand-

ing sentry mid-horns, pointing the wrong way,
frivolous as a boutonniere upon
this "Lord of the Canadian Forest."

4. A Revision After Writing Group Response Responses (three more drafts went into this one).

Another Moose Postcard

Slowly, tundra unfreezes for summer's
snapshot—days like taste of fresh mud, bitter,
gritty.
      Knee-deep in joy-growth of grasses,
near-sighted, anvil-headed, large leaf-shaped
ears, spread-fingers of horn lapped by softest
velvet, bellows-barrel chest, he is caught
in the shutter's instant, then released.
                    The
moose shifts hooves. Framed by a hot breath's dignity,
slow jaw moving across the stick-coarse cud,
he shows white hair, moss greens, whisks head, tail
misses the S-shaped white and gray bird standing sentry mid-horns, pointing the wrong way,
frivolous as a boutonniere upon
this "Lord of the Canadian Forest."

                                    —Wendy Bishop

A Borrowed 10 × 14 slant rhyme Poem

In groups, modify the end rhymes below into slant rhymes (where they are full rhymes—instead of red/head you might try red/altered or red/add). Each group member agrees to write two borrowed sonnets, using words from this list. Write a poem of fourteen lines that fits the end words your group agreed upon. While drafting, you may change any **two** of the fourteen words to make the poem better. You may work with a 10-syllable line or move to lines of any length.

Sample end rhymes from William Shakespeare:

sun, red, dun, head, white, cheeks, delight, reeks, know, sound, go, ground,
    rare, compare

Sample end rhymes from Robert Frost:

heard, bird, again, flowers, ten, past, showers, cast, fall, all, bird, sings, words,
    thing

Sample end rhymes from Floyd Skloot:

wide, legs, hide, begs, mirror, bone, her, grown, know, being, grow, freeing,
    thirst, first

Sample end words from Marilyn Hacker:

wrong, lean, seventeen, belong, school, image, rummage, drool, dropping, in, Insulin, ambulance, hands, shopping

Sample end words from Robert Pinsky:

back, slap, dock, clamber, top, remember, lake, same, cheek, color, name, her, over, her

(W.B.)

Piecemeal Fictions

Use to Write:	Short Fiction; Autobiography; Creative Nonfiction
Ideas and Concepts to Explore:	fragmented narratives; narrative collage.
Authors/Works Mentioned:	Aristotle; Robert Coover, "The Babysitter"; Annie Dillard; E.M. Forster; William Gass, "In the Heart of the Heart of the Country".

For this exercise, begin with an informal survey. Ask a writing partner, "What's a story?" Ask your mother, ask your brother, your best friend, your lover. Ask yourself.

Collect your answers. Write them down. What have you got?

In a previous exercise, "The Perfect Grammar of Form," we talked about the little triangle of rising action, climax, denouement. We talked about the concept of events in a sequence, involving the push toward and away from equilibrium, of placement, displacement, replacement. At least part of this logic derives from Aristotle, who, long ago proposed that the middle of a story should come after the beginning, and the end should come after the middle.

Between then and now, E.M. Forster developed the concept of causality. *The king died, then the queen died,* is a story, he said. But if the queen dies *of grief* because the king has died, then it is a plot, for one thing has not simply followed another but instead has been *caused* by it.

Story writing depends a great deal on plot, but contemporary stories may organize themselves around different kinds of logic, structures and forms than the classic causal triangle we have already described. One common such structure explores fragmented form, or what Annie Dillard calls "narrative collage." Such stories may come together as bits and pieces, sometimes as passages with section titles, sometimes as items in a list, sometimes apparently random, separated from other fragments with just white space. Sometimes the unfamiliar structure of these stories is confusing, but if you read them carefully coherent narrative often emerges, which can be reconstructed with its own beginning, middle, and end.

Indeed, as Annie Dillard argues, the imperative for fragmented texts to hold together may even be greater than we are accustomed to, and we may find them to be even "more highly structured than leisurely traditional tellings."

This exercise is one that asks you to experiment with fragmentation as a formal convention. It proceeds from the assumption that a story will coalesce around randomly (or not so randomly) assembled objects, concepts or experiences to the degree that the writer seeks order.

Begin as a collector.

Collect words: fence, apricot, wainscoting, wren, piecemeal. Gun, rock, babe, icon, shelter. Socks, teeth, pulse, auto club, apostle.

You may collect your words out of books, your memory, a letter from your mother, the evening's newscast. Collect them around a particular theme—a sport, a construction trade, a hobby, a professional discourse. Or just collect them at random.

When you are satisfied with your collection, arrange your words on the page according to some pattern you devise—repetition, alphabetization, numerical sequencing, something random.

Now, write a prose fragment that spins off from the first word, then the next, then the next. Don't think about it. Just start. Like this:

Fence: My father built fences for a living. He was a short man, with thick shoulder, and my most vivid memories of him are of him standing chest deep in the foundation of a fence, sweat pouring off his face, and with a look about him between determined and frantic.

Apricot: If you want to grow apricots, be prepared for three things: blankets of soft rotting fruit on your yard all summer that squishes into mush when you try to clean it up, the ever present stink of apricot sweetness, and that the life of any apricot tree is maybe fifty years. You may outlast it. You may watch as it rots from the inside out.

Wainscoting: In his spare time he built wainscoting, the old-fashioned kind, carving it and working it by hand.

Fence: I did not know then what my father was afraid of, but it lay underground, and for years we both dreamed of its darkness.

Maybe you already have some idea of where this story is heading, something about the loss of a tree, a rebuilt fence, a view of a father and how it changed the summer that the tree died. Maybe you don't yet. Keep adding fragments until a whole story emerges.

How else might you structure your own story? What finally holds it together for you?

Note: Two widely anthologized fragmented stories are "In the Heart of the Heart of the Country," by William Gass, and "The Babysitter," by Robert Coover. What other fragmented narratives have you read?

(K.H.)

Comparison vs. Contiguity: Using Metaphor and Metonymy

19

Use to Write:	Short Fiction; Longer Fiction; Poetry; Creative Nonfiction; Autobiography; Essay/Criticism
Ideas and Concepts to Explore:	metaphor; metonymy; metonymic logic; icon; the image of "the writer"; romantic (as a literary term); Modernism.
Authors/Works Mentioned:	Roman Jakobson; Herman Melville, *Moby Dick*.

As mentioned in this chapter's first exercise ("Dislodge the Icon of 'The Writer'"), most of us begin with some fixed ideas about what a writer is and how we are supposed to be like that. Maybe your image of the writer wears a little bowler hat and smokes a pipe. Maybe she dresses in black. Maybe she's your best friend, the "creative" one, whose work the teachers read out loud the whole time you were growing up.

In my own writing story I started out giving up at sixteen when I read *Moby Dick* and realized that I was neither smart enough nor talented enough to be a writer. For five years after that I did not write, until I met a man who redefined my private concept of what a writer is. He was a smart man, and a gifted writer, and I was in love with him, and so when he told me that he'd trained himself for writing for an entire year by thinking of a metaphor for everything he saw, I thought: by George, I can do that too!

This was in the early seventies, in Santa Cruz, in winter, when late afternoons, high above the ocean, would turn a cool crystalline blue. I was earnest and a very hard worker, and so I started right away and went outside to study a redwood and think up a handy metaphor for it. At the end of ten minutes, I burst into tears, for I'd failed absolutely to come up with anything at all. Without a single metaphor in mind, I knew, once again, I could never be a writer. Was this fate, or was it something flawed in me?

Years later, in graduate school I came across the work of Roman Jakobson on metaphor and metonymy as they manifested themselves in the deranged discourse of schizophrenic aphasics. In his work Jakobson had observed that some of his subjects thought and expressed themselves exclusively in metaphor, and others exclusively in metonymy. Generalizing from this to the work of writers, Jakobson hypothesized that certain kinds of language association may be hardwired in our brains, and that, as a general rule, poets might tend to be metaphorical thinkers, and fiction writers, metonymical thinkers.

While this may seem an odd source of confirmation, it was a great relief to me to discover there were other forms of figurative writing than metaphor, at which I had long before failed. Also, if such thinking were hardwired in the brain, the failure was not really my fault.

But what, you may wonder, is metonymy, and how does it work in writing?

In your literature classes you may have learned metonymy as "part for the whole," which is how we can call the king, the "crown," for it sits atop his head and represents him. More loosely, metonymy can be conceived as a web of contiguity, one thing being connected to the other because, like the hipbone to the thighbone, they touch.

Imagine a dinner setting: spoons and knives to the right, forks, on neatly folded napkins, to the left, glasses to the right, above the spoons, and so forth. In metonymic logic, spoons may read left, to the knife, or up, to the stem of the wine glass, on which the dinner guest's fingers, seductively cupped, read right to the next dinner guest.

Or soccer: the halfback, who defensively boots it to the midfielder, who sends it to the forward, who scores.

Metaphor, a literary trope (trope is a figurative use of language) of substitution and replacement, compares like things to each other in associative leaps. Metonymy is, instead, a trope of combination and addition, where one thing leads inevitably to the other because they are contiguous, because, again, they touch.

For this exercise, pay attention to figurative language. Listen for metonymy, as well as metaphor, in your regular life. "The ducks are on the pond," you may hear yourself cheering at your brother's Little League game. Or, "Fly, baby, fly," as your girlfriend steals home on a bad throw.

Maybe, instead, you try telling your friend a simple story about how you went to the market to get bread and milk, but someone had spilled milk all over the case, and as you were trying to find a carton that wasn't sticky you found yourself eye-to-eye with the dairy man behind the shelves, and he seemed to be whispering something to you that you couldn't make out, and the look on his face, how it scared you.

Now, begin with a word: rock, eucalyptus, salamander. Pinenut. Brother. Sky.

Write your word, any word, and fill the space around it with either metaphors, or metonymies. Don't panic if you draw a blank, but keep moving through the web of words you can associate with the word you started with as quickly as you can, and when you have filled up some space, choose a word from that space and write more comparisons (metaphors), or contiguities (metonymies), fingers for your new word.

When you have filled your page with the connective tissue of language, put it to one side and write a poem off the words that you find there, or a little story, finely crafted, or something that may combine elements of both. Use the web of words to guide your writing. See where it leads you.

Now, try the other logic. If you worked first with metonymy, try metaphor, or the other way around. You may begin with new words, or not. See where this new logic leads you.

Finally, you may want to reflect on how it felt to work this way. Did either writing logic, or the other come more easily to you? What might this reveal about the way your own minds works? How may this be useful in your continued writing?

(K.H.)

Working with Metaphor

20

Use to Write:	n/a [the exercise addresses "metaphor" in general and may therefore be used in connection with virtually any genre]
Ideas and Concepts to Explore:	metaphor (as referring, in general, to comparisons and figurative language); metaphor (as referring more specifically to an implied comparison); metonymy; simile; synecdoche.
Authors/Works Mentioned:	[in this exercise, a brief bibliography is appended].

No doubt you've read about, discussed, and analyzed the concept of metaphor quite a bit already, and you've also probably learned the basic difference between **a** *metaphor* and a *simile*. Virtually every writing class and every writing textbook, including anthologies with glossaries, will take up the subject and also include definitions of more particular types of metaphor, including *metonymy* and *synecdoche*, so we'll skip over the definitions but do so with the confidence that they'll be readily available to you from many different resources. (If you'd like to make a dictionary your first stop, that's fine, too.)

Here is a brief writing prompt that will get you writing with and thinking about metaphor in a focused way.

Directions: Close your eyes and visualize a person you know, a person about whom you have strong feelings. Open your eyes and write the name of or a code name for that person at the top of a sheet of paper. Then quickly write responses to the following prompts:

1. Think of this person as a landscape. What landscape would he or she be?

2. Describe this person as a kind of fruit, a metal, a wood, a time of day, a time period in history, a piece of clothing, etc. Invent other options-for-comparison, if you like.

3. Think of this person in his/her favorite location. Describe it. Have him/her speak? Bring someone else into the scene and let them talk together.

4. What would this person like to say but never says? What does this person dream about? Tell some lies for this person.

This prompt can of course be adapted easily to descriptions of things (objects), events, houses, rooms, public places, journeys, etc.

Additionally, you might "spend a week with metaphor." During this week, go over some of your poems, stories, creative nonfiction, dramatic work, or even course papers and mark every implicit, explicit, buried, effective, ineffective, clichéd, or original metaphor you can find. Brainstorm revision possibilities for each one—sharper comparisons, more subtle comparison, bolder comparisons, better-phrased comparisons, and so on. That is, you'll be reading your work through a lens that focuses only on metaphoric language—explicit or implicit comparisons. In *all* the reading you do that week—newspapers, billboards, textbooks, classified ads (including the personals!), literature, whatever—look carefully at the metaphorical language being used. Make notes about good, bad, confusing, unintentionally funny, and other sorts of metaphors.

For additional reading about metaphors, you might look at the following works, which are widely available in libraries:

The Poetics of Fire, by Gaston Bachelard (1968).

Textbook: An Introduction to Literary Language, by Robert Scholes, Nancy R. Comly, and Gregory L. Ulmer (1985).

Writing With Power, by Peter Elbow (1981).

Metaphors We Live By, by George Lakoff and Mark Johnson (1980).

Women, Fire, and Dangerous Things: What Categories Reveal About the Mind, by George Lakoff (1987).

More Than Cool Reason: A Field Guide to Poetic Metaphor, by George Lakoff and Mark Turner (1988).

On Metaphor, edited by Sheldon Sacks (1977).

(W.B. and H.O.)

Premises, Assumptions, Hypothetical Situations

21 **Y in X-land:**
Dropping Characters into Places They Don't Belong

Use to Write:	Short Fiction; Longer Fiction; Poetry
Ideas and Concepts to Explore:	allegory; analog; extended metaphor; fantasy; parable.
Authors/Works Mentioned:	Lewis Carroll, *Alice in Wonderland.*

Lewis Carroll's fantastical *Alice in Wonderland* remains a widely read, widely known book—for many reasons. It bridges the gap between so-called children's literature and adult literature; it is, like a good dream, at once crazed and internally logical; it opens itself up to numerous rich interpretations; and, not least of all, it's full of wit and humor. Some would argue that part of its lasting appeal springs from its capacity to represent psychological states in terms of vivid physical situations. One example: Alice, an adolescent who, like all adolescents, undergoes enormous emotional changes, finds herself part of an underworld in which beings and situations and language change instantly, wildly, unpredictably. In this way, "Wonderland" becomes a marvelous analog to, almost an allegory or extended comparison of, the sometimes disorienting, dizzy world in which adolescents find themselves.

Much literature represents life in such a way that hidden meanings are exposed and conflicts beneath the surface of ordinary life are revealed. In this particular writing prompt, however, we make more of an obvious, even extreme, attempt to create an underground, hidden world, to drop a character into it, and to see what stories might spring from the experiment.

Develop your own characters who visit their own analog-world, so to speak—an underground, a topsy-turvy world, a hidden world, a world with its own internal logic (or nonlogic). For the moment, consider your character to be "Y" and the world to be "X-land." Begin to fill in particulars of either the character or the analog-world—or both at once. Use the extraordinary world to represent psychological, emotional, or even political situations in unusual ways.

Example: whereas Alice disappears down a rabbit hole and falls into Wonderland, perhaps your character is a college student who disappears through a hidden door of a classroom, falling into an alternate college—Wonder-College, or Anti-College, or whatever. No matter who your character is or what the X-land is, begin to think as well in terms of a journey the character or characters make: a descent into or a tour across this otherworld. What is the nature of the journey, and how might it serve as an instructive, entertaining analog to our so-called real world? As an extended metaphor or allegory, what does the journey through this world start to say about "the real world? That is, for example, what does Character X's journey through Wonder-College say about life in college today? And naturally you need not think in terms of a long narrative; begin with a short, parable-length piece, if you like. Take small fictional steps, even as you make long imaginative leaps.

(H.O.)

▶22 Under What Circumstances Would Someone . . . ?

Use to Write:	Short Fiction; Fiction; Poetry; Drama; Screenplay
Ideas and Concepts to Explore:	circumstances; conflict.
Authors/Works Mentioned:	n/a

You might say fiction concerns *circumstances*—clusters of chance and fate, accident and human will, nature and society that combine to create friction, trouble, conflict. The roots of the word suggest a "standing around," not as in "loitering" but as in "the things—the forces, people, and events—surrounding us," changing each of us constantly.

Sometimes writers can get to "the story" by starting with such a cluster of circumstances, and imagining the circumstances can be triggered by a single question. Following is a list of trigger-questions, all beginning with "Under what circumstances . . . ?" Answer any or all of them—musing on them, scribbling some notes, inventing a character, freewriting, free-associating, or writing a scene. Think of each question as creating a space your imagination will fill. The expected outcome is that, once your imagination begins to fill the space, an idea for a story will emerge and draw you toward a narrative. The more specific the *circumstances* you can invent in answer to each question, the better.

Under what circumstances . . .

1. . . . would someone love a dirty city?
2. . . . would a gift be regarded as a threat?
3. . . . would theft be morally correct?
4. . . . would a party be the most lonely occurrence one could imagine?
5. . . . would someone dread the arrival of Spring?
6. . . . would someone be jealous of a dead cat?
7. . . . would someone kiss a credit card?
8. . . . could someone be said to belch gracefully?
9. . . . would someone play the tuba at a funeral?
10. . . . would someone pray devoutly to a stone?

(H.O.)

23 ▶ Against the Grain: Ignoring Conventional Wisdom

Use to Write:	Short Fiction; Poetry; Longer Fiction; Journal; Drama; Creative Nonfiction
Ideas and Concepts to Explore:	amorality; immorality; morality; conventional wisdom/received opinion; "counter-cosmopolitan"/ provincial; unreflective.
Authors/Works Mentioned:	*The Bible* (Old Testament); Alberto Rios, "The Iguana Killer"; William Carlos Williams, "The Use of Force"; Virginia Woolf, "A Room of One's Own".

Out of necessity, perhaps out of temperament, most writers come to think of "conventional wisdom" as a contradiction in terms. To write entirely outside of conventions, of course, is impossible, and in writing as in life, we are bound by more conventions than we know. But in writing, as in life, we also come to define ourselves by creating a niche for ourselves, a place of our own, what Virginia Woolf literally and metaphorically called "a room of one's own." We create a niche by going against the grain, in ways large and small, by refusing to receive "received opinion." Here are some prompts that invite you to go against—specifically, to write against—the grain. They are merely options from which to choose; feel free to alter them; feel free to spring off them and invent your own prompts for writing against the grain.

One purpose here is to draw on the energy often created by a mood of independence, of going one's own way, of creating one more space in which the imagination can roam. The prompts, then:

1. The Ten Commandments: Read them and then choose one and write a story, a *short-short* story (parable?), or a poem that implicitly supports violating one of the Commandments. Since that may be thunder we hear in the distance, perhaps we might qualify this prompt by suggesting that the trick is not to discount the Commandment, or the Ten Commandments, or the worthiness of moral codes, but to try to *invent a situation* in which the right thing to do, ironically, would be to violate the Commandment. Literature often concerns such ironies. To a degree, the piece will involve not immorality or amorality but moral complexity—perhaps a moral *dilemma*.

2. Write a story or a poem that is implicitly sympathetic to shopping malls and mall-culture, which are routinely ridiculed.

3. Write a story or a poem that is implicitly sympathetic to television, which politicians, intellectuals, educators, and other Serious People love to bash.

4. Write a story or a poem that is implicitly sympathetic to bureaucrats or to one bureaucrat or to a bureaucratic problem.

5. Write a story or a poem that is implicitly sympathetic to someone whom a politician or a lazy journalist might callously refer to as "a welfare mother."

6. One summer a colleague asked me, "Where've you been?" "Alabama," I replied. "Oh gawd," the person said, "I'd never want to go there." *Well, okay,* I thought, *that takes care of that!* I'd been to the Gulf Coast, and I'd visited a town called Fairhope, which has one of the most interesting histories of any community in the nation—the place was founded, in part, as a social-economic experiment. So my reaction was, *But you don't know what you're missing.* Within the framework of this exercise, then, my reaction might be phrased as, *Discovery often means going against the grain.* My colleague's reaction highlighted for me the relationship writers virtually *must* have to a place and to "place." It simply cannot be so automatic and unthinking. Even if a writer ends up mainly despising a place, she or he cannot do so automatically, unimaginatively, partly because writers must work against stereotypes and tired categories. This, then, is one context out of which the following prompt springs:

   Write a story or a poem that implicitly celebrates a place conventionally or unreflectively thought to be "unglamorous" or wanting or unworthy. Examples, leaving aside Alabama for the moment: The state of Oklahoma, which in conventional American wisdom is thought somehow to be less glamorous than states like California or New York; the Central Valley of California (as opposed to Hollywood or San Francisco); the rural south; a small town on the Great Plains; New Jersey (as opposed to that other place across the Hudson); a farming town in Wisconsin; Spokane, Washington (as opposed to Seattle); Oakland, California (as opposed to San Francisco); Frankfurt, Germany (as opposed to Berlin, Cologne, or Munich); Houston, Texas (as opposed to Dallas or Austin); Corvalis, Oregon (as opposed to Portland). No doubt other states, regions, cities, or towns may, in your view, fall into this category, and these examples are meant chiefly to help you get **your own list** going.

7. Write a story or a poem that is implicitly sympathetic to dentists.

8. Write a story or a poem that is implicitly sympathetic toward misbehaving children. (You might take a look at William Carlos Williams' much anthologized story, "The Use of Force" or Alberto Rios's story, "The Iguana Killer.")

9. Write a story or a poem that is implicitly sympathetic to "boring relatives."

10. Write a story or a poem that is implicitly sympathetic to accountants.

(H.O.)

(24) Against the Grain, Part Two

Use to Write:	n/a [the exercise encourages "violating" conventions in any genre]
Ideas and Concepts to Explore:	fairy tale; genre conventions; implicit/explicit "rules" of form; limerick; lyric poem; memo; novel; oath; playful sabotage; prayer; surrealism.
Authors/Works Mentioned:	Jorge Luis Borges, *Labyrinths;* Charles Dickens; Emily Dickinson; James Joyce, *Dubliners;* Walt Whitman.

As mentioned in Against the Grain, the previous exercise, no one could write without the presence of conventions, no matter how anarchist or experimental her/his intentions were. Even the first written texts in history came out of oral conventions, and all writers now work within thousands of written-text conventions—received "codes," if you will—concerning vocabulary, diction, grammar, usage, spelling, punctuation, story telling, plotting, type fonts, language-rhythms, and on and on. Even the most wildly experimental writing owes its existence to what it is experimenting *with,* what it's changing, the rules it's bending or breaking.

The urge to experiment, however, is deep within us. It springs from a basic human need to alter, to challenge, or to play with the boundaries of communities, traditions, various spheres into which we're born. It springs from boredom; it springs from the satisfying nature of a certain tension between a sense of belonging and a desire not to belong, between the tug of individuality and the tug of communal membership.

In some instances, *conventions of genre*—the "rules," explicit and implicit, of lyric poetry, short fiction, drama, autobiography, novels, etc.—can weigh heavily on writers: You might come up with an idea for a story, for instance—an idea that seems fresh, exhilirating, new; but when you begin to write, you feel yourself slipping into conventions—everything from conventional beginnings to conventional dialogue to something as seemingly trivial as capitalizing the first word of sentences. (James Joyce apparently had to fight furiously with the publisher of his short-story collection, *Dubliners,* in order to keep some unconventional punctuation in the stories.) The conventions may seem to conspire to drag the fresh idea down like an undertow, and you feel yourself starting to write "just another story."

The following prompt invites you to take an aggressive attitude toward genre-conventions, in part by "cross-wiring" or short-circuiting the conventions of one genre with those of another. It's playful sabotage, intended in part to take a more assertive, less victimized, stance toward genre-conventions. So, you might write . . .

1. a one-page novel

2. a lyric memo

3. an interpretive essay on a work of literature or philosophy that doesn't exist (Note: Jorge Luis Borges was very good at working such illusory scholarship into his fiction; you might look at some of his stories, especially those in *Labyrinths,* but of course you need not work in terms of *Borges's* conventions!)

4. an adventure recipe (a recipe using the conventions of adventure tales)

5. a shopping list in formal verse

6. surrealistic directions to your house

7. a job-application letter written in the style of Walt Whitman's poetry (you might look at his *Song of Myself;* is it fair to say that, in some respects, job-applications ask us to "sing ourselves?")

8. a condensation, in limerick form, of a Dickens novel

9. a five-word graduation speech

10. a prayer that asks for nothing

11. a disloyalty oath

12. a serious limerick

13. a fairy tale without magic

14. an adaptation of an epic poem or epic tale, written in a series of no more than five haiku, one haiku for each episode of the epic. Here is a haiku by Gary Snyder in this mode, entitled "Trojan War":
moonlight on
the burned-out temple—
wooden horse-shit   (from *The Back Country*)

(H.O.)

The Nonexistent Relative: Viewing "Facts" as Malleable

(25)

Use to Write:	Short Fiction; Longer Fiction; Autobiography
Ideas and Concepts to Explore:	literal vs. fictional "truth"; autobiographical fiction; "breaking from the facts."
Authors/Works Mentioned:	n/a

Write a story, or at least write toward a story, about a relative who never existed. That is, into the matrix of your real family, "drop" a fictional relative. You may define "real family" as you wish—nuclear family, extended family, a sibling group, or whatever.

This tends to be a good prompt for exploring the complexities of drawing on explicitly autobiographical material as you write fiction; in some ways, of course, autobiography is the main reservoir for raw fiction material, because it is "our world," filled with "true stories," parts of stories, narrative legacies. One problem with this obvious resource, however, is that even when we set out to write fiction, we remain loyal to the facts, and, despite our best fictional intentions, we resist divergence from "what really happened."

This prompt honors what is and what was—"the real family," its particulars, its history—but provides a swift, sharp chisel—the nonexistent relative—that can break up autobiography, allowing you to exert control over the facts, keeping some, discarding others, creating an alloy of fact-and-invention.

Ironically, the unreal relative can also be an effective means of seeing your family in clear light, letting you understand things once hidden in plain sight by the mass of fact.

As you invent, shape, and reshape this fictional relative and the story or prospective stories flowing from the invention, always give yourself license to let the "fictionalizing" expand, changing facts as necessary to fit the emerging fiction, giving the relative who never existed lots of elbow room.

(H.O.)

Ambiguity Is Certainly Useful

(26)

Use to Write:	Short Fiction; Longer Fiction; Poetry; Essay; Drama; Journal; Autobiography
Ideas and Concepts to Explore:	ambiguity; conflict (in fiction and drama); ethical dilemma; hypothesis; irrational fear; multi-dimensional responses; "character" vs. "fate"; paradox; subjectivity vs. objectivity.
Authors/Works Mentioned:	Kate Chopin, *The Awakening;* William Faulkner, *Light In August;* Toni Morrison, *Beloved;* William Shakespeare, *Hamlet, King Lear, Romeo and Juliet.*

Hypothesis: *If,* as the axiom goes, literature is all about drama/dramatization, which is all about conflict, *then* our "literary" writing should naturally represent, and/or spring from, strong emotions, which often cause conflict or are symptoms of conflict.

Journalism, too, largely concerns conflict (man bites dog, President bites Congress); and most essays exist to test ideas that are (con)testable—capable of sparking intellectual conflict: debate. Essays interpret fact; interpretation is always contestable; indeed, the hypothesis with which this exercise begins is contestable in several ways. So even in such ostensibly more "objective" writing, we seek the seeds of strong emotion, which is an aspect of subjectivity.

However, in writing, and especially in writing fiction, it's possible to focus too much on conflict, at least in this sense: driven (by ourselves, our teachers, conventional wisdom) in search of conflict, we can be led to pit good against evil (for instance) in such stark terms that the result is almost cartoonish: Conflict is certainly present, no doubt about that, but it's *too* present, obliterating all other dimensions of "story." Conflict becomes the proverbial 900-pound gorilla. We might add that the same thing can happen with journalism, not just in tabloid journalism, which dedicates itself to exaggeration, but with television news-panel-shows and talk shows that obliterate the subtleties of debate and often try to allow only for two extreme positions, thereby guaranteeing a "war of words"—much shouting in a little time before the break to commercial.

Sometimes, therefore, deliberately exploring ambiguity—complex, uncertain, murky, perhaps even paradoxical conflict—can help us produce richer fiction, can help us avoid being mindless adherents to the Conflict Axiom, can help us represent ourselves and the world with greater integrity. To "begin with ambiguity," then, you might . . .

1. Explore in writing something about which you have mixed emotions. "Going home" is a classic example. Whether it's for the weekend or following decades of being away, returning to one's home can call up clusters of emotions and memories that make any single response impossible. And what is "home," after all? The surface simplicity of the word thinly masks all sorts of contestable, shifting, indeterminate definitions. . . . Work, a particular time of year (like holidays), an "era" or block of time (like "high school years"): these are other subjects likely to be haunted by ambivalence or mixed emotions. Essays, poems, or stories springing from this exploratory writing will necessarily have to be multidimensional, not simplistic, in the way they handle subjects of conflict; the notion of conflict by no means disappears, but it gets balanced and contextualized.

2. Write about an irrational fear of something. If there's a fire in your kitchen and you're afraid of it, probably that's a rational fear. But if you're afraid of all spiders, even those that are absolutely harmless to humans, then probably that's an irrational fear—fear based on something besides the facts and logical consequences. The fear is no less real, but the conflict inside you is complicated—ambiguous.

3. Write about an ethical dilemma—a moment in your life or someone else's in which "the right thing to do" was not at all clear and in which indecision resulted not from moral weakness or laziness but from the ambiguity of the situation.

4. Write about "character versus fate." Example: After a long, stormy political career, Richard Nixon became the first sitting President forced to resign, in the face of impeachment. How much of this disgrace sprang from Nixon's character, and how much of it sprang from fate? How much of it sprang from choices Nixon made, and how much of it sprang from circumstances—his upbringing, the era of American history, the nature of American politics? Choose an historical figure, or a friend, or a family member, or a sports figure who did something fine or something disgraceful; debate with yourself about "character versus fate" in the situation; and write a short essay that explains your interpretation. Later you might turn it into a story. Naturally, "character versus fate" also opens up those infamous issues of "free will versus inevitability" (we have control over what we do *versus* we do not have control over what we do) and "nature versus nurture" (genetics versus behavior). "Character versus fate" also opens up issues in literary interpretation: For instance, in works like Shakespeare's *Hamlet, King Lear,* and *Romeo and Juliet;* Kate Chopin's *The Awakening;* Ralph Ellison's *Invisible Man;* William Faulkner's *Light in August;* Tony Morrison's *Beloved;* and so on . . . what are the pressures of *character* and *fate* that bear on the narratives' outcomes, on the particulars of tragedy? And of course, the X versus Y phrasing of these issues is deceptive, masking complexity and ambiguity and the difficulty of defining the terms—as you'll discover all over again as you write.

5. Write of an issue about which you just can't make up your mind. Example: the issue of abortion. From the media we tend to get depictions of fixed, *completely* worked-out positions on the issue: "Pro-Choice versus Pro-Life" is how it's characterized. But then in our own lives, we may listen to a lot of people—and we may or may not be among such people—who just can't decide, who continue to struggle with the issue. Select an issue that has kept you struggling to decide, and write about why you're still struggling. This writing might lead to a poem or a story or an essay.

(H.O.)

(27) Drama = Conflict = Power

Use to Write:	Short Fiction; Longer Fiction; Drama; Screenplay; Performance Piece
Ideas and Concepts to Explore:	drama; conflict; plot; "fictionalizing".
Authors/Works Mentioned:	n/a

Let's call it an axiom, one that most students of literature encounter early on: *The essence of drama is conflict*—forces of one sort or another at odds in one way or another. Broadly defined, such conflict is really any kind of **trouble between people**; "drama" in this case refers not necessarily just to plays but to fictional stories that might take shape in any genre: short story, novel, play, movie, epic poem, dramatic monologue, etc. It would be difficult to find a work in any of these genres that doesn't feature one or more contests, competitions, struggles, or fights: conflict.

The previous exercise concerned the ambiguities often present in conflict; this one focuses on the notion that the essence of conflict is power. *Power* as in . . .

someone has authority over someone else

someone challenges the authority of someone else

an institution or a group of people control an individual's behavior

an individual controls the behavior of a group of people or an institution

someone wants something from someone else

someone uses the threat of physical force to manipulate someone else

someone uses information or money to try to control someone else . . . and so on.

Some situations in these categories are explicitly political. That is, the President of the United States can order U.S. troops into a foreign land; that's overt, plain political power. Others are chiefly personal: A parent says to a child, "Because you didn't do what I asked you to do, I won't let you go to the concert." But of course, something that seems explicitly political can be shaped by all sorts of personal forces, and a supposedly personal or romantic or family-oriented situation can also be political.

Example.

A man who has grown up believing it's all right to strike a woman is not just an individual but an individual who has grown up in a particular social and political moment, not in a vacuum. Yes, he is, or should be, accountable *individually* for what he does, but what he does may also be a part of a larger social or political pattern of behavior. More bluntly put, statistics show that a lot of men, in the United States and elsewhere, think it's all right to strike women, an indication of a broader pattern of behavior. The combination of the personal and the political shows up in literature, too, of course. Shakespeare's *King Lear* indeed concerns a king, a political person, but Lear's fall from his political perch is deeply involved with his personal flaws and with conflicts in his immediate family.

Still other situations seem trivial or even harmless on the surface, but beneath the surface they are filled with power.

Example.

A young woman has just joined a law firm. On a break she goes to a coffee shop, where she encounters one of the senior male partners—one of her bosses, that is. They stand next to each other as they wait to pay for their coffee. If we were to glance at them, the situation might seem almost too ordinary to bother studying, might seem far removed from issues of power and conflict, the axiomatic "stuff" of literature. And yet . . . the woman might be super-alert to what she's saying as she makes so-called "small talk"; therefore, the talk isn't "small" at all because *something seems to be at stake.* Or . . . the man may stand a couple of centimeters too close to the woman, making her uncomfortable, and perhaps he knows he's making her uncomfortable. Or . . . perhaps the partner is an alcoholic and is failing at his work, and the woman is the protegé of another partner, who has the upper hand in the firm: How would this change the "subtext" or "hidden agendas" or the unspoken but palpable forces there in that "ordinary" meeting in the coffee shop?

In literal terms, the two people may exchange a total of fifty words and buy a total of two cups of coffee for what amounts to small change, but in figurative terms, all sorts of conflict may be occurring, all sorts of power relationships may be there, leaking into the moment. And maybe that moment will be a crucial moment—when something is decided, revealed, or what have you. Again, the same process occurs in literature. In John Updike's oft-anthologized story, "A & P," young women walk into a supermarket wearing bathing suits; therefore, the situation is hardly as grand as the plots of *Moby Dick* or *The Iliad.* Nonetheless, obviously non trivial conflicts involving social class, gender, age, and ethics flow from the small event.

Begin by thinking about any and all power situations in your life, ones you've been involved in, ones you are involved in, ones you've heard about, ones you observe up close or from a distance. They can be obvious ones: Someone is fired from a job; power is clearly exercised. Or they can be not so obvious, even masked, like the coffee-shop scene described above. Make notes. Ask, *Who has power over Whom and why? What's the source of the power? How is it being used?* Perhaps you'll want to observe interactions between people, little "ordinary" scenes that begin to seem extraordinary—scenes at a job, in a coffee house, at a bar, at a party, in a library, on a freeway. What issues of power can you detect beneath the trivial surface?

Then ask, *How is the power leading to* or *How has the power led to* conflict? How is the conflict playing out, or how did it play out? Any surprises? Gross injustices? Small or large betrayals? Paradoxes? Strange or not-so-strange reversals of fortune?

As you sift through these particulars, give yourself license to fictionalize, just as we fictionalized the entire *lawyers-in-the-coffee-shop* scene above. Essentially, fictionalizing begins the moment you start making guesses about relationships and motives. Change certain "players," if you like. Remove some particulars, add others. Follow your own interests in power and conflict. In a writerly way, become more assertive and reshape the situation you recalled or observed.

Then work toward situations, scenes, or stories you'd like to invent as a way to dramatize more completely the conflict and power. Maybe the rough shape of a whole story occurs to you, or maybe at the moment just one exchange of words or one scene occurs. There's no telling (so to speak) what sort of story our coffee-shop scene would have led to, especially since we hadn't filled in most of the particulars, hadn't even decided which of the particulars we invented we would keep or discard, hadn't decided who was who and who might do what to whom. We were just getting started. Whatever particulars you start to generate, begin to "write them up." Work toward some sort of "drama"—a short story or a little play, perhaps: a *playing-out* in a specific *plot* of fictional *conflict*.

This is often a good writing prompt for beginning writers who "don't know what to write about." But it can also be a good one to return to for writers who feel out of gas, out of ideas, somehow stuck. Thus, here's another writerly axiom, especially for those of us who count ourselves amongst the Fiction Crowd or the Drama Crowd: *When in doubt, return to the basics of conflict—and power—in human relations.* It is an inexhaustible reservoir of material.

(H.O.)

28 ▶ Story Spinning: 51 Prompts for Story Ideas

Use to Write:	Short Fiction; Longer Fiction; Prose Poetry
Ideas and Concepts to Explore:	epistolary form; e-mail-epistolary form; persona; second-person point of view; compound sentence; complex sentence; recipe story; reverse chronology.
Authors/Works Mentioned:	C.S. Lewis, *The Screwtape Letters;* Samuel Richardson, *Pamela.*

Here is an abundant list of *options,* from which to choose one idea, or more than one, for writing.

1. Write a story in the second person.

2. Write a story organized around a single present moment that extends into both the past and future.

3. Write a story in which one character, in bed with another, reveals a past life to that person.

4. Write a story which begins and ends with the same sentence.

5. Write a story about writing a story.

6. Write a story in which a meal is prepared and consumed, by the end of which: 1) the characters, who barely know each other to begin with, are best friends, or 2) the characters, who had been best friends for years, determine not to meet again.

7. Create a persona—an aging soccer coach, a seamstress, a ten-year-old boy in summer—and write a story in the voice of that person.

8. Write a story you wish you had read.

9. Write a story in the form of a letter to: an old friend, someone you barely know, a lover, an ex-lover, your grandmother, someone famous, your parents, your brother or sister, your brother's or sister's girlfriend or boyfriend,

your therapist, your teacher, someone you made up, yourself. (Literature in the form of a letter or letters is sometimes referred to as "epistolary form," "epistle" being another word for "letter." The well known eithteenth-century British novel by Samuel Richardson, *Pamela,* is an "epistolary novel," written entirely in letters. The more contemporary book, *The Screwtape Letters,* by C. S. Lewis, is another good example.)

10. Write a story in four parts, each 500 words exactly.

11. Write a story, all in compound sentences.

12. Write a story, all in compound or complex sentences.

13. Write a story about the house you grew up in, but before you were born.

14. Write a story about a house you will never live in.

15. Write a story with many different kinds of fish in it.

16. Write a story about something that really happened to you, but mix it up with something that didn't.

17. Write a story about something you saw happen at the grocery store or park.

18. Write an "alphabet story," in which each sentence begins with the letters of the alphabet, in sequence.

19. Write a story based on musical principles.

20. Write a story in reverse chronological order.

21. Write a story using sentences, all thirty words long or longer.

22. Write a story using sentences, all under fifteen words.

23. Write a story for your mother, your aunt, your son.

24. Write a story following a recipe for your favorite casserole, main dish or dessert.

25. Write a story all in dialogue.

26. Write a story with no dialogue in it.

27. Write a story in the future tense.

28. Write a story with someone else, each of you responsible for every other sentence.

29. Write a story in the voices of five imaginary people.

30. Write a story about imagining an historical figure.

31. Write a story using only words found on the front page of today's newspaper.

32. Write a story in which you repeat one or more lines at least seven times.

33. Write a story in which you repeat the word *blue* fifty times.

34. Write a story about weather.

35. Write a story about someone who has an unusual job—underwater welder, horse trainer, orderly in a surgical ward.

36. Write a story based upon the rules of baseball.

37. Write a story in the form of e-mail correspondence between two people who will never meet.

38. Write a story in the form of a list.

39. Translate a story you wrote, from English back to English.

40. Write a story answering a worksheet in your biology lab book.

41. Write a story where everything important happens in the white space.

42. Write a story in which your main character suffers from an unusual affliction, either real or imaginary.

43. Write a story about sleep.

44. Write a story using all the words on a random page of the dictionary.

45. Write a story in which your main character is born without one of the five senses—sight, hearing, smell, taste, touch. (Imagine never having been able to taste, to feel.)

46. Write a story without using the letter "b," the letter "m," or the letter "s." (One, not all, of the three.)

47. Write a story based on a math equation.

48. Write a story about a place you love.

49. Write a story, then take a third of the words out, some words from every sentence.

50. Write a story about ideas for writing a story.

51. "Imagine the imagination imagining." (William Gass): Now, *Write*.

(K.H.)

Memory

Listing and Memory

29

Use to Write:	Poetry; Prose Poetry; Short Fiction; Longer Fiction; Autobiography; Creative Nonfiction
Ideas and Concepts to Explore:	objects and things: their literal (functional) and figurative meanings; prose poem; metaphorical meanings of "belongings," "possessions," and "carrying."
Authors/Works Mentioned:	Wendy Bishop, "Into and Out Of Gillian"; Tim O'Brien, "The Things They Carried."

It has been nearly fifteen years since I inherited the last of my family—mother's and father's—belongings. The corner hutches are gone, but I still have the carved coffee table from Japan, my baby cup from the same place (I've written poems about both), and a shawl that I don't remember but found among my mother's possessions at her death. When my sisters and I cleaned out my mother's closet, we gave away her enormous collection of sale shoes (I wrote prose about this thing-ful event). Even today, I keep an Imari bowl, a broken incense burner, and a memory of her MixMaster mixer. I have things and memories of things, and each item triggers a story and a powerful memory chain.

Once I discovered the power of things, I knew it would be worthwhile to write toward, through, and past them: to list them and consider them, to list them and remember. The first time I recall seeing my mother cry, for instance, is connected to her connection to her things. One of her hutches—stacked in two parts—tipped over as she moved the bottom section to plug the vacuum cleaner into a socket behind the hutch. When she did this, a lifetime of collectibles tumbled onto the rug and the wood floor: china figurines from Germany, her mother's cut glass bowl, some carved ivory netsuke from Japan. These inheritances represented her life and her times—she was a war bride in the late 1940s. Some items broke, some fractured in—to her eyes—irreparable ways. She sat down and cried.

You could say, things overpowered her. They continued to do so each time my Army family moved, 26 times in 20 years. Called on to transplant herself yet again, my mother packed each object and then unpacked it—its shape, its story, its memory, its meaning—and set it out in a new house—much as she set herself out—to disappoint or to please. Eventually, I completed a seven-part prose poem, "Into and Out of Gillian," by writing about my inheritance, my mother's "things." This was one way to get to the heart of her.

Before going on to the set of prompts that follow, you might want to write about the "things of" and "thingness" of someone for whom you, too, have powerful memories and associations.

Next, to uncover more ways of looking at things, read Tim O'Brien's story (widely anthologized), "The Things They Carried." The following prompts were derived from that story.

- List the things that make you hopeful (figurative and literal).
  "They were not love letters, but Lieutenant Cross was hoping, so he kept them folded in plastic at the bottom of his rucksack."
- List the things you have that you keep that you can taste.
  "He would sometimes taste the envelope flaps, knowing her tongue had been there."
- List the things you carry by necessity.
  "wristwatches, dog tags, mosquito repellent . . ."
- List the things that people you know carry, keep, collect, or hold (maybe choose a particular group of friends—for O'Brien, the men in a company in Vietnam—for you . . . ?)
- List and describe five photographs you carry in your purse/wallet, and or/mind.
  "In his wallet, Lieutenant Cross carried two photographs of Martha."

- List things you have, keep, or carry by virtue of your job, profession or special role you hold.

  "As a medic, Rat Kiley carried a canvas satchel filled with morphine . . ."
- List things you keep but wish you didn't, things you think you have to hold on to but hate, things that overwhelm you but you can't get rid of (physical and/or psychic).

  "They carried all they could bear, and then some, including a silent awe for the terrible power of the things they carried."
- List things that compose you and how you contribute to the world. What goes into and out of you?
- List the charms and lucky tokens you collect and keep.
- List the odds and ends of things you can think of—in the drawer, a cupboard, a wallet/purse/backpack, a car, a garage, a room. Explore the meaning of what you keep. Explore the connection between several disparate things.
- List the special equipment you keep and maintain.

  "They carried wiring, detonators, and battery powered clackers. Dave Jensen carried earplugs."
- List things that you have, carry, or keep that are in common with others who are close to you or related to you in some way. As all soldiers carry helmets and weapons, you and ? have, carry, hold, keep ?
- Carry yourself from one time/place in life to another—what did you carry along, abandon behind?
- What stories do you carry?
- What emotions do you carry?
- How are they like or not like the other things you carry?
- What are the things you carry inside?
- Finally, consider the weight (or lightness) of the things you carry.

Take any of these explorations and shape them into fact or fiction of your choosing.

(W.B.)

The Most Important Spectator in Your Writing Life—You

30

Use to Write:	Autobiography; Creative Nonfiction; Short Fiction; Longer Fiction; Journal
Ideas and Concepts to Explore:	"event" vs. "experience"; free association; juxtaposition; "participant" vs. "spectator".
Authors/Works Mentioned:	James Britton; Kim Haimes-Korn; Richard Wright, "The Wonder I Felt".

My friend Kim Haimes-Korn has often organized her writing courses around the observation offered in the following paragraph:

> Each event spoke with a cryptic tongue. And the moments of living slowly revealed their coded meanings. . . . We live in time and as we participate in any event, while it is actually happening, the pressure of participation, the work we do unconsciously to continue to play our part—listening, watching, responding, doing—these make demands of us, of our energy, and of our powers of attention. It is only afterwards, when the event has been swept into the past, when we are spectators of our own past lives, that we can make sense of it: then and only then, can we say it was an *experience* rather than a mere *event*.
>
> —Richard Wright "The Wonder I Felt"

You don't have to agree totally with Wright that experience is more powerful than event to find his distinction worth thinking about. It is a provocative opposition, one that you could explore in writing in the same manner I've encouraged you to explore realization/epiphany distinctions elsewhere in *Metro*. Oppositional terms like these are obviously artificial constructs in that they simplify issues, but simplification can help writers. Wright's passage addresses the much discussed distinctions between showing and telling, explaining and rendering. Such exploration becomes more interesting when you also consider the terms suggested by writing researcher James Britton—participant and spectator. In his research on written texts, Britton found writers shifting between these two stances, moving from that of participant—one who is living—to spectator—one who is writing about the event that was once "merely" lived experience.

To help writers in her classes explore such stance shifting, Kim asks them to experiment with time and distance—by detailing an earlier event and then writing in ways that help them make meanings out of that event.

We could chart these ideas this way:

active	reflective
event	experience
participant	spectator

(perhaps you can add more terms to these columns)

Understanding seems to deepen when your narrative moves between these positions as well as when you weave these positions together (through the use of multivoiced texts or by offering multiple perspectives in juxtaposition).

Some useful words for the reflective spectator who is working to turn event to experience are—detail, shape, engage, revisit, construct, reveal.

Now some exercises, options from which to choose:

1. Create an extended memory chain—detail an event, then free-associate and reconnect, free-associate and reconnect.

2. Set yourself at a certain age: remember and detail your beliefs, way of life, attitudes, etc. Move up to the present and reflect on how those beliefs, actions, attitudes have shifted. Explore why.

3. Distance yourself from an early event in your memory chain—film it, photograph it, tell it from several points of view (yours, your parents, an invented outsider, an animal, an inanimate object).

4. Revisit an actual site. Tell a past story from that site while actually there. Look around you and draw on the present physicality of your location which may help/require that you shuttle back and forth in time—how it was then, how it is now, and so on.

(W.B.)

How New Writing Grows Out of Old

31

Use to Write:	n/a [the exercise may lead to work in virtually any genre]
Ideas and Concepts to Explore:	invention; the personal "writing contract".
Authors/Works Mentioned:	n/a

Students tell me they enroll in writing classes because the classes provide needed deadlines. Sometimes the writing teacher's primary role is that of class "manager," because she sets up the schedule—asking for writing drafts on specific dates. That role allows writers to do what they already want to do, write. In addition, I ask writers to draw up a writing contract that allows them some freedom within class requirements (discussed in a moment). By doing this, the teacher becomes the classroom conductor or coordinator or manager—someone who helps writers meet the writing deadlines that they too often don't allow themselves to schedule into busy lives.

Because our lives are full, they are also good sources for writing topics. If we don't stop to plan our writing before we begin, in a general way, and assess where we've gotten to, at the end, in a general way—we lose some important control of and sense of having developed a writing life. In addition, writers who work only in and for school tend to forget how much they actually have written. They also forget the many things they wanted to write about but didn't: because there wasn't time, because the topic didn't seem appropriate, and so on. All writers find it useful to review their writing—past and present—to see where they want to go next. In this exercise, you'll see how your new writing grows out of your old writing and also how you might better plan a course of work.

For each of the next twelve prompts, write nonstop, remembering what you can. You may want to return later to these lists or titles in order to add more details (this list has evolved from reading books on writing by other writers—you may hear echoes of their prompts in these or you may want to add some prompts that you've found in other books).

Exercise.

Write for approximately three-to-five minutes, nonstop, on each of the following prompts as they are called out in class or as you sit at your computer.

1. List all the things you can remember that you've ever written, from kindergarten to the present. Or, slice your memories into chronological sections— list everything you've written in the last month, then the last year, then in college, then before college, and so on.

2. List your most memorable school writings. Return to the list and note why each was memorable.

3. List your most memorable personal writings. Return to the list and note why each was memorable.

4. List things you've wanted to write but didn't (and why you didn't).

5. List things others have written that you wish you had written (and why).

6. List things you've written that you wish you'd written differently or that you would write differently if you had the chance?

7. List your current obsessions.

8. List some family stories you know/remember/have heard that won't go away.

9. List things you feel strongly about and would speak out about today (if you were to speak out).

10. List things that you're curious about but never take the time to learn more about.

11. List things that repeat and resurface in your writing.

12. List things that haunt your writing (things that you've said or avoided saying).

Using Your Writing to Make More Writing: The Personal Writing Contract.

Writers sometimes think they have writer's block, a lack of topics, nothing worth saying. This exercise should have shown you that's simply not true. Subjects are there; it's a matter of gaining access to them. These prompts may have made some of your subjects more readily available for use.

If so, use these prompts to develop a personal writing contract. To do that, identify the five most powerful subjects on this list and decide what genre you'd like to use to address them (poem, story, nonfiction, play—this choice may be constrained by course requirements) and for what audience. Give your top three topics working titles; then, write descriptive abstracts for them. That is, what could this piece be called and what might this piece look like if/when you write it? List two alternates to write about, as fallbacks, in case the first three don't sound as productive later as they do today. Detail your writing plan in a memo to yourself and/or your writing teacher, explaining how each choice develops needed writing skills or addresses themes that are important to your writing development. Explain the challenges each choice represents to you as a writer.

Remember, you can expand the list you developed in this exercise by completing any of the invention prompts in this chapter.

(W.B.)

Riding the Orange Line

Development and Improvisation

Time

Playing With Time: Some Basic Moves

Use to Write:	Short Fiction; Longer Fiction; (Narrative in) Autobiography; (narrative in) Creative Nonfiction; Narrative Poetry
Ideas and Concepts to Explore:	"back-story"; flashback; fictional moments; focalization; "shoe leather"; "story" vs. "plot".
Authors/Works Mentioned:	Mieke Bal; John Updike, "A & P".

Four subsequent "Telling Time" exercises in this chapter explore notions of time in narration more fully, introducing a wider array of concepts and terms. This exercise serves as a kind of introduction to those, presenting some basic time-issues to consider as you write fiction or use narration in other genres—and *especially* as you work on rough drafts of fiction. Before looking at this exercise, you might want to read John Updike's very short story, "A & P," which is available in numerous anthologies, because it's discussed in some detail here.

Almost all the stories we read and write represent, in one fashion or another, time: things that happen(ed) over a period of time; the experience of a bygone era; an imagined future; crucial *moments* in people's (characters') lives; something as simple as a conversation taking up a few moments of the reader's "real" time, a few illusory moments of a narrative's time.

One way to develop a story that's in draft form, then, is to examine this basic representation of time. Here are some essential questions to ask, but no doubt you can think of others as well (and you'll be encouraged to do so in a moment):

1. **How many different "times" does the story try to represent?** Here's an example: Perhaps the main action of your story occurs in what is *represented* as

roughly 30 minutes or less, as is the case with John Updike's famous story, "A & P." (Sammy the supermarket checker is working the job; some customers come through his checkstand; he jaws with a coworker; some girls come in and . . . there's trouble. All of this is represented in just a few pages, but the pages help us imagine a "time" of 20 to 30 minutes.) But maybe your story also contains a flashback to an earlier "time" and a self-contained event or episode *in* that earlier time. So, from one point of view, your story would then be representing two "times," and within those times, certain very specific events, actions, episodes, conversations. Once you've identified these times, then you can ask questions of your draft to help you develop the story more or differently. Which time seems more successfully rendered than another? Which one needs work? How satisfactory are the transitions between these time segments? Is that flashback (if there is one) really necessary? If there isn't a flashback, might one be useful? How? And so on.

2. Hollywood screenwriters sometimes refer to "shoe leather"—scenes in movies that are "just there," too mundane, wasted screen time. The term comes from watching a character in a film cross a room to open a door. The important stuff will come after that door is opened. In the meantime, the character is just wearing out shoe leather. Sure, on film this may take only seconds, but every second is precious in a film—and in a story. So look at certain scenes, which are really "blocks of time," in your story. (Because of the fluid nature of time, maybe "pools of time" is a better term.) Is there the equivalent of shoe leather? **That is, are you wasting words, narration, description on a conversation or an action that doesn't seem to deserve that much attention?** Put another way, is there a scene that has the effect of slowing down, even bogging down, the movement (the reading, the action) of the story? If so, how can you shrink this scene? How can you make it move faster? What can you cut? Can you delete the whole scene?! If you want to turn this into a specific writing prompt, treat that scene as a self-contained unit; if it's now two pages long, write it in one; or if there's a page of dialogue, cut it to a half page and try to get the same action, information, conflict-development, and/or character-development. And know that the arbitrary goals (reducing two pages to one) are merely provisional, there to help goad you to revise.

3. **Conversely, maybe there's a moment in a story that you've represented too hastily.** For example, you might have a sentence like "At that point, Ray and Phoebe had a fierce argument, which ended when Phoebe threw a vase at Ray." Well, maybe it would be useful to slow down the narration: to pause, if you will, and represent that argument—giving us the who-said-what-to-whom, filling in physical details, building slowly up to that throwing of the vase. You might also provide impressions or perceptions of Ray or Phoebe or both; critic Mieke Bal calls this **"focalization"**—you are imagining for the reader a mind, or a consciousness of a situation. By

providing Phoebe's thoughts about the argument, you are "focalizing" Phoebe: not just narrating a scene but narrating Phoebe's *perception* of the scene. If you want to turn the foregoing discussion into a specific writing prompt, take a sentence or two of narration and expand it/them into a scene of a page or so.

4. **Does your story begin and end at the right moments?** Let's use Updike's "A & P" as an example again. The story ends when Sammy the supermarket clerk quits his job and walks out into the parking lot, where he sees the girls that had come into the supermarket and caused the problem that precipitated Sammy's having quit. He glances at the girls, muses to himself—end of story. This seems to work all right; after all, Updike's story has remained enormously appealing over the years. But another narrative choice might have been to extend the time of the story and have Sammy go over to the girls and talk to them. Still another choice would have been to end the story "earlier." So take a look at your story and lay out some other options for ending it. Maybe you're milking the ending, letting it go on too long? How and where might you end it earlier? Maybe something more is needed—if there were another scene, what would it be and what would it do for your story? Go ahead and draft different endings. Follow the same process for your story's beginning. Could the story start "earlier" or "later?" How? To what effect? Draft different beginnings.

5. **Step back, as it were, from your draft and ask, "Is there a missing moment (scene, episode, segment of narration, key action)?"** If you're even partially tempted to say "Yes," go ahead and "write up" that moment, wherever it might be in the time(s) your story is representing. At the very least, drafting this formerly nonexistent part of your *story* will expand what you know about your characters and about the specific *plot* you've put them in. In a lot of cases, all or part of this newly represented moment will find its way into your final draft. To refer once more to the world of Hollywood, scriptwriters often write "back-stories"—scenes, characters' biographies, brainstorming lists that fill in information about the plot or the characters and provide a kind of reservoir of knowledge on which to draw. And sometimes part of the "back-story" makes its way into a later version of the screenplay and into the finished film.

6. **Make your own list of ways in which to "play with time" as you write, develop, and revise your stories.**

7. **Look at some of your favorite stories or novels by published authors. See how time has been handled in those narratives.** Or pull out a published story that you thought was a real drag, literally: a slow, ponderous, elephantine blob of a thing, no matter how famous it is, how "great" other people think it is. Rewrite a small part of it to make it move in a way you'd prefer.

(H.O.)

Telling Time 1: Order

Use to Write:	Short Fiction; Longer Fiction; Narrative in Autobiography; Narrative in Creative Nonfiction; Narrative Poetry; Literary Criticism
Ideas and Concepts to Explore:	analepsis; prolepsis; flashback; flashforward; to "conflate" time; juxtaposition; narratology; order, frequency, duration.
Authors/Works Mentioned:	Gerard Genette.

"Fiction is the art of making time legible," a student once remarked. She had just discovered time as one of the great pleasures of fiction, falling literally in love with the fluidity of it, its range and possibility, the ease with which, in language, we are able to move through the history of a family or a century in a single breath.

Time: a wave, a digitized frame, a dizzying loop, parallel universes, loss, telling stories. Writers write about losing all sense of time when they are writing; we are in real time (time is passing as we work), even as we work out the magic and complexities of narrative time. In writing time, the past conflates with the present; the future is as knowable as anything else. Time passes.

The next several exercises explore a typology of time, originally described by the French theorist, Gerard Genette. This typology, derived according to principles of *order, frequency* (see Telling Time 2), and *duration* (see Telling Time 3), is highly useful for thinking and talking about how we organize time in our stories.

We begin with *order*, a principle that describes the sequence of events, which are either *chronological* (in order), or *achronological* (out of order). In *achronological* narratives, the temporal order may be altered by moving either backward (called a flashback, or what structuralists call an *analepsis*) or forward (a flashforward, or *prolepsis*). Such movements may be contained by, or extend beyond the time frame represented by, the primary narrative, which itself may be organized around a *present moment,* from which the rest of the time fragments eddy.

In other words, in fiction, we can think back, look forward, loop around a particular event, elide another, swoop and swirl. One moment, you can be in your mother's kitchen, worrying about how, now that your mother is older, she keeps forgetting things. In the next moment, you may be a child again, approaching your mother in a moment of crisis, torn between hope and dread, because, really, you did not mean to soften your clay on the heat register. You did not mean to throw the rock for your sister to squirt with the hose, the rock looping mysteriously back, as if with a mind of its own, toward the new car's windshield. You did not mean to wear your ring to play in the dirt pile. And of course in fiction, in yet another moment, you may be standing by your mother's grave, which you cannot yet bear to imagine, so maybe you write it instead.

For this exercise, imagine a story as a series of plain events in a linear sequence, unfolding from the past toward the present, pushing forward. Make it simple.

For example: Two high school girls are friends. One lives in town with parents who are professionals, the other on a small ranch where she keeps a few horses. The ranch is a poor one, and the girl's father works also as a mechanic to make ends meet. Both girls love the cloudy, wind–swept autumn days that roil over their scrubby foothills and shock everything with the acrid scent of impending rain. On one such day, they take the horses out and get lost. In the late afternoon, they find themselves on the edge of the lake, much farther than they have ever gone before. It will be midnight before they get back, but for now, they sit on a red clay beach and look out over the choppy water. As they eat their smashed sandwiches, the girl from town watches her friend; she thinks about how different their lives are and how much she loves her. By the time they get back, everyone is worried and both know they will never ride together again.

Now, rewrite your story achronologically by choosing a present moment from which to narrate it, moving back and forth from this present moment but always returning to it. Such a present moment may be a particularly charged one, or it may simply function as a narrative anchor. Around it, past and future extend in separate branches.

In the above story, for example, that present moment might be the red clay beach. From there, a series of flashbacks might emphasize the girls' lack of such basic preparation as adequate water and maps, or their day-long growing feeling of becoming lost. The narrative might also look forward to adult lives, characterized by inchoate loss.

Alternatively, the ride itself might function as a present moment for a story that extends beyond the boundaries of that ride, looking back to how the girls' friendship began in biology lab, bonded over dissected frogs, and went on to flourish in marching band. It could also look forward to how their lives increasingly diverged. Or both.

In your own story, now add all new material by going back even further in time than the original sequence of events, some particular moment from childhood, say, that refracts the current narrative in interesting ways. Return to this moment once or several times. How does this extension affect the original story?

Alternatively (or, additionally), imagine a future event, or sequence of events, and write them into your story. If your story is first person, this will take the form of imagination, or conjecture; if in third, your narrator can project beyond what the characters know.

Variation.

Rewrite your original story in reverse chronological order, paying particular attention to variations in nuance as the sequence inverts itself.

Note.

A general rule for temporal transition is the less said, the better.

White space works well, as do simple phrases such as *later*, or *when she was ten*. Remember, this is language. The arc of a single sentence can move time with grace and at will.

(K.H.)

 ### Telling Time 2: Frequency

Use to Write:	Short Fiction; Longer Fiction; Drama; (narrative in) Autobiography; (narrative in) Creative Nonfiction
Ideas and Concepts to Explore:	iterative events; repeated events; singular events.
Authors/Works Mentioned:	n/a

Storytelling is organized in such a way as to create tension and surprise. This is often as true of spoken stories as it is of written ones, and if you've ever been "corrected" in the middle of a story, or told to "stop exaggerating," you already know how this works. As a storyteller, you are more interested in the *felt* than the *literal* truth of events. Some people may call this lying, but they're not storytellers.

One way time can enhance this *felt* truth is through the manipulation of the *frequency* with which events occur.

Singular events, for example, are those that occur once and are narrated once. Maybe during a visit to your parents' friends' house when you were a girl, their dog nipped your elbow, drawing blood. Crying, you ran to tell your mother, who might have been drinking, for she laughed, then seemed angry, and said, "What did you do to provoke it?"

In such a simple story, one thing leads directly to the next and may depend for its impact on simple and singular narration.

Repeated events occur once, but are narrated multiple times throughout the story.

Maybe, instead, you were so traumatized by this dog bite and your mother's response was to have developed a pronounced phobia of dogs that haunts you now as an adult, in love with a breeder of hounds. In such a story, that bite may be repeated multiple times. The event is the same, but each time the story repeats it, something is added, resonance accumulates, meaning changes.

Mysteries, in particular, may depend on repeated events, since often each retelling reveals something new or overlooked about a particular scene. Unraveling a significant enigma depends, in many cases, on reseeing, with a difference, something seen before.

Iterative events have occurred more than once but are narrated only one time. Such events may accumulate resonance through the elision or compression. For example:

"When I was a child, I was bitten seven times by dogs, and my mother always blamed me. She always said, what did you do to provoke it?" (*Iterative.*)

"Yesterday, a boy threw a baseball at my son and when I intervened, I turned to my son and said, 'What did you do to provoke it?'" (*Singular.*)

"All that winter I was so afraid of dogs I couldn't walk down my street, couldn't play in my yard, couldn't even leave my house, so I stayed inside and read." (*Iterative.*)

This is a straightforward exercise, in which you take a simple event—a dog bite, a home run, a kiss, a mountain hike—and construct it, in a story or narrative poem, first as a *singular* event. Each part of it occurs only one time and you tell it only once, as it happened.

Now, return to the same event and write it as a *repeated* element in an expanded narrative. You will have to develop your original story, creating a time and space expanse in which you can return, to tell over again, the simple event you began with. How does this change the mountain hike you took, or that kiss under the street lamp in August?

Finally, construct your original event as an *iterative* one in a story where what happened, the way you first told it, really happened many times in the past. Begin with the iterative moment, and see where it goes. ("All that autumn we kissed under the street lamp at the corner. And then never again.")

Pay attention, in this exercise, to what happens when you change the frequency with which an event either occurs or is narrated. How is the event itself constructed and received differently? What happens to the story that surrounds it, or precedes or follows from it? In what way is the narrative logic changed or charged?

(K.H.)

▶ 4 ▶ Telling Time 3: Duration

Use to Write:	Short Fiction; Longer Fiction; (narrative in) Autobiography; (narrative in) Creative Nonfiction
Ideas and Concepts to Explore:	duration; pause; scene; "real time" vs. "narrative time"; *petite madeleine*; stretch; summary.
Authors/Works Mentioned:	Raymond Carver, "Popular Mechanics"; Marcel Proust, *Remembrance of Things Past*.

In yet another twist on time (see "Telling Time 1" and "Telling Time 2"), narrative events extend over two kinds of "time"—1) the amount of time they would actually take to occur in "real" life, and 2) the amount of time they take for the reader to read. This hypothetical relation between "real" and "narrative" time is known, in narratology, as *duration*. Duration has five dimensions.

1. *Summary,* in which events in real time would take more time to occur than they would to read (real time > narrative time). We tend to think of summary as a bad thing, since we have learned to *show, don't tell,* and telling often takes place as summary. But of course, there is nothing intrinsically wrong with it, and most narratives depend on some degree of summary, which may collapse the events of a summer, a childhood, an evening, a life, into a sentence, a paragraph, a page, or a chapter.

   You may write, for example, "During the course of my middle–school years, we moved seven times in three cities, and each time my mother assured me it would be the last." As you go on to describe the moves, or their aftermath, you will depend on summary, for no narrative will take as long to read as it takes to endure middle school.

2. *Scene,* in which events in real time would take the same amount of time to occur as to read (real time = narrative time). True scene is often characterized by dialogue, since it takes about as much time to read a line of speech as it does to say it in "real" time.

   Consider Raymond Carver's short story, "Popular Mechanics," in which a husband and wife, arguing about who will get the baby in their separation, end by separating the baby. Almost all dialogue, the story completes itself in a single scene.

3. *Gap,* in which time passes in the story, but does not appear in the narration (real time ~~narrative time~~). Gap is frequently marked in contemporary fiction by white space, and can be very powerful. Some stories depend so heavily on this device (gap) that what isn't being said is more important than what is. Gap forces such narrative compression that, in it, our silence may speak louder than our words.

4. *Stretch,* in which events take more time to read about than they would to take place in reality (real time < narrative time). You are probably more familiar with this mode in film as slow motion, but it works the same in language-based narrative.

   In Proust's *Remembrance of Things Past,* for example, there is a passage where the protagonist is eating a small cookie and falls into a pages-long reverie as he remembers such cookies from when he was a boy, their smell and taste, the tea, his mother, the light through the window, and so on. This is a famous passage, painfully familiar to French-language students, who believe themselves, working it, to be failing their translation exams. How, they wonder desperately, can it take Marcel three pages to swallow one bite of cookie? That's stretch.

5. *Pause,* in which the narrative is interrupted to go somewhere altogether different, and then returns to the exact point of rupture as if nothing else had happened at all (narrative time/ $^{\text{narrative time}}$ \narrative time).

Your character, for example, wakes up in bed with a stranger, sheets crumpled and with a sour, unfamiliar smell, the room gloomy from an overcast morning, but she is still wearing her jeans and t-shirt, and her body feels bruised and sore. At that moment, the narrator recalls another incident, many years before, when your character was thrown from a sailboat in winter and awoke with the same bruised feeling. The sailboat, in winter, belonged to her brother, who used to urge her to sail with him, but since the incident, in which she almost drowned, she has not gone near water. You write about her fear. You write about her brother. You write about her struggle in the water, its steel gray color the exact color of the sky outside on this other morning years later. The man beside her wakes and asks if she wants coffee. She looks at him.

She says, "Who are you?"

Or, your narrator may leave a critical moment in a story to comment on the story itself, or the nature of fiction, or why what the reader is expecting will not happen. Or you may write parallel narratives, in which two or more stories unfold in alternating segments, each segment a pause in the other. Or you may interrupt your story with historical notes, or biographical information, or reminiscence, or meditation. The point is that you end up where you began. The narrative has paused, and then continued.

Mostly, we are not so self-conscious about duration when we write. Time tends to work itself out in narrative according to the basic logic and nature of the story. We speed things up, and we slow them down as the story seems to call for it. But sometimes it is useful to practice these effects, for, as in muscle memory, practice creates reflex and extends the range of what seems easy or "natural" to you.

For this exercise, begin with a simple event, or brief sequence of events: You come into your bedroom after school and discover that someone has been there before you, your brother probably, and one of your lizards is missing, and the other has turned from bright green to a dull, mottled brown.

Or: You're sunning yourself on the beach, a bright, scorched day, watching your four-year-old daughter build sand castles when your son runs up screaming he's got sand in his eyes, and by the time you rinse them out with fresh water from the cooler, your daughter has wandered out into the waves, where even from that distance you can tell that the next one will come crashing down over her head.

Or: Your husband, drunk again, is in a rage, and you know that if you move, he will strike.

Write your story, or small sequence of events, first as *summary*. Get the facts down, what happens and how. Do it quickly. Use compression to your advantage:

> When my husband gets like that, he hits me. He works up slow to it, almost always. You know, comes home late, smelling like he does, and tries to honey me up. But the smell, and his hands, when he's like that, they get clumsy. He says something. I say something back. We do this a few times, then the next thing I know I'm in the bathroom, my nose bleeding into the sink.

Now write the same events as *scene*, filling them out, paying strict attention to detail, timing the narration to the actual logic of real time:

"Don't you come near me," I yell. I turn my face away from the smell, something like medicine but sweeter, more familiar than a recurring dream.

"Aw," he says, "honey. Aw honey."

"I mean it this time," I tell him. "You can sleep on the couch. I've had enough."

"Enough what?" he says, coming closer, backing me toward the wall

He has that look in his eyes, and though I know I should not be afraid, that there's more danger in being afraid than in just, for example, walking out, I do not walk out.

Instead, I say, "The pillows are in the hall closet," and that's when he hits me.

Now write the same events as *gap*. Here you will have to write parenthetical events that are powerfully suggestive of his rage:

In the shelter, everyone was kind, but I missed him. They kept trying to make me remember. They made me talk to counselors. They showed me pictures.

One woman (I'll call her Grace) had a little deaf girl with her. That girl was so blondheaded that when the sun hit her hair it could be blinding. She loved the sun, that little girl. She used to go from room to room in the shelter, looking for little scraps of sun in from the windows on the floor. Then she'd squat there, playing jacks. You could come up right behind her, and she wouldn't budge, nor even blink.

That was the first night in so many nights, months it seemed stretching to years, he wasn't home by dinner, by nine, or ten, or midnight. I should have known by midnight what to do. My own sister lived down the street.

When that girl's mama told me that she wasn't born that way, not deaf, born instead with all her hearing, that's when, for the first time, I wanted to cry. I wanted to gather her up in my lap and cry out loud for every one of us, but there's something wrong with my eyes these days and they don't tear up right.

Take the same events, or a portion thereof, and *stretch* them out into slow motion:

It's like, you see it but you don't see it. Everything gets quiet and far away and even the words coming out of your own mouth aren't your own, it's not your voice, this isn't even your life. Because it's all in that instant when he raises his hand against you, but you don't really believe it, the drawing back of his whole arm—shit, you have seen this before, run girl run. But you don't. It goes back sure and fast, almost like pitching a baseball, but there isn't any ball in his hand. His hand is the ball, all round and white, but you're not the hitter, he is.

"I mean it," you tell him, even as the ball is floating all round and white toward the plate, which is you and you don't duck.

Experiment with *pause*. Interrupt your scene with information about violence against women—statistics, relation between such violence and alcohol abuse, psychological profiles, and so on. Or go back to your character's girlhood nosebleeds, an identical white sink and the flow that could not seem to stop. Or try something self–reflexive, like:

> How do I know her, this woman, who endures the force of her husband's fist not once but many times before ending up in a shelter, a small blondheaded deaf girl in her lap? You may think I don't know her at all, and of course you will be right. I have made her up, yes, but I can never know her, just as I will never know the force of a man's fist. That's what she said too, before she married him. Never, never, never, is what she said before she married him. I shouldn't even be writing this. I cannot possibly know.

Story Development.

Write a story, or prose narrative, in which you deliberately use all five dimensions of temporal duration.

Write them down on separate slips of paper: *summary, scene, gap, stretch, pause*. Fifteen slips of papers. Three times each. Scramble the slips of paper in a box, or hat, or envelope, draw ten out at random, arrange them before you (*scene, summary, summary, gap, stretch, summary, scene, pause, stretch, scene*) and write.

Repeat as necessary until you have a story.

(K.H.)

5 ▶ Telling Time: Down and Dirty

Use to Write:	Short Fiction; Longer Fiction; (narrative in) Autobiography and Creative Nonfiction
Ideas and Concepts to Explore:	gap; pause; repetition; scene, stretch and summary; to "violate" chronology.
Authors/Works Mentioned:	n/a

In the past four exercises, we have discussed different organizational concepts of time—"real" time vs. "fictional" time; order; frequency; and duration. But of course these things do not occur in isolation, so let's get them all (and see them all) working together—by writing.

Review the list below, select five, and write. You don't have to do this in any particular order, and you don't have to limit yourself to this list. But play around with time as much as you can. Violate chronology. Collage a timeline of your story. Stir things up.

1. Present summary
2. Present scene
3. Present stretch
4. Present gap
5. Present pause
6. Past summary
7. Past scene
8. Past stretch
9. Present gap
10. Present pause
11. Future summary
12. Future scene
13. Future stretch
14. Future gap
15. Future pause
16. Repetition

(K.H.)

Developing Characters, Points of View, and Other Elements

Character Witness: 20 Questions

Use to Write:	Short Fiction; Longer Fiction; Drama; Experimental Fiction/Performance Piece
Ideas and Concepts to Explore:	antagonist; the concept of "character" in fiction and drama; protagonist; stereotype; stock characters.
Authors/Works Mentioned:	n/a

Most writing of short fiction and novels depends significantly on creating a sense in readers' minds that characters in a narrative are indeed people—physical, emotional, intellectual *presences*. The better we are at creating this illusion, the easier it is for the audience (the reader) to "suspend disbelief," as the 19th century British poet and critic, Samuel Taylor Coleridge, phrased it. Essentially, when we suspend disbelief we forget or at least ignore the fact that we're in a theatre, and we allow our minds to become fully involved with the play; or we forget/ignore we're in a cinema complex in which light merely dances on a screen, and we "fall into" the story, feeding our mouths popcorn absentmindedly; or—to focus on the matters at hand, reading and writing—we forget/ignore that what's before our eyes is just paper and ink, and we fall through language into story, into a narrative taking place in our imagination.

And yet, at the beginning of the writing process, the writer often knows as little about these illusory entities, *fictional characters,* as the reader does. At the beginning of the process, the writers themselves might have one heck of a time suspending disbelief, might be self-conscious about how artificial "characters" are. The pressure of stereotypes and stock-character prototypes can also inhibit a writer's ability to create a character because these, too, highlight the artificiality of characters.

But the opposite situation can also be a problem: A writer begins to develop a highly particularized, hardly stereotyped character, only to have that character change, or "resist" certain plot ideas; or the character might "have ideas" that change the original narrative all around—almost like a real (stubborn, willful) person! Yes, it's true that a character is only an illusion created by words—your words, over which you allegedly have control. But it's also true that as you develop the illusion with your words, your words and the developing illusion can seem to have a life of their own, a kind of protean force outside the reach of your will and your creative control. Usually writers want and need to pursue some sort of middle course between the **sterile control offered by stereotyping** (almost all control, virtually no imagination) and the **mercurial chaos** of a character who dodges, disappears, fizzles, or morphs (almost no control, virtually all unbounded imagination). The following writing prompt is one way to chart that vast middle course; that is our purpose.

The prompt can be used at almost any stage of developing a story or a novel, but in my courses students have used it most often after they have already begun to think and write about a story: after *something* to do with plot, narrative voice, scenes, "trouble" (conflict, problem), or character(s) has begun to take shape; after a draft of a narrative has at least begun to emerge.

The "rules":

1. You need to have one character in mind; preferably this will be a significant character, perhaps what we sometimes refer to as a "main" character or "protagonist." But other characters will work, too.

2. You must *write* answers to the following questions—even if the writing is scribbling, mere notes. The physical act of writing tends to force your imagination to be more specific than it might otherwise be.

3. You must answer quickly and authoritatively. If you feel as if you're bluffing, that's fine; at least *pretend* to be authoritative. As in acting, there's naturally a lot of bluffing in storytelling, story writing, especially at the invention-and-development stage. Bluffing is in the job description. Part of the rationale here is that *quick* answers are often *intuitive* answers, and that intuitive answers are often surprisingly on target—often "feel right." Another part of the rationale: Answering quickly keeps your energy up, and to a degree, character invention depends on energy, a kind of forward drive into this

process of creating the illusion of people, of "a world." When in doubt, have fun with the prompt. Stay loose, stay quick, keep the brow unfurrowed.

4. Don't worry about contradictions between answers. They can be sorted out—or perhaps not sorted out but used—later. Movement, speed, and answering quickly are key to this prompt. Paper & pen; typewriter; computer: ready? *Go.*

20 Questions About the Character In Question.

1. What is the *exact* age of your character—years, months, days?

2. A place where your character is living or visiting begins to burn. The character has a few moments to escape. What does he/she grab—save?—before getting out of the fire? Why?

3. The character enters the room in which you're sitting. Sits down near you, places his or her left hand on a table or desk near you. Look at that hand. Describe it in as much detail as you can. *Quickly.* Go.

4. This may go against your nature, but let's at least *pretend* you're a real snoop. You have access to a wallet, a pocketbook, or a purse belonging to your character. You have an opportunity to go through it, and—being a snoop—you seize the opportunity. What's in the wallet, pocketbook, or purse? Take the stuff out and put it on a table. Describe it. If there's lipstick, say what kind, what color, what kind of container. Money? How much—exactly?—and how's it organized? And so forth. Is there something about which the character would be especially embarrassed? If so, what? If not—what do you make of that?

5. You walk into a room in which your character's napping. Without waking the character up, you lean down, put your nose close to one side of your character's neck—just below the ear there—and sniff. *Describe what you smell.*

6. Describe one meal or type of food your character really likes to eat.

7. Describe the social, political, and economic background of one of the character's parents, one of the character's siblings, one of the character's friends, or one of the character's rivals (defining "rival"—antagonist—in a way that makes most sense to you).

8. Describe one scar—it can be a very tiny one—on your character's body and how it was acquired.

9. Describe in detail one thing your character would enjoy reading, or some kind of text your character would enjoy examining—a text that might exist within the text of your story.

10. Your character laughs at something. What is it? Exactly why does your character think this thing—joke, event, sight, whatever—is funny?

11. You are invisible; your presence is unknown by your character. You are observing your character look into a mirror. Describe your observations.

12. "France." Your character hears that word. What, if anything, comes to your character's mind? Be as specific as you can.

13. "I remember . . . ." Your character says or thinks these words. Now provide a list of at least five things your character remembers.

14. Describe one *not-so-obvious,* not-so-easily detected nervous habit of your character's. Toe-tapping and drumming-of-fingers-on-table are probably too obvious, too conventional, for example.

15. A sound that's especially pleasing to your character—what is it? Why is it so pleasing to the character?

16. What is your character's middle name, and what is the brief history—if any—of that name?

17. Describe (compare, contrast) the ways in which your character sneezes in private and in public.

18. Who was the first American President of which your character was aware, and what is one image or memory your character has of this president?

19. Describe a piece of jewelry your character might wear or buy for another person or admire or dislike. (It's all right to answer all four options, too.)

20. Provide one more telling piece of information about your character.

What To Do With This Information.

1. Use your own judgement, of course; when my students have used this prompt, several particulars seem to leap out, and the authors immediately think of ways the particulars might fit in with, might alter, or might figure significantly into the story-in-progress. Often the information tells the writer immediately how to use it.

2. Some of the information you invented will seem hollow, flat, faked, half-hearted. Some of it, for whatever reasons, will seem *right on target*—will have a feel of the genuine about it, will somehow fit with this illusion of a character you're building by accretion. At least save the information that seems "right"; you don't necessarily have to try to work it into the story immediately. But keep it handy. Let it simmer. Trust your instincts.

3. If you've been working on a draft, have several pages, but for some reason seem stuck, **start a new section of the story** using a piece of the information you generated. The new part of the narrative can seem out of place, and you don't have to be sure how or whether it will fit into the existing draft or even into the existing concept of the story. (Believe it or not, building a bridge—later—between two parts of a story that don't seem to fit yet can be enormously pleasing; probably you've done this already.) But at the very least, writing the new section may reignite your interest in, your authority over, the story-in-progress. Call it a "jump-start."

4. A piece of information you've invented may lead to a whole "side" or cluster of traits or problems or a whole segment of personal history. If this is a

possibility, zero in on that piece of information and do another whole round of brainstorming based on it. That is, there's no need to rush back to the story if more invention and development seems like the next writer's move to make.

5. If you're in a metafictional, postmodern, jazzing-around mood (that's quite a mood!), write a story in which the narrative is somehow based on these 20 questions; you could even make the numbered list the structural foundation of the narrative.

(H.O.)

⟨7⟩ Building Character

Use to Write:	Short Fiction; Longer Fiction; Drama; Creative Nonfiction; Literary Criticism; Performance Piece
Ideas and Concepts to Explore:	the idea of "character" in fiction and drama— especially character as . . . "noise," "verbal energy," and "controlling conception."
Authors/Works Mentioned:	William Gass, "The Concept of Character In Fiction."

Part 1.

To live in a family, any family, is to participate in the making of myths. The two sets of grandparents who met and married in the small mining town subsequently flooded behind a dam engineered by the first–born son, the grandmother who decorously lit the wicks of candles before she put them out (to prove they were not just for show), the mother who chased neighbor children with a pitchfork—all these stories come together differently in each family member. You tell one story, your sister tells another, and each telling constructs not just the myth, but the teller: We become the stories we tell.

Writing is part of that myth-making process. In Section Twenty-Five of Chapter Two, the exercise, "The Nonexistent Relative," works with ways of "fictionalizing" families. This exercise works more directly with family stories and with the powerful, resonant language in them.

Directions.

1. Select a family story that has been told and retold, over time and by many family members—Aunt Ethyl's one true love, an MIA in Vietnam, for example, or why the Brewer twins refused to dress alike anymore in high school. This should be a story about which there is some disagreement. It was the best thing that ever happened to Aunt Ethyl, when that man did not come back from Vietnam. The Brewers got mad and stayed mad at each other, or their mother, depending on who is telling the story. Now, assume the persona

of one of the central characters—Aunt Ethyl herself, or one of the twins—and write a letter to another family member who has a different view of the story than you in which you explain your own version of the "truth" of exactly what happened. That's it. Don't overthink. Just write the way you'd write any letter to someone about whom you care a great deal and whom you suspect won't entirely believe you.

2. Select a writing partner and exchange letters. Read your partner's letter; then write a response in the persona of its addressee.

Part 2.

In "The Concept of Character in Fiction," William Gass argues that character is not "a mirror or a window onto life," not a reference to a person, not in any sense mimetic, but rather, "first of all, the *noise* of his name, and all the sounds and rhythms that proceed from him (or her)." This noise is a *proper name*, and a proper name, properly speaking, is nothing more than "a blank, like a wall or a canvas, upon which one might paint a meaning." The character is the painting of that meaning. The character is also, for Gass, a *source of verbal energy*. Some words, he argues, appear to "gravitate toward their subject like flies settle on paper, while others seem to emerge from it." Thus, the character becomes a *controlling conception*, a "primary substance to which everything else is attached." This could be a hotel, this could be a feeling; we think of characters as people, but for Gass a character is a constellation of words.

In the first part of this exercise, between your partner and yourself and your separate texts, you created a new character, the person who wrote back. Maybe this character utterly surprised you; maybe she fit your Aunt Ethyl to a T. Whether or not you recognized her, she provided new perspective on the story-making elements of your family life, their mythologizing aspects, and where to go from there. For though you invented her, the person you wrote first to, neither you nor your partner could control who she became.

Now think about that character, not too much, and not the one either of you made up, but the one that emerged in the empty space between your correspondence. Don't try to know everything about her. Just give her a name—Ramona, Aunt Ethyl, Wren—and start writing to see what words to emerge from that name for the length of a paragraph, at least half a page.

Maybe your character inflects up at the end of her sentences, as if she were asking a question. Maybe he's a heavy-footed man, whose steps reverberate throughout your house. Maybe he sired a pair of twin girls. Maybe she's a spinning ballerina.

At the end of this paragraph, have your character interact—speak, act, touch, etc.—with another character for twenty lines or more.

Interrupt this interaction in the middle of something, and write a paragraph in which words settle like flies on sugar upon your original character. Her sentence goes flat. He stops stomping. The girls take his hand. She stoops to unlace her pink slippers.

Repeat until a story emerges.

This exercise depends upon your willingness to let your character guide you and not the other way around. Physical characteristics, familial relations, past and future experiences, gestures, temperaments, desires, or shames provide areas of language from which you might draw. The words themselves will build the character you find. (It may be possible to link this exercise with some of the work in "Character Witness," the previous exercise in this chapter.)

If you fall in love with her, so much the better. Become the settling fly, the force of language emerging from your name: Castro, Hubert, Sky.

(K.H.)

Pardon Me, Your Nemesis Is Showing

8

Use to Write:	Autobiography; Creative Nonfiction; Short Fiction; Longer Fiction; Performance Piece
Ideas and Concepts to Explore:	irrational distrust; the Jungian Shadow; nemesis; provoke/provocation/provocateur.
Authors/Works Mentioned:	Edith Hamilton, *Mythology*; Carl Jung.

X, class president, valedictorian, and point guard for the basketball team, dropped out of engineering school at X-State (rumors of too many keggers and wet T-shirt competitions). He enrolled at the business school at the regional university; now he sells medical equipment (or is it auto parts?). He married his high school girlfriend (after several messy breakups), has three daughters, lives in a three-bedroom house with two-car garage, and rides a lawn tractor over his ½ acre lot on summer Saturdays.

Y, class vice president, salutatorian and editor of the sports section of the year book, went to Saint Paul Bible College, narrowly avoided becoming a missionary, got a master's degree in English (at the same university that X got his business degree), earned a Ph.D. at Z University, and is now an assistant professor at T State University. He has never married and lives in a 1920s house, surrounded by more phlox, hostas, lilies, and peonies than he can find time to tend.

A nemesis may be a bad thing to have in your life: the person who always seems out to get you, who is valedictorian to your salutatorian, who gets the better job, partner or salary, who cuts you to the quick and cuts you off at the pass. But a nemesis may prove to be a fine thing for your narratives. You can use a nemesis to show real or imagined persecution that creates drama (when imagined, of course, the nemesis takes you into the provocative mental lands of quasi paranoia, long a staple of suspense and horror writers). You may think "nemesis", as did my friend whose "thumbnail sketches" from a 10th reunion I share above, and later find out you misunderstood that competition, finding that the nemesis has turned into a misunderstood side of yourself or discovering that he was someone who offered no actual threat to you.

When I told one of my *Metro* coauthors I wanted to discuss how writing about a nemesis can provide rich food for narrative speculation, he laughed and said he could write all day about his. In fact, we even had some in common from the time we were in college writing–classes together.

Does someone you know provoke you in strange ways? Let him or her provoke you aloud in your nonfiction or provoke a character in your fiction. Have you encountered nemeses from earlier years in later years? Accidentally on the street of your town or at a professional event, a class reunion? Write a poem or a sketch about who you each were, who you each are now, and how you've both changed (or not changed).

Does considering the human competitors you've had (or imagined you've had) tell you anything about the human condition? Do you think you were paranoid? That is, did you experience a clinical (or intellectual or emotional or aesthetic, non-clinical version of a) "disorder characterized by delusions of persecution grandeur, often strenuously defended with apparent logic and reason"? Are there times in your life that you rightly or wrongly (or your character, friend, lover—rightly or wrongly) experienced an extreme, irrational distrust of others?

Have you or your friends, lovers, characters, actually experienced a nemesis—an opponent who (seemingly) cannot be beaten or overcome, one that inflicts retribution or vengeance?

You might want to do some investigation into the derivation of this word—from the Greek goddess of the same name (Edith Hamilton's *Mythology* is always a good place to start on such a quest). You might also consider the subject from a psychological point of view and familiarize yourself with Carl Jung's notion of "the shadow." For example, Jungians might say that our reactions to nemeses—indeed, our creation of nemeses—reflect something in this other person that is also inside us, whom we have repressed or otherwise buried in our subconscious mind.

Where would Odysseus be without Cyclops and Circe? Samson without Delilah? What does the story of Cain and Abel teach us? Think of a part of your self that creates a self–nemesis—the Hyde to Jeckle, your secret sharers and *doppelgängers*. (And you might take a look at the exercise, "Shadows, Doubles, and Others" in Chapter One—"Riding The Blue Line.") What of evil twins and any superhero and archrival? What politicians are without nagging detractors and athletes without brushes with destiny via capable opponents?

Is there life without a nemesis? Let your nemesis show and find out. More specifically, and with regard to *developing existing drafts*, examine the ways in which characters in your narrative seem to overreact to one another, or ways in which the narrative already contains the seeds of a nemesis relationship. Or perhaps a nemesis relationship already exists in the story, perhaps even dominates it, but so far the plot does not account for or support the relationship. In such a case, you might need to change how you are representing "character" in the story, or provide more motive, or otherwise account for the "fact" that a nemesis has taken shape.

Additionally, you may want to experiment with, make notes about, and draft different ways in which the nemesis relationship will play out, will—or will not—be resolved in your narrative.

(W.B.)

Turning the Lens: Framing Narrative Perspective

9

Use to Write:	Short Fiction; Longer Fiction; Literary Criticism; Journal
Ideas and Concepts to Explore:	cognition; focalizer; focalized; point of view.
Authors/Works Mentioned:	n/a

Narrative perspective, or what we know as "point of view," is frequently described as the "eyes" through which the story is being seen, something like a camera, a fixed lens. But language is not the same as a camera, and just as you need to know how to adjust a camera lens for light and distance, you need to know how to work with the separate properties of language.

Another way to conceive of narrative perspectives is as "focalization," a triadic relation among a narrator (who tells), a focalizer (who sees), and a focalized (what is seen.) Focalization is informed by five dimensions: time, space, cognition, emotion, and ideology.

Maybe you're telling a story about a fight your mother had when your brother dyed his hair purple and she called him white trash. You'd never heard your mother use the phrase "white trash" before. Your brother's purple hair was positively glowing.

Imagine how the telling of this scene would change if you, as both narrator and focalizer, were telling it just after it happened, or a week later, or after you yourself have become a parent (time). Imagine how it would change if you were sitting right there at the dinner table, watching the whole thing up close, or if instead you were watching tv in the next room, catching glimpses of it through the open door or outside in the garden, watching through a window (space).

"Cognition" describes what you—or the person whose perspective through which the story is being filtered—can be said to know. Maybe you were there and saw it all. But maybe what you, as the focalizer, can't know (but the narrator can) is that your mother's own mother, in an alcoholic rage when your mother was fourteen, called your mother a slut because she refused to take her curlers out to run an errand. And maybe you weren't there at all but have only your mother's, or your brother's, version of the story. Whose?

Now add a little brother to the scene. Let's say you weren't there, but you heard the whole thing. You're telling the story, but you want to filter it through your little brother's perspective. Let's say everyone in the family adores your little brother, but your little brother hates the brother with the purple hair. Let's say, instead, they're aligned against the mother, comrades in rebellion. Imagine how your telling of the story will be changed by these emotional or ideological elements. (Personally, we're on your brother's side, though we can also understand how your mom feels.)

This is a practice exercise, designed to flex your focalization muscles. In doing it, be aware that focalization is never static but shifts all the time, all over the place.

To begin, imagine an incident from your own life, or one that you read about, or just made up for this purpose. It should be simple, but charged: You're the starting pitcher for your Little League team, your father is the coach, your mother is watching from the stands and this is a play-off game. You're one of the best pitchers in the league, and you've held a six-run lead since the bottom of the first, but now, in the last inning, you can't throw straight. One batter after another, you walk away the game.

Or: You have a wisdom tooth that has moved into your sinuses, pushed there by a dentric cyst. You have arrived early at the surgical center, where the tooth is to be removed, but your oral surgeon is there before you. To pass time, you chat in the pre-op room—you in your surgical gown, your surgeon in her scrubs, your husband in the corner, wearing street clothes. Your surgeon is telling you about this day-long horse-jumping clinic she is scheduled to take with an equestrian who won an Olympic medal. She tells you she wants to drop three to five pounds by the end of week so she will look cute in her outfit.

Or: Writing your final history exam on the decisive battles of the Civil War, you glance over at your best friend and notice he's copying from something you can't see. When you look toward the front of the classroom, you notice your TA is watching you.

In each of these scenes, it is clear that each of the characters will perceive the events differently. Imagine your own scene, and choose a character through whom to "focalize" the events. Try writing it with the character being physically very close to the event. In the three scenes above, for example, the dad (focalizer) might be watching from the third-base line, or you might be sitting right next to your cheating friend. Now, write it again from a greater physical distance. The dad joins the mom in the stands, your cheating friend is sitting clear across the lecture room.

Do the same thing with time. Describe your event as if it were happening right now, yesterday, a year ago, ten years ago, a lifetime ago.

The following option will be harder, because it has to do with attitude, but let's say you focalize the Little League game through your dad, who also failed in an important game when he was a boy. Or maybe, instead, he pitched a shutout. Let's say you, listening to your surgeon, suffered for years from an eating disorder, or are completely phobic regarding any procedures of the mouth, or once had Olympic aspirations yourself. Let's say when you catch your friend cheating, you're cheating yourself, or have just received an award for good citizenship.

In other words, in the scene you are imagining, try positioning the character who is "seeing" the events as sympathetic to them, or strongly opposed to them, either emotionally or ideologically.

Try writing your scene from as many different perspectives as you can. What do you notice about them? How are they alike? How different?

This is an exercise to which you may return many times. It is designed to help you practice certain modes of perception. The goal is to become so proficient in a wide range of narrative perspectives that they become, in your writing, second nature.

(K.H.)

Narrative "Voice" and Listeners Within Stories

10

Use to Write:	Short Fiction; Longer Fiction; Poetry; Autobiography; Creative Nonfiction; Literary Criticism
Ideas and Concepts to Explore:	the concept of literature as a "funhouse"; narrator; narratee; narrating persona.
Authors/Works Mentioned:	T.S. Eliot; Francois Camoin; Joseph Conrad, *Lord Jim*.

. . . there are four ways of thinking: to talk to others, or to one other, or to talk to oneself, or to talk to God.

—*T.S. Eliot*

Writers talk a lot about finding their "voice," as if the process were a rite-of-passage, like turning old enough to vote or drink, or passing the bar exam.

If you think about it—your physical voice—it's just how you sound. It comes out of a box—your voice box. Maybe you like yours, maybe you don't. If you are male, you remember when yours changed.

Ostensibly, your writing voice is something you can "find". You can practice it, and stretch it, and work it out. But maybe sometimes we think it is too much about speaking.

Sometimes it is useful to stop thinking about who is speaking, and start thinking instead about who is listening.

One way to imagine voice is as a *conversation* between who is telling the story to whom, and why. Sometimes we call this *narrative stance*. The teller is the *narrator*, or *narrating persona*; the listener is the *narratee*. In actual life, we adapt our speaking voices to our context, but in writing, too often, we proceed as if we're writing into some sort of vacuum, a neutral space where all writing sounds alike.

My teacher Francois Camoin used to say that if you want to build a funhouse, you're better off with a set of blueprints than with some vague *idea* of what a funhouse is supposed to *feel* like. The blueprint for any story is defined at least in part by its narrative stance. Narrators may be straightforward, loud, muted, deceptive, and so on; narratees, less apparent, may nonetheless call attention to themselves in a variety of ways. Sometimes, the narrator may actually be speaking to another character, or group of characters (as in Joseph Conrad's, *Lord Jim*), in which case, he is a literal storyteller, who hunkers down and says, "Let me tell you a story." Or the narratee may be more implicit, or he may actually be so effaced (neutral) as to be what we call a "zero-degree" narratee. The point is that while it is the narrator who calls the shots about the telling of the story, what to put in when and how, and what to leave out, it is the narratee, deeply embedded in the story, who often determines the choices the narrator makes.

Take, for example, the case of an oral history class, where the professor and students (all women) engaged in a project to record the story of how each of them lost their virginity. The project took place at the professor's house after a potluck dinner that featured large quantities of wine. Imagine how each student must have framed her story for this peculiar narratee—the professor in her house, her fellow students, the tape recorder, wine, her final grade. Imagine, too, how differently that same woman might tell the same story to, say, her current lover, her best friend, her therapist, her sister, her mother. Between the speaker and the listener, "voice" is formed.

Consider the following situation: A white guy and girl, drinking in a bar in Montana, hook up with a Blackfoot, who is also drinking. After the bars close, the three drive around mountain roads and keep on drinking. Eventually, they stop at a lake, where the white guy and girl get it on and the Blackfoot gets excited and starts talking about Native Americans to no one in particular and no one pays attention until he says, "All this land belongs to the Indians." Then he pounds on the truck and says, "Even this truck belongs to the Indians." So the white guy, who later reports having been in a subtle state of mind, shoots him, protecting his truck.

Even "character" in this situation is a participant in the story (many stories), as well as an observer. If the white guy remembers what happened with the girl at some later date— the next day, five years hence, in 2020—one story will emerge. If the girl instead is the narrator, and the white guy the narratee, a different story will develop. But what if *he* speaks, instead, still drunk, to the dead Blackfeet Indian? What if *she* tells the dead man's mother how it happened that her son was killed? What if the story comes out in a court of law?

While the events themselves remain constant, how they unfold in the telling changes a great deal depending on, among other things, who is listening. This exercise explores the concept of listener.

For it, imagine a story, maybe something that really happened in your family, and write it first to a zero-degree (neutral) narratee. Concentrate here on the facts, the events. Make it straightforward and simple.

Now, write the story again, but as if you were trying to convince a relative, who sees it differently than you, that your version of events is really the truth. Now write it as if you were telling it to a close friend who has never met anyone in your family. Now write it as if your were "talking" to someone as closely involved in the event as you were, remembering it together, as it were. Write it to yourself.

To your dying grandmother. Your therapist. God.

What other ways could you frame your story? How would this change things, if you did?

Like the exercise, "Turning the Lens," this one is designed to help you develop and practice certain strategies of perception. You will not always want to be self-conscious about your narratee, but sometimes just imagining a little guy listening on your shoulder—who he is, what he's wearing, his whole investment in what you have to tell him—will help you know better how to proceed.

Variation.

Revise a story you've already finished by selecting a new narrator and narratee from among the existing characters. Try changing the narratee only. What do these different stories share in common? How are they different? In what ways do they reflect on one another? Which do you prefer? Why?

(K.H)

11 ▷ Using Delay As an Organizing Principle

Use to Write:	Short Fiction; Longer Fiction; Autobiography; Creative Nonfiction; Literary Criticism
Ideas and Concepts to Explore:	delay, enigma, proairetic, hermeneutic, reference, semic, suspense, symbolic: all in the context of narrative theory.
Authors/Works Mentioned:	Roland Barthes; Julio Cortazar, *Hopscotch*.

In his book, *S/Z*, French theorist Roland Barthes developed a theory of narrative around five codes. These are (and though the names might seem hard at first, don't be put off): *proairetic* (plot, what happens), *semic* (character, who it happens to), *reference* (cultural, Coke bottles and McDonald's franchises and libraries and such), *symbolic* (what we recognize as literary language, tropes and so on), and *hermeneutic* (enigma). While these codes are largely arbitrary, (you could make up your own if you wanted) they can help organize our experience of reading. Among them, Barthes gives special value to the hermeneutic code, because it is the code of suspense and surprise.

According to Barthes, certain elements in narrative texts open up enigmas—questions, or riddles, or just things that you wonder about in your reading—and these enigmas are one source of pleasure in reading (as well as, we would add, in writing). They are what engage us, take us up. But the pleasure lies not so much in the enigma itself, but in the variety and complexity of ways the text delays answering its questions. Pleasure springs from the delay itself, the putting off of closure, what remains open. Suspense.

Imagine ice cream, maybe Baskin-Robbins, maybe Häagen-Dazs. Imagine a warm summer evening, with time on your hands and a sweet breeze, and you decide on a whim to go get an ice cream cone. The pleasure of that cone does not lie so much in the ice cream itself as it does in everything it sets into motion, beginning with the whim, the actual moment you decide to go out for it. It is hot, and you are bored inside watching t.v. reruns, and August has never seemed so long. Then it pops into your head, the possibility of ice cream, you imagine the cone, you decide why on earth not. So you enlist your roommate, your sister, or your lover, and together you go out into the balmy night. This is pleasure, the balmy night, the drive through the overhanging trees that darken the night sky to a lacy pattern, the anticipation of ice cream. And you think: *single scoop, double, triple?* You think: *double chocolate, pralines and cream, Reese's peanut butter cup, boysenberry swirl?* You remember the feeling of the ice cream excursions you made as a child in a different part of the country. You remember the feel of the coins your mother pressed into the palm of your hand.

All this is pleasure, but not so much, finally, the ice cream itself. For after all of that, you will almost inevitably choose the wrong flavor. The scoops will be smaller than you remembered, and they will cost a lot more. The ice cream will drip down the side of the cone and the napkin all the way to your wrist before you can stop it. And how unimaginably young are the ice cream attendants who scoop it out behind the counter, just boys.

There are ways in which writing is not unlike math. You start with a problem, the more you try to solve it, the more complex it gets. Then one day you figure out it was never really about x at all, but about the process you go through to solve for it. Even as x continues to recede, you keep moving toward it in increasingly more interesting ways.

For this exercise, think of x as an instance of the hermeneutic code, an enigma, something you might wonder about in a story.

Why was Aunt Rachel's red polka-dotted lingerie hanging in the cherry tree this morning?

How can you write a story where the end is the same as the beginning?

Begin with a table of kumquats. What are you to do with all those kumquats?

You are visiting the deathbed of your grandmother. You have it in your mind that the salvation of her soul is in your hands. She looks at you and says, "No Jesus today, please, thanks. Tell me a story. Make me laugh."

You have never been told the truth about your life. You were born an identical twin, and your sibling lived for three months before dying. How do you know this?

On the top of a volcano you find a rock with some kind of image etched into it. What does it mean?

Your character coughs, but the sound is like something you have never heard before.

You are digging in your garden and you uncover—what, a small stone statue of a horse? someone's ring? the bone of a small animal?

Would I find La Maga? (The opening sentence in Julio Cortazar's *Hopscotch*.)

For the exercise, treat "x" as an unknown you don't want to know. Try inventing as many ways as you can to put off discovering what you seek to know through your writing.

The story you make up, for example, to tell your grandmother on her deathbed, will not be so interesting as why it makes her laugh. What made the etching on the volcano stone—a person, an animal, the volcano itself? Who is La Maga?

Fiction is almost always indirect. Write away from the story, not toward it. *Look for* satisfying enigmas *in existing drafts of stories.* Put off the end as long as you can, and when finally get there, be aware that a story ends, as it begins, with only the sound of its last sentence.

(K.H.)

Writing What Cannot Be Filmed

Use to Write:	Short Fiction; Longer Fiction; Creative Nonfiction; Autobiography; Journal; Film Criticism; Literary Criticism
Ideas and Concepts to Explore:	cinematic/filmic; surrealism.
Authors/Works Mentioned:	Saul Bellow; William Gass.

What the writer must do, of course, is not only render the scene, but render the scene inseparable from its language, so that if the idea . . . is taken from the situation, like a heart from its body, both die.

—*William Gass*

We once heard novelist Saul Bellow talk about writing. He wore a little bowler hat, very dapper, and spoke with gentleness and conviction. At one point he noted that he and Updike and other writers of his generation had assumed the deliberate challenge of writing stories that could not be filmed. When they were young, he said, movies were taking over, the hottest thing and so exciting. How could the written word compete? Now writing had to be something altogether different: the word had to be what it was.

Narrative, of course, is story, and story is fundamental, maybe even natural, probably universal. In the early days, before the written word and printing press, narrative moved through the culture orally, people telling stories to each other in groups. Thus, narrative was both a communal and a unique experience. However many times a storyteller might tell a story, each telling would be different, one-of-a-kind, just as no two theater productions are ever the same. Books transformed the way stories move because in them the same story could repeat itself exactly, widely, and eventually cheaply. But reading, as Walter Benjamin has argued, is a solitary activity, which isolates the reader with her story. Movies brought narrative back as a communal experience, but with the uniformity of written texts. Video has returned us to our isolated cocoons even as it has worked to further mass-produce the culture.

And then there is radio, t.v., the internet. We have become a culture glutted with story. What can writing possibly do that other forms of narrative cannot?

To write what cannot be filmed.

Bellow used, for an example, the famous surrealist cinema shot of an eyeball being pierced by a blade. The blade approaches the eye, coming closer and closer. You can't believe that it will pierce the eye, and for an instant, the eye turns into the moon. Then it is an eye again, and the blade does what you cannot imagine: it slices the eye.

But for writing, Bellow said, imagine a panoramic view of an old house with a long, green, sloping lawn. On the lawn, hardly big enough to see, and far too small to film, is a dog worrying something, chewing and playing and tussling with it. The dog romps around, as gradually the narrator reveals that what you can't see the dog chewing is in fact a human limb.

Some things that cannot be filmed might include: the thoughts of a character, two parallel scenes unfolding simultaneously, a paradoxical perspective (as in the example above) where you know what you cannot see, the scientific principles of a geologic event you are depicting, language as pure sound or image.

Elsewhere, we have warned against running a movie through your head when you are writing, though like all rules, this one is sometimes good to break. But mostly, we should learn to pay attention to what makes writing, writing—sound, rhythm, words—*what cannot be filmed.*

For this exercise run a movie through your head and write it down, the looks on your characters' faces, what they do with their hands, how their voices sound when they speak, all the visual and cinematic qualities.

Now, add another element that you couldn't, strictly speaking, film—a sense like taste or smell or touch, memory, thoughts, something going on in another place or time, sound patterns.

Add again.

And again.

And again.

How is your final draft different from your first? What more can you add?

Variation 1.

Reverse the above exercise, writing first a text that could never be filmed, and then turning it, step by step, into something more visual and cinematic.

What happens to the writing?

Read the two versions to somebody else and compare.

Variation 2.

Write the two scenes I've attributed to Bellow's descriptions above—the razor in the eye, the dog chewing on a human femur. Can you feel the distinctions he is making? Which feels, in writing, more "natural" to you? Do you agree that the razor in the eye image is potentially more powerful in film?

(K.H.)

A Certain Conventional Element

13

Use to Write:	Short Fiction; Literary Criticism
Ideas and Concepts to Explore:	*histoire;* metaphor; metonymy; point of view; *recit;* time-tampering.
Authors/Works Mentioned:	Anton Chekhov, *Uncle Vanya;* William Gass; Suzanne C. Ferguson, "Defining The Short Story"; Norman Friedman, "What Makes a Short Story Short?"; Susan Lohafer and JoEllen Clary (eds.), *Short Story Theory At A Crossroads.*

We all know that short stories are, well, short. But what *makes* them so? And why?

In "What Makes a Short Story Short?" Norman Friedman argues that there are two reasons for the shortness of the genre: ". . . the material itself may be of small compass; or the material, being of broader scope, may be cut for the sake of maximizing the artistic effect." In the first instance, the distinction inheres in the "story," itself, that is, its sequence of events—what *happens.* (This is what narratologists may refer to as *histoire*). In the second, the distinction inheres, instead, in the telling, how the events get expressed on the page (*recit*).

In "Defining the Short Story," Suzanne C. Ferguson argues that the modern short story shares certain impressionistic characteristics with the modern novel, only to a heightened degree. Some of these characteristics include rejection of chronological time ordering, formal and stylistic economy, the foregrounding of style, self-conscious manipulation of point of view, and increased use of metaphor and metonymy.

William Gass says that "the material that makes up a short story must be placed under a terrible compression, but it must not simply release its meaning, the way a joke does."

Many of us feel, to varying degrees and at different times, isolated in our writing, on our own and sometimes adrift. But writing never takes place in a vacuum, and it is useful to imagine it instead as a conversation with all different kinds of writing—texts from several centuries ago, Grace Paley's stories, what the other students in your class are writing, Stephen King and the latest *New Yorker* and *minnesota review.*

You know the way it is with conversation. People do not talk the same at the barber shop as they do at the beauty salon. What you talk about, and how, in class just before the professor arrives is not the same as what you talk about, and how, after she gets there. And if you're hanging out at the mall you will have a different conversation with your friends than if you go to the ballet or a ballgame, or if your little sister is hanging around.

Conversation follows rules, the same as any discourse, and if you want to be able to speak up, you have to be able to recognize the rules and know the kind of conversation you are in—shop talk, for instance, as opposed to repartee.

Writing, too, has its rules. This book is full of them, explicit and implicit, and you have probably also heard that you have to "know" the rules to "break" them. Just as you "learn" not to discuss astrophysics with your baton-twirling neighbor, somewhere along your development as a writer, you also "learn" to show, not tell, to avoid flat characters, and to limit your use of dialogue to move plot along. (Do you agree with these rules, or not? Why, or why not?) Still, you may find that the rules and conventions of writing, just like your baton-twirling neighbor, may well surprise you.

This exercise began by describing certain conventional elements of the short story—compression of material or expression, foregrounding of style, time tampering, self-conscious use of point of view, formal and stylistic economy, emphasis on metaphor and metonymy, artistic effect. This list, not at all comprehensive, gives us a place to start.

In this exercise you are encouraged to play with these conventions in a story. Use them to drive and organize your work. See how many you can use and explore.

For example, years ago when I was young and vain about my hair, I let it grow and grow until it fell all the way down my back. Then one day I decided, for vaguely anarchic reasons, to have it cut off at the local beauty school. This was well before inch-long hair was hip, but I kept thinking my trainee could fix what she had done if she would just cut a little more off. Finally, she refused, and I left, a ragged clump of tears.

Several days later I went to see the Chekhov play, *Uncle* Vanya, in which a character laments, "When a woman isn't beautiful, people always tell her she has beautiful hair."

Not long after, a friend of my sister's approached me with a look on his face between shock and horror. "What have you done to your hair?" he cried. "You used to be so beautiful, and now you are so ugly."

If I were to include this in a fiction, I might begin with the image of myself in the mirror at the beauty school, watching my hair grow shorter by the inch (*time tampering*). Or I might mix perspectives and voices, including mine and my mother's, the girl's who cut my hair, my sister's friend who found me now ugly (*self-conscious use of point of view*). I might, instead, choose to expand the material, writing a whole story about hair (*metaphor*), with this a tiny anecdote, compressed between the one in which my mother called my sister a "slut" for going out in curlers, and the one in which I cut my own grandmother's hair after her last stroke left her bedridden (*metonymy*).

These are just a few of the ways I might explore short story conventions in such a fiction. What about you? What story might you write, and which of these conventions might you use in its telling?

Variation.

Revise a story you've already written according to one of the elements above. If the point of view is large and telescopic, make it small. If time is treated chronologically, mix it up. If the style is expansive, make it economic.

And so on.

You may find this an awkward way of working, but resistance can play to your advantage. Imagine you're a poet, working out a sonnet form. Imagine how the form works first to frustrate, then to guide, finally to dazzle you.

Be dazzled.

This also gets easier the more accustomed you are to seeing, or hearing, or thinking the conventions you are using, for the success of any conversation depends on you knowing its terms. Look at any lumpy story and you'll often find a story at odds with its own conventions. This exercise is just part of learning some of the rules that work for us in our writing.

What other conventional elements of short fiction can you identify?

If for some reason you become semi-obsessed with defining this mercurial form, short fiction, you might look at *Short Story Theory At A Crossroads,* ed. by Susan Lohafer and JoEllen Clary (1991).

(K.H.)

Deconstructing and Reconstructing

Things Are One Way, Then They Are Another

14

Use to Write:	Alternative and Experimental Forms of Fiction
Ideas and Concepts to Explore:	*histoire;* metonymy; narrating persona; *recit;* Structuralist poetics.
Authors/Works Mentioned:	Samuel Delaney; Richard Hugo; Alain Robbe-Grillet.

Many of us come to writing in the first place with the fierce desire to communicate. But, "If you want to communicate," Richard Hugo says, "use the telephone." However powerful a motivator self-expression might be, when writers write, it is typically far from their mind. They are too busy thinking, instead, about what they are "making." Or, as Samuel Delaney has described the process:

Story, as it's usually conceived, seems to me the most boring thing about fiction. Story is a way of talking about the experience of "story" at very few points in the text—often only for a moment or two, sometimes just at the very end. Get back from the writerly canvas and you'll see certain things. One thing that emerges, when you're at a certain distance, is, of course, the "story," so at least it's a real category for *readers* to think about. But for the writer who has to work right up next to the canvas all the time, story dissolves into so many other things that it's almost pointless to think about it directly. From the viewpoint of the writer, I'd say "story" doesn't even exist. It's just not a valid writerly category. Writers face off against the page, put one letter down after another to make a word, one word after another to make a sentence: the sentence has to have a certain shape, a certain melody. Then you have to make another sentence. Then you have to make sure the two of them harmonize—at every level, from sound to semantics. Story vanishes in this process. Move back far enough and, yes, a "story" emerges at a certain point—in the same way that, if you move back even farther, you can see the story's theme; and, if you get back even farther still, you can see its genre. But up close, it's just words and sentences and sounds and syntax, one following another in a variety of patterns, while you try to make those words relate to all the others you've put down in a variety of ways—a very few of which *may* relate to story.

We do not need necessarily to agree with Hugo's remark about "communication" or Delaney's view of "story" in order to benefit from focusing on the "up-close" work of manipulating language itself. This exercise will concentrate on that work once we briefly discuss some terminology that may prove useful.

Structuralist poetics describes a relation between the story, known in French as *histoire,* and its discourse, or *recit.* Technically, *histoire* is what happens, the basic events of the story itself, the boy meets girl part, and the fall in love part—or what Delaney calls the "most boring thing about fiction." *Histoire* is the narrative sequence of events, but rearranged chronologically, as if they might have really happened in life.

Recit is the *made* story as it refracts the *histoire. Recit* exists on the writerly canvas—all those words and sentences—where it orders and selects according to principles of narrative convention, sound and rhythm, syntax, pattern, harmony, and so on. Between the narrator and narratee, *recit* is the story as told, the literary artifact, deliberately crafted.

"Real writers don't have anything to say," says Robbe-Grillet. "They just have a way of saying it."

Recit is the way you have of saying a thing (the language itself); what you say is the *histoire.*

When writers first start out, they have a tendency to work too far away from the writerly canvas. They're afraid of being boring, they want to move things along, they believe they will better express themselves if they make sure to cram their message in. All of which tends to result, ironically, in labored and unconvincing writing.

This exercise, then, is designed to bring you back close to your canvas and, in so doing, let your story breathe again.

Begin with a 3 to 5 page story, either a new one or *one you have already written.* Something simple, like: You go into a restaurant, order coffee. The waitress brings you tea instead. A man at the counter in a silver bolo argues loudly about an item on his bill. When you go back out again into the midday sun, hundreds of birds swoop past high above, shimmering like the man's bolo.

Or: your mother calls you in the middle of the night, alarmed that the creek is rising. It has been raining for days, and you know the danger is real. There is something in your mother's voice that has been there since your father died last year, only now it is worse, close to panic. You go out to help your mother, hoping the rain will stop.

Or: you meet a guy at work, tall and lean, in a white Oxford shirt and brilliant, silk tie. He's soft-spoken, and you become friendly. When he takes you out for drinks, he asks you all about you—where you grew up, what books you read, how you imagine your future. You know this is the man you want to be with for the rest of your life. The next day, you run into him in the company gym and his whole body is covered with tattoos.

Reread your story carefully, and then revise it according to one or more of the following variations. Repeat several times, or as often as desired.

1. Rewrite it in sentences of thirty words or more.
2. Rewrite it in sentences of ten words or less.
3. Alternate sentences of fifty words or more with sentences of fifteen or fewer.
4. Eliminate all dialogue.
5. Rewrite the story entirely in dialogue.
6. Concentrate on all five senses (touch, taste, smell, hearing, sight), but avoid adjectives.
7. Rewrite the story in a different person—first, second, third.
8. Use all one or two syllable words.
9. Rewrite the story backwards.
10. In fragments.
11. Rewrite it as a single sentence, making sure it is grammatically correct.
12. Put a color in every sentence.
13. Use only one-sentence paragraphs.
14. Rewrite the stories in paragraphs that grow incrementally: the first paragraph is one sentence, the second is two, the third, three, and so on.
15. Rewrite it all as questions.
16. Repeat one sentence, always the same sentence, in every paragraph.
17. Rewrite the story as a fable or a fantasy.
18. As a news report, from the paper or the radio.
19. As a secret, something forbidden.
20. Change the tense—present, past, future, conditional.
21. Rewrite the story as a letter to your lover.
22. Work through the alphabet as you rewrite your story, beginning each sentence with the subsequent letter. Start your first sentence with an *A* word, the next sentence with a *B* word, the next with a *C* word, and so on.
23. Put a metaphor in every sentence.
24. Tell the same story, only fifty years later.
25. Rewrite it in rhyme.
26. Use metonymy (see "Comparison vs. Contiguity: Using Metaphor and Metonymy," Chapter Two) as an organizing principle.

27. Rewrite the story in seven numbered parts, each part a complete autonomous segment. Don't fill the space in between.
28. Rewrite the story, leaving out everything you've already written, and putting in everything you've so far left out.
29. Write it in a circle.
30. Reverse everything in your story.

What other variations can you think of for your writing? What happens to the story as you adapt it to a style, strategy, or technique? What determines the choices you make in the way you proceed?

Variation 1.

Choose a writing partner and exchange stories. Rewrite your partner's story, according to one of the variations above, or one of your own devising. (You and your partner should both use the same variation on each other's stories.)

Compare your results.

Variation 2.

Form a writing group with four members. As a group, choose a variation from the list above, or invent one collaboratively. Pass your stories clockwise, and revise the story you receive according to the principle the whole group has agreed on. When you are finished, pass the original story to the next group member, who will also revise it, and then the next, and the next, until each story has been revised by all the group members.

Compare your results. Not focusing on the *histoire,* what do you find appealing in the *recit* of different versions? Why?

(K.H.)

Fiction Backwards and Forwards: Interlocking Narratives, Prequels, and Sequels

15

Use to Write:	Short Fiction (including short-story "cycles" or series); Longer Fiction; [while the exercise does not mention autobiography, the concepts here can easily be adapted to work in that genre]
Ideas and Concepts to Explore:	"backwards" time and "forwards" time in fictional characters' lives.
Authors/Works Mentioned:	William Faulkner; Søren Kierkegaard; John Updike, the "Rabbit Angstrom" novels.

The Danish philosopher Søren Kierkegaard once observed, "Life can only be understood backwards, but it must be lived forwards." There is a forward and a backward in the "lives" of characters we invent and represent in fiction, too. Often what we try to represent in a story is a crucial interval in a character's life; often we try to create the illusion, through narrative, of a pressure point between a character's "backwards" time and her/his "forwards" time; and often the pressure point represents a tension between understanding life and living it.

One useful development question to ask of a story draft (especially an early draft), then, is, "Am I representing the right interval—if this is the *one* time in this *one* character's life to be selected and given a narrative, have I chosen well?" As you answer this question in a variety of ways, you may be led to pick up the story "sooner" or "later" in this imaginary life. Or you may be led to bring in a piece of "backwards" time—with a flashback, for instance. Or you may decide you have indeed chosen well but still need to represent (describe, structure, narrate) the well-chosen interval better. Finally, you may decide that you cannot yet decide—that you need to keep writing *toward* the story, toward that "time" that somehow insists upon being represented.

Also, some writers are drawn to a character's "life" so intensely that they choose to represent several key intervals of it. So they may write a series of interrelated stories about the same character. Or the imaginative world expands to such a degree that the writer sees how key intervals in separate characters' lives overlap, or influence one another, or cause a chain reaction. So the writer might create a group of interrelated stories with a different character at each story's narrative center. Or the writer might produce a novel—or several novels: John Updike's "Rabbit Angstrom" novels are one example. Think of interrelated novels or story-series to which you've been especially drawn. Consider filmmaker George Lucas, who did not create "Episode One" of his Star Wars myth until he had created several "later" episodes first.

William Faulkner is one of the best examples of a writer whose imagination created vast webs of characters and narratives. He wrote about different intervals in a single character's life, and he also wrote about the intertwined intervals of many characters and of families. No wonder Faulkner scholars are sometimes enticed to design maps, diagrams, and genealogies; what they're really mapping is Faulkner's busy imagination, which roamed restlessly through all kinds of imagined "backwards" and "forwards" times. Sometimes all the characters who lived in his imagination and emerged onto his pages seem related by blood, marriage, or tragic histories of one kind or another. For Faulkner, "backwards" and "forwards" times seemed to represent an endless process of imagination. But let us move now from Faulkner's vast interconnected fictional world to three specific areas you might explore in your writing:

1. You need not be a sufferer of Faulkner's Syndrome to experiment with interlocking narratives; you might in fact do something as simple as writing two stories about one main character. Many of my students have found this to be an enormously satisfying process, and often they have set the two stories at significantly different "times" of a character's life. An interesting variation is to make the character who is "main" in the first story less central in the second one, giving way to another main character. Or, to explore the intricacies

of narration, you might narrate the first story in first person and the second story in the third person; in this way you're experimenting not so much with backwards and forwards time as with how point of view shapes the representation of time.

2. It may also be helpful to use the backwards/forwards notion to do another "round" of invention after you've drafted a story. What more might be useful to know (invent) in the character's past? In your evolving representation of the character, how does he/she see the future, what does he/she expect from, want from, fear about, or dread in the future? Invent several scenarios of the future "after" the interval your story represents; this work may refine the way you see the crucial interval.

3. Finally, it may be useful to ponder whether your story and the construct of "the character" seem more backwards-directed or forwards-directed. One way of rephrasing this is to ask whether your character is more preoccupied with loss, memory, nostalgia, or past trauma than she/he is with desire, ambition, hope, acquisition, planning, or quest—and vice versa. Sometimes the answer is surprising and allows you to make significant changes in the narrative. Sometimes the answer reaffirms your sense of the story but nonetheless allows you to refine and focus certain things. In other instances, the answer may be difficult—a revenge story might perch precariously between the backwards and forwards zones—but that's fine: probably your narrative is about that difficulty, that precariousness. After all, Kierkegaard's comment, with which we began "back there," concerned in part the precarious balance between living life and understanding it, and such is often the situation with the characters we invent.

(H.O.)

When Losing Control Is About Finding It Again

16

Use to Write:	Autobiography; Creative Nonfiction; Essay; Fiction; Journal
Ideas and Concepts to Explore:	ghost paragraph; post-outline; what a paragraph "does" versus what it "says".
Authors/Works Mentioned:	Pat Macenulty; Mary Jane Rayals; [the motion picture, *The Piano,* directed by Jane Campion, is also mentioned].

It can be hard to write. Sometimes you have to just let go, let loose, follow an uncertain idea, trust your skills or your desire, launch out into writing, and write some in order to write more. Other times you know what you want to write and where you want to get to—but not how to get there. Perhaps this is because you're entering new-for-you-territory, without compass or map.

For two very different reasons, you have come to the same solution. You just start. You trust and go on. You say to yourself. "Okay. Good enough. For now. I'll just write."

Then, you share your writing with others. You're fond of some parts, worried about others. But you're ready to share, you need to share what you've written. They read, and you listen. Together you search for the central importance of what you said; you seek to balance the parts and sections, now, in retrospect, after the heat of composition, through revision. You're ready to combine where you went the first time with where you need to go the second time.

This is not about writing down a thesis statement and then trying to fulfill its promise, ready or not.

This is about discovering your point, your center, putting your finger on the precise moment or place where things, stuff (how are those for imprecise terms?— but they're the right ones for this uncertain moment) start to work.

Where and when you find your way in a text sometimes feels miraculous. But you can usually find it better with the support of careful readers. There's no surprise in this—it's not easy to read yourself, to take a step back into critical distance.

Often, reading like an editor, I'll tell a writer, "Amputate that first paragraph. I know it hurts. But here—in the second paragraph (or page, or draft) the work begins to come alive for me as reader. Here. Right here."

I'll read a line, a phrase, a paragraph aloud and try to tell the writer why the text begins to move at just this point. Then I suggest some of these strategies:

1. Pull the new line or paragraph to a blank page of the word processor and write a new ghost paragraph. Perhaps this is a new opening paragraph. Perhaps this is a new self-promise about the direction the new draft might take.

2. Post-outline your work—or ask someone else to provide you with a paragraph by paragraph paraphrase—"I see this paragraph doing this, this one this, this one this," and so on. You as writer may be delighted with what you heard or horrified or indifferent. But often you'll start itching to take the text back, to find a way to control it again (if only temporarily—another day and you may need to lose control of that text again in order to amplify or further explore). Teacher and scholar Ken Bruffee recommends that writers ask themselves what each paragraph is *doing* and what each one is *saying*. The "doing" relates to the effect of the paragraph on the reader, the paragraph's rhetorical function. The "saying" relates to what the writers want to get across. Although the distinction is somewhat artificial, or at least too simple, it serves as a way into analyzing paragraphs, provides a useful provisional tactic. So, for example, you could be saying what you want to say, but something still could be wrong about the way the paragraph "hits" the reader, or about its placement in the essay, or about its structure. For another example, a paragraph could seem to work splendidly for a reader. It could be doing its rhetorical job, but it may misrepresent what you had wanted to say.

Here's how variations of these suggestions worked for two writers in a nonfiction writing group. We met last Sunday to discuss Pat Macenulty's essay. We were reading a narrative written a year or more previously in order to help Pat decide what to do next with this temporarily abandoned text. All five readers, male and female—those who had worked with Pat in writing groups before and those who never had—said many things about the text, but we kept circling back to a single sentence found on page ten of a sixteen-page work.

The essay, in part, recounts Pat's experiences as a visitor to Japan. On page ten, she says: "For a trip to be successful, you must meet someone you'll never forget, but I don't think that's going to happen to me in Japan. I'm too isolated, too obvious."

Her original draft opens with an explanation/description—why she has joined her husband in Japan, and what they see in the first few days of the visit. The essay closes with a visit Pat takes alone to a shrine in another town. But we readers all kept coming back to the provocative sentence on page ten.

After this workshop, Pat rewrote her essay. For now, she has moved that key sentence forward, adding issue to her original situation and scene. She has dropped the descriptive one-and-a-half-page opening, set in Japan, and now begins her essay by considering what brought her to Japan in this manner:

> For a trip to be successful, you must meet someone you'll never forget. In Nicaragua I met a man who made his living chauffeuring the American press. His back was covered with scars from the cattle prods of Somoza's men. When my husband and I came back to the States, we sent him a stroller for his new baby. In Ireland before I was married, I hitchhiked across the country. I only had one ride. His name was Michael; he was an executive for a large Irish manufacturer. We had the freshest salmon I've ever eaten and I was introduced to a cinnamon-flavored liqueur that I drank regularly for the next few years. In Jamaica, I met a European man and his Jamaican wife who raised polo ponies. And in St. Thomas, a guitar player who took me to a Calypso party. But when I went to Japan a couple of years ago with my husband, I had serious doubts about the potential of an encounter that would fit my definition of success. After all, I didn't know the language, I didn't have an itinerary, and my husband, who was more familiar with Japan, would be busy working the entire time.

This new introductory paragraph of Pat's essay strikes me as much more tightly controlled, enhancing the intriguing draft our group originally read. She is ready to write again—not by abandoning her original impulses and words, but by improving on them—by aligning, in Ken Bruffee's terms, the "doing" and "saying" of a group of sentences, a paragraph.

Mary Jane Rayals's essay posed a different problem. She was in the process of turning an informal conference talk into an essay for journal submission. When delivering this text before an audience, she had been able to juxtapose and weave together information about and critical responses to Jane Campion's movie *The Piano*. During the talk, Mary Jane showed clips from the movie. Now the text had to stand on its own, mute, without the physical support of hand and eye gestures, voice modulation, or film clip illustration.

The rhetorical situation and challenges were quite different for Mary Jane than they had been for Pat—though in this instance Pat was one of Mary Jane's readers just as Mary Jane had been one of Pat's readers. Still, we pushed Mary Jane for similar things, asking for more focus in the next draft, more of a center or context, or issue, or theme around which to develop our reading responses.

Again, several of us pointed to a telling sentence in Mary Jane's original draft: "I think Campion does something entirely new by giving voice to the land in this film." We thought Mary Jane might start with this sentence in order to go more deeply into her essay's spaces. And she did in her next draft. She didn't only move the sentence from back to front, though. Instead, she pulled crucial ideas from two different sections—early and late—to develop her new essay, beginning it in this manner:

Original paragraphs:
Paragraph three on page one:

Unlike Native American Indians shown in U.S. films where the Indians were either something to shoot or something to weep over, the presence of Indians meant something to me. It was of particular interest to me, as I have Native American ancestry and because my major area of study for my English Ph.D. emphasized Native American literature.

Paragraph two on page thirteen (of a fourteen-page paper):

I think Campion does something entirely new by giving voice to the land in this film. "The bush," she says in the interview, "has got an enchanted complex even frightening quality to it, unlike anything that you see anywhere else,"

The new opening paragraph:

As I watched Jane Campion's "The Piano" I became haunted by the Maori people in the film. They appeared in more scenes than they did not, spoke in their own language untranslated, gave impetus for action in the children's drama when they interpreted the drama of murder as real life, and tried to save the actress from the ax wielding actor. The Indians argued with white people over land, they sang to the piano, they banged on the piano. Campion seemed to insist on their presence, even if they weren't actors in the main drama. This did not fit the role of Indians in U.S. films, where Native Americans were people to kill or pity or revere.

It reminded me of my relation to my eastern Creek Indian great-great-grandmother, Ocana. She died at 33 having given birth to nine children, and I had heard nothing about her. The silencing of her story was so effective that I hadn't even known her race until I became an adult, typical of the American south's attempts to often hide the truth. Any culture passed on by her has apparently disappeared. I have the stereotypical coal black hair, and not much more Indian than that. So I made Native American Literature the major area of study for my English Ph.D.

The film reminded me that some things need to be heard and aren't heard because no one is listening. And that some things speak to us even if they seem silent. And that it matters that we listen.

Both these writers trusted themselves to draft and explore, losing themselves in their text, before finding and gaining control again. Through this process, and with the help of careful readers, they came to productive new beginning places for their writings, just as you will.

(W.B.)

More Work with Language Itself

The Fat Draft and the Memory Draft:
17 ### When Energy Runs Out

Use to Write:	n/a [can be used in connection with drafts in virtually any genre]
Ideas and Concepts to Explore:	"fat draft"; "memory draft"; reader-response protocol.
Authors/Works Mentioned:	Nicole (a student), "Process Note".

There's nothing like realizing your typing fingers are keeping up with your composing thoughts or that your thoughts are racing ahead and calling your words to come after: *hurry, fast, this is it, this is exciting.* But for every drafting sprint, there are times when we slow and stop before we're really finished.

Perhaps we didn't leave enough time. We didn't start in the right place. We were in the wrong mood. Sometimes, we lose our breath, our energy, our idea; sometimes, despite wanting to write, we can't quite get to where we thought we should be. Sometimes, we want to have finished more than to start. So, despite having made a good beginning, despite having produced "something" we no longer know where to go.

At this point, when first drafts run out, when enthusiasm requires a reader's spark or a writer's revived energy, try composing a fat draft and/or memory draft.

- **A fat draft** asks that you arbitrarily double your text. Turn a one-page poem into a two-page poem. Turn a five-page essay into a ten-page essay. Turn a one-act play into a two-act play. *It doesn't have to be "good" or "better" or "finished;" it just has to be honestly twice as long.*

- **A memory draft** asks that you read your text carefully. Say two times. Once silently. Once aloud. Then you put it away. Immediately, (or if you prefer, after you've dreamed upon it), you sit down and write another text of at least the same or longer length—you can try to "remember" your text, go off on a tangent, or do both. This is a memory draft—it may closely shadow the original or strike off in a new direction. Again—*this does not have to be "good" or "better" or "finished" it just has to be as long or longer and written without a single turning back to the original,* except for what you have retained in memory.

- In fact, you may want to write a memory draft first and then a fat draft of the memory draft. Or do both, working from the original. Your goal is to create additional text—the words that create a high-calorie, high-octane fat draft, or the new ways of saying what you discovered within the memory draft.

- Now, do what you will—weave parts of the two drafts together, abandon one and go with the other, take something from all three, and/or follow either of the two procedures again.

Last semester, a writer in class gained experience with both these types of draft, one intentionally, one accidentally. Here's what she said about fat drafting, assigned for this class:

I sat again at my computer and took out the drafts that were commented on by my group members. I incorporated new sections in response to their suggestions but still found myself running short of doubling my draft. So I sat there pretty blank and typed some nonsense. Then I pushed away from what I was actually writing and went back to some childhood memories that related to my "theme" on literacy for my paper on speaking out. I began to write about that and my paper became a little more visual and fun again. I started to show instead of tell—like I did in the beginning.

(Nicole, Process Note)

This process note refers to Nicole's first essay of the term. For her third essay, she chose to return to and expand on a piece she had started in another class. However, the night she went to find the essay on her computer, it wasn't there. She explained the next day that she forced herself to sit down and rewrite the original text from memory. The next morning, on her computer again, she found the original, seemingly lost file and printed it out. She brought both drafts to class. Nicole had invented the memory draft for herself, and she was quite excited by what she learned in comparing the two drafts. Things she thought important in the first draft had faded, and in the new draft events took on new significance and were discussed in unexpected detail. For her final paper, Nicole borrowed from the original and from the memory draft.

As you can see, fat drafting encourages you to add significant detail, to explicate and explain what you thought might not be needed by a reader (but so often *is* needed). Memory drafting asks you to let your subconscious mind retain what's truly important so you can focus on it further, encouraging you to let the dross, the unimportant, the fussy detail drop away as you resee your draft. Together, they help you develop *and* refine—the two goals of a midlevel draft (before you travel on to edit and proofread).

As always, with these drafts, you're better off if you share with readers. For instance, here is a reader's response protocol writers in classes can use to ask necessary questions about a text (P.S.—while this is set up for a peer reader, you can complete one of these sheets for yourself to get some distance from your text and ideas for re-revising):

Writer's Name: _____ Title of Text: _____

Who do you imagine as the "best" audience for this piece?_____

Your (Reader's) Name: _____

To the Reader: For today's "fat draft" (or "memory" draft) response session, please complete this sheet by **answering any five of the following questions** (write the question down again as you answer, please).

1. What part of the essay (poem, narrative) do you remember best (and why)?
2. Be nosy. What do you want to know more about? Think of three questions to ask the writer about his or her piece?
3. Was there anything that you didn't understand? If so, what part(s)?
4. Which sensory details were most effective?
5. What do you wish the writer would leave out on the next draft? Mark it in [brackets] on the text.
6. Suggest some aspect for the writer to experiment with. (Examples: past to present tense, change point of view, serious to sarcastic tone, first to third person, move ending scene to the beginning, emphasize a different theme, etc.)
7. If you could have lunch with one of the characters in the essay (poem, narrative), which one would it be? What would you talk about?
8. What do you think about the beginning? What made you keep reading? What did you think of the end? Did you wish it had continued? Ended sooner? Or . . . ?
9. If this were your paper, what would you do next?
10. Tell the writer what he or she does best and encourage her to do it some more.

Use the front and back of this paper—and feel free to add your own other observations

(W.B.)

---

18 ▶ Thinking Poetically to Develop and Improvise

Use to Write:	n/a [may be used to develop drafts in virtually any genre—not limited to poetry
Ideas and Concepts to Explore:	cognate subject; collage; hypertext; parallel texts; subject positions; triggering texts.
Authors/Works Mentioned:	Ai, "Guadalajara Hospital"; Louis Crews, "Thriving As An Outsider"; Thom Gunn, "The Feel of Hands" and "Yoko"; Marilyn Hacker, "Elektra On Third Avenue"; Peter Meinke, "Untitled"; Richard Rodriguez, *Hunger of Memory;* Sheila Ortiz Taylor, "Re/Collection"; Van Mong Trinh, "You and I—Our Different Worlds".

In the same way that computer hypertext lets users access multiple levels of a text, readers can use invention for developing and revising their texts. Poetic invention techniques work particularly well for this, allowing you to explore and find places for expansion within the draft you already have in hand. By freewriting about key words, reading poems on cognate subjects, responding to a text from different subject positions, and so on, you can create parallel or triggering texts that can be added to the original draft or collaged into an entirely new draft that creates original ways of seeing a formerly predictable subject. When you, the writer, explore the poetic hypertexts that can be found in all own texts, you learn ways of uncovering significant details, creating quirky angles and perspectives, and learn—as we know you always do through revision—what you meant to mean in the first place. (P.S. You can use these techniques, too, when conferencing with another writer about his or her piece of writing, either or both of you composing these inventions).

Developing a (too) predictable essay, poem or narrative.

1. Write a fifteen sentence portrait to help you "see" better (complete prompts can be found in *Working Words*). In the case of these examples, imagine that Pepper is your dog and you've chosen to write an essay that explores your relationship to/with Pepper:

   Example: Choose the most vivid sentence (or phrase) from your draft: "Pepper looked like a little gray and white fur ball and his cropped ears were sticking straight up in the air."

   Next continue the portrait: Write a sentence with two colors in it. Next, write a sentence of more than 40 words. Next a sentence of less than 8 words. Use a sentence with a simile (like or as). The next five sentences should use all of the five senses—taste, touch, sight, smell, sounds. The next sentence, (and so on—these prompts can be structural, leading to interesting sentence variation, and/or poetic, leading to concrete images and exploration of particular details).

2. Draw a floor plan of the house where you lived with Pepper. Number each room. Make notes toward a story of you and Pepper for each room. Freewrite about the two stories that you have not thought about in the longest time.

3. Take Pepper's point of view and write a paragraph describing each member of Pepper's "family."

4. Write haiku—image poems of 5, 7, 5 syllables (approximately)—first take them from the original essay, then take them from your new freewrites.

Dog Sitter

Grapefruit and oranges
Payment from elderly owners
for watching Pepper.

5. Write cinquains—poems of 2, 4, 6, 8, 2 syllables—first take them from the original essay, then take them from your new freewrites.

First Dog

Grapefruit
and oranges. Payment
for watching Pepper. When
owners stay in Florida.
He's mine.

6. Freewrite the plot of every dog story and dog movie you've ever seen. What elements are common to them all? What made each different? Look for places in the Pepper essay where there's a chance to tell a "different" story—choose a sentence from each and freewrite, extending the essay deeper: "Pepper on the other hand, paid no attention to her"—why did the dog never spend time with the sister? "The elderly couple"—what do you remember about them? How did they talk to Pepper? As a child, what did they seem like to you? "The night walk"—what would you see? Where did you live? What plants, what kind of neighborhood? What did you think about on those walks? Did you talk to Pepper? What did you say?

7. Revise the original essay (poem or narrative) using parts of these explorations and/or write a new essay (poem or narrative) that uses parts from at least four of the six exercises you completed.

Developing an overly predictable five-paragraph multicultural essay on a teacher-set reading (Sample: You're told to write your response to *The Hunger of Memory: The Education of Richard Rodriguez*).

1. Redraft a paragraph of your current draft in Spanish and in English. What does that do to the meaning, voice, juice, energy of the piece?

2. Write a letter to your parents or write a letter to Rodriguez, addressing him directly.

3. Write about your neighborhood. First, draw a map of it—try to remember all the houses, stores, meeting spots, special places. Name families and family members, special neighborhood characters, pets and animals. Draw in the vegetation (if any). At the edges, indicate the climate—were days mostly sunny, stormy, snowy, etc. Use a sentence from the essay: "We used to greet each other with a kiss. . . ." and freewrite more details of the neighborhood, using the map you drew to prompt you. Then, look for places where you found missing or forgotten details. Pull those to the bottom of your writing and freewrite about them some more.

4. Look at the poem "You and I—Our Different Worlds" by Van Mong Trinh and use it to write your own poem about cross-cultural differences.

5. Find five key words in your essay—translate them into Spanish, and then, in either language, freewrite about each one: strength, Hispanic, self-esteem, family, language.

6. Find five key phrases or sentences from Rodriguez—free write about each.

7. Combine exercise 5 and 6 into a collage of associations.

8. Revise the original essay using parts of these explorations and/or write a new essay that uses parts from at least five of the seven exercises.

Developing needed distance and detail for a (possibly) too confessional essay (poem or narrative). (Sample: "Positive Bleeding"—story of a young man dealing with the painful pleasures of sexual orientation and getting his nipple pierced).

1. Read poems by Thom Gunn, Marilyn Hacker, and others about coming to terms with one's sexual orientation. After you read each, explore a single line in connection with your own life.

2. Read poems by Ai, Sharon Olds, and others that explore the connection between bodily and mental pain. After you read each, explore a single line in connection with your own life.

3. Expand on the visit to "VENUS: BODY PIERCING"—write this as if you are a film photographer, scanning the room, recording details, and sounds, and scents, dialog. Make readers feel like they are there. Do not make any editorial comments or judgments.

4. Like a painter, complete a series of self-portraits in words over the course of three days. Day one, look in a mirror and try to record the details of what you see. Day two, sit somewhere public and try to define yourself by the way you respond to the environment. Day three, interview family members and friends, ask them for memories or descriptive details they'd use to describe you. Don't respond, just record these. Then, compose this portrait using the words of others. Day four, try to collage the three portraits into a single portrait.

5. Consider audience—write a letter that tells this story. The first audience is your parents. The second audience is a lover who is at a distance. The third audience is a young cousin who asks you about your life. The fourth audience is a magazine that wants your view.

6. Rewrite your essay (poem or narrative) using any materials generated. Avoid rhetorical questions and state your intended audience/potential place of publication.

Sources for poetic invention techniques:

Behn, Robin and Chase Twitchell, eds. *The Practice of Poetry: Writing Exercises from Poets Who Teach*. NY: Norton, 1992.

Bishop, Wendy. *Released into Language: Options for Teaching Creative Writing*. Urbana, IL: NCTE, 1990.

——.*Working Words: The Process of Creative Writing*. Mountain View, CA: Mayfield, 1992.

Drury, John. *Creating Poetry*. Cincinnati, OH: Writer's Digest Books, 1991.

Weathers, Winston. *An Alternate Style: Options in Composition*. Rochelle Park, NJ: Hayden, 1980.

(W.B.)

19 Word-Surfing Safari: Playing with Language

Use to Write:	Short Fiction; Longer Fiction; Poetry; Autobiography; Creative Nonfiction.
Ideas and Concepts to Explore:	sprung rhythm.
Authors/Works Mentioned:	Amiri Baraka; Lewis Carroll; Emily Dickinson; Gerard Manley Hopkins, "The Windhover" ; Langston Hughes; James Joyce; Pablo Neruda; Dr. Seuss; Gertrude Stein; Dylan Thomas; Walt Whitman; John Edgar Wideman, "Surfiction" and *Collected Stories;* [saxophonist John Coltrane is mentioned, too].

It's easy to get so preoccupied as writers with technique, phrasing, plotting, planning, rhyming, making things grammatically correct, etc., that we drift away from the enormous jazzy, funkified joy of *language itself*, this strange, wonderful capacity we have, this linguistic *thing* that is its own inexhaustible, internally logical, coherently chaotic force: a sort of ocean, is language.

Children, especially those age 2 to 5 years, are experts at what one might call "surfing" this ocean—riding its currents, going with its flow, flowing with its go, testing its energy. They play so well at language, are so unintimidated by it, that they don't know not playing at it is an option. For lots of reasons—some good, some bad; some necessary, some not—adults come to *work* at language and some-times lose the knack of language play, of "surfing," altogether. Writers, who are among those who can least afford to lose this sense of play, are also ironically among those most susceptible to the play-killing effects of work—self-consciousness, phoniness, plodding dullness, worry, pretentiousness.

Gertrude Stein was one of the great artful drudge dodgers. Implicitly, her texts shout, "Whatever else writing is or is not, it better be fun." She maintained a word-surfer's attitude. Her power as a writer sprang from many sources, and no doubt she worked as hard as anyone else, but she didn't allow the work to be a killer of play or a thief of linguistic pleasure, and arguably the prime source of her power as a writer was her connection to language's oceanic force. A brief, inadequate, impromptu homage to Stein might read *About what did she write she wrote about Paris, not Paris but language, not about language but of language not of language but language, she wrote language languaging in Paris, Paris France Paris Language paris france paris language she wrote about what she wrote about writing, she did write she did.*

In a much different way but with as much generosity of spirit, e.e. cummings was also a word-surfer. So is Amiri Baraka; he's a social critic as well as a poet and dramatist; indeed he works at language, works at making it do things in the world; but he's also playful—and knows something about the politics of play, in jazz and in writing. Read his poem on John Coltrane. Out loud. Out very loud, very.

Gerard Manley Hopkins. Personally and culturally, he's about as different from Stein and Baraka as George S. Patton is from Ghandi. But he was a word-surfer of the highest order, too, ripping along the edge of something he called "sprung rhythm." Read "The Windhover" and other of his poems. Other writers I'd place in a loose word-surfer category are Dr. Seuss, Lewis Carroll, Emily Dickinson, Pablo Neruda, Langston Hughes, James Joyce, Dylan Thomas, and Walt Whitman, each in her or his peculiar way. Contemporary writer John Edgar Wideman has a story called "Surfiction," available in his *Collected Stories.* You might read, or read more of, works by these writers; but more importantly, start your own list of word-surfers, writers who have some kind of strong connection to the playful heart of language, a connection with which *you* in turn connect. A smile on your face as you read is a good warning sign that you may be in word surfing territory. Perhaps tap into the word-surfing power of modern-day scat singers, or Rap or Hip-Hop artists.

Draft poems or short-short stories that, no matter what else they do, draw on the deep play of language, its currents and recurrences, its absurd surprises, its inside jokes. Slip along the waves, rip across the roaring surface. Keep a separate notebook, if you like—and if you're worried you might "contaminate" your other writing, name it "Improvs," or "Surfings," or something better you'll come up with.

Existing Drafts

If you have some corpse-like drafts of poems or stories lying (literally) around, mur-dered by Technique or Seriousness or High Ambition (perhaps an English teacher was an accessory to murder), lift them off the autopsy table, give them big jolts of linguilectricity; indeed, a monstrosity may result: *It lives!* But so what? You can't fail because you started with a corpse. And at the very least you will have shrugged off the barge-like, drudge-sludge weight of *working so hard, so joylessly* at language. More than at the very least, you'll have discovered some stylistic range, some word-surfing muscles you didn't know you had.

Set aside a block of time and . . .

1. Rewrite a one-page poem, concentrating on the play of language, the pleasure of rephrasing. And/or . . .

2. Rewrite the first sentence of a story several times, focusing just on the play of language itself. Read aloud as you rewrite. And/or . . .

3. Choose one of your stories that contains a lot of dialogue. Rewrite the dialogue, concentrating on subtle changes of phrasing, vocabulary, pace. And/or . . .

4. Choose one of your academic essays and, still keeping it within the accepted rhetoric of academic prose, rewrite at least one of its paragraphs, making the sentences more supple, more pleasing to read, more rhythmic, more taut.

(H.O.)

Riding The Red Line

Revision and Editing

Strategies: Different Approaches to Revising and Editing

The Executive Summary: How to Respond to Workshop Criticism

(1)

Use to Write:	n/a [the exercise will apply to virtually any genre]
Ideas and Concepts to Explore:	"executive summary"; "global" vs. "local" response/revision; workshop.
Authors/Works Mentioned:	n/a

Workshops: Writers love them and hate them. Where else can we receive such attention to our work? Small group to large group—four respondents to twenty-five, each will tell us something about our writing that we didn't know; each will bring a reader's expectations to meet (clash with, collide with, support, subdue) our expectations. Each—if the workshop is composed of enthusiastic colearners—will bring insights to bear at the global (did we say what we wanted to say?) and local (does that dash really work in that sentence?) level. After the workshop, the formerly nervous writer (that we all are) returns to a text, needing to make decisions, to sort out emotional reactions, and to draw energy from what was said and suggested.

To get some needed distance from the workshop situation, we suggest writing an executive summary and revision plan. Some writers need to do this just once, to internalize and formalize a process of sorting and weighing advice. Other writers will find this a useful sequence to follow after each workshop, particularly if they need to delay revision to a later time—the executive summary can keep revision ideas fresh and well ordered.

Here's how the sequence works. Remember, this is just a single sample of the many ways a writer can summarize comments. Different writers in different genres use these steps, but differently—it's the thinking process that's important. Develop one that works for you.

After each workshop, do the following within 24 hours:

1. Read all the written responses and write an executive summary by listing and tabulating comments and numbers of times you received them:

   Example.

   Suggested Changes

   - find a title that helps readers more (two people)

   - maybe find a way to change opening to the same tone as paragraph 3 (1 person)

   - lots of small punctuation changes (sixteen people marking different spots—check which I agree with)

   - confusion about why I believe it's problematic that the parents don't appear in the story (4 people)

   Strengths

   - liked the way I used a story to show how maturing is impossible in a relationship like this (5 people)

   - thought the piece should be sent to *The Kudzu* (3 people)

   - liked the title (1 person—what am I supposed to do?)

   - would have liked to read even more, didn't think it was too short (7 people)

   - liked my descriptions

   - thought my single sentence paragraph in the middle was effective (1 person)
     [Remember—there are various ways to present these summary lists but it should be easy to skim to get a general impression of agreement and contradictions—you'll receive both.]

2. Write a short response to the workshop and then discuss what you think about contradictory suggestions.

3. Write a detailed one-page revision plan and revision timetable.

4. Revise. Follow your plan if it helps. Remember, it's a plan, an aid, not a straight jacket. Like a diver who "imagines" a dive before executing the dive, you're "imagining" the revision in great detail before executing it. But when you dive [write], you work to do the best you can at that instant.

(W.B.)

②▸ The Voices of Revision: What to Do with Advice

Use to Write:	n/a [the exercise will apply to virtually any genre]
Ideas and Concepts to Explore:	deify; demonize; imagined/internalized advice.
Authors/Works Mentioned:	n/a

I remember getting *so* much advice when I first began in earnest to write poetry—advice from teachers, classmates, friends, family; even imagined advice from writers whose work I admired. In one sense I sought out and thrived on the advice because it was a form of recognition. In another sense I came to dread it because it all tended to cancel itself out and confuse me. In this latter regard, I was as much at fault as anyone because I turned everything I read into advice to myself—the poet or critic or poem I read the night before became implicit advice about how I should write the morning after. I wasn't always good at knowing how to sift through responses, knowing what to do with all the voices of advice I heard. Like many writers, I also had to learn that often there's quite a difference between advice and genuine teaching.

Probably almost all writers go through such a process, go through phases where they seek help, desire "trade secrets," want approval from writers perceived to be successful, need to be made to feel "talented" (whatever that means)—and then go through phases where they're apt to turn away, turn inward, get prickly, forge their own way, walk a lonesome valley for a spell.

Sometimes it's good just to be aware of how many "voices of revision"—voices telling us what's good and bad about our writing—are speaking to us, are inhabiting our minds, regardless of where we find ourselves on the continuum between desperately wanting and needing advice and wanting to ignore the world of advice. Mainly it's good to identify the voices *as* voices so we can avoid either deifying them or demonizing them.

So: choose a poem or a story, perhaps one you've just finished. Then for each of the real, imagined, and composite readers in your writing life, write a short monologue in the first person, "spoken" by the reader whose voice you imagine, a voice commenting on the story or poem.

Your list might include . . .

one or more classmates

one or more professors/teachers

a friend who never reads your writing (but you can imagine what she/he would say)

a friend who reads your writing

a parent or two

a sibling or two

a writer whose work you admire (dead or alive)

a writer whose work you don't admire (dead or alive)

a public figure whom you detest

a spiritual figure

a stand-up comedian

your first-grade teacher

your ideal editor . . .

. . . and so forth

After you've replicated some or all of the "voices of revision," some of the following outcomes may result:

1. Just writing these short monologues should be cathartic, should get those voices out of your system, should make you feel more in control of that chorus, should help you distinguish between and among voices.

2. You might discover one or two voices that are too powerful—ones that somehow make you quake, that offer advice you're likely to take automatically, without thinking. Analyze the reasons behind the power.

3. You might discover that a voice you usually trust has a consistent bias, always comments on the same aspect of your work, always overlooks other elements, always rides a certain hobby horse. Consider how you might adjust your response to or use of the comments offered by this voice.

4. You may discover that a voice you rarely if ever take seriously actually has something valuable to say about your work. In such cases, concentrate on the message, not the messenger.

5. You may have fun—parodying a voice-of-advice you are, temporarily at least, fed up with. This is healthy. Turn this into a poem, a story, a performance piece, whatever.

6. You may decide to write three versions of a poem, each for a different reader: "variations," in the musical sense of the word.

7. You may get a clearer picture of where *your* voice—that voice of self-criticism—stands among these voices, what your strongly held beliefs about writing are, set against the backdrop of other readers. Identity, in this case the identity of your self-critical voice, is to some extent a matter of context.

8. You may discover you cannot be or do not want to be the sort of poet or story writer a certain reader wants you to be, regardless of how much you admire this reader otherwise. This realization may allow you to establish some necessary independence.

9. You may discover very specific, practical advice about revising and editing. Perhaps, via a monologue, you've discovered that "My friend Irving would

say to start this story on what's now page two—and you know, I think he's right this time." That's the sort of specific advice I have in mind.

10. You may want to stitch together these voices to make a poem or story—revising a lot or a little, depending (naturally) on the advice you get and the advice you choose to accept. A collage of advice. Or write a piece of "metafiction," in which voiced criticism of a story is woven into the story itself.

(H.O.)

③ Radical Revision: The Strategy of Risk

Use to Write:	n/a [the exercise applies to virtually any genre]
Ideas and Concepts to Explore:	audience; generative revision; genre-shift; graphics; layout; radical revision; syntax; tone; topography; voice.
Authors/Works Mentioned:	Don DeLillo, *Mao II;* bell hooks; James Joyce, *Ulysses;* Herman Melville, *Moby Dick;* Gertrude Stein, *Tender Buttons.*

The radical-revision exercise asks you to stop worrying about success (or grades or writing perfection) and focus on what can be learned by trying something difficult and/or risky in your own writing. Risk-taking delivered, eventually, for Herman Melville in *Moby Dick,* for James Joyce in *Ulysses,* for Gertrude Stein in *Tender Buttons,* for Don DeLillo in *Mao II.* Poet e.e. cummings radically revised his signature (and poetic style), as has feminist-critic bell hooks. And old ideas are radically revised through parody and the use of multiple media in the work of (in)famous media ad execs and by journalists and the designers of MTV videos. To older generations, it almost always seems like the younger generation is intent on radically revising the world. Revision is natural, thought- and text-provoking, and it can become one of the most generative parts of your writing process.

However, while most of us learn from mistakes, we don't often get rewarded for mistakes or the learning they engender. This exercise asks you to take an already "finished" or "successful" piece of writing (generally one completed earlier in your writing life) and to challenge yourself in how you choose to revise it. You have nothing to lose since you already have the completed, successful product. But you have much to learn about revising as you take this revision journey. Here's how:

1. Choose an earlier (or older) piece of writing. It should be something finished enough that you're not liable to want to replace it with your new draft. Sometimes, it helps to choose a piece that you're sure is done but is not necessarily your "favorite"—since this exercise asks you to dismantle the text. If you're too fond of the text, that can be too hard to do.

2. You will revise this piece in a way that challenges *you* to take risks and try something you've never tried before. For some writers, choosing a more con-

servative form may represent risk (one writer we know found the five-paragraph theme a challenging form that he tried for the first time) though for most of us attempting a new genre, writing a double-voice text, writing from a new point of view, will prove more challenging. You can find examples of many of these techniques in the *Metro* anthology. In fact, reading through the anthology, you should think of the works there as a style-bank—an arena for borrowing.

3. The revision can end up less effective than the original (there's no real risk-taking without the possibility of failure).

4. The core of the assignment is your process cover sheet where you recount what you chose to do, why—why is this a risk/challenge for you as a writer, how it worked, and what you learned. More or less, this is the story of what you learn as a writer while completing this project.

To revise radically, choose one or more of the following revision strategies, before you redraft. Try to stick to your self-promise and take the text as far as you can, keeping composing notes for your process essay all the while.

Try:

Voice/Tone Changes.

double, multiple, meta-voice, interrupting voice, change from first to third or try second singular or third plural; write as a character, change tone (serious to comic, etc.), change point of view from conventional expectations, Socratic dialog, change ethnicity, change perspective, use stream-of-consciousness, use point of view of something inanimate, use a voice to question authority of the text.

Syntax Changes.

alternate sentence length in planned patterns; sentences in arbitrary lengths (all 7 words); use computer spellcheck alternates to distort tone; use spellcheck alternates to insert "nonsense" words; translate into another language (and maybe translate back again), double columns to highlight double voice.

Genre Changes.

nonfiction to poem to song to ad campaigns, bumper stickers, fables, letters, sermon, journal, fairy tale, recipe, prayer, cartoon, and nontext genres—dolls, origami, game, . . .

Audience Changes.

(sometimes really variations of tone/voice changes?)
change from adult to child to alien, fracture or change tone, try parody, imitation

Time Changes.

future (flashforwards, flashbacks), continuous present, parallel times, simultaneity, tell backwards, situate in different era or point of time, change expected climax point of narrative

Typography/Physical Layout.

different fonts for speakers or emphasis, one sentence per page, large margins and illuminate, cyber text, lengthen, space differently, shorten/compress

Multimedia/"Art" Piece.

performance, play, audio and/or videotape, art installation, sing-along, write on unexpected objects (shirts, shoes, walls), choral performance, mime.

push your text, fracture, bend, flip, break conventions to learn about them
(W.B.)

Sentence Sounds:
Exploring the "Conjunctive" and "Disjunctive"

4

Use to Write:	Short Fiction; Longer Fiction; Autobiography; Creative Nonfiction; Essay
Ideas and Concepts to Explore:	"conjunctive" vs. "disjunctive" modes of writing.
Authors/Works Mentioned:	Raymond Carver; Michael Collins; Don DeLillo; Robert Frost; Ernest Hemingway; Richard Hugo; Nancy Krusoe; Jan Ramjerdi; Christa Wolf.

I give you a new definition of a sentence:

A sentence is a sound in itself on which other sounds called words may be strung.

You may string words together without a sentence sound to string them on just as you may tie clothes together by the sleeves and stretch them without a clothes line between two trees, but—it is bad for the clothes. . . .

. . . The ear does it. *The ear is the only true writer and the only true reader. I have known people who could read without hearing the sentence sounds and they were the fastest reader. Eye readers we call them. They can get the meaning by glances. But they are bad readers because they miss the best part of what a good writer puts into his work.*

—Robert Frost

Some of the finest prose-writers think first of themselves as "sentence-writers." They are writers full-blown in love with the arc of a sentence, what can be done with a subject and verb, how it feels in their mouths and their ears, the sound and the cadence of it. Although otherwise like many people you may know, they dream of themselves curling into their syntax as they push at the envelope of sentence possibilities. They hear the siren call of sentence sounds, and this, more than anything, makes them the writers they are.

Two prominent modes of American sentences are "conjunction" and "disjunction." Twentieth century disjunctive prose descends directly from Hemingway to Carver. Disjunctive sentences are short and hard edged, often with a little space—or gap—between them. Often, this space—or gap—reverberates. Disjunctive sentences use mostly Germanic-rooted words. Their style is spare and lean and highly suggestive. They characterize much minimalist writing.

Listen, for example, to these:

> The end of the world was a school day. There was even home work due. It seemed strange.
>
> —Michael Collins

> The restaurant was not very gay. It was in a large square room on the first floor of an old house. Ben led her to a table near the wall and told her to sit down.
>
> —Jane Bowles

> She met him at a dance. Pretty, too, and young. Said he worked in a restaurant, but she can't remember which one. Geraldo. That's all. Green pants and Saturday shirt. Geraldo. That's what he told her.
>
> —Sandra Cisneros

> It shows a man driving a car. It is the simplest sort of home video. You see a man at the wheel of a medium Dodge.
>
> —Don DeLillo

Conjunctive sentences, on the other hand, are long, loopy and mellifluous, interconnected with multiple coordinate and subordinate conjunctions. They are complex, with many clauses. They are lyrical and often Latinate. They come to us down through Faulkner, dense and evocative, poetic.

Listen, for example, to these:

> Why is it that we can't bear being the victims of chance. I sat down at my desk to finally read the morning mail, among other things a letter from that woman, over eighty years old, who writes to me from London in her generous, aged handwriting, and whom I would so much like to see—a wish I nourish within me without yielding too much to the doubts that stir within me the longer her illness, we both say "exhaustion," lasts.
>
> —Christa Wolf

> All right, man, so I'm busing down tables—we gotta do our own here, and we gotta sweep, mop, wash dishes, and do just about everything else,

too—*and* I'm trying to keep flies off my arms and the sweat out of my eyes and the seam of these polyester monkey-suit pants from working in the crack of my ass.

—Reginald McKnight

I am thinking of the walk to Rose Point, the narrow path along the cliff, the bright green shoots, the noise of new earthen flowers in wet environments, where all things disintegrate, she didn't love me dearly, I'd have to say, I played at being cheerful, land, I would cut in space new landscapes, explain that: Everything changes where something appears in the interval: the little round RV with blue curtains in the rear window: memory-images; some thing that would sever the bonds between remembrance and the present reality.

—Nancy Krusoe and Jan Ramjerdi

In this revision exercise, experiment with conjunctive and disjunctive sentences by rethinking your story entirely at the sentence level. Write it first disjunctively; then rewrite it conjunctively. Set yourself word limits—ten, no more than fifteen in the disjunctive mode; thirty, forty, fifty, or more, in the conjunctive mode. Pay attention to ways you can combine the sentences of your "disjunctive" text to make it more "conjunctive." Play with the connections, their flexibility and nuance. Stretch.

As you work, think about what happens when you write in different kinds of sentences. What do you have to add, leave out, rearrange, transform? How are the different elements of your story changed?

Don't worry if the story you're revising turns into a whole different story. Revision is like that.

So, for that matter, are stories.

(K.H.)

Getting Unstuck: Slowing Down To Pay Attention

5

Use to Write:	Short Fiction; Longer Fiction; Poetry; Creative Nonfiction; Autobiography; Drama
Ideas and Concepts to Explore:	moveable type; resiliency of the text.
Authors/Works Mentioned:	Raymond Carver; T.S. Eliot; Ernest Hemingway; Samuel Johnson; Gore Vidal; Eudora Welty; [Johannes Gutenberg is mentioned; the Sumerians are mentioned].

Even before Johannes Gutenberg became the first person to print with moveable type (in the 15th century), but especially after he did so, writing and reading in Western societies became linear practices. No wonder, then, that we sometimes get locked into one way of writing a particular story, essay, poem, or what have you: That is, a text appears upon the page (or, nowadays, the screen); we revisit it; but even if we are determined to change it, the text takes on a hardness, a resiliency, a palpable existence of its own in the world. Our texts are certainly more fluid than what some regard as the first texts in history—clay tablets scribbled on and then baked by the Sumerians over 3,000 years B.C.E. Nonetheless, for other reasons—perhaps more psychological than physical—our texts take on a baked permanence, too: Our eyes travel fast along those Gutenberg highways of type—printed lines—and what may have begun with grand hopes of "global" revision becomes light editing, cosmetic adjustment. There's a sense in which the text starts writing us or at least resisting us.

Such a situation is only made worse if we give into a temptation from which no writer is immune: being smitten by our own writing. "Read over your compositions," advised eighteenth-century British writer Samuel Johnson, "and when you meet a passage that is particularly fine, strike it out"—a quintessentially Johnsonian way of suggesting that we need to fall *out* of love with our writing sometimes, and that we need strategies for penetrating the hardness of existing drafts.

You don't necessarily need to follow Johnson's brutal advice and strike out fine passages, but as you read over drafts, sometimes it's good to slow down to a tortoise's pace, and to look at each part of a text as an opportunity to pause and to invent as many revising *options* as you can for that particular part. For example, . . .

1. In a short story, let's say you've come to a passage that is essentially a scene of one sort or another. *Stop there.* Think of different options for representing a character in that scene. Jot down notes about how you might show what you want to show about this character by means of. . . .

   a. speech—if the character is mostly doing something in the existing draft, how might you revise to have her say more? or

   b. action—if the character is mostly speaking, how might you introduce a physical action that would advance the drama? or

   c. setting or place—let's say that without thinking about it too much, you have put your character(s) in a restaurant, mainly because that seemed like the next place the plot should take them. All right, they're in the restaurant. Forget about the characters for a moment and "stroll" around the restaurant. Furnish it—tables, chairs, lamps, plants. A beer sign. Something in the kitchen back there, making noise. The light in the place—what's it like? After you've done this work, ask yourself how you can use some of the stuff you've invented to enhance the scene. Maybe for some reason the beer sign makes a character think of something to say— something he or she shouldn't say, or should say. Maybe there's a candle on the table and a character fidgets with it and the hot wax spills—to what effect? Think of such places as a source of abundance—abundant images, narrative choices, opportunities; or

   d. memory, daydream, desire—in the scene as it exists now, the character is doing or saying things pretty much in the present moment of the narrative, the "here and now" of the plot you've invented. But perhaps now her mind wanders—a powerful memory overtakes her, she daydreams, or she desires something or someone: Revise and let the narrative follow that memory, daydream, or desire; if the revision is big enough and good enough, if it earns its place in the narrative, it may become a new section, perhaps a flashback. Maybe it's good but small—a moment's pang of desire; still you would keep it. Maybe it invites you to leap out of naturalism or realism into a Kafka-like mode or into what's now known as magical realism: A snake talks, an armored *conquistador* clanks from one reality into another, a neighbor acquires a wolf's face.

e. metafictional hijinx—have some postmodern fictional fun. If you're reading over a draft and your writing seems to be, in Gore Vidal's words, "good gray prose"; if you have this nagging feeling that you've written "one more pretty darned good story"—then break the frame of the narration, expose the man (or woman) behind the curtain, treat your reader's disbelief without utmost callousness. You could write something like . . . *Here is a message from the Emergency Fiction Network. The reader is instructed to choose from the following list of things that might happen next to Our Character, Amanda.*

1. *Amanda marries Steve.*

2. *Amanda makes a sandwich.*

3. *Amanda marries a sandwhich.*

4. *Amanda begins to sing.*

5. *Amanda gets in a taxi and is never heard from again and the story is taken over by another character; these things happen; fiction isn't fair.*

6. *A guest-writer—Mr. Ernest Hemingway, ladies and gentlemen!— appears and writes the next paragraph:*

   Nick took Amanda fishing, and it was good. The water was cold. Amanda shivered. Nick never knew what to do when Amanda shivered. The color of the lake changed. When the color of the lake changed, you knew the fishing was going to be no good. Still Nick and Amanda had gone fishing and the fishing was all right for a while.

7. *The story has become a movie, and Amanda is now played by a young successful actress getting paid 5 million dollars to play Amanda.*

8. *The movie of this story has been made and appeared in theatres and is now on television and in the movie-story-television-narrative, Amanda has just kissed Steve and now a commercial has come on and you, reader, wherever you are, get up and go to a kitchen, your kitchen, and what do you fix yourself there? and now the movie-story-television-narrative has become your life your story and what is happening?*

Sometimes such metafictional messing-around is just silliness, granted. But even as silliness, it can help your writing by sweeping some cobwebs out of your mind, by giving you an edgier attitude to your own fiction, by putting you in a healthily mischievous mood—a mood in which you're more likely to be inventive, crafty, alert.

2. Reading over a draft of a poem, pause at a line that seems really interesting to you but somehow unwieldy. Arbitrarily tell yourself you're going to rewrite the line 10 times—different phrasings, different rhythms, different lengths, plain style, jazzy style, led on by meaning, led on strictly by sound, as T.S. Eliot would write it, as your neighbor down the street would write it, and so on. Abundant options.

3. If you're a little unsure of yourself as a writer of dialogue, pause at a scene and just let two or more characters talk on and on, as might happen in real life. Maybe five pages of dialogue, some of it (perhaps) completely unrelated to the plot as it now exists. A real bull-session. Will you keep all of or even most of it? Probably not. But "letting characters talk" is a great way of expanding your notions of them, of discovering speech rhythms, of stumbling on some great dialogue that never would have come to the surface when you kept traveling fast through the draft. Raymond Carver's stories often bear the stamp of a writer who has let the characters talk in draft after draft. So do Eudora Welty's. (An expanded version of this idea is in a piece appearing in the magazine, *The Writer*, Vol. 99, December 1986, pp. 11–12; 44).

4. Let's say you're writing an autobiographical piece, and let's say you're writing about a house or some other abode in which your family spent many years. One common way to write about the house would be to place the self you are now at the center of the narrative and then survey different memories of the house. You might, however, slow down and write brief monologues, in the first person, "spoken" by different selves: Yourself at age 6, yourself at age 9, yourself at age 13, for example. This tactic takes your present self out of the center of the narrative—something that may seem unsettling at first. But it has the potential of unearthing more memories, different memories; and it expands the range of choices you have in writing and revising because it increases the number of angles from which the house is seen. It also allows you to experiment with imagining—inhabiting, if you will—the voices, the outlooks, the preoccupations of your different selves, according to stages in your life. Naturally, we're just using the house as one example here; you could do the same for incidents, relatives, household routines, a Big Event, and what have you. At the very least, the monologues will comprise a reservoir of material to be drawn on, but you could also include some of them or parts of them in the autobiographical piece—offset, perhaps, in Italics, adding significant texture and depth to what you're writing.

(H.O.)

6	**Quickness As Complementary To Complexity**	
Use to Write:	Short Fiction; Longer Fiction; Autobiography; Creative Nonfiction; Essay; Literary Criticism	
Ideas and Concepts to Explore:	"category fiction"; crime novel; elision; episode/episodic; fantasy novel; "genre fiction"; "interior" drama; melodrama; "lightness" in narrative; mystery novel; plot-twist; "revolt against plot"; romance novel; science fiction.	
Authors/Works Mentioned:	Richard Brautigan, *Revenge of the Lawn;* Italo Calvino, *Invisible Cities* and *Six Memos For The Next Millenium;* Albert Camus, *The Fall, The Plague,* and *The Stranger;* Anton Chekhov; Guy deMaupassant; Ernest Hemingway, "A Clean, Well-Lighted Place" ; O. Henry, "The Gift of the Magi"; Langston Hughes, "On the Road"; James Joyce; Yasunari Kawabata, *Snow Country* and *The Sound of the Mountain;* Pär Lagerkvist, *Barrabas, The Dwarf,* and *The Sibyl;* Clarice Lispector, *The Passion According to G.H.;* Katherine Mansfield, "The Fly"; I.B. Singer, "Gimpel the Fool".	

Critics and literary historians sometimes speak of a "revolt against plot" that occurred in the 19th century, when several European and Russian writers—Anton Chekhov premier among them, perhaps—wrote stories in which not much traditionally defined "action" took place but in which the drama of people's interior lives took center narrative stage. Specifically, this revolt seemed to be against narratives dominated by melodrama, fast-paced episodes, rather predictable plots, "twist" endings, and other elements contributing to an easily digested tale. These same elements still dominate much of American television and Hollywood movies, by the way, and are still important to so-called "genre" or "category" fiction: thrillers, mystery novels, crime novels, westerns, horror fiction, some science fiction, and some fantasy and romance.

Terming this other kind of fiction a *revolt* is to some extent an overstatement and no doubt oversimplifies the differences between a writer like Guy de Maupassant and one like Chekhov. Nonetheless, literary short fiction did indeed come to focus on more subtle characterization, evocative imagery, symbolism, polished prose style, psychological complexity, and intentional ambiguity. Telling a rousing, fast-paced tale came to seem less important. This new general way of writing fiction blossomed fully in the first half of the 20th century in the work of James Joyce, Katherine Mansfield, Ernest Hemingway, and many other writers. Contrast Anton Chekhov's story "Gooseberries" with "The Gift of the Magi," by O. Henry, who was more of an old-fashioned story teller, and you'll get a strong sense of the different attitudes toward narration. (Both stories are widely anthologized, easily available in libraries.)

Some modern writers have been able to have it both ways, however. They write stories that are intellectually complex and socially current but that also draw on the plot-driven quickness and attention to speed found in the work of O. Henry and in earlier narrative modes, such as folktales, fairytales, and parables. In this category of modern writers, I'd place Langston Hughes ("On the Road," "The Blues I'm Playing" "The Ways of White Folks"); I.B. Singer ("Gimpel the Fool," among many stories); Richard Brautigan (look at his collection, *Revenge of the Lawn*); Italo Calvino (*Invisible Cities*); and Clarice Lispector (*The Passion According to G.H.* and *Soul Storms*). You might also look at Calvino's essay on "lightness" in writing, part of his nonfiction book, *Six Memoes for the Next Millenium*. Indeed, some stories by the writers mentioned in the previous paragraph are good examples, too: Mansfield's "The Fly" and Hemingway's "A Clean, Well-Lighted Place" are two that spring to mind.

The short novels by French writer Albert Camus (*The Plague, The Stranger, The Fall*), Swedish writer Pär Lagerkvist (*Barrabas, The Dwarf, The Sibyl*), and Japanese writer Yasunari Kawabata (*Snow Country, The Sound of the Mountain*) blend quickness and complexity in marvelous ways, too. These books are widely available in translation.

It's as important, if not more important, for *you* to find examples of quickness in short-story writers and novelists you like, in works with which you especially connect.

Then start using quickness or "lightness" (in the way Calvino uses the term) as a guide to revision. Look for opportunities to condense, to make leaps, to make elisions, to play with the representation of time, and so forth, even as you keep what is complex and subtle in your fiction. Conversely, maybe quickness and lightness come easily to you but come at the price of losing some complexity, texture, or depth; in such a case maybe the challenge is to add the complexity, texture, or depth while maintaining the quickness that comes naturally to you. Begin with just one story, perhaps—one that seems either a little slow, thick, or dense or quick but facile, thin, simplistic. Zero in on paragraphs or pages or scenes in which you think you can combine quickness and complexity, speed and substance.

(H.O.)

Forms Within Formlessness: Seeing the Potential Shapes of a Poem

7

Use to Write:	Poetry
Ideas and Concepts to Explore:	amorphous; "beats" (stresses) in a line of poetry; the credo, *make it new*; free verse; half rhyme/partial rhyme/slant rhyme; iambic trimeter/tetrameter/pentameter; "leaping" poetry; Modernism; surrealism/surreality—especially in relation to questions of form.
Authors/Works Mentioned:	Robert Bly, *Leaping Poetry;* Emily Dickinson; John Hollander; Langston Hughes; Richard Hugo; Ezra Pound; Stevie Smith; William Wordsworth.

American poet and critic John Hollander, among others, has made the point that for the better part of a century, so-called "free verse" has dominated the writing of poetry to such a degree that poets don't give enough thought to the shapes of their poems. In earlier times, that is, poets often *began* with the idea of shape—by writing in the sonnet form, to cite just one example. This approach had its drawbacks, too, naturally; in some ways, the rise of free verse was a response to—a reaction against—slavish, formulaic attachments to traditional poetic forms. When Ezra Pound and other Modernists rallied around the idea of *Make it new,* they were reacting against centuries of work within forms that seemed exhausted or that at least seemed to have been taken up by exhausted writers.

Hollander and others look at the present situation and argue for a return to writing in received forms, or at least for putting a lot more effort, study, discipline, and energy into the idea of form. It's really not an either/or, all-or-nothing proposition, however; that is, in order to give more thought to form, writers don't need to abandon free verse and write sonnets (for instance) exclusively. There's a middle way, and this writing prompt attempts to explore one version of it.

Take an existing draft of a free-verse poem—a draft that now pretty much exists as "a bunch of lines," a kind of amorphous unit lying there on the page. Ask yourself how many potential shapes (forms) are lurking there, masked by *apparent* formlessness. I'll use one of my rough drafts, lifted straight out of a notebook (this will be painfully apparent) as an example, warts and all:

[no title]

Consider the arbitrariness of cedar
trees, and women's long hair:
there comes a time when all
the work society concocts provides
nothing to you. You want to visit one
small lake hidden by willow and pine,
look down in water past reflections, see
bugs maneuver and waterlogged wood
blend into mud. What comes next in
your life isn't the point: it could be lightning,
long storms, or merely autumn. What matters?

Such a raw draft—such a lump! Only a beginning, mere notes. "Chopped prose," as Hollander might say. One way to begin revising would be to jump in and start adding and deleting. This would be like kneading dough, in a way—taking the existing lump, working with it, pushing it around. Another way, however, is to choose not to see the draft as a whole but to try to see some parts and patterns, some potential forms. Let's try that. Here are some things I see, phrased as notes to myself:

1. Eleven lines. How about putting it in ten lines—five unrhymed couplets? Try that.

2. I see three parts. Part one begins with "Consider." Part two—"You want to visit . . . ." Part three—"What comes next." These are shifts in rhetoric or thought—even shifts of scene. Try the poem in three numbered parts? Make each part more of a list. A: List of things to consider. B: List of what the "you" wants. C: List of "what comes next." (At the very least, revising this way would invite a lot of brainstorming, a lot more material with which to work.)

3. Still playing with these three parts: Write the draft backwards. Start the poem with the question, "What matters?" Write backwards through autumn, storms, lightning, waterlogged wood, bugs, the lake—all the way back to women's long hair and cedar trees. Try that.

4. Some partial rhymes (half rhyme, slant rhymes) are in there, hidden: Cedar/water. One/pine. Wood/mud. Revise the poem more aggressively than options 1 to 3 suggest, concentrating on using these rhymes. Maybe couplets, maybe not.

5. How about turning "Consider" into a marker, a signpost—a provider of form? Keep repeating "consider," organize the poem around that directive.

6. "Strip the poem for parts" (Richard Hugo's term). Use the parts for a series of haiku. Example:

cedar boughs
women's long hair—
storm coming up.

lake surface: reflection.
—past this, bugs in mud,
waterlogged wood.

7. Beats. In a lot of the eleven lines, there seem to be three beats. Line three is even in strict iambic trimeter verse. Try a version of the poem that gravitates toward strict iambic trimeter? Or at least try a version in which all lines have three strong beats?

8. A more deliberate move: Start to nudge the draft toward a more traditional verse form —a sonnet; a modified sonnet, unrhymed, in iambic tetrameter or pentameter; a quasi-ballad form that, although unrhymed, takes cues from William Wordsworth, Emily Dickinson, Langston Hughes, or Stevie Smith. A step in that direction:

There comes a time when all the work
The world assigns dissolves the soul.
That small lake, then—you must go there—
remember? Cedars swim the sky.

9. In the last line above I made a move that has something to do with form (iambic pentameter) but also something to do with the deeper movement of poems. I used that cedar-tree image from the notebook draft, but I made what

Robert Bly calls a "leap." Actually, he might call it only a "hop." (See his *Leaping Poetry*, Boston: Beacon Press, 1978.) If I were to do what poets hate to do—paraphrase or self-interpret—I might say that the image of cedars swimming in the sky captures some of the fluidity of cedars, which can be construed as erotic trees (now *there's* a leap, eh?). The real point is that the leap, "cedars swim the sky," resists paraphrase, expands the psychic space of that little stanza, makes the poem less earth-bound. This is what I mean by the deeper movement, deeper form, of a poem. When you leap, of course, you're more likely to fall—no risk, no gain. Maybe I fell when I took that leap; many readers might think so. I might think so. That doesn't mean I or you should be afraid to leap, however—to associate, to involve *sur*reality, intuition, the subconscious. Naturally, this technique is pretty far afield from the more obvious considerations of form we've discussed, but it is hardly unrelated to the task of seeing potential forms within existing drafts of poems.

Okay, your turn, and "your turn"—not my draft—is the real point of this exercise: Find a draft, a "lump." Pick it up and look at it from different angles. What shapes are in there? What potentially more "form-full" ways of revising occur to you? What are some different ways the poem seems to "want" to be written or rewritten? Are there many poems in the one poem? What images or moments in the poem invite you to "leap"—associate rapidly, expand the space of the poem? In any event, *go for it*.

(H.O.)

⑧ Old Faithfuls: Some Enduring Approaches to Revision

Use to Write:	[the approaches may be applied to work in virtually any genre]
Ideas and Concepts to Explore:	n/a
Authors/Works Mentioned:	n/a

A few effective approaches to revising prose and poetry are so uncomplicated and have been around so long that they are easy to overlook. We place them last in this "strategies" section to highlight them.

1. Read your work out loud often. After completing a draft of a poem, read the draft out loud; almost always, just reading it aloud will reveal certain necessary revisions—the need for a different word here, better phrasing there. The same applies to drafts of stories and essays. Read out loud, the story will "come to you" in a fresh way, certain things will sound great, others won't, and a few ideas for revising will become immediately clear.

2. Listen to someone else read your work out loud. As you listen, try as hard as you can to pretend that you did not write the poem, story, or nonfiction piece. What comes across well? What doesn't? What suddenly sounds clumsy, unintentionally funny, or inappropriately vague? Where does the other person stumble—or pause, out of confusion, as she or he is reading? What pieces of dialogue sound wooden or otherwise just don't seem to work? What words, phrases, or sentences sound forced, unnecessarily tangled, pretentious, unhinged? At what point do you feel the need for—the urge to supply—more detail? Figuratively, where and why does this piece of writing sound "out of tune" to you?

3. As you revise pieces of prose, always look for unintended *shifts of verb tense*. For example, you may start to write a story in the present tense but then, because telling stories in the past tense comes so naturally to all of us, you may shift back to the past tense without meaning to do so.

4. When we draft poems or pieces of prose, we believe we are beginning where we need to begin, but in fact a "real" (better, more appropriate) beginning appears several lines into a draft of a poem or a paragraph or two in a piece of prose. We write our way *into* drafts, so to speak. Such an occurrence is so commonplace that making a habit of looking for that "real" beginning is one reliable way of approaching revision. Discovering such a place in a draft does not, of course, preclude other sorts of revision.

5. Some errors in punctuation, spelling, grammar, and vocabulary haunt us. We commit the same ones over and over again, often even when we understand why the error is an error; habit can overwhelm knowledge. So keep a list of the errors you make repeatedly; make sure you know why they are errors; and then *expect to find them* in your drafts. Expressly look for them and correct them as you prepare a final draft of a story, a poem, or another piece of writing. Counteract one bad habit with a good one; devote one specially targeted reading of a draft to finding such habitual errors, which, because they are habitual, are likely to go unnoticed when you are reading drafts for other purposes.

(H.O.)

Tactics: Specific Tasks of Revision and Editing

The Arbitrary Reviser Looks at Fiction

Use to Write:	Short Fiction; Longer Fiction
Ideas and Concepts to Explore:	arbitrary revision; "free agent"; "wild ingredient".
Authors/Works Mentioned:	n/a

One way to revise a story is to keep going over it, moving parts around, adding something here, taking something else away there, and generally working within the narrative that already exists. This is a commonsensical, practiced, comfortable way of revising for many writers. Sometimes, however, our stories—or our perceptions of our stories—can benefit from a jolt. After all, revise means re-vise, re-visualize, see again, see afresh. Hence the potential benefit of a tactic that jolts us *into* seeing afresh. Common sense dictates that revision should not be arbitrary, that it should arise from a familiarity with the story—that it should be intentional and studied. True enough, often enough.

Sometimes, though, it can help to introduce a free agent into the process, an arbitrary move, a wild ingredient to inflame the chemistry. Such a move can make us see something new in a story, and sometimes, in trying to make the arbitrary move fit the "logic" of an existing narrative, or to have the narrative accommodate the wild ingredient, we can take that narrative into more original territory—in spite of our natural resistance to making a story vulnerable to something foreign, accidental, or not part of an existing foundation. Here, then, are some prompts for such arbitrary moves, such less orthodox revision. They are merely options, of course; you may choose one—or more; you may invent arbitrary moves of your own or have a writing colleague invent ones for you.

1. In the first paragraph of your story, introduce a question at some point. If nothing else, rewrite a statement as a question.

2. A flower. A coin. A beautiful stranger. A bird. An odor. Flip through your draft and, as randomly as you can (randomness is difficult), point to a passage, paragraph, or scene. Introduce one of these "things" (flower, coin, stranger, bird, odor) into that narrative place. Work to *make* it fit—as difficult as this may seem at first.

3. Make yourself introduce some kind of *list* into an existing draft of a story.

4. In an existing dialogue between two characters, make something "come off the wall," as it were. That is, look at the setting and have something happen in that setting that intrudes momentarily or radically on the dialogue. A cat knocks a cup off a table. Hail hits the roof. Someone at the next table collapses. A chair breaks. A spider crawls across a hand. A terrible odor comes out of nowhere. One of the characters gets a sudden pain in her toe (in this case the body is "the setting"). Or have something in the dialogue itself come off the wall; that is, have a character say something out of context. After all, people say such things quite often. How does this utterance affect the dialogue? Is there a way to keep it in there? Does it open up options for revision?

5. Let's say you have a draft of one medium-length story. Turn it into three compact narratives that tell the same story but in different ways—three different, even contradictory, versions of the fictional truth.

6. Arbitrarily cut out all the adjectives in a draft. See what happens.

7. Make your own list (arbitrarily!) of possible arbitrary-revision tactics. Then try them out.

(H.O.)

Paper, Tape, Scissors:
The Arbitrary Reviser Acquires Tools

10

Use to Write:	n/a [the exercise applies to virtually any genre]
Ideas and Concepts to Explore:	collage; "first form".
Authors/Works Mentioned:	n/a

I drove once on a field trip for my son's fifth grade class to the studio of an artist named Vasa. Vasa works in huge acrylic sculptures—bright colors, clean forms, clear light. I had seen his work before at school auctions and did not find it interesting, but in the studio, white-walled and with ceilings almost clear to the sky, washed by the sweetest light, the colors and shapes were serene and moving. I came to appreciate not only the concept of his medium, but also how wrong I had been to dismiss it.

Vasa is soft-spoken, maybe sixty, an immigrant from Yugoslavia when Yugoslavia was still a place. All thirty children were uncharacteristically subdued and respectful when he spoke. When they asked about his process—his "inspiration"—he was thoughtful. It was not what they might think, he said. It came from everywhere, unexpected, abstract. Then he paused and told them that much of his art came from accidents, or mistakes, that occurred when he was doing what he didn't know how to do. Two colors he hadn't intended might look good together, and so they would stay.

Mistakes that occur in the process of doing what you don't know how to do: If this is art, surely it is writing too.

But writing, as we know, has a tendency to stick to its first forms—the first way we imagine it—as if it has to be that way and no other. Sometimes this is because we are so close to our work we can't really see it. Maybe we think if we touch it we will ruin it. Sometimes we're just plain stuck.

This is an exercise in getting unstuck by experimenting with the possibilities of accident. For it you must be willing to approach your writing in the spirit of free play. You need an already written text (be sure to keep a copy for future reference), a pair of scissors, some tape, and a partner.

Begin by exchanging your texts—you take your partner's, she takes yours. Then each of you cut up the other's text into at least twenty small pieces. It is fun to watch this part of it, your work being turned to a pile of scraps. Now, close your eyes and select five of the scraps from the pile of your text, crumple them up and throw them away.

Have your partner do the same.

What each of you now have before you is a pile of incomplete text fragments. Your task is to rearrange them according to the principle of accident. Arrange arbitrarily. Use tape. You may write into new spaces to smooth out jagged or incomplete seams, or work entirely with fragments, juxtaposition, collision. Prose may ease into poetry, and back. You may or may not make sense.

The point is not to make a piece of finished writing (though that sometimes happens) but rather to explore strange connections among words and the unexpected outcomes of textual collage.

Mistakes that occur in the process of doing what you don't know how to do. Share what you assembled with your partner, and if you like, start over again.

Variation 1.

Proceed as above, but instead of discarding text fragments, commingle yours with your partner's. Exchange them, piece by piece, until you have in equal parts fragments from each text.

Rearrange as above.

Variation 2.

Proceed as above, but in groups of three or more.

(K.H.)

Directed Revision and Editing: Variations on Arbitrary Revision

11

Use to Write:	Short Fiction; Longer Fiction; Poetry; Creative Nonfiction; Autobiography; Essay
Ideas and Concepts to Explore:	adjective; "domesticated" draft vs. "wild" draft; iambic pentameter; *modus operandi;* prepositional phrase; prose poem.
Authors/Works Mentioned:	Richard Hugo, *The Triggering Town.*

Often it's fine for us to be guided in our revision and editing by our own instincts and experience, our own *modus operandi,* as just mentioned in the previous chapter, "The Arbitrary Reviser." However, sometimes being forced or nudged to revise or edit in specific ways can help the drafts at hand and also sharpen our instincts and broaden experience. Here are some revision-and-editing tasks we've offered to writers over the years. Sometimes they will overlap with other exercises in this chapter, but that's all right. Sometimes they will make you think of other methods and tasks of your own, and that's more than all right. Try them out on specific poems, stories, or nonfiction prose pieces on which you're at work:

Poetry, Prose Poetry, Prose Sketches and Short Fictions.

1. Experiment with adjectives: remove all the adjectives (or adverbs or both) from the text. Or, if you tend not to use them enough, try using more, or try using adjectives in pairs.

2. Rearrange a poem so that the line breaks come at the end of sentences. Then arrange the same poem in ten-syllable lines. Try it in two- or four-word lines. Finally, space it by phrases and move the lines across the white space. If you often break lines at the end of sentences, do the opposite. Or if you follow other patterns repeatedly, break the pattern. Read all the versions aloud and try to explain how each works or does not work. Ask others what versions they like and why. For prose, change the margins and indents (try hanging indents and seeing where the lines break with different margin sizes).

3. Remove all *ands, the's,* and prepositional phrases (ex: around, under, over) from the text.

4. Cut the text in half (condense to half as many lines) while trying to maintain the original intensity.

5. Try turning an unmetered poem into one composed in iambic pentameter (or vice versa). Turn a prose sketch into a lined poem. Add to a poem and turn it into prose.

6. Write a paragraph description of what you intended to say in the text without the work in front of you. Compare the description to the original. How successful were you?

7. Write some poems (or paragraphs) as spontaneously as possible (perhaps one each morning for a week). Do not revise them at the time. Then, a week later, look carefully at the faults and strengths of each, and revise them if you wish. Perhaps try to "stitch" some of them together, according to surprising connections.

8. If a text seems good but somehow too safe or careful or predictable or "well-mannered" to you, revise it roughly, feverishly, using free association, tapping into a more surrealistic area of your imagination. Think of the draft as *domesticated,* then return it to *the wild.*

9. Strip some other of your poems or short prose for parts, to borrow Richard Hugo's analogy. Take parts (lines, images, phrases) from different texts and assemble a new text from them.

Fiction and Nonfiction.

1. Write a dialogue between two characters already "in" one of your narratives, without using names or identifying tags and even, if you like, without thinking of the current plot/essay organization as it stands.

2. If you have a fairly long dialogue in your text, tell yourself you're going to make it as short as you can while still having it contribute to the narrative in the way you think it should. Make it a challenge: *How little dialogue can I get away with?*

3. Rewrite a scene from an existing narrative that's in the first-person point of view and make it second person. Then make it third person. Or turn third person into first person, and so on.

4. Explore "poetic" technique as you revise a longer narrative—leaving out (or including more) adjectives, having some characters rely on cliché in their speech, describing a character/person you know by using an extended metaphor (technically called a poetic "conceit"), paying a lot of attention to rhythm in dialogue, and so forth.

5. Basic polishing: Look for places where you've begun a parallel structure but not finished. For example, you might have a series such as "Mike wanted to go fishing, hunting, and take a hike" and simply need to replace "take a hike" with "hiking." Many modal verbs ("could see") can be revised into simpler, swifter forms ("saw"). Often we use two adjectives when one will do—and do better: "burly" instead of "big and burly," for instance. Look for lapses in pronoun agreement and reference and in subject/verb agreement. Use descriptive dialogue tags sparingly (she hissed; he roared; he said, sneeringly); edit out as many of these extras as you can, and let the words of the dialogue themselves suggest how someone speaks.

Remember: Out of context, discussion of such elements is usually boring, but in the context of your own writing and a specific draft, such "clean-up" work is crucial.

(W.B. and H.O.)

Writing Between the Lines: Revising as "Adding To" Not "Taking Away"

12

Use to Write:	n/a [the exercise applies to virtually any genre]
Ideas and Concepts to Explore:	revision-as-discovery; "re-envision".
Authors/Works Mentioned:	E.M. Forster.

How can I know what I mean until I see what I've said?

—*E.M. Forster*

Maybe you've heard that real writers sweat blood when they write, slaving over their texts. Maybe you've been told you must be willing to kill off your (text) babies. It is common knowledge that whatever you love best about your writing is the first thing that should go in revision. And yet, we remain of several minds about it.

One:

Though the golden rule here is *revise, revise, revise,* sometimes we would argue: *just don't do it.*

Sometimes revision takes all the best energy out of your writing.

Sometimes writing is better left alone because too often what happens in revision is we try to "fix" our texts according to some vaguely articulated concept of an ideal—the perfect poem, the shapely story, the moving memoir. If you write with others—a class or writing group—the group will establish the ideal, derived not only from our current writing culture (what gets good reviews or made into movies), but also from the "best" writers in the group. In either case, such "revision" turns into a process of trying to make your writing sound the way it's "supposed" to sound and soon you lose your way in it.

And sometimes it is better to know when to move on to the next writing project, having already learned from your current one the best of what it has to teach you.

Two:

Think of revision not as "fixing," but as "re-making."

In most cases we think of revision as an odd kind of writing subtraction in which, if we just take out all the "bad" parts, the writing will say what we mean. Here we propose, instead, a radical logic of addition that depends instead on our not always knowing where we're headed.

Imagine revision as a wresting apart, a prying open, a writing into the locked spaces of the text in which we may discover something quite beyond our already-known purpose, a wonderful surprise that awaits in the always-writing more.

In this exercise, begin with a text you have written, any kind of writing—a poem, or a story, an autobiographical fragment. Begin by telling yourself you don't really know what it is about. Now, begin writing between lines of your text. Between every two lines, insert an additional line of writing.

Something new.
Something borrowed.
Something more.

Repeat as before, as many times as necessary, until the writing saturates itself.

Variation 1.

Break each sentence in two, completing each as necessary.

Variation 1a.

Where you have split the sentence, add a sentence between each new sentence.

Variation 2.

Identify the basic organizing unit of the text: paragraphs, stanzas, prose fragments. Open the text at the joints of each unit, and write a new one at each break.
Repeat.

Variation 2a.

To explore and revise your writing according to mixed-genre conventions, add units of different organizing logics. Between paragraphs in prose, insert poem stanzas; between stanzas, insert paragraphs.

Variation 3.

Have someone—your teacher, friend, or writing partner—make random slash marks on your text. Then break open the text at each mark and write yourself into that space.

Variation 4.

Invent your own variations of revision that proceed from a logic of opening up, adding to, reexploring. Know that revision, too, depends on discovery.

    Remain open and interested in the jagged edge of text. Suspect seamlessness. Write on.

(K.H.)

---

⑬ "Blowing Up" Your Poems: Large-Font Revision

Use to Write:	Poetry
Ideas and Concepts to Explore:	font; stanza.
Authors/Works Mentioned:	n/a

Computer technology has made writing-revision almost miraculously easier than it used to be in what now seems like the Stone Age of handwriting and typewriting. Ironically, however, new drafts of things we write are so easy to produce that we sometimes overlook some additional ways in which the computer can help us revise more rigorously. Here is one of those ways.

    Bring an existing draft of a poem up on your monitor. Probably it will be in 10- or 12-point font. "Blow it up" into a huge font—18, 20, 22, 24. Suddenly you will be looking at the poem as if through a magnifying glass; each word will seem massive. Almost automatically, you will find yourself asking, "Is this word really necessary?" or "Can this phrase be tightened?" Also, you'll discover that if, for example, you have a poem in stanzas of four lines, the large font will force lines to spill over, meaning that in order to preserve the four-line stanzas, you'll have to shorten each line by removing words or at least replacing words with shorter ones.

    But wait a minute: Should a low-grade robot be allowed to force a writer to make cuts simply on the basis of font size?! No. But forcing yourself to say, "I don't care if this line *does* spill over—I need every one of those words, and I need those exact words" is a good exercise, a healthy *process* of revision; call it "defending the words." It makes you justify each word; it makes you reexamine every move you've made in the poem; it asks you to have a reason for being loyal to a certain word or phrase.

    Not least of all, magnifying the poem by means of a large font will also generally make you see the poem afresh, whereas even if (or especially if) you've taken the poem through several revisions, you will have seen the text so many times that it becomes a bit of a blur. We tend to memorize our texts.

In sum, then, an aspect of word processing that seems entirely mechanical, graphic, even trivial can be used to achieve a poem that's more linguistically and intellectually challenging.

(H.O.)

(14) **Revising Openers in Prose Genres: Eight Options**

Use to Write:	Short Fiction; Longer Fiction; Creative Nonfiction; Autobiography; Essay
Ideas and Concepts to Explore:	formulaic; personification; riff; voyeurism; writer/reader "contract".
Authors/Works Mentioned:	[each of the eight numbered tactics includes a quotation from a story and identifies the author].

It's obvious how crucial the first sentence, first few sentences, and/or first paragraph of short stories are. "Openers" begin that precarious contract (always subject to immediate cancellation) between the narrative and the reader. Sometimes as we revise, therefore, it's good to focus even more than usual on the story's opener. Here are some "templates," if you will, for opening up narratives. They are substantially revised versions of ones that appeared in *Writer's Digest* (June 1991), pp. 37–39. A list of eight "model" openers may seem a little too cut-and-dried or formulaic, but that's not the purpose; over the years, looking at such models has helped students first to remember they have available to them more than one way to open for the narrative they're working on, and second to analyze "openers" they have already crafted. So these eight narrative tactics are *not* offered as "sure-fire bets" or "quick (and slick) fixes" but as one picture of the *range* of options open to you. You might choose a story you're working on and begin by seeing if only *one* of the options below might work, by improvising upon it, and by seeing what effect it has on the narrative and how the narrative might have to change to accommodate the new opening tactic. Or you might situate the opening sentences of an existing draft among the options. Experiment. (And with some adaptation, some of these tactics may work well with nonfiction writing, too.)

1. Conflict; or "Tell, Don't Show"

    You might call this the "keep it simple" opener: state a conflict or a problem flatly in the first sentence, and as you revise from there, see where the paragraph seems to want to go. This also allows you to ignore, *for the moment,* that "Show, don't tell" advice that seems ubiquitous in writing classes. For example, the first sentence of James Purdy's story, "Cutting Edge," is:

    Mrs. Zeller opposed her son's beard.

Nothing fancy here! Purdy's narrator doesn't "work up" to anything. Sometimes such unadorned bluntness is refreshing—both to you, the writer, and your readers.

2. Character

In "Everything That Rises Must Converge," Flannery O'Connor places her reader inside the mind of the main character, Julian, and also quickly suggests the complex relationship he has with his mother:

> Her doctor had told Julian's mother that she must lose 20 pounds on account of her blood pressure, so on Wednesday nights Julian had to take her downtown on the bus for a reducing class at the Y. . . . Julian did not like to consider all she did for him, but every Wednesday night he braced himself and took her.

The "problems" suggested here aren't as out-in-the-open as the "problem" stated in Purdy's first sentence, but there is a sense in which a variety of pressures are beginning to build. If you've read this story, you know how crucial buses and blood pressure become in the plot (I won't ruin it for those who haven't read the story), so O'Connor's opener is also efficient, economical, in the sense of getting to what is, what will be, crucial as the narrative plays out. Maybe you can revise an opener so that it locates itself "inside" a character or represents one character's view of another.

3. The Daily Double: Conflict and Character

Here's how John Updike's well-known story, "A & P," begins:

> In walks these three girls in nothing but bathing suits.

Hmmm. The "stated problem" isn't as blunt here as it is in Purdy's first sentence, but we know something's up. And we don't get the psychological quicksand suggested by O'Connor. But we get an appealing blend of character and conflict, for there's a strong hint of personality, of a voice rattling off a story, and the action described gives us the sense that we're at least rolling toward a problem, a conflict, a collision of some kind—doesn't it? What do you think? If you have a first-person story going, you might try something breezy and quick like Updike's opener and see how it works.

4. Talk Is Good, Not Just Cheap

E.B. White starts "The Second Tree From the Corner" this way:

> "Ever have any bizarre thoughts?" asked the doctor.
> Mr. Trexler failed to catch the word. "What kind?" he said.

Almost regardless of what they're saying, *two-characters-talking* has a way of jumpstarting a narrative. Often the effect is one of "beginning in midstream" (*in medias res*). Maybe it's that we feel we're listening in, eavesdropping. I don't know for sure. Maybe it's because in virtually every dialogue, every exchange of words, there's the potential of conflict—misunderstanding, disagreement, overreaction. It could be that "buried" several paragraphs into your story there's a dialogue; you could try starting your story *there*. Give yourself and your reader two voices to listen to.

5. Nobody Home, Just Yet

Often when I read stories or novels that begin by deliberately establishing the setting, I get a little bored—because I want to get to the representations of people, characters, the actors in the drama. There are times, though, when description of setting brings its own drama, as the following opener from Ernest Hemingway's "Hills Like White Elephants" does (in my opinion):

> The hills across the valley of the Ebro were long and white. On this side there was no shade and no trees and the station was between two lines of rails in the sun . . . .

For me, the extremity, the severe sparseness of the setting, begins to build a tension of its own here. (For similar reasons, I also liked the opening scenes of the so-called "Spaghetti Westerns" of the late 1960s and early 1970s—many featuring Clint Eastwood, many directed by the Italian, Sergio Leone, and most shot, ironically, on the turf of Hemingway's story, Spain.) And the imagery is striking while not succumbing to the temptation of *personifying* nature; personification often comes off as forcing the drama, as does a gothic description: You know—thunder, wind in big trees, lightning flashing to reveal the outlines of a big ol' house. Try opening with setting description, but be a tad sly about it.

6. Characters On a Landscape

This tactic is another daily double, if you will: It starts fairly conventionally, with characters in the drama, but it views them from a distance, as part of the landscape or setting and creates some subtle suspense. The example I've chosen is from Alice Adams' story, "At The Beach":

> The very old couple, of whom everyone at the beach is so highly aware, seem themselves to notice no one else at all.

The tension here is refreshingly simple, the implicit message being "We watch them but they don't watch us"—a hint of mystery, a hint of voyeurism, drawing us into the narrative. We like to watch people, don't we—to spy a little bit? You might capture that feeling in an opener that shares some elements with Adams'.

7. Desire

Desire is ubiquitous in fiction. Sometimes I think, "What else is fiction but narrative expression of what people want but can't have, what they get but don't want (while they want for something else), and so forth?" So why not "begin with desire?"—as Walter Howerton does in "The Persistence of Memory":

> Sometimes I wish I had gone to Viet Nam . . .

The first person narrator here wants something, yes, but also he wants something complicated, even counter-to-common-sense: to have fought in a war, and not just any war but the Viet Nam war. It's hard *not* to be interested in this expressed desire and the narrative flowing from it.

8. Theme

Especially after decades of literary criticism that has deflated the importance of, even the very concept of, "theme," this opener may seem old-fashioned, belonging to the age of Jane Austen (*Pride and Prejudice* begins, "It is a truth universally known that . . ."). For that very reason, however, it can be a refreshing opener because it gives the reader what the reader may least expect—a kind of thesis statement, which is supposed to belong to the domain of essays, not stories. Surprises are good. The example I've chosen is from the story, "Widow Water," by Frederick Busch:

What to know about pain is how little we do to deserve it, how simple it is to give, how hard to lose.

As you revise, try some of these. Experiment with them. Just as importantly, start your own list of openers you like (or don't like). Take them apart, see how they function, see what narrative moves follow them, improvise, "play riffs." How to *open* a narrative is endlessly fascinating, terribly difficult, charmingly challenging, almost always important as you revise and edit.

(H.O.)

Union Station

Alternative Guided-Writing Scenarios

Multiauthored Texts

 Coauthoring—Some Whys and Wherefores

Use to Write:	n/a [while much discussion is given to poetry, the exercise applies to work in virtually any genre]
Ideas and Concepts to Explore:	collaboration; call-and-response; "chimings"; collage; pastiche; writing "across" texts.
Authors/Works Mentioned:	Basho; Wendy Bishop, excerpts from several works; Andrei Codrescu, "Nostalgia For Everything"; Pamela K. Gordon and Monifa Love, "I Grew Two Voices"; Gary Snyder, "Four Poems For Robin"; Henry David Thoreau, *Walden;* Rex West and Devan Cook, "Patrimony: Patrimony."

Coauthoring breaks down our (false) beliefs that writers always write (best) alone. They don't. They don't have to write alone. There is the immediate example of this book, for instance. Although many sections are authored separately, the book was conceptualized and realized collaboratively. None of us had all the exercises or all the answers (we still don't). We pooled our resources in the interests of diversity, complexity, and encouragement. We also wrote across each other—that is, some of my words have been changed (for the better) by the overall editor; we've all critiqued one another's writing; we've all influenced each other's thinking as we've worked through numerous drafts.

Many of my best writing ideas have been borrowed from my other coauthor(s) who are longtime writing friends. We exchanged these ideas over many years before they were reborn here in my (seemingly singular) voice.

We all benefit from coauthoring, whether we pair and pastiche and weave together our formerly separate words (but can still see the parts, the person, the edges) or whether we collaborate entirely, becoming unable to say what is what, whose is whose piece of writing. Knit together or Cuisinart-ed, there's much to be learned about words and sentences and the ways they deliver up (or don't!) our ideas and messages. Coauthoring lets us learn more, faster, because we're usually articulating writers' decisions as they are negotiated.

So, now, imagine you are hearing this small portion of the transcript of a five minute collaborative poetry audio tape titled "I Grew Two Voices" by Pamela K. Gordon and Monifa Love. The poem is recited over a background of instrumental jazz:

(Voices should follow the notations but only as general parameters. The voices should begin and end together. Call and response and meanderings of the spirit are integral parts of the piece.)

Voice #1	Voice #2
She sits straight-backed in the	jump back sally sally sally
rusty old red and white porch swing	jump back sally sally jump
her long zebra-stripped hair	jump back sally sally sally
brushed into a neat bun	jump back sally sally jump
a bowl of snapbeans in her lap	
creaking back and forth	who is sally?
as the long green tubes pop in half	
Her ancient bronze hands work	Great grandmother
rhythmically	stone-faced and gracious
She looks so good for her 81 years	snapbeans in her lap
"My life has been so fruitful" she tells	daughters at her feet
Her blue and white checked sack dress	
has risen above her knees	Any y'all named sally
exposing the tattered garters	
holding up her stockings	
I wonder what will I be like when I	
become her age?	Little sally walker
	sitting in a saucer
	rise sally rise

This project allowed two poets to pool their strengths. As you look at this transcript you can imagine that surely it is possible that one coauthor did more of the work. Perhaps Pam (or Monifa) wrote it all, and Monifa (or Pam) just stopped by for a few minutes to help to record the product. Perhaps friends who were listening as they recorded suggested alternative readings, chantings, singings? How will I as a writer or teacher of writers ever know? And to what degree does it matter? Authors have often resisted coauthoring because "institutions"—teachers, bosses—have not known how to evaluate who contributed what to a coauthored project. That problem can be solved pretty easily—each author can trace her "ownership" and her learning in a process journal, or write a summary essay reporting on her learning. So I think we're unnaturally suspicious of collaborative writing. Perhaps your first thoughts were "This is strange? How do I read it?" Texts that are unexpected, seldom encountered, or even surprisingly pleasurable can cause such a reaction.

Why don't we see more of this type of work? First, collaborative writing takes different time commitments. Second, since writers have few naturally occurring literary models of collaborative work—novelists are "supposed" to write their own novels, poets their own poems, etc. (though I should point out they have strong models of collaborative performance via rock videos)—they need to be allowed a great deal of experimental space. Equally, writers who would experiment need to train themselves to read and respond to collaborative writing carefully, sensitively, like they read and respond to any other writing.

First, the time issue. Quite simply, it takes a different type of time to participate in a successful collaboration. Collaborative projects will demand better planning and less procrastinating. The smaller the work group—pairs or trios—the easier the work is to schedule and accomplish. The simpler the technology or media—two writers at one computer screen or swapping text over e-mail, or audio tape rather than videotape—the more writers can focus on composing (performing) and revising texts and the less they have to focus on arranging for and mastering the technology.

Learning and work styles come strongly into play for collaborative work. Work with someone you can work with. This is simple advice that is sometimes impossible to put into practice until after you have worked with that other author and find out he or she is incompatible with you. But realize that if you're a procrastinator, being yoked to the detailed scheduler can create untold crises and recriminations. Within real limits, choose as wisely as you can.

Second, the models and reading problem. Experimental work taxes our reading expectations (see "Responding to, Evaluating, and Grading Alternate Style" on the Blue Line of *Metro* for more on this issue) instead of providing quick, reliable matches. When writing experimental collaborative texts, you are asked to—and readily and stylishly do—break conventional text expectations. How do you, your collaborator, and your readers know if/when you've "succeeded?"

If you take the "anything goes" approach to collaborative craft—well, then anything will go—some of it terrible, ill-conceived, and/or downright boring. Teach yourself to read collaborative work and ask appropriate questions. Ask what being coauthored seems to have contributed to this project. Ask what aims the project announces as it opens. Does the text teach you to read it? It probably should, since we all need help navigating the textual universe. And so on. Designing new questions can teach you to have patience and tenacity as a reader of these sometimes demanding works (for instance, the transcript above probably communicates more fully as performance) though this won't be true for all coauthored/collaborative works, like this book, for instance. Foremost, set aside judgment for a while as you name, investigate, and evaluate the convention making and breaking the authors were engaged in.

Coauthoring With Yourself: Autobiographical Collages

- To explore your personal archeology, write a name acrostic poem (this is found on the Blue Line of *Metro,* also) on what your name means to you or on how you were named; next, write an imitation/parody of a writer whose themes or language are important to your life. Or write a self-portrait, compose a text about heirlooms or talismanic objects, write a narrative poem that tells a family or neighborhood story, and so on. That is, do a series of inventions from the Green Line and shape them all toward exploring your own life.

*   Combine sections, portions, fragments from these texts into an autobiographical collage. To do this, consider collage techniques: linear, spatial, and chronological order, listing, genre pastiche, dialog, interrupting narrators, and so on.

In this project, then, you are coauthoring with your own selves, the you of previous times in your life. (To gain a humorous sense of this, you might locate Andrei Codrescu's short "Nostalgia for Everything"). Essentially, you're collaborating with different aspects of your own identity and with your past(s), discovering that you are not mono-vocal and at the same time exploring the boundaries of genres. Here is a section of Sean Carswell's collage:

Depression: I once wrote a poem called "All I Have to Say About Depression":

I close my eyes
and see nothing
I open them
not much better

but that poem was written a long time ago and my record needle was broken.

Breeding: I have three Peter, Paul and Mary albums, and I blame that on my breeding. "Where Have All the Flowers Gone" is one of my favorite songs in spite of myself. I know all four verses to "Home on the Range," and I almost ran away from home several times because of this.

Poetic Evolution: The first group of poems I handed in was during my senior year of high school and I titled it *Assorted Genius by Sean Carswell.* A poem I wrote last week describes me as:

Etherized and I feel
Like I should just join the rest of my poetic
Generation and just write song
Lyrics.

Influences: While reading *Walden,* I decided I should move to the woods and live deliberately, but I should wait until the end of the semester to do it. I felt the ghost of Henry David Thoreau slap me upside the head.

I'd never read any Gary Snyder before this class, but after reading "Four Poems for Robin," I wrote this poem about the time I hitchhiked two hundred miles to see a girl I thought I loved:

Sometimes when   the air is cold enough
and it tickles   my nose enough
to smell like   melancholy the fruit
I think of her   the frozen waterfall

The time I thumbed   two hundred to turn around
the mountains and   the beds of trucks
the sheet rock hanger   the Cherokee reservation
and her mother   telling my future
I wonder why her   mother didn't warn me
but the bed was warm   if the face wasn't
and I guess I mistook   stick-to-itiveness for love.

Start Together and Work Alone (and Come Back Together): Drive Words, Poetry Trading Cards, and Group Poems

- First, list single words that are important to you in a variety of categories—favorite colors, smells, sounds, months, types of weather, etc.—40 to 50 words total (example, flannel, shattered glass, potatoes, collard greens, Texas, October, panty hose, cats, belly or belly button, pool cue, calluses, saliva). You are working to develop an evocative set of primary concrete nouns (mostly nouns although drive words don't have to be limited to nouns).

- Next, review your list and write your most interesting words on a set of ten three-by-five Poetry Trading cards.

- Find several partners and together read each other's cards/words and negotiate a common list which must have some words from each member (example: Pool cue, shattered glass, okra, sandpaper dry, camel hair, nails, thighs, panty hose, bus fumes, liquor store).

- After compiling this list of ten words, each group devises its own composing rules: members can change word tenses, from nouns to verbs or not; in the poems group members write, they must use eight out of ten words, all ten words, etc.

- Groups reconvene to examine four individually authored poems, which still utilize agreed upon drive words. A sample of a draft goes like this:

Reading Detective Fiction into the Night

requires a street,
straight as a **pool cue,**
lined with leaves
and heaps of **shattered glass.**
Here **okra**-shadowed curbs of Saturday night.
Here the pimp in a **camel-hair** double-breasted coat . . . .

(continues, using the rest of the words)

Work Together: Coauthoring Poetry

- Choose a medium for coauthoring—text, audio, video, dance, etc.

- Decide whether to use previous work—matching, weaving, amplifying, annotating—or whether to compose completely new work by writing side-by-side on a set theme, using inventions from the Green Line, and so on.

- Look at "The Narrow Road to Mixing Genres" in Chapter One, The Blue Line; using Basho's work as a backdrop, the exercise includes some possibilities for collaborative writing.
- Read your work to each other, separately, in parts. Maybe even read it aloud together, listen for chimings, overlaps.
- Talk about what you could do. Talk about what you hear. Talk about what's missing. Talk about when you'll meet. Consider individual and coauthoring responsibilities. Make lists. Draft more. Find time for more meetings.

You get the picture—there are no hard and fast rules. You can coauthor at a distance (on the phone, through the mail, over the internet, by FAX) or in person, each handwriting, each computing, taking turns at a computer, passing a pad back and forth. Try as many forms as you can.

For example, Pam was taking poetry writing for the first time; Monifa was an experienced and published poet. Pam first wrote a prose poem for class about her grandmother that did not strike anyone—Pam included—as successful during a class response workshop. She revised the prose poem and she and Monifa used it for a base, Pam refining the imagery as Monifa added African American chants and songs. Together, they produced a piece that highlights their talents.

Here is a portion of a collaborative poem by Rex West and Devan Cook. They achieved entirely different—but I think equally effective—poetic effects. Rex and Devan used no background music and did not overlap their voices when they recorded this poem:

Patrimony: Patrimony

Reader #1	Reader #2
The road slinks, a sheep trail	
dropping between two bare hills	
	covered by sage grass—
	blades bend and rattle
The mine is hidden	
	and the town that went with it.
My father was an engineer.	
I am a writer. I lie.	
	My great-grandfather was a coal miner.
	I am a writer. I lie.
We're all concerned more with	
what works than *why* it works	
	Don't let the facts get
	in the way of the truth.
In his career my father invented new processes	
for producing phosphate;	
he mined mountains, aspen leaves yellowed young,	
fell through still air to creeks fuming black	

from smelter runoff: in snow melt spring floods
washed the bank with water that killed
everything. At the plant, two men died
in thirty seconds from a phosgene leak.

> Words explode, white-hot scraps of poems
> scatter.

My father's leg burned white to the bone;
bandages off, he went back to work
like the others wearing melted skin, welts,
scraps of hair, boots that glowed.
This all disappears when it snows.
Everything buries quietly
But mines are full of holes.

> My great-grandfather said the first steam engine
> pumped water out of a mine
> the first canal was cut to carry ore from Worsley
> to Manchester,
> the first railroad—at Newcastle—took coal from
> pit mouth to river.
> He had a human voice.
> A collier, he said, is a coal miner
> and gets used to being damp.

I like coauthoring because it allows me to pay a different type of attention to my writing. I think much more about issues of influence, authorship and intertextuality—who wrote before me, who writes beside me, and how will my writing be read? And too, I keep an eye out, looking for peers who might be a congenial or challenging collaborative partner because with a coauthor, everything I've done before becomes new, everything I've tried, can (and probably should) be tried again.

(W.B.)

2   **Dream Wandering: Writing with a Group**

Use to Write:	n/a [the exercise concerns surrealistic processes and techniques applicable to a range of genres]
Ideas and Concepts to Explore:	*des rives*; nodes of energy; surrealism.
Authors/Works Mentioned:	Basho, *The Narrow Road To the Far North*; Herman Melville; Jan Ramjerdi.

It is not down on any map; true places never are.
(Queequeg's island, Moby Dick)

—*Herman Melville*

For this exercise we are indebted to writer Jan Ramjerdi. Frustrated with the failure of a class to relate to one of her favorite books, Basho's *Narrow Road to the Far North,* Ramjerdi imagined a contemporary, student-centered version of the 1950's French Situationalist's "mapping" activity, known as a *"des rives." "Rives"* translates as "rivers," and a *"des rives"* is known, rather crudely, as "a wandering." But in fact *"rives"* is very close to *"reves,"* which means "dreams," just as in English "wander" is very close to "wonder."

In this exercise, we wander, like a river, dreaming, in a state of wonder.

In the 50's, in Paris, groups of artists and writers would wander through the city, dreaming it out the tips of their fingers, in paintings, poems, collages, texts, sketches—any and all kinds of artistic responses to the places they saw and were in. Their intent was to "map" the city, but with a difference, to map the heart of it, which could not be mapped.

Basho wandered, too, looking closely at the world.

In Los Angeles, Des Moines, or Tallahassee, we have, many of us, gotten out of the habit of looking. Maybe this is because America has become so homogenized that Minneapolis' shopping malls are indistinguishable from Albuquerque's, and a strip is a strip is the same fast food joints, no matter if it's in Montana, Mississippi or Rhode Island. But the commercial landscape of this country hardly scratches the surface of our worlds, and writers everywhere must learn to look closely and pay strict attention.

Ramjerdi sent her students out on a *"des rives."* She told them to wander for at least four hours, not talking, just writing and drawing, collecting, collaging—mapping the path of their wander. They were to record not just the world they saw, but the world they sensed and felt and remembered and dreamed—the unmappable true heart of things. When they wanted to know how they'd be graded, she told them if they wandered off completely and were never heard from again, they would all get "A's." From that time on, it is said that her students wrote like angels.

Writing like an angel depends, in some important respects, on cutting loose from familiar moorings, learning to drift beyond the pull of both gravity and intent. Wandering through your world in the company of others, not talking, just recording and listening and gathering, can help you do that.

Begin by setting group rules for your *des rives.* Think about the boundaries within which you will agree to wander, and why. Set a time limit. Decide whether talking will be allowed, and what kind. You may want to share your work as you go. Most importantly, you must decide how you choose where to stop, and for how long. Typically, this is the prerogative of any member in the group. The Situationalists themselves stopped at what they called "nodes of energy," places or points in the wandering that called out for attention, for recording, for something to be made at that exact spot. In your *des rives,* look for such "nodes of energy," stop and make something, whatever you choose. Then proceed to the next such spot.

The product of this collaborative wandering will be an assemblage of some kind. In our own classes, *des rives* have included text-inscribed mobiles and found-art sculptures, multidimensional verbal collages, interwoven written texts, virtual hypertexts constructed on walls, a totem pole, performance, and more.

What you make is up to you. In this exercise, the important thing is your process, how you renegotiate and reenvision your world, what grows out of it. You're not alone on this journey, and what you're looking for, you have never really seen. The point is to look and listen, then map what cannot be mapped—the true place where you are.

(K.H.)

▶ ③ Public Poetry

Use to Write:	Poetry Performance Piece; Drama
Ideas and Concepts to Explore:	poetry slam.
Authors/Works Mentioned:	Allen Ginsberg; Homer, *Illiad*; Robert Lowell.

In virtually all cultures, written poetry can be traced back to oral poetry—songs, tales passed on in an oral tradition (Homer's *Illiad* is a good example), chants, spoken accompaniments to dance, creation myths, prophecies, curses, incantations. These forms of oral poetry were—by definition and necessity—public: situated right in the middle of one kind of community or another.

Once songs became texts (ballads are a good example), once poetry became primarily a written-down art form and then a printed-up art form, a gap of varying size developed between truly public poetry of oral traditions and poetry-on-the-page. Nowadays, for instance, it is quite possible for a poet to write down a poem, never speak it out loud (though it is true most poets speak their drafts), and have it published in a small magazine that only a handful of people will read—silently, to themselves. In such a case, the poem is certainly made public (published), but the public is small and fragmented, and there is an almost private, certainly *unspoken* aspect to the process.

It's often helpful to our writing, and to ourselves as writers, to experience something more like the public (oral) poetry of old. Poet Robert Lowell was already experienced, widely published, and acclaimed when he traveled to the West Coast of the U.S. and attended readings by the so-called Beat poets in the late 1950s and early 1960s; the Beats are often credited with getting poetry back on stage, as it were, making it more of a community art form. Lowell by no means embraced the Beats' way of writing or their way of looking at the world, but he later credited the experience with loosening up his style, opening up more possibilities for using casual speech rhythms in his verse, and allowing him to improvise as he gave readings. The point is that while Lowell remained essentially the same poet and was by no means the sort of performer Allen Ginsberg was, the experience of "oral poetry" helped him in general.

To some extent, poetry classes give us some experience with performing our poetry, hearing ourselves read it out loud, hearing others read it, hearing how others read their poetry, and so forth. But poetry classes tend to be an odd mixture of the public and the private, are still enclosed, in a way; so it's good to seek other more truly public opportunities, including the following:

1. Get some fellow poets together and give a reading on a campus radio station—live, preferably; recorded, if that's more practical or, at first, less scary. Notice how you'll look at your work differently and select poems with a different sort of audience and presentation in mind. Tape the reading. Yes, you might be mortified by how you sound, but you'll also hear your poetry as you've never heard it before; build on strengths, learn from weaknesses of presentation.

2. Go to a poetry reading—on campus, at a bookstore. They're usually free, so there's that. Review it—privately or for a newspaper. Go to a few more. Start determining what kind of poetry-reading style you like. Write a poem about one of the readings.

3. Go to a "poetry slam," a more juiced-up, competitive version of a reading. Slams take place now in just about every large or medium-sized city and sometimes in towns, too. After you go to several, or maybe after going only to one, you might find yourself getting up there, experiencing the adrenaline rush, adapting your work to the audience, including the audience in ad-lib compositions. Even if you don't choose to participate, you can note what sort of poetry is read, how it's adapted, what styles of reading are used, what styles you prefer, what you do and don't like about the slam-poetry, what the audience is like, in what ways the experience is different from reading poetry on the page. Write a poem about a poetry slam.

4. Write or cowrite some short poems (using washable chalk, please) on public sidewalks, such as those on a campus. True, this is still an example of print culture, not oral culture, but it's still public. See what kind of reaction you get. Have people read the poems out loud. Ask them what they think. Invite them to write their own or cowrite poems with you. Maybe videotape the whole thing, maybe make it a class project.

Through it all, see how you can let experiences of public poetry influence your poetry-on-the-page in ways large and small, regardless of whether you're the "performing" type or not.

(H.O.)

4▷ Video Poem: Let Each Medium Teach The Other

Use to Write:	Video Poem; Screenplay; Drama; Multimedia Performance Piece
Ideas and Concepts to Explore:	authorship/"author-ity"; Imagism; Modernism; realism; surrealism.
Authors/Works Mentioned:	William Carlos Williams.

Modernist, early twentieth-century poets still have enormous influence on how we write poetry today. Their insistence on close observation and imagery has had a particularly lasting effect, William Carlos Williams being one of the primary advocates for the ethos, "no ideas but in things," and for having our poetry honor, as it were, those aspects of experience that may not immediately seem significant: red wheelbarrows, bits of glass, rows of suburban houses, cold plums pilfered from the refrigerator. One offshoot of so–called "imagism" was an attempt to make poetry cinematic, to make it appeal to the eye in ways analogous to the appeal of cinema.

Now, of course, we are in an age of The Video, when our every waking moment seems to be deluged with a flood of video images. Poets and other people who work with the written word, therefore, can feel endangered in this world of "pure" visual imagery.

Maybe one rationale behind making a video poem is "If you can't beat 'em, join 'em." Less fatalistically, however, we might say that working with video can teach us to make better written art. Or we could say that our choice is not necessarily EITHER video OR the written word. Put another way, maybe poets and other written-word types can influence the way video is used, and maybe numerous kinds of hybrid forms are possible.

On your own or with a group, make a video poem. Define "video poem" however *you* like. How do you start? Well, borrowing a video camera (camcorder?) and a blank tape is a good beginning. Otherwise, there are as many ways to begin a video poem as there are to begin a written poem. You could just start shooting footage. Or you could brainstorm ideas. You could use your own poetry as a kind of script.

One poetry class I had met in a room in a sports complex called The Fieldhouse. When the class decided to make a video poem, it began close to home, as it were; it began with the odd physical circumstance in which we found ourselves. The students started with the title "Fieldhouse" and shot some footage in the weird little classroom, which was adjacent to a basketball court. Then they recorded each other reading poems out on the court; in the background, someone zoomed by on a skateboard on that polished, well-lit floor. Someone else shot an imaginary freethrow. Someone else declaimed a poem from the bleachers.

Did much of the footage seem chaotic, pointless, and silly? Of course. But it was an exploratory draft—on tape, as opposed to on a computer monitor or on a page. Gradually, as the class shot more footage and started editing and splicing, adding music, and mixing video technology with computer technology, patterns began to emerge; a coherent draft took shape. Because this was a collaborative project, arguments also ensued about the direction in which to take the video poem. Ensemble art can be counted upon to create both enormous energy and vivid personality conflicts. Along the way, we discovered other things:

1. Everyone loves to appear on video. No one seems immune from being starstruck.

2. Making the video made us look at poetic technique from different instructive angles: elements such as rhythm, pacing, symbol, repetition, contrast, surrealism, realism.

3. Everyone had to learn to be better speakers, better readers of their own work (in instances when they read their work for the camera). If nothing else had come of the project, this in itself was a healthy result.

4. As with poetry, discovery is almost everything. We discovered what we wanted to "say" by just shooting some footage. Chaos led to a plan.

5. What happens to "authorship" in the age of the video? When we write a poem all by ourselves, we find it easier to claim that we are the god of the poem, that we are the sole creator (even though we're working with words shared by millions of other people, even though we're enormously influenced by what we've read, etc.). But who's the creator of a video poem? The person on camera? The person operating the camera? The person with an idea about editing or music or graphics? All of the above. Illusions about sole creatorship are harder to maintain. For this class, making the video poem was a concrete exploration of "authorship" and "author-ity," of letting go of control, of true collaboration, of ego-management. In the end, we came up with a presentable, often hilarious, occasionally fascinating, sometimes original "product"; but the real benefits came from the process itself.

So get a camera and a blank tape and start to "write" a video poem.

(H.O.)

Experimental Forms and Less Familiar Modes

Writing from Your Autobiography Box

5	
Use to Write:	n/a [the exercise may lead to work in virtually any genre]
Ideas and Concepts to Explore:	assemblage; "combinatorial logic".
Authors/Works Mentioned:	Italo Calvino; artist Lisa Bloomfield is also mentioned.

. . . And then there are boxes, which contain things, or hold them together.

In the Japanese culture, the gift box is as important as the gift. Covered in elegant papers, cut and folded according to a complex origami logic, the box is itself an external expression of gratitude, love, celebration, respect.

When you are young and on the move, you scrounge boxes at the grocery or the local liquor mart. You crush and recycle the wine bottle inserts and cram your books and other personal belonging where they were. Much later in life, you may purchase any boxes you need, or use the ones the moving company provides.

Maybe you keep jewelry in a hinged rattan basket, Little League game balls in a shoebox, fluorescent rocks in a cardboard file with a peephole, glowing other-worldy beneath a UV lamp. Outside the box they are common and dull.

Artist Lisa Bloomfield uses autobiography boxes in her photography classes. There is a writing practice that turns the box itself into a 3-D story.

This exercise is not about the story—or the poem—that the box is, but about the writing that grows out of the box, which you will assemble over time.

For this exercise, become a collector of things to keep in your box. You alone will know them, what belongs, what defines you, what has energy and resonates for you: the perfect tiny conch shell you found on a fogbound island one summer in Maine, a mottled gray-green Western seagull chick's feather, one shard of Mimbres pottery, a tiny rusted tin saltshaker from a turn-of-the-century mining camp dump, baby hair, a scrap of green silk, some skin of a grapefruit, raw umber paint, dried leaves, lava, a rock like the mountains of Montana. Ticket stubs, old shoelaces, marbles, pressed butterflies, a lipstick, some thread and sequins, sports medals, ribbons. You may want to include old things you have saved and that have great sentimental value—your baby's hospital bracelet, your army induction notice; or you may want to collect things, instead, at ran-dom, a round ocher-yellow pebble, cactus spines, sweet-smelling soap.

Some care, too, should go into the selection of the box. A Nike shoebox is big-ger than the box your graduation watch came in, but either might do for this exer-cise. You may wish to build your box out of paper, cardboard, wood, scraps of fabric. Remember that the outside of the box is also space, and that each surface is like an artist's canvas.

Italo Calvino has said that writing is a process of "combinatorial play" (see "The Possibility of Play," later in this section) in which the writer tosses words together until they make that spark that takes the writer down into the space where writing happens. In your box, you toss objects together just to see what will happen.

To begin:

Imagine your box as a private space for writing into which you can slip and work your way, at odd angles, into memory and language.

Principle:

A person never simply speaks; there has to be a context in which that person feels privileged to speak. Here you create that context.

Directions:

1. Open your box in front of you and write without stopping for half an hour. Let yourself be guided not only by the objects you've collected, but also by the space itself, a container for yourself and for the words that spark and play there, your own language.

2. Same as above, only multidimensional. Include objects from your box in your text, whatever you can glue on, weave into, or somehow reassemble. Write around the objects of your box. Write on your box.

3. Choose a writing partner, exchange boxes, and write yourself into this new and unfamiliar space.

4. Choose a writing partner, combine the contents of both boxes in yet another box, and write off the collaborative box.

5. Choose a writing partner and share objects from your boxes. Draw at random, or give as gifts. Proceed as above.

6. Form a writing group with several members. Spread out the contents of everyone's box and write a seamless narrative that combines all that you see before you into one seamless narrative.

7. Form a writing group and make a text that weaves together elements from everyone's box. This is not a seamless, but a braided text. Each person's box narrative remains discrete within it.

8. A "class monitor," eyes closed, takes something out of everyone's box. Write around the missing object, the empty space it leaves.

9. Pass boxes randomly around the room until a monitor cries *stop*. Study what's before you, write off that. Then pass again, stop, and write.

10. Construct a class sculpture of the contents of everyone's box and write.

This exercise can be repeated many times, and in any combination of the above. Pay attention, in it, to how fluid are the lines of your own life. Though you begin with an autobiographical assemblage, as you alter and reassemble its essential parts and share them with others, the elements of your own life in writing will shift and change.

The memory of your first high-heeled shoes—red, with two-inch spikes—for example, may combine with someone else's of the arc of her first childhood hand-spring. One person's lilac tree may be joined to another's twelve home-run baseball season.

Maybe this will help you help "let go" a little of your single sense of how things have to be. What butts up against something else—in your writing as well as your box—may surprise you. What you learn is that in writing, you own, paradoxically, nothing and everything.

This may help you turn the paradox to your advantage.

Variation:

Finish your box and first writing at home, then bring the box to class in a paper bag. Have your teacher mix the bags up and then take out the boxes, arranging them where everyone can see them. Read your texts out loud. See if the class can figure out which text goes with which box.

Or, pass your texts around, no names on them. Read them at random, out loud. See if the class can figure out which text goes with which box? Which writer?

(K.H.)

Parodies—Pushing Imitation to the Edge

Use to Write:	n/a [the exercise may be applied to parodies in virtually any genre]
Ideas and Concepts to Explore:	imitation; nuance; parody.
Authors/Works Mentioned:	Will Baker, "End Note" (a parody of William Carlos Williams' "This Is Just To Say"); Raymond Carver; Emily Dickinson; T. S. Eliot, *The Waste Land;* Robert Frost, "Stopping By Woods On A Snowy Evening"; Ernest Hemingway; X. J. Kennedy; Christopher Marlowe, "The Passionate Shepherd to his Love"; Flannery O'Conner, "A Good Man Is Hard To Find"; Sir Walter Raleigh, "The Nymh's Reply To The Shepherd" (parody of Marlowe's poem); Leo Tolstoy; Eudora Welty [a "works cited" also appears at the end of the exercise and includes titles of anthologies of parodies].

Parody can instantly place you into the intricate decision-making world of writers with the added benefit that this form of imitation is enjoyable. It asks us to play, to push, to observe nuance, to uncover irony, to understand decisions the "serious" writer made, only now we rediscover their meanings by putting tongue-in-cheek and putting their words our way.

To parody Robert Frost, for instance, you have to delve to the core of "Frostness." You cannot simply analyze "Stopping By the Woods on a Snowy Evening" mechanically, checking off theme, symbols, form (stanza, line, and meter) and then leave Frost behind as you go on to lunch or to Calculus. To write a parody of Frost (or any other writer), you must engage fully with the writer to learn for yourself how Frost achieved his effects and chose his directions. You mine his obsessions (and we all know obsessions can quickly become inverted into humorous commentary). By actively parodying him, you live with Frost and his concerns for a while. How, you must ask, does he develop his signature tone, use his landscape, set his mood? These are not easy questions and in one sense, the surest way to approach answers is to write the parody.

Some Ideas About, Directions For, and 2nd Thoughts on Writing Parodies

I've learned that it's easiest to write a parody about a text you have strong feelings about. However, strong negative feelings will sometimes lead to heavy-handed or simplistic satire. Making fun of a writer in lieu of understanding him does not seem to lead to greater understanding for writers or for readers. X. J. Kennedy reminds us of the pitfalls of simplistic parody:

Rather than merely flinging abuse at another poet, the wise parodist imitates with understanding—perhaps with sympathy. The many crude parodies of T.S. Eliot's difficult poem *The Waste Land* show parodists mocking what they cannot fathom, with the result that, instead of illuminating the original, they belittle it (and themselves). Good parodists have an ear for the sounds and rhythms of their originals. . . . (636)

To develop such an ear, you need to read more than a single poem or prose passage to come to an implicit and then an explicit understanding of a writer's craft.

Freewriting, brainstorming, and nonwriting percolation time can help you get going. Directed freewriting after reading a large selection of the writer can help you analyze the author's work informally.

Next, in a brainstorming session, list topics or moments that could be approached in a Frostian or Plathian manner (or in the manner of another author you choose). In the two short samples below, writers seemed decided to undertake political commentary and modernizations. They turned locomotive to airplane and horse and buggy to a car.

Freewrites and brainstorming for parody can be augmented by reading classic examples of poem and parody/responses like Christopher Marlow's "The Passionate Shepherd to his Love" and Sir Walter Raleigh's "The Nymph's Reply to the Shepherd" to distinguish the tradition of poetic imitation.

To parody, you can focus on one poem in particular for imitation (focused parody), which will require close analysis of the poem, beyond tone and theme, as you study technical devices (line, meter, imagery, metaphor). Or you can decide to write an overall parody of the poet (general parody), which works to capture the poet's representative tone, themes, form, and topics. When you do this with prose, you'll be rewriting Flannery O'Conner's "A Good Man Is Hard to Find" in a contemporary setting but keeping the same number and types of characters, the same plot, length, tone, and so on—focused parody—or for general parody, you'll write your own life story in Hemingway's short-sentenced, staccato, guy to guy voice). First time writers of parody often choose focused imitation while advanced practitioners seem to move toward general imitation.

After freewriting and brainstorming, I suggest that you percolate—that you wait. Donald Murray claims that sometimes *not writing* is a powerful heuristic and not the writer's block we too easily associate it with. I think you benefit greatly from this waiting, from playing in your head with lines, approaches, attitudes. Write several first lines and then rewrite them; take a walk and daydream in your favorite place, and so on, before you sit down to a full drafting session. In this way, you collect notes, lines, scraps, rhythms. Sometimes useful: memorize all or part of a poem or a prose passage you intend to parody and deliver it aloud to the snow and trees on a morning walk.

Finally, you learn a lot about parody by writing about the process of parody—this act of imitation at the humorous edge of another's domain. So, when you're done, write a one-page process summary. What did you do and what did you learn?

Here is a parody from a student in a college level writing-with-literature class (readers benefit from parody as much as writers do) followed by the poem the parodist imitated:

Parody of Emily Dickinson

I like to see it drink the air—
And push the clouds away—
And land to feed itself at tanks—
And then—prodigious leap

Above a pile of mountains
And supercilious peer
At Trees—stretched below the clouds

[parodist is changing Dickinson's locomotive to an airplane]

(original)

I like to see it lap the Miles—
And lick the Valleys up—
And stop to feed itself at Tanks—
And then—prodigious step

Around a pile of mountains—
And supercilious peer
In Shanties—by the sides of Roads—

And here is a parody of a poem by a writing friend of mine, again followed by the very well-known poem he parodied:

End Note
Apologies to WC Williams

The refrigerator
   you thought would be
under this note
   is gone.
So is the CD player
and the rugs, my skis
and the guitar
all the interesting books
and the beanbag chair.
   They're in the trailer
behind the van, which
   is also of course now
leaving the state
   with me.

And oh yes what was left in the checking account
   forgive me but
that was so sweet
   so cool.

                       —Will Baker

This Is Just to Say

I have eaten
the plums
that were in
the icebox

and which
you were probably
saving
for breakfast

Forgive me
they were delicious
so sweet
and so cold

                 —William Carlos Williams

No, parodies usually do not result in great poems, though often they provide great humorous pleasure, the kind I take in Will Baker's poem. And the first time you write one, you may—as in the first sample—feel most comfortable sticking closely to the original, a little like taking a dance lesson from Fred Astaire but because it's a parody—an imitation for learning undertaken in fun—you can laugh if you don't quite get the steps or the rhythm right. You don't have to be Ginger Rodgers, this time. But the careful imitation of sounds and attention to line turns in parodies actually do broaden your writing repertoire, and for some writers (Dave Barry, for example, parodies just about everything he gets his hand on; and, more classically, *West Side Story* parodies *Romeo and Juliet*) parody eventually becomes a favored form. Besides, this stuff isn't really as easy to write as it seems. But somebody's gotta do it. Try a parody.

                                               (W.B.)

Works Cited

Kennedy, X. J. *Literature: An Introduction to Fiction, Poetry, and Drama*. 3rd. ed. Boston: Little, Brown 1983.

Murray, Donald M. "The Essential Delay: When Writer's Block Isn't." In Mike Rose (Ed.), *When a Writer Can't Write* (pp.219–226). New York: Guilford Press, 1985.

Note: You might also track down *The Brand-X Anthology of Poetry—Burnt Norton Edition: A Parody Anthology,* ed. by William Zaranka. Cambridge, Mass.: Apple-Wood Books, 1981. More recent is *Very Bad Poetry* ed. by Kathryn Petras and Ross

Petras, New York: Random, 1997. Less recent, but especially appealing to anyone reading or writing literary criticism or "literature papers," is *The Overwrought Urn: A Potpourri of Parodies of Critics Who Triiumphantly Present The Real Meaning of Authors from Jane Austen to J.D. Salinger.* ed. by Charles Kaplan. New York: Pegasus, 1970.

⑦ Palimpsest: Writing "Over" the Forbidden Story

Use to Write:	n/a [the exercise involves work that deliberately blurs lines between and among several genres]
Ideas and Concepts to Explore:	"faction"; imperatives; inscription; "problem of material"; prohibitions.
Authors/Works Mentioned:	Michel Foucault; David Jones; Grace Paley, "A Conversation With My Father."

Our making is dependent on a remembering of some sort. It may be only the remembering of a personal emotion of last Monday-week in the tranquility of next Friday fortnight. But a "deed" has entered history, in this case our private history, and is therefore valid as matter for our (writing). To become a making or poesis, *then, the deed must be shown forth as a "thing;" some abstract quality must cause it to have "being" or presence. And it must be offered "not merely utile, but with significant intent;" that is to say a "re-presenting," a "showing again under other forms," an "effective recalling" of the deed must be intended.*

—David Jones

I would have preferred to be enveloped in words, borne way beyond all possible beginnings. At the moment of speaking, I would like to have perceived a nameless voice, long preceding me, leaving me merely to enmesh myself in it, taking up its cadence, and to lodge myself, when no one was looking, in its interstices as if it had paused an instant, in suspense, to beckon to me. There would have been no beginnings: instead, speech would proceed from me, while I stood in its path—a slender gap—the point of its possible disappearance.

—Michel Foucault

In writing, brother—since you ask—we are more and more obliged to act the part of the writer and, by falling out of character, to pull off our masks, to let our authentic self shimmer through, between the lines which follow the social code, whether we want to or not. We are mostly blind to this process. A day like this, paradoxical in its repercussions, forces us, forces me to make the personal public, to overcome reluctance.

—Christa Wolf

This is a multipart exercise designed to help explore a variety of questions raised by the hypothetical genre, "faction." Neither fiction, nor nonfiction, faction combines elements of both. Proceeding from the old creative writing cliche to "write what you know," faction demands that we foreground the problem of material by asking ourselves not only what we know, but also how we know it. *Is it "true?"* is one question. An entirely different one is, *how can we tell?* For in several important respects, any distinction we make between what we believe to be true and what we assume we make up is arbitrary and unstable, and raises critical questions about the genres that divide "fact" from "fiction."

Take, for an example, the argument your mother had one fine spring evening with your sister about your sister's pierced eyebrows and nose. In your memory of this evening, the light was sweet and limpid as your mother screamed names at your sister, including both "slut" and "whore." Your mother says your sister threw a hairbrush at her. And your sister swears your mother yanked her nosering until it drew blood.

Whose version of this story is "true?" How will you ever know?

For many writers, this "problem of material" is compounded by what might be called the paradox of family—its prohibitions and imperatives—as a source for writing. While novice writers often privilege the concept of "invention" over "inscription"—writing what you "make up" over what "really happened"—experienced writers know that we really *know* (as in "write what you know") is often grounded in some element of "reality" or "truth." Simultaneously, the most powerful material often carries with it the most inhibiting proscriptions. For what is it you really *know,* if not your own family story (read *family* as a metaphor for whatever is forbidden)? And how can you possibly tell it, for won't they all want to read it?

This is a four-part assignment:

To begin, identify a story you have long wanted to write, something that may really have happened and about which you feel strongly, but which you have never been able to write. Think of this story as your "forbidden story"—the story you're "refusing to write." Maybe it's too personal, maybe your mother will be embarrassed by it, maybe you're not "good" enough to do it justice. For whatever reasons, you have kept it to yourself. Now is the time to bring it out.

Consider the Grace Paley story, "A Conversation with My Father" (see anthology), in which a dying father asks his writer-daughter to write an old-fashioned story, sad enough to break your heart. His strongest desire is that she should learn, before he dies, to look tragedy in the face. But she, willy-nilly, writes three parodying drafts of a story that is not at all old-fashioned and persists in irony and hope. They love each other fiercely, this father and daughter, and in the course of their "conversation" we are ourselves forced to look tragedy in the face. The father's heart is wearing out, and because this is what the daughter cannot bear to see, she instead writes a story of refusing to face it—an old-fashioned story sad enough to break your heart.

Your "forbidden" story need not be anything dark or dramatic. Often we may avoid certain stories because they seem sentimental, unimportant or boring. Whatever your reticence or hesitation, this assignment asks you to find a way to write what you have not been able to write by writing over it many times.

1. Decide on your story.

    You may know right away what story you'll choose, or you may have to think about it for awhile. You will be spending some time with this material, so pick something you really do care about. Think about your story.

    Now write it. In this part of the exercise, just write the facts—who said what, and what happened, and why this haunts you and what makes the story both difficult and important for you, what compels and confounds you in it. Write down every detail. Tell it all. (You don't have to show this story to anyone if you don't want to.)

2. Now, write your story as if it were fiction. Imagine you invented the whole thing. Construct a little triangle—rising action, climax, denouement. Tell your story around it, but feel free to embellish with all the lies and inventions you want.

3. Write the story of how you wrote the story, your feelings, your discoveries, your fears, your archaeological dig, as it were, into this story you are writing.

    Here you may want to construct yourself as a self-reflexive narrator, even locating yourself within the framework of this assignment. Or write it journal-fashion in your unmediated voice. Or tell it as if it had happened to someone else. However you find to do this part of the story, reflect directly on your process—what it has felt like to bring your story out, how it is different in the first part and the second, where you think this may be taking you. Turn this story into a story.

4. Make a text that combines parts of all three of your prior texts.

(K.H.)

The Possibility of Play and the Play of Possibilities: Trying Writing Games

8

Use to Write:	n/a [the exercise applies to work in virtually any genre]
Ideas and Concepts to Explore:	"combinatorial play"; hermeneutic; proairetic; semic; symbolic.
Authors/Works Mentioned:	Roland Barthes; Italo Calvino; James Joyce; Carl Jung.

It is the childish delight at combinatorial play that induces the painter to try out patterns of lines and colors and the poet to attempt combinations of words. At a certain stage something clicks, and one of the combinations obtained by its own mechanisms, independently of any search for meaning or effect on some other level, takes on an unexpected sense

*or produces an unforeseen effect that consciousness could not have
achieved intentionally.*

—*Italo Calvino*

For the purposes of this exercise, we will take the metaphor of play in writing
literally.

Consider Calvino's description of "combinatorial play" above.

Once psychoanalyst Karl Jung was treating writer James Joyces' daughter for serious mental illness. As he described the affliction to Joyce, Jung used a diving metaphor.
Unable to see the problem, Joyce said, "That's just what I do when I write."

"The only difference is," Jung replied, "you're diving, she's drowning."

An open spirit of free play may enable us to dive in our writing without drowning. Play is being playful with your word choice or your syntax. It is sending your
characters off to the zoo just to see what they will do there, what will happen. It is
being willing to try one word (or image, or sound, or idea, or memory, or true fact,
or name, or point of argument, or credo, or hypothesis, or dance step, or figure) in
place of another out of curiosity, to see what it will be like, the sound and the shape
and the rhythm and the meaning of it. Play is being willing not to know. Play is risk
and whim and absolute conviction. Play is both/and, never either/or. Play is your
tongue on the roof of your mouth, trilling. Play is when your chest meets (smack)
the soccer ball.

You may grab words randomly from here or there just to see what will happen
when you put combustibility next to green, fluteplayer alongside flood, gaggle with
over–the–top. We know writers who work with all their best-loved books open
before them, looking for sentences, or passages, or collisions or juxtapositions that
may set off writing. In Calvino's concept of play, some spark occurs that takes the
writer down to where writing can take place.

And we can do this without drowning because we can play.

This exercise asks you to take the concept of play as far as you can to a game of
writing. Begin with paper and pen, maybe some dice, your own ingenuity and a
lively sense of fun.

Refer, for example, in Chapter Three—The Orange Line, to "Using Delay as an
Organizing Principle," and Roland Barthes' concept of narrative codes: *proairetic*
(plot, what happens), *semic* (character, who it happens to), *cultural reference* (Coke
bottles and McDonald's franchises and libraries and such), *symbolic* (what we recognize as literary language, tropes and so on), and *hermeneutic* (enigma). How
could you use codes in a game of writing played with dice?

One way might be to make a set of code cards. You roll seven on the dice. The
dealer deals through the deck, handing you the seventh card. You get *semic* code, so
you start up a character, a thin woman with a goiter on her neck.

Now it's the next player's turn.

Use a timer. Set a limit, one to three minutes. Get your story rolling. Write fast.

Let's say the next player draws the hermeneutic code. This woman with her
goiter has something hidden in her hand, and she is trying to give it to a little boy,
but the little boy keeps shaking his head. He looks afraid of the woman.

Next player. New turn. Culture-reference code: he kicks his new white Nikes over and over into the dirt, scuffing them, but not looking up.

Roll eleven, lose your turn. Roll three, you have to take something out of your story. Roll doubles, draw get two cards. Make your own rules and see what they write.

Make another set of cards using units of narrative temporality (see Chapter Three—The Orange Line, "Telling Time: Order," "Telling Time: Frequency," "Telling Time: Duration"). Make some for aspects of focalization (see Chapter Three—The Orange Line, "Turning the Lens: Framing Narrative Perspective.").

Invent a set of rules based on trading cards.

Make some random cards with lines of actual text you will have to use if you draw them: *the blue-eyed stranger with the jagged limp .... "You think so?" he said, with a sneer. At that time, I had no way of knowing ....*

Maybe make a board to play along. Take an old *Chutes and Ladders* or *Candyland* or *Risk* and fill in the template with writing prompts.

The game is over when you win the card marked *conclusion* or *the end*.

For poets, use poetic terms or writing prompts. The play's the same, just a different set of cards.

Or mix two decks and see what happens when the lines between your genres blur and you have to hold them together.

Nonfiction with your fiction?

These are just suggestions. Your exercise is to invent your own game of writing, as elaborate or simple as you want. That's the first part.

The second is, you play the game. You roll the dice. You write.

Exchange games with another group and play the game someone else invented. Still, you write. Do you want to play again?

Note:

Any game you invent may be played either collaboratively or individually. In the first instance, you work together to "write" a single story or poem. In the second, you work on your own text. Whoever writes the "best" text wins.

(Who decides?)

(K.H.)

Multimedia, Cross-Cultural Writing

Use to Write:	n/a [the exercise may lead to work in virtually any genre]
Ideas and Concepts to Explore:	cross-cultural; Eskimo; Yupik.
Authors/Works Mentioned:	Wendy Bishop, "Cross-Cultural Genres"; Carolyn Kremers.

I borrow this idea, with thanks, from another writing teacher, Carolyn Kremers, who developed it for a class on teaching. To complete this exercise, you need to do as Carolyn did, collect materials on another culture. Some of you grew up within two or more cultures, some of you traveled to other cultures, some of you lived with military parents stationed overseas or overland, and some of you have just always been curious about another culture or felt an affinity for another culture—maybe because some of your ancestors came from that faraway place.

To give us insights into Eskimo culture, Carolyn—who had taught in the Yupik village of Tununuk—shared slides and an audiotape of a village elder telling a story in the Yupik language. And we, listeners, all responded to what we saw and heard in our writing journals. Then she passed around photo books about Eskimo cultures, and an Eskimo language ABC book. Finally, she gave us a list of cultural stereotypes—that worked in both directions, those Anglos held about Eskimos and Eskimos about Anglos. We all wrote some more. If it had been possible, she might have brought artifacts (clothing, carvings, and so on) or food (moose stew, Eskimo ice cream). What is important in this exercise is that writers have stimulation from multiple media sources. For your presentation, you can find recordings at the library of the culture's music, or perhaps folktales. You can prepare foods to bring to share with writers. You can do research on the World Wide Web—talking to individuals in that culture, reading their home pages, "visiting" their countries in this manner. You can collect photos (if you've been there) or guide books (if you hope to go there) and so on.

Here's a prose poem that resulted from being immersed in Carolyn's love for Yupik speakers and Eskimo culture. You may find yourself writing prose or poetry in response, wanting to collect more photos, do more research, or to plan a time to visit that culture.

Cross-Cultural Genres

Here is an Eskimo ABC book. Here is Tununuk graveyard, filled with snow, blown in shapes of animals moving just beneath the cold skin. Picket fence pierces like spearheads, herds life toward an orthodox cross.

Houses in a white on white landscape sit as square ships, antennae pointed toward outer space which doesn't exist in a land where "they deny planning." The universe exists, yet an elder's narrative seems, unfairly, a mouthful of glottal stops, remolding my conception of story—plot, tension, dramatic moment—I drift and slip into another meaning system with Adam Fisher, nasal laugh and nasal laugh and nasal laugh.

We have no real patience for stories. We who "always talk about what's going to happen later" never stop to examine what is. She's young—just started having periods. Shimmies skinny slim hips, squeezes them into comfortable straight Wranglers, walks different but like her older brother, calls electricity to the ends of crackling black hair that she smoothes in hanks.

Silence is built into the land, pale off-tan grass, gathered Sundays after the traveling priest moves out of the village on a snow machine. The machine sputters and shrives silence then engulfs the Bering Sea while Adam Fisher tells a story, nasal laugh and nasal laugh and nasal laugh. Things with hair stand out: musk ox, seal, men, women. Perspective is plotted by color of bronze skin and enlivened faces against muted palate of weathered buildings, steam of sweat houses, undergreen of tundra, far gray of airplane shadow. "They are too indirect, too inexplicit. They don't make sense. They just leave without saying anything." In the Tununuk grave-yard, snow shifts shapes, graves fill, grass bows down, As Bs Cs tussle with sea wind. They leave, they leave without saying anything.

(Published in Tonantzin 6.3 [1990]: 17.)

After reading this poem, you can see how the cross-cultural prompts worked their way into my text, created my text. I start with the Eskimo ABC book, something I had never seen before, and a photo Carolyn had taken of the graveyard opens and closes the poem. The name of Adam Fisher comes from the elder who is speaking on the tape she played for us. The statements in quote marks come from the list of cul-tural stereotypes. I invented the young girl in Wranglers, borrowed from my time liv-ing on the Navajo reservation and in Fairbanks, Alaska—real observations transposed. The same for the musk ox, found in a musk ox farm near the Fairbanks campus. I knew about snow machines in villages from my students' freshman English compositions. I borrowed some ideas from a poster I kept (and still keep) in my office of Alaska natives in a rope tug. The story of the traveling priest is one Carolyn told as she showed us slides and spoke of her own teaching/living experiences in Tununuk. Together, Carolyn (and the pieces she shared) and I created a prose poem portrait. I suspect much writing works this way—and this exercise can prime you to do, simply, what writers do: borrow, study, learn, transpose, and amplify.

(W.B.)

⑩ The Virtual Hypertext Game

Use to Write:	Alternative and Experimental Narrative/Prose Forms
Ideas and Concepts to Explore:	"author function"; hypertext; interactive; virtual.
Authors/Works Mentioned:	Julio Cortazar, *Hopscotch*; Michel Foucault; Deirdre McNamer, *Rima In The Weeds*.

You'd have to live in a cave these days not to know that the world is a-changing. Faster than fast computers. All the information in the world delivered to your finger-tips in the comfort of your home: mellaluca trees, cartography, photographs from space, stock market quotes. Instant communication. On-line romance. Sometimes tedious or harrowing, sometimes benign or beatific, whatever we may feel about it, technology has changed forever how we do things.

This goes for writing as well.

Think, for example, about its effect on how texts circulate in the world.

A long time ago stories moved orally through the world, permeable and fluid. People told them. In some cases, special people, storytellers, told them. But in others, anyone could tell them, and anyone could change them.

Then came the printing press, and suddenly, stories could be duplicated many times over, exactly as the writer wrote them, and they could be linked to that writer. Now written texts could be copyrighted and owned, sold and distributed, giving rise to what Michel Foucault calls the "author function." Stories, in their written form, had become inextricably affiliated with whoever wrote them.

Several centuries would pass before things would change again, but here we are in this historical moment where books are so expensive few people can afford them, movies dominate narrative, and writing itself moves instantaneously, freely, and anonymously on the Internet. Anyone with a modem and computer can produce it. Though it is still impossible to know what this will mean, a great deal of interest has already been provoked.

Advanced technologies have also made possible whole new genres: CD rom, multimedia extravaganzas, hypertexts more complex than a nerve, the sometimes mind-boggling convergence of text, image and sound. It is all out there, all possible, and it is both seductive and confusing. If writing no longer progresses along the linear path of the page, but can respond to the whim of the reader at the click of a mouse, what obligation does it have to hold together anymore, or in old-fashioned terms, to make sense? The temptation to go with the flow is enormous. Click here, link there. How fun it is on the cutting, cutting edge.

Hypertext is a form of interactive writing that allows the reader to click on highlighted words and follow a self-selected path of reading. Each click will follow a link to a different place in the text, and each reader determines which links to follow, choosing from between an often wide array of options. Paths can be programmed to move deliberately or at random. They can be intricately woven. They can work to control their own porosity, or they can be absolutely open. They can circle; they can all loop back to their beginnings. But someone "writes" them, just as someone still writes the words they follow. And none of this—not the fancy graphics or the stereophonic sound or the freewheeling razzle-dazzle of it—mediates the obligation of the writer, well, to write.

Back in the sixties, Julio Cortazar wrote a long novel, *Hopscotch,* loosely based on hypertext principles. At the front of the book, Cortazar outlined an alternative order of chapters which would produce a different novel than the one produced by linear reading. We heard about this book for years before we ever read it, and so were mildly surprised to discover that the "alternative" novel was much like the linear one, but supplemented with some additional chapters from the back. The second order of reading consisted of a more or less straightforward progression through the original novel, with these extra chapters interspersed.

In such a novel, it is easy to see clearly the author's hand in the whole scheme of things. Hypertext may hide this presence, but it is still there, and still always crucial.

Maybe you are a technological whiz; maybe you don't even own a computer. The principles of hypertext, especially as they are defined by the capacity to link things, one idea or textual fragment to another at the discretion of the reader, does not depend on sophisticated equipment but rather on the willingness to let things open up in the reading.

For this exercise you will play produce a virtual hypertext, according to the rules of the following game.

Play is designed for three to six players.

You will need a set of dice and a three-minute timer. Each player will also need a story she has written, a pair of scissors, a high-lighter, one large sheet of paper to serve as a story board, tape, paper and pen. Novice players should begin with stories three to five pages long; more advanced players may experiment with longer texts.

The goal is to create a virtual hypertext. First one finished wins.

There are four basic moves in the game: 1) **define a word-link,** 2) **add a text-link,** 3) **lose a text-link,** and 4) **return.** These shall be determined by rolls of the dice: 1–3 will denote **define a word-link;** 4–6, **add a text-link;** 7–9, **lose a text-link;** and 10–12, **return.** A **word-link** refers to the highlighted word that directs the reading elsewhere; a **text-link** refers to the text arrived at by following the **word-link.** Note that **word-links** may be embedded in **text-links** as well as in the "original" (but soon-to-be-lost) text.

To begin: roll the dice to see who goes first. Play proceeds to the left.

Each player shall begin by rolling the dice. If you roll 1–3, **define a word-link,** roll again to identify a reader among the other players. If there are four players, Player 1 shall be identified by the numbers 1–3; Player 2, 4–6; Player 3, 7–9; and Player 4, 10–12. If you are Player 1, for example, and you roll a 7, you will hand your text to Player 3, who will begin reading until she comes across a word that strikes her fancy as a link. Player 3 will highlight the link and pass the story back to Player 1.

If you roll, instead, 4–6, **add a text-link,** the timer will be set for three minutes, during which time you will: 1) find a text-link later in your original story, or 2) write a new one, on the spot. If the text-link already exists, it may be moved, with scissors and tape, or it may be copied, word for word, on the story board, off to the side of the original passage, with arrows to designate the connection.

Let's say, for example, your story begins:

> March, that year, was full of wind that rolled across the world with a sound as clean and lonely as rushing water. It rocked the stripped cotton-woods, hurried clouds across the sky, sprayed gravel against bare legs. You walked into it with a forward tilt.
>
> —*Rima in the Weeds,* by Deirdre McNamer

The reader-player, for example, may highlight the word *wind, lonely, cotton-woods, you,* or any other. The writer-player must then look for something else in the story to complement the link, or write new text to add in for a link: something about cottonwoods, loneliness, "you."

Arrange the text on the story board.

Play now moves on to the next player.

If you roll 7–9, **lose a text-link,** you must go to your story board and take out a link you have already connected or written.

And if you roll 10–12, **return,** you go back to the point in your original text where this last set of linking began.

If your move is impossible—you roll, for example, lose a text-link before any are written, or add a text-link before you have any defined word-links—you lose your turn.

Play is limited to three minutes a turn.

Designated player-readers may read aloud, but may not solicit advice from the other players, unless agreed upon beforehand. As the texts develop through the game, players will read from the growing story boards rather than the original texts, though these "originals" will continue to provide material for text-links, as well as points of return.

Texts may be read in any order that follows a developing pattern of links. Remember that word-links may be defined in other text-links, so that the story will tend to spiral, rather than develop along a more linear pattern.

The game ends when one player finishes a story, or when no new links can be found in a text. It is optional that play should continue until all players have finished.

Important note:

The *Virtual Hypertext Game* is conceived of as a collaborative game. Also, feel free to talk out your strategies and motivations.

Consider putting your winning virtual hypertexts on-line. How are they different, in the ether?

(K.H.)

Fortuitous Textual Coincidences; or, When Fragments Collide

11

Use to Write:	n/a [the exercise may lead to work in virtually any genre, and to multigeneric work]
Ideas and Concepts to Explore:	epiphany; narrative collage; prose assemblage.
Authors/Works Mentioned:	Katharine Haake, "Arrow Math"; [artist Lisa Bloomfield is mentioned as well].

Elsewhere in this book we have referred to "narrative collage" as an assemblage of fragmented prose segments, little bits and pieces of writing that, brought together, make a story, or maybe a piece of creative nonfiction or personal memoir. Another form of narrative collage proceeds from a logic not so much of assemblage as of collision. In this exercise we explore what happens when different kinds of texts are arbitrarily jammed together in a radical collision, just to see what comes up.

I learned this principle one morning at dawn years ago, after a long night of writing during which an intruder appeared at my door just as an intruder appeared in the story I was writing.

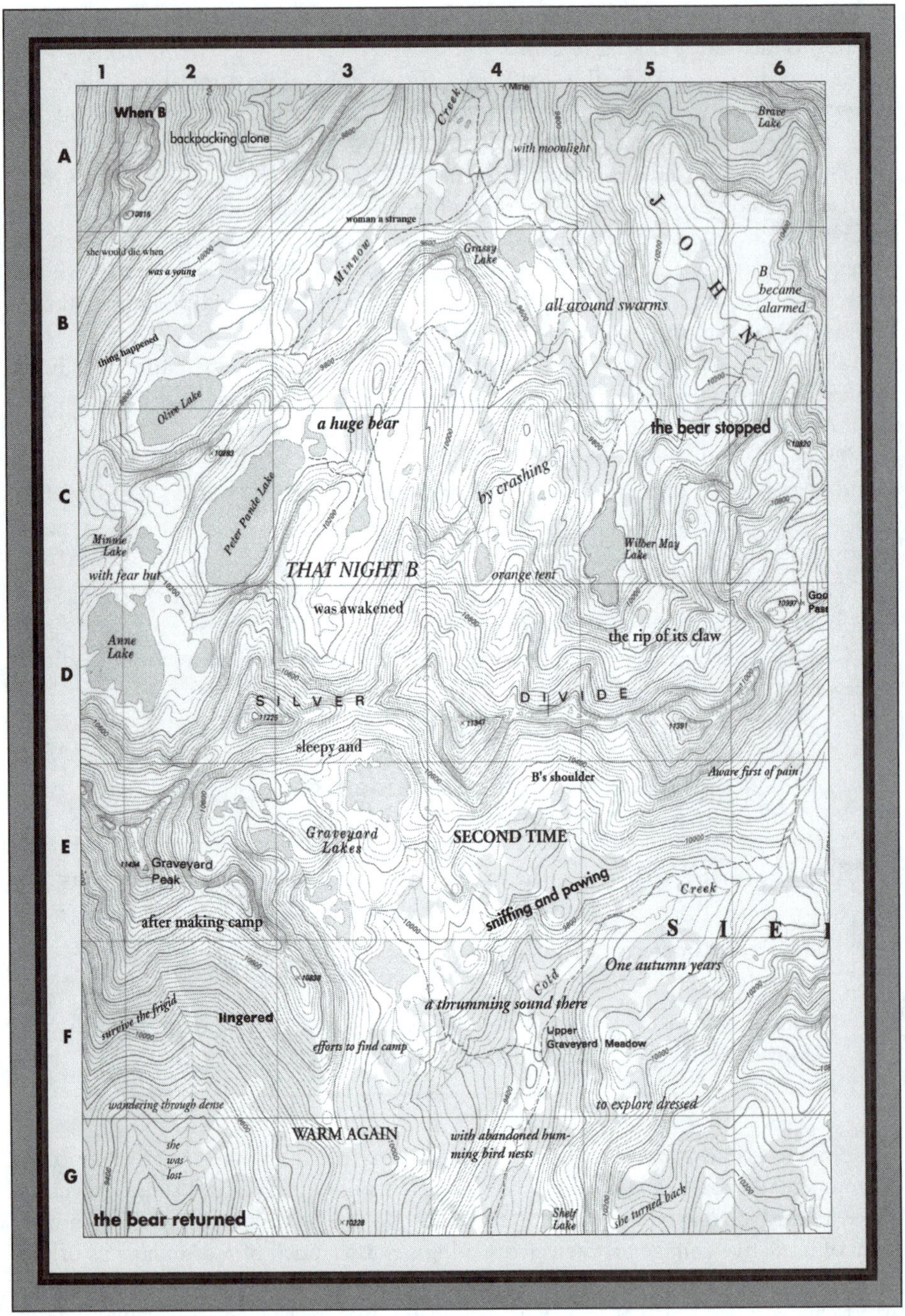

Figure 5.1

FEATURE	GRID		FEATURE	GRID	
			When B	A	2
			was a young	B	2
			woman a strange	A	3
			thing happened.	B	1
			Backpacking alone	A	2
E-13			into a remote	C	7
			wilderness	B	3
			she came	D	12
			to a perfectly	F	22
			round lake milky	L	28
			and jade-colored	A	19
			from glacial runoff.	A	21
			All around swarms	B	5
			of humming-	K	14
L-11			birds dived	K	14
			and hovered and	I	19
			the air was	Y	2
			thick with	Y	13
			the pulse	N	21
			of their wings.	L	29
			That night B	C	3
			was awakened	D	3
			by crashing	C	4
			and through	S	13
			orange tent	C	4
			walls bright	T	4
			with moonlight	A	4
			she saw	B	19
P-3			a huge bear	C	3
			rummaging	U	3
			through her gear.	C	19
			When it reared	E	29
			B's body went	Q	2
			cold and unfamiliar	R	5
			with fear but	C	1
			the bear stopped	C	5
			short of the tent	R	17
			sniffing and pawing	E	4
			the ground as	T	9
			inches away, B	G	21
			imagined	V	9
			the rip of its claw.	D	5
			In that instant	P	1
			the bear	J	20
			arched to rub	Q	6
			its haunches against	L	22
			B's shoulder	E	4
			through luminescent nylon	R	4
A-6			and B was filled	S	7
			with a peace that	G	25
			lingered	F	2
			long after	T	4
			the bear	U	7
			had lumbered away.	D	22
			One autumn years	F	5

FEATURE	GRID	
later B hiked	H	14
to another round	M	21
lake and another	P	14
strange thing	B	20
happened.	S	9
After making camp,	E	2
B went off	T	11
to explore dressed	F	5
in a thin	L	20
flannel shirt	I	22
and was soon	P	9
wandering through dense	F	2
manzanita draped	P	6
with abandoned hum-	G	4
mingbird nests.	G	4
All afternoon	T	2
she searched for	E	12
the source of	A	13
a thrumming sound there	F	4
and by the time	R	7
she turned back	G	5
she was lost.	G	2
As night fell	B	24
B became alarmed	B	6
she would not	R	11
survive the frigid	F	1
temperatures	S	17
and redoubled her	T	3
efforts to find camp.	F	3
Aware first of pain	E	5
then numbing	D	21
in her extremities	P	7
she felt certain	K	23
she would die when	B	1
she found herself	T	8
again among humming-	D	12
bird nests.	B	8
Seeing they were made	Q	1
of soft dry	S	17
moss B stuffed	H	24
her clothing with	D	26
them and tied them	A	23
in place with strips	P	7
of green bark.	R	3
Soon she felt	T	11
warm again	G	3
and very	L	27
sleepy and	D	3
it was in	J	23
this state that	Q	6
the bear returned	G	2
to her a	A	25
second	E	4
time.	E	4

Near midnight, in my story I typed, "It doesn't matter who he is. He's here. He could be dangerous."

At my door came a violent knocking, then a strange voice called out, "It's me. Let me in. Let me in."

After the police had come and gone, finding my little house and its environs safe, I surveyed my options and determined that, since the story was due in the morning, I could not, in good conscience, go elsewhere to sleep. But just in case my intruder came back, I'd stay up all night and finish my story.

So I got back to work, and I wrote all the way until dawn, which when it came at last I'd been writing more than eighteen hours straight, well near to the point of exhaustion and far beyond the reach of my internal censor. After eighteen hours, an intruder, and no sleep, I was willing to write just about anything. The problem was, I was so near the end of my story it would only take a scene or two, hardly more than a page, but I found myself plumb out of sentences, deserted by whatever muse had stood by me through the night. I flat out wanted to call it quits and go to sleep.

On the corner of my desk lay a small autobiographical fragment I'd written some months before. It was just an account of an adolescent experience, a stand-alone epiphany of sorts. I'd written it, I think, to appease the force of memory, and probably also to write myself out of one kind of writing slump or another. Now, it was just some random pages on my desk.

So what I did (I don't know why I did this), I took the fragment off the corner of my desk, and jammed it on the end of my story. First I wrote: *Here is my story.* Then I jammed the two together. They were unrelated—one in third person, the other in first, with different characters, one fiction, the other memoir, and so on. But once they were together, a kind of resonance occurred between them that framed the main story with such a difference that it was as if transformed—and so, from that point, was writing for me.

Years later an artist friend, Lisa Bloomfield, asked me to collaborate by writing a piece for a text-based image she was working on with maps. We talked for awhile, then I wrote her a little narrative about a woman named B. who finds hummingbird swarms on two separate backpacks, separated by many years. In the first, there is a bear; in the second, she gets lost, but wraps herself in moss from the hummingbird nests to stay warm.

Bloomfield liked the story, but the project stalled, and several years passed. Then one day I found myself at the end of a story with no way to end it. Not being one to waste writing, and with Lisa's work on hold indefinitely, I pulled out B.'s little story, just to see what would happen if I used it.

This splicing took a bit more work. I had to change B.'s gender, turn her into someone's father, give the story a reason for being. But otherwise, the text itself is virtually unchanged from the one Bloomfield eventually used when her project got back on track.

Compare its two incarnations, above in the art work and at the end of "Arrow Math," in the anthology. In each case, the words and the events are virtually identical, but how different the effect in different contexts.

For this exercise, write a textual fragment first. A tiny story, a memory, something you heard in the news. This can be a poem, or it can be a prose fragment, or it can be a whole tiny story. Read it out loud as you craft it. Make sure that every word counts.

Now, find at least two different spaces to jam your text into, one made of language, the other made of something else.

First, add it to something else you wrote. Don't change anything. Just link the two texts together.

Then, have someone read it for you. Listen closely to her comments. How do the pieces work together? What does each teach you about the other? How has your old work been made all new?

In the second part of this exercise, find a physical space for your initial text you wrote: a t-shirt, a sculpture you make out of found objects, a painting, a wall space, a mirror, transparencies with images beneath them. You may work with someone else, or on your own, but try to participate in the actual transfer of your words to a surface that is not blank paper. Use your own paint brush. Cut your own stencil. Think about not just the different textual spaces brought together in this project, but also their materialities, what they are made of, how they feel and look.

Now, hang it on your wall. Wear it. Use it.

Live with whatever you have made.

Same text, different context.   How are they the same, and how different?

(K.H.)

What the Words Grow Out Of: Building Multidimensional Collages

12

Use to Write:	Alternative, Experimental Forms of Writing
Ideas and Concepts to Explore:	epicenter; sculpture-as-writing; writing-as-sculpture.
Authors/Works Mentioned:	Jan Ramjerdi; Wallace Stevens.

This exercise grew out of the Northridge earthquake, the largest natural disaster ever to befall an American university campus. At five o'clock in the morning of January 17, 1994, just beneath my campus, the earth shifted to the power of 6.8 on the Richter scale, and everything crumbled.

In days that followed, we were teaching in mud fields and construction zones. Perched on the end of corrugated culvert pipes, we shouted to be heard above the roar of bulldozers, hydraulic equipment, buzz saws, hammering and all the rest of it. Just beyond, half-installed trailers were clotted with piles of multicolored electric wires, and just beyond, a multilevel parking structure continued to crumble, steel beam by buckling ribbon-like beam.

This was in February. Sometimes it was raining, and if you had a night class, the fields stretched pitch black around the place where someday soon you might have a classroom trailer. Some of us taught with flashlights. In the open, the aftershocks were not so terrifying.

It wasn't raining the day I first met with the theory and writing class Jan Ramjerdi and I were coteaching, but it had been raining. Everything dripped, the piles of construction trash and half-constructed trailer eaves, the bulldozers, the caution tape, students, us. Ramjerdi and I slogged through the mud, wondering what we might do for our first day of class.

Then it struck me. "Build," I said.

"What?" she said.

"I don't know," I said. "Something. Out of this. " Which was, after all, what everyone else around us was doing—building something back out of the rubble.

And so we did. And so, before long, all sixty creative writing students had formed small sculpture-building groups and were roaming their devastated campus in search of scraps of lumber, odd pipe ends, sawhorses, Pepsi cans, electric wires, cigarette butts, black roof paper, nuts and bolts and yards and yards of the yellow caution tape that delimited the boundaries of their lives. By the time we were done, our dank trailer was filled with sculptures and writing. They wrote on everything, the wood, the caution tape, scraps of soggy paper. They wrote, for the most part, about what had happened to them, and what had happened to them had happened, for the most part, to all of them together. Then they read from their sculptures out loud to the class, and then they talked about what they had done.

This exercise is based on the sculptures our students continue to build, large ungainly things, still assembled from the perpetual detritus of a campus remaking itself. They are made of wood, and trash, and metal scraps, and flowers, and the words the students write on them grow out of the sculptures themselves. Sometimes they grow into interconnected "hypertext installations," with links made of rope, or wire, or wilting daisy chains. Sometimes they are built to deconstruct, and sometimes they become permanent fixtures in our offices or classrooms: a totem pole, a mobile, a map.

This exercise is simple and proceeds from certain logics of boundaries, crossings, and weather.

For, as Wallace Stevens tells us, "The gods grow out of the weather."

And as we know from the world we move through, between words and whatever sparks them is sometimes a palpable line, something you can touch, hold, know somewhere outside language, in your body.

The point, in this exercise, is to cross that line and back, to build links between the physical world and the concept-driven world of language, and to explore this space not alone, but with others, to hold a conversation that grows out of the stuff you find to build and what you build with it, and then to link it with someone else's conversation on the other side of your classroom.

In this exercise, you need not assume that what you build must come out of chaos or ruin, for the world all around us offers a rich and varied canvas for writing. When my son once had a school assignment to "build something out of something that would be thrown away," we went to the desert and came back with deadwood, and rusted tin cans riddled with holes, bullet casings, colored glass shards worn smooth and translucent from the sun, rocks. What can you find in the place where you live? What is natural to its geography? What has been brought there, and left?

For this exercise, form a group, or choose a writing partner, and go out into your world to collect some materials for building. Use your imaginations, and whatever manual skills you might have to build a sculpture, large or small, of what you find.

Admire your handiwork.

Now, add text, found, or invented, or both.

When you are done, share your work with others.

Link your work with other sculptures, crossing the space between them with twigs, or twine, or bottle top or rubber band chains.

Hang text from the chains.

Document your work with videotape.

Write about what you have done.

Add to your sculpture over time, more material artifacts, more words, more links.

Take the words off your sculpture and rearrange them on paper.

Take the whole sculpture apart and put it back in the world.

(K.H.)

Flooding Yourself: A Strategy to Gather, Freewrite, Assemble, Construct

13

Use to Write:	Alternative and Experimental Forms, Chiefly Narrative Poetry; Performance Piece
Ideas and Concepts to Explore:	collage; "flooding" as a writing technique.
Authors/Works Mentioned:	Jill Giegeric; John Mandel.

This exercise is borrowed from artists John Mandel and Jill Giegeric.

Despite the paradoxical sound of it, the advice given writers—*Just Don't Think*—is often useful. Some kinds of thinking can get in the way of the words, binding you too rigidly to some original intent, cutting off the possibilities of surprise. Artist Jill Giegeric has developed a strategy for making art that depends on overloading as a means of suppressing negative hyperconsciousness. This technique, which she calls "flooding," systematically creates and organizes chaos in an attempt to create a working climate generative of surprise.

It works like this: Giegeric goes to the library, sets herself a time limit (maybe half an hour; the point is to work fast), picks an arbitrary section (medical texts, geology, math), and pulls down and looks through as many books as she can, marking passages of interest or at random. Then she spends time at the copy machine, again working fast, copying hundreds of pages to take home and sketch off. Hundreds and hundreds of sketches, as fast as her fingers can work. A sketch or two a minute. Pages torn off and flying around. Giegeric floods herself with images and sketching, and in the end her final product is collage.

For this exercise, try it yourself. Go to the library. Pick a section, any section: gold mining, astronomy, local history. Pull down a lot of books, book after book after book. Flip through them, fast. Faster. Mark pages, what you notice as of interest or just at random—diagrams and photographs, charts, phrases, titles, facts you would never have imagined, not in a million years.

Little yellow post-its will help.

Work fast. Faster.

Move to another section: biology, poetry, sports. Try art, the children's section, rare books. Music. Dance. Current events.

Faster.

Now, fill your arms with books and copy as many pages as you can afford. Don't be stingy. Copy. Copy. Copy. Then get home as fast as you can get there safely, spread your copies all around you, and start writing. Fast.

Faster.

As you work, you may want to cup your copies up and scatter them before you. You may want to tape them together. Be sure to include visual as well as textual material.

Write twenty short poems, twenty pages of prose. Pronto.

Work in whatever form you want, but use as much of your library material as you can, letting it prompt, guide and organize your work.

Wait a week. Then go back and see what you've done.

Now you can begin to craft and shape it.

What surprises you about this work? What about it satisfies you?

Variation 1:

Work at the library. Don't go home until you've got a pile of writing.

Variation 2:

Write things out by hand on handmade paper and make your own collage.

Make a book of your collages. Stitch it by hand.

(K.H.)

Vantage Points on Language

The Center Holds:
Weaving Multiple Discourses in a Single Text

(14)

Use to Write:	n/a [the exercise may lead to work in virtually any genre]
Ideas and Concepts to Explore:	"braid" vs. "plough" as metaphors for "story"; continuity/discontinuity in writing.
Authors/Works Mentioned:	Katharine Haake, "Arrow Math."

This exercise explores a writing principle we call "braided narrative."

Braids, or other forms of weaving, depend upon logics of both continuity and discontinuity, of bringing things together from wildly different modes of being or spaces. We knew a weaver once who would loop tiny sequins or beads, gold or silver bangles or threads into her brilliant silk fabrics. This juxtaposition of disparate elements would take one's breath away. To touch her work—a blanket, a small pillow, a decorative throw—would open something, like pleasure, inside you.

Or if you will, imagine hair: elegant, upswept French braids, poky pigtails, a thick single braid down your back.

Perhaps you have heard the term "watershed story," which describes the kind of story in which a writer's whole writing life shifts. Almost always, such stories are marked by difficulty and resistance to the most concerted efforts, as well as by what opens up when they finally yield.

One day we wondered: why can't a story be more like a braid than a plow (see Chapter Six: Exact Fare, "What's In a Sentence: The Possibilities Exposed by Breaking the Rules").

In my own work, writing "Arrow Math," I kept pushing myself to see how many disparate elements it could hold together without flying completely apart: facts about Mt. St. Helens, mathematical il/logics, reflections on poetry, people I made up, my own children. For my braid, I reached far into different worlds and their discourses. I let myself be curious, open and receptive. And when I got to where I couldn't take it any further, not yet entirely sure what I'd wrought, I went back into my pre-existing files (see Chapter Five: Union Station, "Fortuitous Textual Coincidences; or, When Fragments Collide") for an ending.

The part of the braid that comes from way underneath—the most radically different, the most unexpected—is always the most interesting part. The same is true for writing as it is for hair or fabric, and this exercise explores exactly how.

Begin, then, by gathering materials—multiple stories, disparate discourses, things that are "true" and things you "make up," odd bits of information that somehow spark, what you know a lot about as well as what you have just discovered. What interests do you have, for example, that you may not yet have considered for your stories or your poems?

For this exercise, notice things: baseball, architecture, topiary, rock climbing, antique tools, the rain forest, crossword puzzles, Hale-Bopp, Frank Lloyd Wright's destruction of the box. Rocks. White-water rafting. How to graft plants.

Make a list of at least three different "things in the world" you would like to explore: dams, the history of the building that you live in, marching bands.

Try five: Mono Lake, the Fourth of July.

Now do some research. Make lists of amazing facts. Pay particular attention to the language or the discourse of your subject. What specialized words or expressions does it use. How does it organize itself?

Now weave them all together in a story. Send a fictional character out to the local dam to look for Hale-Bopp one night. Comets. Where do they come from? How do they behave. And what about you, have you ever seen a comet or a dam? What is the relation between you and your character. If your character were real, would you be lovers, or long lost best friends, or people who stand in line next to each other at the market without speaking, not exchanging a single mortal word?

Put it all in your story, every bit of it.

Use comet lore as section titles to "organize" your story. Or the different parts of a marching band. Or the various declining species of Mono Lake.

Look for odd connections. Be prepared to respond to where one thing sparks another. Go there.

See how much you can jam into this story and still have it hold together. Engage the world, yourself, and your imagination all at the same time and in the same breath.

Now, ask yourself: *what have you wrought?*

Variation:

Using the process described above, write a poem. How is this different, and how the same, from the story?

(K.H.)

15 ▸ Warp and Weft: More On Weaving

Use to Write:	n/a [the exercise may lead to work in virtually any genre]
Ideas and Concepts to Explore:	alternating narratives; intersections and junctions in narratives.
Authors/Works Mentioned:	Hans Ostrom, "Grammar J, As in Jazzing Around"; Robert Farris Thompson, *Flash of the Spirit*.

Perhaps you know someone who weaves. Perhaps you have watched her work, the spindle skimming back and forth between the shimmering warp and weft, the thwump and clack of the shifting loom levers lifting a space for the carved wooden cradle—wool wrapped cocoon-like around it—to shoot through, like a fish for a fly.

Or perhaps you remember, instead, school weaving projects, those bright construction paper strips and your fingers all clotted with paste. Over and under. Warp and weft. Over and under, warp and weft, over and under. It is such a stunning logic, charged with both simplicity and grace, and something, maybe, luminescent, about it.

I once saw an ancient Arab tapestry, hung between two vertical panels of glass and woven to represent the Tree of Life. On one side of the tapestry animals nestled in the tree limbs by day, and on the other side, by night, one lit by the sun, one by the moon, one with the animals active and eating, one with them curled asleep. Between your clumsy fingers with grade school construction paper and that ancient Arab weaver, a whole world of interconnectedness ravels.

Writing has its own warp and weft, and this exercise asks you to explore it.

Begin by selecting two poems you have written with the same number of lines. (If you don't have two such poems, you will have to write them.) Then, quite simply, weave them together, alternating lines or weaving images in and out throughout. Over and under, over and under. Warp and weft. Warp and weft.

Try working with three poems.

When you've woven them together (over and under, warp and weft), the next part of the exercise is to erase one entire strand that you have carefully worked into the poem. Study the negative space left behind. What does it look like? How does it sound?

Alternative:

Try this exercise in prose, splitting a story , or two, into columns. Read them down. Read them across. Study the warp and weft.

Or, try alternating narratives—one line, one story; the next line, another. Back and forth, over and under, warp and weft. Remember to read your work across, and down, and diagonally. Look at the junctions and intersections of words and sentences. Pay attention to what's happening in the language.

Now, erase for negative space. Does it disappear, or does it echo?

Variation 1:

Work with another person or a group, either in prose or poetry. Weave your separate texts together, back and forth, over and under. What have you made? How many other ways can you imagine weaving your text with another, or with several others?

In the second part of the exercise, as you go through with your eraser to create negative space, pay attention to what happens when yours is the warp that is erased. Now, put it back and take out someone else's.

Over and under, warp and weft. Warp and weft.

Variation 2:

Weave together texts of different genres—poetry and prose, fiction and nonfiction, autobiography and prose poetry.

Over and under, warp and weft

Another word for weft is woop.

Further Reading:

Flash of the Spirit, by Robert Farris Thompson (New York: Vintage, 1984), is a landmark book concerning a wide spectrum of artistic and philosophical principles in African, African American (both South and North), and Caribbean cultures. The book includes excellent studies of "rhythmized textiles" and "rhythmized dwellings." It also contains a fascinating chapter on the folk art of Henry Dorsey, an African American artist who essentially took "junk"—everything from hubcaps to coat hangers—and created astoundingly original, improvised sculptures. See also

"Grammar J, As in Jazzing Around: The Roles Play Plays In Style," by Hans Ostrom, in *Elements of Alternate Style: Essays on Writing and Revision,* ed. Wendy Bishop (Portsmouth, N.H.: Boynton-Cook/Heinemann, 1997), 75–87.

(K.H.)

(16) What Hands Make: Using "Instructions" as a Model for Other Writing

Use to Write:	n/a [the exercise may lead to work in virtually any genre]
Ideas and Concepts to Explore:	"intention" in writing; instruction-poem.
Authors/Works Mentioned:	Francois Camoin; Ivy Goodman, "Family Remnants."

The student who learns that he has no intentions worth talking about—that he has nothing to say when he sits down at the typewriter, only something to make—will write much better fiction.

—Francois Camoin

Perhaps when you were nine or ten you had some private lessons to learn a particular skill: maybe how to play the saxophone or pitch a baseball, maybe sewing from a tiny Spanish woman in a musty one-bedroom apartment filled with apple-head dolls in varying stages of desiccation. What you learned from your saxophone teacher, the tall jazz musician with tiny round glasses, or the hunkered over pitching coach three times your size, or the tiny Spanish woman was how to use your body to make something—a mellow note, a perfect pitch, a gathered skirt on an empire bodice. Around you, the cored apple heads of the dolls filled the room with a decaying sweetness, and though you longed to know the secret of their pinched eyes and noses, you knew as well your proper business at your lesson was to master first pins, and then seams.

Years later, you find yourself slicing zucchini, and the rounds fall off your blade, perfect quarter inches. As they steam in the pan you know you are indebted to the woman who taught you how to sew, who resisted your complaints and made you start out with a simple A-line skirt, and who later, with infinite patience, waited out your frustration at tiny tucks and plackets. Perhaps you remember unfolding your first dress pattern, all that recalcitrant tissue that looked nothing at all like the dress you'd imagined, and wanting to weep. Perhaps you remember, too, that before you were done with your sewing, you had learned to pick out fabric by walking between bolts with your eyes closed tight, hands extended to either side of you, running your fingers along the various materials until something felt good to the touch. Then you looked.

Or the baseball, firm inside your hand just before you let it fly.
Or feel of your sax in your arms, just before you let it wail.
What is it you know how to make?
Fish flies? Angelfood cake? Hinged wood boxes with decorative carvings? Car
engines? Quilts? Musical scores? A perfect dive, or arabesque, or slam dunk?
And how did you learn how to make it?
When you make the thing you know best how to make, is the memory in your
fingers? Does your body precede your least thought? Is it a different kind of knowl-
edge than what you know with words? How can the two kinds of knowledge work
together to illuminate each other?

For this exercise, think about the thing you know best how to make. (There's a
chance you've already considered this ability of yours if you worked with the exercise, "Writing from Expretise, Not Just from Experience," in Chapter Two—The
Green Line.) Imagine yourself making it. Feel it first, without any words, in your
fingers, your body, the arch of your neck over your work space, the tension at the
back of your knees.

Then, refer to an actual set of instructions, or write one in the manner of a technical training manual for whatever it is you are making. Use these instructions, or
fragments thereof, as section titles for a narrative. Then write it.

Maybe your instructions on how to tie a fish fly can structure a fly fishing story.

Maybe your famous family pound cake can provide a framework for the family
story about how your mother left her family home in Georgia and came all the way
west to California.

Maybe your engine tune-up manual can hold together the story of the summer
you spent drag racing up and down the southern states.

As you write this story, let yourself respond to the relation between you
making what it is you make, and writing the story that grows out of it. Bring
examples of both to class: what you wrote, and what you made. Be prepared to
talk about both.

Variation 1:

Write an "instruction poem" in which you explain how to make what you know
how to make, something palpable and physical, something you can hold or touch.
Don't refer to the thing itself, or name, except by metaphor, its separate parts. Have
your reader guess: what is it?

Variation 2:

Write an "instruction poem" from which someone might actually learn to make the
thing you know how to make. Teach someone how to knit with your poem.
Actually have them learn the complicated mechanics of the backstroke, the butterfly
stroke. Eat cake.

(K.H.)

In The Same Breath:
Rewriting as Part of the Conversation

17

Use to Write:	Short Fiction; Longer Fiction; Tales; Creative Nonfiction; Autobiography Journal; Literary Criticism
Ideas and Concepts to Explore:	"gestures of affiliation"; intertextuality; writing as "conversation with other writing".
Authors/Works Mentioned:	Francois Camoin; William Shakespeare; *The Fox and the Grapes; Hansel and Gretel; Little Red Riding Hood; The Seven Swans; The Tortoise and The Hare.*

To some extent, this exercise echoes ideas that appeared in the first chapter ("reading") and the fourth ("revision and editing"), but we place it here because it invites you to try a particular kind of experimental, or at least less conventional, writing.

That writers engage in a conversation with all the rest of writing is not a new idea, but I heard it first from Francois Camoin. When that conversation is deliberately invoked, we call it "intertextuality"—a fancy term from theory that describes the way a particular text will echo or refer to another. As writers, we may find this unsettling, preferring to think of our work as "original." But however much we may want to be unique, others will have been there before.

Imagine, then, the writing conversation. How overwhelming it can seem! There are so many voices, who could ever sort it out? much less get a word in edgewise. Or maybe you're the shy type, who goes quiet at dinner parties, keeps checking her watch, longs for escape. At least in writing, you do your talking at home alone, and the writers you talk with may be centuries dead.

This conversation saturates your work, whether you think about it consciously or not. When you adopt the conventions of naturalism in your fiction, for example— abundant detail, "representational" language, characters at the mercy of a disinterested, "natural" world—you locate yourself in a literary tradition that makes certain assumptions about the nature of literature and its relationship to the world. That New York woman, for example, who pauses on her brownstone steps, arms loaded with bags of fresh produce, to admire the roses blooming in the small patch of earth beside the building, has plenty of literary company.

The same goes for writing a confessional poem, experimental prose, minute stories, sonnets, free verse, minimalism. Your work is full of echoes when you write. One way to hear them more clearly is to imagine which shelf in the bookstore your writing would go on? In which section, what shelf, between what other writers?

Another is to go back to our beginnings and have a little fun, for most of us begin our experience with other writing with nursery rhymes, Dr. Seuss, fairy tales or fables. They're all in it too, that vast dictionary of texts we draw from when we write.

This is a simple exercise designed to help you explore some of the basic organizing principles of all the other writing in your writing. Begin with a well-known fairy tale or fable: *Hansel and Gretel, Little Red Riding Hood, The Tortoise and the Hare, The Fox and the Grapes, The Seven Swans.* Now, rewrite it in contemporary terms—both language and situation—without reference to the original tale, just as if your story were new.

All new material. All your own.

You might want to prepare for this exercise by rereading some fairy tales—Hans Christian Andersen, the Brothers Grimm. Spend a night with tales you've forgotten. Immerse yourself in their language and stories. Then see where it goes in your writing.

Variations:

This exercise will work differently for recent immigrants or for those whose heritage is not Western European. Part of the point of this exercise is to experiment with aspects of cultural and literary contexts as they organize writing, so if you feel oddly dislocated inside these "well-known" tales, explore that dislocation in your own retelling.

Then, refer to your own "original" stories, the stories you learned stories with: Native American myth, African folk tales, Chinese legends. Rewrite one of those. How does it feel to you, writing it? Is there an easy "fit" between the story you are writing and a more dominant "North American" aesthetic? Do you have to make adjustments in your telling, or can you play off certain aspects of its dissonance?

For those of you whose heritage is Western European and who have grown up in this country not the children of immigrants, try reading folk tales from another culture and then writing one in contemporary language. How does this feel to you, writing it? What kinds of adjustments do you have to make? How can they work to your advantage?

Now, try weaving the tales of two different cultures together, still in a contemporary language and situation.

Think about this experience when you are done, especially in terms of your relation to the various materials you used. What feels "natural?" What do you, properly speaking, feel like you "own?" What comes more easily, and what comes harder? What is more interesting to you? What is more familiar? What longings does this stir up inside you?

(K.H.)

18 ▶ Silence

Use to Write:	n/a [the exercise may lead to work in virtually any genre]
Ideas and Concepts to Explore:	mute; mystical; paradoxical; the rhetoric of silence; silence.
Authors/Works Mentioned:	Parts 2 and 8 below list authors and works; [George Kalamaras, *The Rhetoric of Silence,* is also mentioned].

For writers and critics alike, the topic of *silence* is a source of fascination because of its mystical connotations and because of its paradoxical nature: All texts are silent insofar as ink and paper are literally mute, and yet stories and poems and other writing can make us *imagine* silence as well as noise. Also, how odd and terribly human of us to want to *discuss* silence! And finally, there is the paradoxical rhetorical power of silence: In many situations where people are silent, they convey meaning, they assert themselves, or they control argument and discourse. In other instances, of course, silence is a sign of oppression—rhetorical or political powerlessness. Remaining silent can be respectful, honorable, and right in some instances while in others it can be disdainful, dishonest, and wrong. (George Kalamaras recently published a fascinating study entitled *The Rhetoric of Silence*). It's odd but true that there are different kinds of silence—and different kinds of silence evoked in writing and used by writers. It's good sometimes, therefore, to examine, work with, and play with different notions of silence as we write—and even to use silence to help us write.

Here are some possibilities:

1. Perhaps with one or more poems, you've felt you were "talking too much," felt the poem is too thick, too dense, too wordy. Work at trying to let some "silence" into the poem, perhaps by erasing certain logical or grammatical connections and creating places where the poem leaps, where there are intended gaps in continuity, where there is the effect of open spaces. Or perhaps you could simply find ways to slow down the poem, creating more pauses, allowing the poem (and the reader) to breathe, as it were. Or maybe you don't know when or how to end the poem, so you just keep going, repeating yourself, tying things up too neatly, explaining the poem, pressing. See how early you can end the poem, leaving a kind of space, an illusion of inviting silence after the last word, where the reader's mind can linger.

2. You might also read some taciturn poets—poets of relatively few words: Jon Skelton, Matsuo Basho, Emily Dickinson, Langston Hughes, Tomas Tranströmer, Philip Larkin, Edwin Arlington Robinson, Stevie Smith, Stephen Spender, William Carlos Williams, and John Haines come to mind. See the different ways these and other poets create illusions of silence, of space, of laconic speech, of saying a lot in a few words. See what sorts of moves they make and try out one or two as you revise.

3. Work with silence in your fiction: Characters who use silence in a variety of ways; the "presence of silence" in certain scenes; how silence might be interpreted differently by different characters and therefore be a source of conflict; the role the illusion of silence might play in phrases, sentences, dialogue, paragraphs, and other units of a story.

4. In your notebook, describe, categorize, meditate on, or speculate about different kinds of silence you experience or observe. This writing may feed into subsequent poems, stories, or nonfiction prose.

5. Write "in silence" beyond the usual silence in which you write. Choose a time when and a place where the quiet is pervasive if not total. What do you hear

beneath the silence? Are there faint noises you hadn't observed before? Are you a person who needs noise—why? Are your thoughts noisy sometimes—why? Be patient. Just sit. Maybe write a line and let it "sit in silence," inviting it to tell you—as it were—what words might come next. Let ideas, images, and words come slowly, advancing into silence like wary wild animals entering a meadow.

6. Write, shoot, and edit a short silent video.

7. Watch television or a video with the sound off. Invent your own dialogue for dramas or invent your own newscasts and "talk" on talk shows.

8. Find and read as many poems as you can that concern, in one way or another, silence. Perhaps start with Robert Frost's "Stopping by Woods . . ." or Robert Bly's "Silence in the Snowy Fields." Or read poet Adrienne Rich's book, *On Lies, Secrets, and Silence.* Write a reading-journal entry or an essay about one or more of the poems or other works related to silence you read.

9. In your view, to what extent do the following kinds of punctuation suggest different kinds of silence? Speculate (and have a bit of fun).

  a. ( )
  b. .
  c. :
  d. [ ]
  e. { }
  f. ????????
  g. &—
  h. " "

(H.O.)

Exact Fare

Guided Writing Related To Selected Matters of Grammar, Precision, Style, and Punctuation

Note: Because the topic-area of this chapter is so carefully circumscribed, we have dispensed with the standardized headings concerning genres, key terms, and so forth.

Behold the Sentence

The Care and Feeding of Sentences

English teachers have a reputation, at least partly deserved, for killing creativity like a late frost—an obsession with grammar and punctuation ("G & P") being the chief murderous trait. Later in this chapter, we have a separate section on grammar and punctuation, but the "G & P" we mention here is the perceived obsession with Correct English that makes students sometimes dread *any* discussion of "the sentence." Writers, especially fledgling ones, often come to associate G & P with boredom at best, pain at worst. And it seems not to do much good for teachers and experienced writers to yammer about *You can't write well without knowing the basics of the language!* because the yammering sounds like another parental pronouncement in the genre of *Sure the medicine tastes bad, but it's good for you—trust me!* The teacher/student relationship is different from the child/parent relationship, of course, but talk of G & P can call up unwanted parallels and make everyone concerned rather ornery.

The more writers write, though, the more likely they are, gradually, to come to look at G & P from the inside out. Bad memories of . . . English teachers, horrifying red ink, tortuous quizzes, and dull handbooks fall away. The writer starts to see things from the sentence's point of view, believe it or not. G & P emerge as a way to observe and channel the strange, mercurial energy of sentences, of written language.

For language *is* movement and energy, no doubt about that. Sentences move through time and across space, whether they're pushed by tongues and mouths or computer cursors. Sentences represent linguistic creativity, a transfer of mental energy into sound and symbol, a creativity as basic as electrical fields.

And when it comes to G & P, it's almost always best to start with *your* sentences and then, if need be, consult a book about something you don't know—such as what a gerund is, or what the deal is with semicolons. When studies of the sentence become an end in themselves, sure they can get boring. But if they're treated as a means to examine the wiring of *your* poetry and prose, they're as interesting and satisfying as any fine, necessary tool in a project you desire to pursue.

Here, then, are some ideas for engaging the energy of your own sentences:

1. **Circling.** Something inexplicably listless or flat about a draft of a poem or part of a narrative? Try this: Circle the verbs (not the wagons). After they're circled, preferably in vivid ink, see what they're up to. When students have done this circling in my class, invariably many of them say, with surprise, "There are so many verbs!" So just the circling itself provides some interesting instruction about how crucial verbs are to writing; in general, of course, we know this already, but the process of circling drives the point home.

   Are there other verbs that might do a better job? Maybe, for some reason, "torched" works better than "ignited." That sort of thing.

   Might a modal verb ("could see") be boiled down to something simpler ("saw"), increasing the power and speed of a sentence?

   In a poem, can you move a verb from the end of one line to the beginning of another? Verbs have a way of driving a line, making it jump, when they're at the front there.

   At any rate, once you've circled the verbs, isolated each of them, a lot of revision possibilities usually emerge, rising out of those circles on the page.

2. **Cross-wiring.** Find a poet or prose-writer with a distinctive style. It can be a style you like or one that seems downright strange (not that you might dislike something downright strange). Possibilities: Emily Dickinson, Ernest Hemingway, Gertrude Stein, Philip Levine, William Faulkner, Alan Dugan, Jack Kerouac, Hunter Thompson, John Milton, Raymond Chandler, Ralph Ellison. Be sure to look at very particular examples—a specific poem or poems, certain pages of a specific novel, and so forth.

   Then take an existing draft of your own—poem, *part* of a story, *part* of an essay, whatever—and rewrite it as if you were that other author. Try not so much for parody (exaggerated imitation) as for likeness—though some attempts at making your stuff like his or her stuff are bound to make you laugh. So much the better—when was the last time work with G & P made you laugh?

   After you produce an imitation that seems to hang together, analyze it— line by line, sentence by sentence, quirk by quirk. In terms of very specific choices—vocabulary, sentence construction, usage, grammar, punctuation— what seem to be the key determiners of this style? Put another way, what writerly moves did you have to make to begin to make your poem "Dickinsonesque," for example?

   The point of this cross-wiring is NOT to get you to write like Dickinson or Chandler, even if that were truly possible. Instead, this is a way to get familiar with the concrete elements of a style. And it's a roundabout but ironically easier way to see your own habits and quirks afresh. Maybe you're a person who records music, and you've wanted to get a sound on tape that you've heard another artist produce; you analyze how that's done, and you learn more about your own style. Or maybe you're a painter and want to try to get the shadows to be like those in a painting you admire; you find out you can't exactly imitate the technique, but you still learn more about creating the effect of shadows. This is really what we're up to in this kind of imitation.

3. **Stretched Sentence.** Write a one hundred word sentence that makes sense and that is grammatically sound and punctuated properly. For a slightly greater challenge, write the sentence using "and" only twice. Uncertain about what punctuation marks to use? Consult a handbook—but only *after* you've written the sentence.

4. **Effect vs. Transciption.** "Rules of grammar" are only provisional rules, based on longstanding conventions that have evolved and that will continue to evolve. Indeed, there are many grammars; when we indicate that "ain't" is "incorrect," for example, we really mean that it doesn't fit the grammar of mainstream formal English, but it certainly does fit the grammar of other kinds of English that are spoken, understood, and even appropriate in a variety of places and in a variety of circumstances. Writers have to be aware of these other grammars, language groups, and rhetorical situations. Writers of fiction especially need to perfect the art of "incorrectness"—the art of creating the *effect* of slang, dialect, or accent without bogging down the narrative in transcription-like representation, where nearly every word might be misspelled, according to mainstream convention.

Langston Hughes, William Faulkner, Eudora Welty, Zora Neale Hurston, Sandra Cisneros, and Fae Mae Ng are examples of writers who have worked with different kinds of so-called non-Standard English. Glance at their work and try to determine some of the techniques they use to create the effect of such language without making their texts too dense and without caricaturing or stereotyping people they are attempting to represent. Also, what sorts of non-Standard English do you encounter in your day-to-day life? In a notebook, try to capture some of it in brief sketches of people, brief captured dialogues, and so forth. Remember: Unlike a social-linguist who might make a *transcript,* you are more likely to want only to create the *effect* of the person's or the group's use of non-Standard English.

5. **Weakness Into Strength.** Maybe you've never quite understood how to use a semicolon properly. Maybe you don't know the difference between "lie" and "lay." As a result, you never use a semicolon, and you "write around" situations that call for the use of "lie" or "lay." Or you write to avoid having to make other choices concerning grammar, usage, or punctuation. In tennis, such avoidance is called "running around your backhand."

At certain intervals (weekly? monthly?) choose just *one* element of grammar, usage, or punctuation that you feel chronically uncertain about and make it a strength. If a teacher is always nailing you for the "comma splice," not only learn what that is, once and for all, but also write as many sentences as you can that *demonstrate* your new-found knowledge; and as you read, look for sentences that do the same thing. That is, a person who just bought a blue Toyota is likely to notice all the other blue Toyotas on the road. Whatever your weaknesses are in G & P (make a list), turn them into strengths, one by one. Turn each one into a blue Toyota. You might even play things more broadly and, after having learned the difference (once and for all time) between "lie" and "lay," write a poem in celebration of the event.

(H.O.)

Sentence As Style

Consider this a kind of continuation of the first exercise in this chapter.

I don't just read and write sentences (nor am I particularly good at analyzing them using the conventional terminology of grammar books), but I find sentences sculptural: clay that writers bend, shape, and mold to their purposes. In a way, sentences seem alive, responding here when pushed there, resisting here and obliging there. My argument: if you start to study sentences as a writer does, you'll see that they're more varied and flexible, a better instrument for exploring and expressing thought, than maybe you ever knew. The rules we're "given" can only address a small part of our language repertoire and are most often constraining and constricting rather than elucidating and explaining. It makes sense to follow the rules to get to where you want to go—especially during initial drafting, *for if you don't know what you're saying, your reader surely won't.* But later, as you revise, the possibilities of language should make you want to play, to match meaning to your own sentence magic, to create what we call style—your own best way of saying.

Here's another analogy. It makes sense that when we sit down together at dinner, we're more comfortable if everyone eats in a fairly civilized way—spoons, forks, or chopsticks, food moving from plate to mouth in a compact and regular manner. I don't want spaghetti splashed all over the wood floor and staining the carpet, and it would make me queasy to eat off someone else's greasy plate. Fine. But there are occasions when such an orchestrated eating arrangement may be less than useful (or pleasurable): don't sit me on the back patio eating a wonderful summer watermelon with a tiny silver spoon and a napkin. Let me take a chunk in my fingers and bite into the red meat with my teeth and enjoy the sweet drip down my chin. I'll wash at the hose in a minute.

The same with sentences. If all our sentences, all our prose, followed "the rules" and showed good taste and fine manners . . . we'd lose something. We'd be bored to death. We wouldn't "hear" much from texts. But, luckily, that's not how it works.

• There are a lot of rules about sentence length and complexity, but the usual urge is for sentences that are not too long, not too short, and not too complex. Clear, concise, coherent. Following is a rule-breaker, a labyrinthine sentence that includes a sentence within a sentence. Citations refer to works listed at the end of the exercise.

> Gardnar Mulloy, tournament tennis player incarnate at eighty-two—**he is six feet one, thin, and trim, walks with the spectacularly balanced gait of a confident athlete, and has a thick mane of white hair**—came up from his Miami home last week to the US Open to start things off on Opening Day with the traditional hitting, together with Bill Talbert and Frank Parker (still only in their seventies), of tennis balls from the Stadium Court net to the spectators.
>
> (Talk 33)

The labyrinthine sentence, properly handled, can be elegantly elaborate. And it sounds quite different from the short, sharp sentences of the detective novel that seems to thrive on what can be damned as "primer prose"— short Subject + Verb + Object sentences. However, this short, hard-hitting sentence remains the building block for creating the terse, self-reliant detective we know and love. And notice another characteristic, the one sentence paragraph:

> Sayres had gone to Doron White, founding partner, previously my ally, and made his argument: I was doing pro bono work without the firm's consent; Crosetti's controversial politics might offend our corporate clients; and I had again placed the firm under the jeweler's eye of publicity.
>
> **Doron had agreed.**
>
> **I'd made the firm a lot of money. I'd made the firm famous.** But all it took was one refusal to back down and I was out the door.
>
> I'd been forced to choose between what mattered and what looked good. I'd chosen not to become Steven Sayres.
>
> (Matera 8)

And to prove that neither short nor long, simple or complex, can possibly be the rule, sentences can have complicated rhythms and balances, parallel structures, teetering and tottering to create an effect:

> I expected this to be an **easy book** to write. To portray the life story of **one woman—why should that** pose any serious writing problems? I also expected this to be a **short book.** The life story of **one woman—why should that** require a very **long book?**
>
> Of course, I ought to have known. Didn't my **comadre** keep telling me I was bringing back a **big book?** "*Se lleva una historia*

muy grande, comadre," she'd say, and she was absolutely right, my comadre. This is a **big book.** Everything seems to have found its way into these pages, even the kitchen sink. I'm afraid there's nothing I can do. You don't **choose** to write **the books** you write, any more than you **choose** your mother, your father, your brother, your children, or your **comrade.**

(Behar ix)

- In fact in many sentences, you find curled up and waiting for you a sense of the persona the author is trying to create. For instance, the repetition, alliteration, word play, punning—self-conscious high-spirited writing—in this excerpt seem to be part of the act of reviewing—that is, selling—a new novel but also of "selling" the author's view; reading his style helps you know if you're going to like Nick Hornby's first novel:

Can a man hope to sustain both a record collection and a relationship? Nick Hornby's first novel, "High Fidelity" (Riverhead; $21.95), turns on this **racking** question. The man on the **rack** is Rob Fleming, ex-d.j., college dropout, "Reservoir Dogs" fan, and owner of a failing London record store, who finds himself alone on his thirty-sixth birthday with a "Robocop 2" video and a phone call from his mom. His girlfriend has gone off with the tenant upstairs, and Rob begins to wonder if his **low-fidelity** relationship isn't a casualty of his devotion to **high fidelity.** "What came first," he asks, "the music or the misery?"

In the space of two books, Hornby has established himself in England as a **maestro** of the **male** confessional. His first, the autobiographical "Fever Pitch," took readers on an uproarious journey through the **mental wasteland** of the sports bore . . .

(Nixon 91)

- Which doesn't mean that a persona isn't also created in a less rococo text. Here, the conversational, parenthetical, and rhetorical work of this text seems to suit (wears the suit of) the interested, technologically inclined reader:

What does Microsoft Windows 95 mean to you as a participant in the PC software business?

If you are a software developer or entrepreneur, the brief answer is that Windows 95 should make you nervous (**unless you work for Microsoft, or have invested in Microsoft stock, or both**). At the very least, Windows 95 will change how you sell software and what sort of software you develop.

Windows users (**I mean, consumers**) should welcome Windows 95 as a big improvement over previous versions . . .

(Schulman 3)

- Sometimes this persona is developed by putting on the cloak of another genre, as when this tile–setting expert opens his introduction using story-telling conventions, transposing them to a work setting in a way that actually makes me want to read his primarily how-to book. A tile setter with a heart and a good ear for language, I'm doubly interested as someone needing to set tile but wanting to do it with style:

> **Over 20 years ago,** unable to find any certified training in tile setting and confused by conflicting information, **I set out to find** the best way to install ceramic tiles. **Since boyhood,** I had been attracted to the beauty of tiles, and **as a young man,** I would do whatever was necessary to learn the tricks and secrets of installing tile and mosaics over thick slabs of mud. No mastic jobs for me! I **wanted sand, cement and tradition.**
>
> (Byrne 2)

Now I've wandered from rule-breaking to style-making, and no one but the author of these excerpts can tell me if the sentence moves I found and admired were *intentional*—but by studying them, I can steal them and make my sentences more supple, more responsive to my writing desires.

Okay, professional writers in all venues, all genres, play with sentence variation. What happens when you do the same?

Try the following first by writing a new paragraph (you might do this in a writing class—say everyone writes one paragraph about coffee, using only words of a single syllable) and then trying the variations below. Even more revealing about your writing, at home, begin with a favorite opening paragraph from your own work to see how what you thought you already liked can take different forms and resonances. Then try the exercises with a paragraph that isn't working to see where simple experimentation can take you.

Exercises.

1. Recast your paragraph into words of one syllable.

2. Recast your paragraph using words of two or more syllables only.

3. Recast your paragraph into a single, labyrinthine sentence.

4. Recast your paragraph into a fragment, then a longer central sentence, then end again on a fragment.

5. Recast your paragraph into a series of balanced sentences—modifier, main clause, modifier—say; do the same for at least two other sentences in the paragraph.

6. Break your paragraph down into constituent parts by dismantling to smaller and smaller kernels. ["I went to the store to buy bread" becomes—"I went. I went to the store. I went to buy bread."]

7. Rebuild your paragraph from the dismantled parts, looking for different ways to combine and modify (called sentence-combining).

8. Recast your paragraph to use parentheticals, slang/conversation, and/or lots of repetition (choose your effect depending on your subject).

9. Look at all your experiments and write your final best paragraph and a note on why you chose the sentence structures and patterns you chose.

Works Cited

Behar, Ruth. *Translated Woman: Crossing the Border with Experanza's Story.* Boston: Beacon Press, 1993.

Byrne, Michael. *Setting Tile.* Newton, CT: The Tauton Press, 1995.

Matera, Lia. *Face Value.* NY: Simon and Schuster, 1994.

Nixon, Rob. "Revolutions Per Minute: Love, Nostalgia, and the Records People Play." *The New Yorker.* September 11, 1995: 91.

Schulman, Andrew. *Unauthorized Windows 95: A Developer's Guide to Exploring the Foundations of Windows.* San Mateo, CA: International Data Group Books Worldwide, 1994.

"The Talk of the Town." *The New Yorker.* September 11, 1995: 33.

Note: You may also want to consult *Shaping Sentences: Grammar In Context,* by Stephen Tollefson (New York and San Diego: Harcourt, Brace, Jovanovich, 1985); any of William Strong's several works on "sentence-combining"; and sentence-combining material in *The Writer's Work* (several editions), by Frank O'Hare and Dean Memering (Engelwood Cliffs, N.J.: Prentice Hall).

(W.B.)

What's in A Sentence:
The Possibilities Exposed by Breaking the Rules

Sentences are where stories start and stop, often what they even grow out of. They have their own sounds. They are infinitely flexible and positively porous. And they begin, as we all know, with a capital letter, end with a period (or other final mark of punctuation), and express a completed thought or action.

William Faulkner said that a sentence should head straight through to its end, like a plow in a furrow. Trinh Minh-Ha describes herself as a "sentence-thinker" but as "one who so very often does not know how a sentence will end. . . . And as there is no need to rush, just leave it open, so that it may later on find, or not find, its closure." Between the one and the other, where does the logic of sentences lie?

Examples.

I stood at the window the curtains moved slow out of the darkness touching my face like someone breathing asleep, breathing slow into the darkness again, leaving the touch.

—William Faulkner

I had not the slightest desire to know who had possibly been buried here forty years ago, rolled up in a blanket or simply stuck in a cardboard box, I did not want to know that his sister's name had been Anneliese, that she had been only three years old, and that they just didn't have anything for her to eat, I know those stories, I was there, you wasted away to skin and bones, brother, in the typhoid hospital in H., where I was taken before you, I almost didn't recognize you when I finally managed the thirty steps down the corridor to your room, now this man with his little olive-green coat should leave me alone with his sister Anneliese, I came here in search of perfect slumber, I don't need his descriptions of starving little girls.

—Christa Wolf

The fields were rolling and grassy and the grass was short from the sheep grazing.

—Ernest Hemingway

Each of the above sentences is, with regard to grammar, seriously flawed. They are run-ons; they have punctuation errors. You would probably get marked down for them in your composition class, and while creative-writing teachers might be a bit more flexible, you can't always count on that, and anyway, their rule is that if you make grammatical errors, you should do so to create a particular effect—a consistent character voice, a certain urgency of meaning, visual experimentation.

Flannery O'Connor once made the observation that writers can get away with anything they can get away with, the only problem being that no one has ever gotten away with very much. Grammarians may think that, on the contrary, we're getting away with far too much. But every experienced writer knows that there are times to follow rules and times to break them. And one very good way of learning rules is learning, instead, how to break them.

The above sentences are all run-on sentences, though each of slightly different kinds. A standard run-on sentence is called a "run-on sentence" precisely because it runs two complete sentences together, linking them with a coordinating conjunction (*and, or, but, for, nor, so, yet*), but without any mark of punctuation. A coordinating conjunction links grammatical structures of equal value together, such as independent clauses or parallel elements in a sequence.

Two specific kinds of run-ons are *comma splices* and *fused sentences*. A *comma splice* links two complete sentences together only with a comma. And a *fused sentence* links complete sentences together without any conjunction or punctuation. The sentences just flow one to the other, without any pause or indication.

The Faulkner sentence above is a "fused sentence." "I stood at the window" is one sentence, and "The curtains move slow out of darkness . . . ." is another. What is the effect of running them together as he does?

Wolf's sentence contains many comma splices, and the Hemingway is a classic run-on, which would be easily corrected by placing a comma before the second "and." Again, what is the effect of running these sentences together as they do?

For this exercise, experiment with voice and punctuation by writing a prose narrative that has as many run-on sentences of as many different kinds as you can make quite necessary to the narrative and voice. Play with the notion of urgency, or things running together in a blur, or voice. Try to make each run-on both essential and effective.

Now, write a text using as many simple run-ons as you can. Write one using comma splices. Write one using all, if you can, fused sentences. How do these different kinds of sentences work differently? Does a fused sentence really have a different kind of impact than a comma splice or a run-on? Can you say what it is?

In the final part of this exercise, revisit each text you wrote and punctuate it "properly." What happens to the voice? Does "proper punctuation" affect what you have written? In what ways? For better or worse?

(K.H.)

Building-Block Stories: Practice Mixing Sentence Styles

This exercise is designed to keep you writing, in Richard Hugo's terms, "off the subject." It assumes that: 1) your subject will prevail in your text only if it is somehow protected from most earnest intentions, and 2) the smallest unit of particular attention in fiction is the sentence. It is adapted, in part, from a similar writing exercise developed by Ken Waldman.

Below, find a number of opening sentences for the exercise. Select one and go on to the following directions. Work to develop a narrative sequence—that is, each sentence should lead to the next. In the end, does a story emerge? What can you say about it?

Note: You may need a dictionary and a book of English usage.

The First Sentences.

One day I was listening to the AM radio.

—Grace Paley

The last time I saw my father was in Grand Central Station.

—John Cheever

I started when I was six.

—Jane Martin

The quail came just before the lilacs bloomed in the green time of their first year married.

—Rolf Yngve

No one knows what they are about or, for that matter, where they come from.

—Tom Whalen

We decided to stop drinking and spend Sunday at the zoo.

—Stuart Dybek

The bank robber told his story in little notes to the bank teller.

—Steven Schutzman

My sickness bothers me, though I persist in denying it.

—Max Apple

She knew it was only boys in the field, come to watch them drunk on first wine.

—Jayne Anne Phillips

For my eighteenth birthday Jack gave me a five-year diary with a latch and a little key, light as a dime.

—Elizabeth Tallent

Hecht was born a late bloomer.

—Bernard Malamud

One of Irina's grandsons, nicknamed Riri, was sent to her at Christmas.

—Mavis Gallant

One morning Senorita Cordoba received a letter from her mother.

—Jane Bowles

In Palm Springs the poor are as dry as old brown leaves, blown in from the desert—wispily thin and almost invisible.

—Alice Adams

When you're the sheriff of Nowhere, you encounter strange crimes.

—Hans Ostrom

Karl kept one cannon on the front porch and one on the back.

—Chuck Rosenthal

Early that day the weather turned and the snow was melting into dirty water.

—Raymond Carver

For years the children whimpered and tugged.

—Barbara L. Greenberg

Lately I begin each day beside myself with a question: so, what is DeVeda Spaulding to me?
We live with acts of God.
I talk to my tumbler of Dewar's.

—Darrell Spencer

Optional.

Look for your own first sentence, one that compels you. Or write one yourself.

The Directions.

1. Write a sentence that repeats one word, but no more than one, from your first sentence.
2. Write a sentence that repeats one word, but no more than one, from your second sentence.
3. Write a sentence that repeats one word, but no more than one, from your third sentence.
4. Write a sentence that includes: a place name.
5. a dash.
6. a color and a name.
7. more than thirty words.
8. less than ten words.
9. a colon.
10. a part of the body.
11. the conditional tense.
12. a first person pronoun.
13. an interruptive clause.
14. quotation marks.
15. two interruptive clauses.
16. three articles of clothing.
17. a simile.
18. any form of the word "try."
19. a geographical formation.
20. italics.
21. a dictionary definition.
22. a metaphor.
23. a parallel structure.
24. exactly twenty-nine words.
25. exactly seventeen words.
26. exactly five words.
27. a comma and a semicolon.
28. the same words four times.
29. a second person pronoun.
30. a question mark.

31. reference to a past event.
32. a familial relationship.
33. parentheses.
34. alliteration.
35. a paradox.
36. exactly ten words.
37. exactly twenty words.
38. exactly thirty words.
39. exactly forty words.
40. exactly fifty words.
41. a comma splice.
42. two dashes.
43. something seen.
44. something tasted.
45. something heard.
46. something touched.
47. something smelled.
48. an equivocation.
49. the future tense.
50. the present tense.

Write a sentence, a paragraph, a page, and finish. Remember that the rules are minimums.

Don't cheat.

(K.H.)

Animal, Vegetable, Mineral?
Writing Using Only Question Sentences

"The difference," Geoffrey Hartman has said, "between what we mean and what we say may constitute the only depth in us."

If this double-edgedness of language ranges, in life, from a certain playfulness to a survival strategy, in writing it is deliberate and fundamental. Consider the Jack Matthews story, "A Questionnaire for Rudolph Gordon," which appears in the minianthology. Composed of one hundred questions, it depends on a narrative strategy that is indirect, implicit, and eerily efficient. Rudolph Gordon's story emerges intact from such suggestive questions as: "Did he hurt you, carrying you so roughly down the rocks and pine trees to the back of the cottage?" and "Where were your real parents?" Of course, the effect of the story also depends on its second person narration, which constructs the reader as the subject and demands a response.

A question is a sentence in interrogatory form. It ends with a question mark, and, in general, seeks to discover.

What did you eat for breakfast?

Where are you going? Where have you been?

How do you solve for x?

Sometimes the principle behind a question is discovery: there is something the interlocutor does not know and is attempting to find out. Sometimes a question frames its own answer. Either way, it depends on its context.

When a mother inquires of a son where he went with the next door neighbor girl the evening before and if they had fun, it is a different sort of question than when the son's girlfriend asks him. Between the one and the other lies something of what the evening was really like.

Consider the children's game, *Animal, Vegetable, Mineral*. You are thinking of animal. You tell the others, "Animal."

Are you a mammal? they ask.

Are you bigger than a bread box?

Do you live in Africa?

Are you striped?

Are you a zebra?

For this exercise, you will play both sides of the game. You will imagine a character, complete with history and conflict.

Example.

Your character has just found out that what he told his Little League coach about Danny Morales' birthday has resulted in his being disqualified from play. (Danny Morales is the boy who walks to the park after school to play baseball in your league because his father can pick him up there after work and because they don't have Little League where he lives). Maybe your character heard the parents talking behind the dugout about how Danny doesn't even know his real birthday because his documents were lost in Guatemala, and his mother is dead, and his father is really his uncle who was living in the US when he was born, and anyway, his documents are forged. Maybe Danny is really a better pitcher than your character. Maybe your character never meant to tell the coach, but it just slipped out when the coach replaced your character with Danny in a tight game.

Or, another story, maybe your character's mother has begun to hallucinate again, but she won't admit it and your character is the only child still living at home.

Or maybe your character knows that his brother's girlfriend is pregnant, but his brother doesn't know yet and maybe there's some question about the father.

Now write the story in questions. Leave as much out as you can, and still get it all in. End every sentence with a question mark. See what you can find out about your character and story that you don't already know. See how the story unfolds. For example, notice how an implied story emerges from the questions below:

Example.

How long have you known Danny Morales? Was he always in your grade in school?

How's Danny's English anyway? Is he the one that told you, "Too much beaches where I am born?"

Do you know where Danny's from—Mexico, Guatemala, El Salvador?

What does Danny bring to school potlucks?

How long have you known your coach?

Do you love baseball more than life?

Does he?

And so on.

Where are you going? Where have you been? How is your story turning out to be different than you imagined when you began?

(K.H.)

 ## Dueling Banjoes: The Use of Parallelism

If elements in writing "hold together" according to the logic of their organizing structures, why not start with outlines and just follow them? The familiar structure of an outline makes good sense to us—all those Roman numerals, followed by capital letters, followed by Arabic numerals, followed by lower case letters and so on, all in a neat linear sequence, all branching out from a central (organizing) idea. Elegant, symmetrical, this kind of structure helps ground us and clarify our thinking.

But there are other kinds of structures that also serve to ground us and organize our thinking, even if we don't know what to call them. Some of these are external and may seem arbitrary in relation to the problem at hand. For example, the earlier exercise, "What Hands Make: Using 'Instructions' as a Model for Other Writing" (Chapter Five), explores the use of instructions as an organizing principle in narrative. Sometimes even just the arbitrary logic of a number line will provide adequate structure in a story to move it along and hold it together. Sometimes a structure will even seem *dis*organized because we are not familiar with its organizational logic. Sometimes this logic is deeply embedded in language and form, but we will know it even so, as if by instinct, the way we know a natural movement of the body, like walking or turning toward a sound.

Maybe this is what Trinh Minh-Ha means by the "coming into being of the structure of the moment." Maybe it's related to what some people call "organic form." Maybe this is where writing comes from, but if so it throws the logic of the outline right out the second-story window.

What is "structure," anyway? How does it organize anything?

Perhaps you have heard the term "parallelism" applied to writing, maybe in your composition class, maybe as an "error" on a paper. Maybe when your teacher wrote it in the margin, you didn't know exactly what she meant, but you wouldn't have argued with her if she'd have told you that "parts of the sentence expressing ideas of equal importance should be in the same grammatical structure." And you would probably never write a sentence like, "Release the clutch slowly, and at the same time feeding a little gas."

Parallelism is one of those organizing principles, deeply embedded in language, that derives from a fundamentally symmetrical logic of grammar. If you make a list, the different items should take the same form. If you write a sentence, all its different parts should be alike. But if parallelism is about symmetry, it is also about order of an almost architectural elegance. That order structures our patterns of thinking, and it is there, in the way language works.

Just as parallelism structures syntax, it often works to organize larger narratives. In "Song of the Fluteplayer," for example, Sharman Apt Russell writes, "In that interior world, that landscape which is another home, two men live inside me"—Kokopelli, the Southwestern humpbacked fluteplayer, and Russell's own father, an air force test pilot who crashed in the Mohave in 1956. "As they walk bare-boned hills and clamor up banks of sand to new vistas," she continues, "I doubt that these two ever meet. More truthfully, there is much about them I do not know." As the essay progresses, Russell explores the stories of both men, not just to discover what it is she does not yet know about them, but also to develop her own story, which takes shape around these two other parallel stories.

Parallelism, in this larger sense, is an effective device not just to hold a narrative together, but to guide you through it, framing your ideas even as they come into being. Such a structure depends on a particular kind of narrative resonance, where what happens in the writing also happens in the interplay between and among parallel narratives, as well as in the space that opens out around them.

For this exercise, study Russell's essay, and then write a narrative framed by two others that share both sameness and difference and that have long haunted you. You may write in any form—fiction, poetry, nonfiction—but choose narratives "of equal value" that can be constructed along parallel structural lines. Let the three stories play freely, and pay particular attention to those odd moments when each resonates with another, as in a call and response or an animated contest between dueling banjos. Imagine those banjos: one plays, the other plays back, back and forth and back and forth. In the space between the two, another song—your own story—emerges.

Russell herself has said that not until she wrote it in this essay did she ever even try to imagine her father's plane crash. Writing took her there, along with those two men who still haunt the desert in which she lives.

What haunts you? Where will it take you in writing?

(K.H.)

Sentence Economics

"Show me the money!" Such was a buzz-phrase spread by a popular movie across the land a few years ago. Some writers have been known to express such a sentiment; some have their agents express it. Other writers focus less on money, though they need to eat and to pay the rent, too. Still other writers are mightily conflicted: "No one but a blockhead wrote except for money," pronounced Dr. Samuel

Johnson, way back in the eighteenth-century. A good, hard-headed Johnsonian commandment—except that throughout his career, Johnson toiled long and hard for not much money, and he worked on one of his most famous and most remarkable projects—a dictionary of the English language—for what amounted to pennies. A labor of love.

Those things inside writers' heads—images, sounds, obsessions, memories, stories, dreams—they say, "Show me the money!", too. Except they want to be paid in language, in sentences.

Probably because notions of narration naturally bring with them all sorts of chronological and sequential expectations, writers often think in terms of episodes, scenes in a series, pacing, transitions, and so forth.

One less orthodox way of looking at narrative is essentially "sentence economics," the basic question of this vantage point being, "How many sentences do I want to spend?" That's the implicit question we're made to ask by those things in our writerly heads. We rarely think of writing in a way that's as obvious and mechanical as the phrasing of this question, of course. But indirectly, sometimes subconsciously, we constantly consider how much language—how many sentences—to devote to different elements of a story as they occur to us. In a sense, then, sentences become the coin of the writing realm, and one way or another, writers have to master sentence economics.

Some of us may horde; others may save and spend prudently; some may go on spending binges but become remorseful; others may spend guiltlessly like there's no tomorrow and, when tomorrow comes, keep spending. Through the process of revision, we may well spend a lot of sentences, but only provisionally, "calling in the loan" as we revise and cut and trim.

Let's begin with a simple example: two versions of a narrative interval. The narrative "moment" is rather trite: a character wakes up and is already in a particular emotional mood. But at the moment we're concerned only with sentence economics, not with originality.

1. Collins woke early, sat up, stretched his arms, and coughed. He tasted how badly his breath smelled, felt how dirty his hair was. The bedroom seemed burdened with an enormous weight, as if the house were pressing in, as if other houses were pressing against his house, as if the city pressed against this neighborhood and the sky against the city. "I can't . . . ," Collins mumbled, and he lay back down.

2. When Collins woke up, he was already fed up—with everything.

In number one, I spent sentences generously, to say the least. In number two, I was a tightwad. The difference in "spending habits" raises other questions, of course. For example, does version two represent Collins, his state of mind, in the same way—and if not, what's lost or what's gained? Also, conventional wisdom has it that good fiction gives us concrete imagery, so if we went with the conventional wisdom, we'd keep version one, but we might want to ignore conventional wisdom, long enough at least to ask what version two provides aside from concrete imagery.

Does the lean sentence-budget of version two achieve something for our story that we want to hang on to? Finally, of course, we can consider more than just these two models of sentence economics.

Indeed, I could spend even more than I did in version one—could conceivably write a long narrative just about Collins waking up. (To what end and who might enjoy reading such a story are separate questions.) And I could be even more tight-fisted as I rewrote version two: "Collins: awake, oppressed."

From one angle, a person might argue that almost all writers, but perhaps especially writers of fiction and autobiography, concentrate a great deal of energy on managing sentence economics. How many sentences to spend, and where and how to spend them—and for what purposes? To some extent, this question—if not in so many words—underlies numerous choices writers make. But enough prelude. Time for you to work explicitly with this idea of sentence economics. Here are some options:

1. Do what I did: Imagine a narrative interval and spend different quantities of sentences representing "what happens," knowing of course that the "what happens" will shift and be stretched or shrunk like silly-putty, depending on your spending patterns. Try at least two versions, but you needn't limit yourself to two. Then step back and evaluate each version for what it achieves for you, for how it brings forth a narrative moment.

2. Take an old, young, or middle-aged draft of some kind of narrative you've written. Apply sentence economics experimentally—increasing slightly the number of sentences here, drastically cutting the number there, and so on. Part of the experiment might even be counterintuitive: you might arbitrarily say, "I'm going to rewrite this scene in precisely three sentences"—a crazy way, on its face, of writing. But sometimes such an unimaginative, arbitrary goal can help solve a narrative problem or indirectly ignite your imagination. License yourself to treat this draft rudely; don't try to protect it; experiment recklessly.

3. Let's say you feel trapped reading a narrative by a published writer, perhaps a very famous published writer. Maybe this person is a real big sentence-spender. Ask this person what time it is, as the saying goes, and he or she will first describe how to construct a watch. Think of an author and one of his/her works that seems to fit this profile. (Alas, many students I've known would probably choose Herman Melville's "Bartleby the Scrivener.")

   Then identify some narrative intervals on which, in your opinion, the writer has spent way too many sentences. Get some revenge: Be a real sentence-economics tightwad and revise (cut) these intervals.

   Or work the other way around: Take a narrative that seems too spare to you and rewrite some parts, spending sentences much more freely.

   Revising such published, even famous, writing may not turn you into a fan of an author whose work you don't like, but it may well let you see the author's approach to sentence economics from a different point of view and come to understand the rationale behind it.

4. Apply everything we've discussed here to...an economics of words. Instead of narrative and/or its intervals, moments, and scenes being the unit on which you spend "currency," now the sentence is the larger unit, and words are the coin of the realm. Develop your own rules, strategies, tactics, or experiments for working explicitly with word economics.

(H.O.)

Grammar, Punctuation, and Creativity

 Grammar-Check Your Favorite Author

You like a writer. You imitate that writer, consciously or unconsciously, using one of the *Metro* exercises (parody, for instance) or on your own. You read a favorite writer's work aloud and you read your own. Yet you wonder. What is it—what is he/she doing and what am I doing when the two of us write "this way"? Well, use your technology as a tool—grammar-check both texts. We hasten to add that this nuts-and-bolts analysis of style is not intended to replace the mysterious pleasure of reading a favorite author, of being drawn in and along by style, and of accounting for style by means of criticism or theory. Indeed, while grammar-checking a favorite author can demystify some aspects of the writing, it can also demonstrate that many elements of style are elusive. Also, there's a bit of whimsy involved in juxtaposing sentence-scanning software with the idiosyncratic linguistic world of one writer.

I borrow this grammar-check idea from Nancy Reichert who used it in a paper I heard recently. She compared the prose style of William Faulkner to that of one of her writing students who had been sorted by test scores as being not highly proficient, and she found that Faulkner's writing and the student's writing weren't all that different—at least in one category: long sentences. Faulkner got away with rule-breaking and took his work farther, because, no doubt, he had written his long sentences (135 words, all one sentence) intentionally while the student writer lacked that control in his equally long sentence (128 words with one run-on and one fragment).

Now run-ons and fragments are no longer considered inherently wrong although formal grammar books still teach them as such. A more sophisticated view requires that we evaluate these rule violations in context. They're "wrong" if they derail meaning, are used awkwardly and unintentionally. On the other hand, published writers everywhere use run-on sentences (or darned long ones like Faulkner's, so long the grammar-check cannot process them well) and fragments. Like the ones you'll find in many sections of *Metro* as we coauthors use them for emphasis and demonstrating language play. (The preceding is a sentence fragment.)

Anyway, Nancy illustrated that Faulkner in some ways wasn't much different from her student writer. Faulkner skipped school and dropped out. He earned a D in English. Eventually, he went on to become a venerated writer (as I hope *128 words/one run-on and one fragment* will do).

You (and Faulkner, were he alive) might enjoy putting your favorite authors through the grammar-check of your computer. Then put your own prose to the test. Analyze prose of your own written in more than one genre. You will learn something about grammar and sentence construction or the limits and possibilities of grammar checkers—or all of the above.

Here are samples of what this exercise looks like:

You like a writer. You imitate that writer, consciously or unconsciously, using one of the *Metro* exercises (parody, for instance) or on your own. You read a favorite writer's work aloud and you read your own. Yet you wonder. What is it—what is he/she doing and what am I doing? Well, use your technology as a tool—grammar-check both texts.

[*Metro* author]

Grammar-check data (selected):

The Microsoft Word grammar-check stumbled on the next-to-last sentence, suggesting that the writer might "Consider **is** or **are** instead of **am**" [what **is** I doing? what **are** I doing?], citing "Rule: Subject-Verb Agreement—subject and verb must agree in person and number." The grammar-check seems to have read "what" as the subject of the clause, not "I." The grammar-check also informs us that there is an average of 9.8 words per sentence, that the Flesch Reading Ease rating is 73.5, that the Flesch-Kincaid Grade-Level is 5.4, and that the Coleman-Liau Grade-Level is 8.0. Our own view is that this paragraph is colloquial, chatty, accessible and that the conversational repetition of "what" in the next-to-last sentence threw off the grammar-check. The Reading Ease rating and the grade levels indicate accessibility. So much for the self-inflicted test run; now on to Edith Wharton.

The observance of Sunday at Bellomont was chiefly marked by the punctual appearance of the smart omnibus destined to convey the household to the little church at the gates. Whether any one got into the omnibus or not was a matter of secondary importance, since by standing there it not only bore witness to the orthodox intentions of the family, but made Mrs. Trenor feel, when she finally heard it drive away, that she had somehow vicariously made use of it.

[Edith Wharton, *House of Mirth*]

Grammar-check data:

The (Microsoft Word) grammar-check warns that the word "observance" "may be confused with observation." Tragically (we jest), the second sentence "was too long to process for grammatical structure." Clearly, the grammar-check can handle only so much improvisation and complexity. The Flesch Reading Ease rating drops to about 54; that's not a defect, of course, but it does support what our intuition may tell us—that the paragraph has a certain formal, even academic, personality. The Flesch-Kincaid Grade-Level is 8.7, and —get this!—the Coleman-Liau Grade Level, which for our sample paragraph was 8.0, is 55.8! Apparently, according to C-L, one has to be in the 55th grade to understand Wharton. (Apparently C-L overreacts to formality and complexity). If one were to imitate Wharton, one might consider adopting a formal, quasi-academic tone, using some abstract, Latinate words, and not shying away from sentences with multiple clauses and phrases; and one would want to load description and scene-making with implicit analysis, telling "what happens" and "what the *what-happens* means" both at once. At least that's one interpretation: what do you think?

> The lights come up and a thing curtain covers the screen, but the sign behind it telling everyone to please visit the concession stands in the lobby while they're getting ready for the next feature can still be seen, and the ripply picture on it of a huge drippy banana split, which they don't even sell as far as she knows, makes her stomach rumble loud enough to give a zombie hiccups, so she decides to go out and see what she can find with less than six zillion calories in it. Her friend, who's flirting with some broken-nosed character a row back in a high school letter jacket and sweaty cowboy hat, turns and asks her jokingly to bring her back a salty dog—"Straight up, mind!"—making the guy snort and heehaw and push his hands in his pockets.
>
> [Robert Coover "Intermission" from *A Night at the Movies*]

Grammar-check data:
The (Microsoft Word) grammar-check began by saying that the sentence was too long to process for grammatical structure. Then—and here's an instance when computers seem to have personality—the grammar-check seemed to get a little miffed: "Consider revising sentence. Very long sentences can be difficult to understand."
How would *you* imitate Coover?
What are your observations, based on this data—and on data you acquire from grammar-checking other authors, including yourself?

(W.B.)

This Adventitious Music: Exploring Grammar with Nonsense Writing

> In the act of love, as in all the arts, the soul should be felt by the tongue and the fingers, felt in the skin. So should our sounds come to color up the surface of our stories like a blush. This adventitious music is the only sensory quality our books can have. . . . No artist dare neglect his own world's body, for *nothing else* about his book is physical.
>
> —William Gass

For if, as Susan Sontag has argued, we need an "erotics" (blood beating through the body of our work) in place of our present "hermeneutics" (dry intellect) of art, we must apprentice ourselves first to the materiality of text, which begins as with the presence of sound.

So, this exercise is simple: it is to make a purely physical text.

What I mean is, make a piece of writing that sounds beautiful and absolutely necessary just the way it is, but is, in its meaning, utter nonsense. Give all your attention to the sound and rhythm of it, its ebb and flow. Listen for your sibilants, your gutturals, and uvulars.

Alliteration.

Rhyme.

Balanced parallelisms.

Assonance and dissonance.

Rhythm and meter.

Cadence.

Sounds that open way back at the back of your throat and those that pop out from your pursed-together lips.

Syllables. Syllables. Syllables.

Vowel sounds.

Consonants.

Work out loud, just as if you were playing a solo concert, heartfelt and inside the very sounds of it.

Feel it in your mouth, your throat, your chest, on your trembling tongue.

Let it transport you with its rolling, rolling, its fine tonalities, the very breath of it.

Breathe.

But be sure it means nothing, nothing at all. It must be completely meaningless, sheer and utter nonsense.

There is only one more thing, a small thing, but important: your text must be grammatically consistent and correct. Just get your verbs and nouns and all in right relations to each other, and then just let them sing, a little bit like angels.

(K.H.)

By All Devious Means
(But With Grammatical Consistency)

10

A "bricoleur" is someone who works with his(her) hands and uses devious means compared to those of a "craftsman" or engineer. S/He is a handy-person, then, who may, unlike the craftsperson, use a piece of wire where the craftsperson would use a screw. The bricoleur can perform numerous tasks, diverse tasks. Unlike the engineer, s/he does not limit herself to the "availability" of materials, but instead she makes do with what happens to be around, "that is to say with a set of tools and materials which is always finite and is also heterogeneous because what it contains bears no relation to the current project or indeed to any particular project."

The engineer questions the universe while the "bricoleur" addresses himself to a collection of oddments left over from human endeavors . . .

In the art world *bricolage* is a term used to define any unexpected use made of ready-made objects. Some of the dynamic of this art is in the "fusion of estrangement with recognition" (Dada).

—Mona Houghton

Something of a *bricoleur* herself, Houghton pulls this definition from Levi-Strauss, *The Savage Mind.* The writer is a kind of *bricoleur* as well, bound to the primacy of other people's words and all forms of language, from those of the most beloved literary texts to what's on the back of this morning's cornflakes box.

This exercise is simple. It asks you to proceed as the perfect postmodern writer, one who sifts through, collects and reassembles, by all devious means, the preexisting texts that surround you. If you need a screw, and you've only got some wire, use the wire; and if you lack that, use twine.

Here, you should steal language, proceed without remorse, take anything you can and record it in a notebook. Maybe you hear someone say, "It was yellow from the day we arrived." Write it down. Maybe you read in the paper, "From gun ports, police fire back with plastic bullets." Write that down, too. Or in a book, "I believe I have some knowledge which you gentlemen should have." Or titles: "The Sonnabend Model of Obliscence," "Bertha Spins Chaos," "No Caviar for the Butcher."

Listen for phrases, snatches of words you catch on the wing. Look for unexpected language, anything that grabs you, what is lovely. Eavesdrop. Watch cartoons. Pay attention to the menus you order from, the cautionary warnings on your household products, the names of businesses you frequent, the sound of someone talking on the phone, all the most unlikely places you can think of. Be vigilant and exhaustive.

Write it all down in your notebook, noting the source and, if you will, the date and time, for your records. Then, when your book is full and you are sated, go back and weave a text of the tissue of quotations you've collected.

There are only a few additional rules:

1. The text must be *grammatically consistent,* and you may alter tense and pronouns to achieve this.

2. When necessary for "making sense" you may add a few of your own words, but at least 90% of your text must be generated from your work as a "writer-*bricoleur.*"

3. You may substitute a single proper name for disparate ones among your textual fragments if you need to.

4. Do not be afraid to take risks or make extravagant linguistic leaps, and consider playing with the appearance of the words on the page in the manner of collage.

5. Feel free to make up your own rules, and, as always, to break them.

(K.H.)

The Problem (Okay, One Problem) With Punctuation

One problem with punctuation is that maybe you have always used it right, or maybe you have always used it wrong, but either way it's mystifying. Its rules seem odd and arbitrary. You know that there must be a logic to this complicated system, but you can't quite figure it out. You believe that if you could figure it out, many of the other mysteries of the universe would miraculously sort themselves out.

At least we suspect that this is how you feel, because we feel the same way—when confronted with new e-mail punctuation, for instance. At least it seems a form of punctuation, but who can really say, this set of notations of virtual moods. If there are any rules for it, we'd really like to know. Instead, we have a list that looks like this:

:-)	happy
:-(	sad
:-O	surprised
:-\	undecided
):->	devilish
:-|	ambivalent
:-&	tongue-tied
%-)	silly
|-O	bored
:*)	clowning
:-C	bummed out
;-/	skeptical
O:-)	angelic
:~/	mixed up
;->	sarcastic

If you are one of those for whom cyberspace has always already been familiar, maybe this above makes perfect sense to you. Maybe you "get" their logic; maybe you intuitively understand the rules. But if you're not, you may have a hard time knowing when to use a parenthesis and when to use a slash.

Standard punctuation rules can seem like that as well, and when you learn them without learning why they are the way they are, they will seem arbitrary and hard to remember. Why, for example, do we use semicolons and not commas to link closely related independent clauses? And what exactly is a "clause" again? (A group of words that includes a subject and a verb.)

In addition to having seemingly endless rules, punctuation is expressive and based on a logic all its own. Sometimes it is useful to imagine punctuation marks as having personalities and temperaments, just like friends and relatives. Sometimes this can help us remember how to use the marks correctly and tell them apart.

Imagine the *period,* say, as a good father, definitive, stable, just this side of stolid. He says what he means, and he means what he says, and he comes to full stops in between. A father's way of being in the world is full of independent clauses, absolutely certain where one ends and another begins.

Commas, on the other hand, are flexible and ever so accommodating. They are used in so many ways—to separate things in a list (words, phrases and clauses), before coordinating conjunctions (*and, or, but, for, nor , yet, so*) linking independent clauses (clauses that can stand alone as complete sentences), around interruptive phrases, and so on. Commas are like the classic middle sibling, peacemakers, smoothers-over, the ones who hold everything together, but gracious and full of discretion.

Semicolons, used between independent clauses not linked by a conjunction and to separate items in a complex list, are like well-intended stepparents. More dogged and insistent than commas, they are also more forceful. The little dot above the line is the glue of their will to keep the blended family in tact.

Colons are used between two parts of a sentence when the first part creates a sense of anticipation about what follows in the second. Imagine the colon as some exotic lover, probably an artist, a dancer, or a rockclimber, nameless, whose every move anticipates bodily pleasure. Either that, or an eccentric uncle who has the infuriating habit of always changing the subject to his advantage.

Dashes make an even sharper break in the continuity of the sentence than do colons, and *parentheses* make the sharpest of all. These could be cousins who are twins, Tweedledum and Tweedledee, who if one says something, the other contradicts her, back and forth, back and forth as if in a single breath.

Ellipses . . . An absent minded professor who never can finish her sentences.

Quotation marks: A good friend who never stops talking.

Question marks: An insatiably curious mother-in-law or brother-in-law.

Exclamation marks: A father again, but this one a strict disciplinarian. Or maybe an acquaintance who gets excited just too easily.

For this exercise, imagine a family—either your own, or one you know or invent. Who, in it, is the comma, the colon? Who is the question mark? Name them, and tell why you chose them.

First write a simple story in plain language; then rewrite the story in the voice (or voices) of your imaginary friend or relative punctuation mark. Do this in as many of these as you can, and in each, use the punctuation mark in question as often as you can. Try to use each mark correctly, and with absolute precision, but also, have fun.

When you are done, read aloud what you wrote and see if your listener can tell which punctuation mark you are using. If she can, what are her reasons? If not, what have you left out? Has this exercise changed the way you feel about punctuation marks? If so, why?

Examples.

A Simple Story.

I went to the park, where boys were playing baseball. There were five dia-monds in use, and children of all ages. It was a lovely day. The sun was shin-

ing and there was a slight breeze. In one game I watched, the bases were loaded, with two out, and the boy who was pitching had a look of concentration about him. Then he struck the batter out, and the fans went wild.

My Father, the Period.

I went to the park. It is a municipal park. It is run by the city. This park is a real asset to our community. Many sports leagues play there. In the fall they play soccer. In the spring they play baseball. Now it is spring. It is a lovely spring. The sun was shining. The breeze was cool. Boys were playing baseball on five diamonds. My own son was a Little League pitcher. I watched that boy load the bases. He walked two batters. Then he gave up a single. He was in a tough spot. My son got himself into plenty of spots like that. Bases loaded. Two men out. But he struck the third boy out. Then the fans went wild.

My Sister, Edith, the Comma.

In the spring, when the weather is fine and the sun is shining, I like to walk to our local park and watch the boys play at their sports, usually baseball, this time of year, but some of them still play soccer, or basketball, or roller hockey. As a girl, I didn't have much chance to play sports, though I was on a tennis team in high school, not that I was any good at it, but I did like the short, white skirts I got to wear, and the coach, who was a friend of my father's and who had three gorgeous boys, near my age. The boys playing baseball remind me of those boys, for they are young, and strong, and they carry themselves with such authority and grace, and when I went to the park that day, there were boys of all ages playing on every diamond, and there was one game I watched, so exciting, the bases loaded, the boy on the mound with such a look of concentration on his face, how my heart went out to him, but, amazingly, he got his third strike out, and then how the fans went wild.

My Brother, Frank, the Colon (With a Little Help from Tweedledum and Tweedledee).

I went to the park—the same park where I spent my time in Little League—to watch the boys playing baseball. I remember my first coach: backwards baseball cap, baseball shorts, the whole shebang. He used to say he wished life was like a Disney movie: you take a ragtag bunch of kids and turn them into a championship team in under two hours. We didn't exactly come through like that: by the end of the season, we were dead last in the ranking. This team looked pretty good: the pitcher had a few bad calls, but he didn't lose his cool, and his fielders were right there behind him. But he was in a bad spot: ducks on the pond. I had my fingers crossed for him (and every time he threw the ball, I'd whisper, "Jinx," under my breath to the batter). I could tell that last pitch was a zinger: it had a perfect arch, and man, it flew! I cheered right along with the fans: those were the days, all right, those were the days!

My Mother's Friend, Agnes, Quotation Marks.

"I went to the park," she said.

"Which park do you mean?" he said.

"You know, the one where all the kids play baseball? It must cost the city a lot," he said. "They have five diamonds, and real stands."

"What do you know about baseball?" he said.

"Who, me?' Quite a lot actually. All my boys played Little League, you know, all five of them, and three of the four were pitchers, and all but one made All-Stars, even City All-Stars. But we'd get whumped every time we played boys from somewhere else. They took their baseball seriously, those other leagues, believe you me. Anyway, so I spend many years and who knows how many hours, sitting in the sun, watching boys at play in the field. My youngest is still playing in high school, and sometimes his brother's still go to watch. He's one of the pitchers, so my heart really went out to that boy. He couldn't have been more than ten. Imagine the pressure on him. Really, I just loved the excuse to sit there in the sun for a couple of hours, doing absolutely nothing. You never really get time to do nothing in this life, not when you have five boys, you don't. And you know, I got to admire them too, in ways I really hadn't been able to since they were babies, crawling around on the floor. Especially the pitchers. They stand out on that mound and you watch them, and your heart stops every time, just like it did when the tumbled as a two-year-old and scrambled those beautiful brains of theirs. Oh, but that boy. He was a small one, and he was so intense. I loved it when he struck that third boy out, but even so, my heart did go out to the other boy. I didn't even know what the score was. I think I saw the boy who struck out start to cry. When he got out of the cage, he threw his hat on the ground and his face screwed all up. Really, it's a tough sport. I do love that park."

My Friend, Linda, the Question Mark.

Did your boys play baseball? Was it baseball they were playing in the park that day? Or maybe it was softball? But girls play softball, don't they? Don't boys almost always play baseball? Is it three strikes, or more, and you're out? And what happens when the bases are loaded? Does the pitcher feel tension, I wonder? Does the sun get in his eyes? Does his young heart start to pound, with such excitement? And if the umpire calls a ball, does he want to cry? Does he want to stomp off the field, and bury his face in his mother's lap or punch his father for yelling so much useless advice? Was that the end of the game, when he struck that poor boy out? What must the final score have been? And why were the fans so excited?

(K.H.)

In Praise of Punctuation

In his tongue-in-cheek (comma-in-sentence) short essay in the anthology, "In Praise of the Humble Comma," Pico Iyer claims, "the comma gets no respect." Endlessly assigned prescriptively, punctuation rules are overapplied like cheap syrup to the pancakes of our sentences. In fact, punctuation imperatives have nearly killed our enjoyment of the perfectly deployed exclamation point or the well formed semicolon. This exercise asks you to change that, by reveling in different punctuation marks, the better to learn how to use them. Going by the theory that it takes excess to curb one's enthusiasm back to controlled usage (according to William Blake, at least, "The road of excess leads to the palace of wisdom"), I'd like you individually (or with a group of writing friends) to assemble a chapbook of essays on punctuation in the manner of Iyer's essay.

Write short paeans, praise-paragraphs, or longer explorations devoted to the following marks (and, like Iyer, utilize the mark strategically but also all over the place, to excess; also like Iyer, you may choose to digress and wax philosophical about the uses of your punctuation mark of choice).

Write then, in praise of: ! ' __ . —; : " ? ( ) [ ] , and so on. If you must, you could even write in praise of E-mail emoticons like sideways smiley faces {a parody of Iyer might be in order here : ;-).} Someone, too, might want to take on the powerful absence or quiet or purity or deviousness of the punctuating empty white space.

In a follow-up exercise, take a current poem or poetic prose passage of your own and load it up and down and sideways. Make it heavily exclamatory. Turn statements into questions. Join the several sentences into one long elegantly orchestrated snake of an exposition. Or, eliminate punctuation entirely and make line breaks and/or syntax shifts do the pausing and turn-signaling for your wary or unwary reader. Read these versions aloud to hear better what you say in this way.

(W.B.)

Word-Choice in Particular, Language-Awareness in General

Words: Choice and Precision

Words, we've been telling you, are everything—when we haven't been contradicting ourselves, as teachers and writers do, by saying that something else, such as *the sentence,* is everything; but then (they said, trying to cover their tracks) sentences are made out of words. For the moment, anyway, we're fixated on *words.*

Which words? Whose words? Your words. Your word choice matters. You've heard people talk and judged them (often wrongly) on their words, their accents, dialects, vocabulary choices, indifference to or attention to words. Words color our texts and also the impressions of those who receive our words. Have you ever been at a loss for the right word? Sometimes I'll wander around chanting—that is, intoning, vocalizing, singing—a word and its alternates to see which one really says what I want to say, also to see if what I want to say can be improved upon. That's why a thesaurus, carefully used, can be a writer's friend (poorly used, used without a dictionary to help calibrate precise meanings, without attention, why a thesaurus can make a sentence and sentence-writer sound down right silly—ludicrous, witless, fatuous—because the writer doesn't know what's being written). Writers pay attention when they choose nouns and verbs. I can go swim or I can much more precisely:

dog paddle

tread water

float

go for a dip

do laps.

I can admire the bird outside my window or I can much more precisely admire a:

goose (if I'm on a farm)

pelican (if I'm at the beach)

crow (if I'm in the desert or on a deserted highway)

or more precisely:

stellar blue jay (if I'm in the western Sierras).

More simply, we all know that the word *stink* encompasses smells as varied as a skunk's self-protective stench and the dizzy smell of rotting apples beneath an unharvested tree. Or, take the color red:

ruby

crimson

cherry

scarlet

carmine

sanguine

cerise

pink

ruddy

Some of these "reds" will work or not work for your writing. Each has a precise denotation—it means a certain generally agreed upon shade, but each also has connotations—ruby comes with the baggage of Dorothy's slippers; cherry evokes the fruit and has sexual overtones as well as being the slang word for praiseworthy;

carmine is a less used, more exotic word with mobster overtones (for me) and pink evokes girl babies, Barbie dolls, frivolity (again, these are evoked for me). Denotations develop over time and are regularized in dictionaries; connotations are never exact. They depend on the interaction of readers' and writers' experiences.

So, what's a writer to do? Certainly, don't hold back, experiment. And experiment through revision and word exploration. Here are some exercises you can try. Though illustrated with prose, they can be used for poetry, fiction, and nonfiction. I provide brief examples of the techniques using the opening paragraph from a piece of my own nonfiction, titled "Sewing" that runs like this:

> In the darkened interior of my mother's trailer, we are cleaning out her possessions. This is five days after her death and before the used furniture dealer arrives. Before my sisters and I part ways after several days of sorting and talking and claustrophobic reacquaintance. We empty closets and cupboards, clean under bathroom sinks and push dampened washcloths into the depths of high cupboards that we are releasing from the burden of my mother's lifelong rummage sale collections.
>
> (*Puerto del Sol* 29.1 [1994]: 497.)

1. Fill in the Blank

   Take a piece of your work and blank out certain words—try a paragraph where the adjectives are gone or the nouns or the verbs. Circulate the paragraph (or poem) around a group, asking each writer to fill in the blanks in his/her copy. Then compare your choice of descriptive words. In this sample, I'll eliminate adverbs and adjectives.

   In the _____ interior of my mother's trailer, we are cleaning out her possessions. This is _____ days after her death and before the ____ furniture dealer arrives. Before my sisters and I part ways after _____ days of _____ and _____ and _____ reacquaintance. We empty closets and cupboards, clean under bathroom sinks and push _____ washcloths into the depths of ____ cupboards that we are releasing from the burden of my mother's _____ rummage sale collections.

2. Substitute

   Play with a thesaurus. Look up substitutes for words in your text. Redraft once to the point of wildness or silliness—push your text as far as you can, choose an unexpected register (formal or archaic or rococo words if you're normally plainspoken or plain if you normally elaborate more than you need to).

   In the shadowy core of my mother's trailer, we are purging her belongings. This is five days after her death and before the used furniture dealer arrives. Before my sisters and I part ways after several days of discarding and conferring and claustrophobic reuniting. We cleanse wardrobes and credenzas, clean under washroom sinks and push dampened cloths into the depths of high cabinets that we are liberating from the load of my mother's lifelong rummage sale collections.

3. Pare Down

Recast your text without any adjectives or adverbs. Then, make sure your nouns and verbs really do their work by picking the best ones you can.

Inside my mother's trailer, we are cleaning out her belongings. Five days after her death and before the furniture dealer arrives, before my sisters and I part ways after brief reacquaintance, we empty closets and cupboards, clean under sinks, and push washcloths into cupboards that we are releasing from our mother's rummage sale collections.

(W.B.)

Figures of Speech

Throughout this book we have talked a great deal about language, our medium, our nature, who we are. The concept, for example, that writing proceeds from language as well as from image, has been explored here in a wide variety of ways. Here we want to talk about figures of speech—idioms, colloquialisms, slang, cliche, and other basic elements of our daily argot.

Years ago when our kids were learning how to talk we learned to pay a new kind of attention to language.

"Mommy," they would say, "what does *kit and caboodle* mean?" Or *fit as a fiddle,* or *an apple a day,* or *the Milky Way?*

"Oh that," we would say. "That is just an expression."

For the most part, people recognize idioms because we are part of a community of speakers familiar with basic conventions of language. Metaphor informs many idiomatic expressions, where things are used in place of other things that they are "like:" *light as a feather, red as a beet, strong as an ox.* But there are other idioms that come to us out of nursery rhyme, or history, or myth, while others seem more purely arbitrary: *hold your tongue, dead as a doornail*—is it *bran,* or *brand new?* (A new brand, or bran, new on the stalks?)

Even so, if you say, "My sixth grade teacher was a bear," most people will understand that the teacher was not literally a bear. Maybe your sixth grade teacher was a strict, mean teacher, and so you have remembered her as a "bear."

In an ESL class, a fifty-something upper-class Colombian woman, nearly fluent in English, asked what *shout it out,* means. The teacher explained about calling out in a loud voice. No, no. The student knew all about that, she said. But she'd seen it on t.v., for a stain removal ad. The product was called *Shout.* And the ad copy ran, "Shout it out."

The teacher, who had never seen the ad, was unfamiliar with the product.

"Oh, that," the teacher said, "that's just an expression."

Some other figures of speech are:

He's a good egg.

Turn the other cheek.

The cat got out of the bag.
Now that's a horse of a different color.
Hell-bent for leather.
Hell on wheels.
It's raining cats and dogs.
The sky is falling.
I smell a rat.
tongue twister
It's a jungle out there.
tickled pink
dig it
d'uh bomb
This car's a lemon.
Two heads are better than one.
His eyes are bigger than his stomach.
Cat got your tongue?
Leave no stone unturned.
running like a house on fire
Play it by ear.
something up your sleeve
the harder they come
in a pickle
skeleton in the closet
I'm losing my head.
My heart's not in it.
I'm so hungry I could eat a horse.
splitting hairs
take a load off
Follow your nose.
pie in the sky
Word!
the apple of my eye
larger than life
Chill, will you?
dirty dozen
foxy lady
good as gold

going cuckoo
Birds of a feather flock together.
Mind your own business.
keep your oar out
up a creek
for heaven's sakes
in a tizzy
lost in space
for crying out loud
holy mackerel
hot diggity dog
right-on
take a chill pill
Your pad or mine?
to be buggin'
spin on a dime
in other words
no reason on earth
I'm toast.

For this exercise, make your own list of idioms (or add to this one). Listen closely to the people and language all around you—movie titles, advertisements, television, sports announcers. Play. As you collect your idioms, let them echo off each other to see how many will grow out of one.

Then write a story or a poem using as many idioms from your list as you can. Use them self-consciously. The deliberate use of cliche, for example, will call attention to its status as cliche. Notice the way this affects both how you write, and how you read what you have written. Notice, too, how the self-conscious use of idiomatic expression also sharpens the way you think about language in general— and about expressions you once used automatically.

Remember your senses of humor.

But this need not be only a joke. For an example of how idiomatic expression can be used to create a highly stylized and ironic effect in writing, see Jane Bowles' puppet show, "A Quarreling Pair." In the Introduction to her *Collected Works,* Truman Capote observes that Bowles' use of language is so original and odd that it seems as if translated from a foreign language. This is at least in part a function of her use of idiom, always at a slant, sounding skewed.

Imagine yourself translating from English to English. See how it sounds.

(K.H.)

15 ▶ The Opposites of Everything

This sickness to express oneself, what is it?
—Jean Cocteau

. . . the science of the various blisses of language.
—Roland Barthes

I told a woman who plays in the orchestra how uncapturable music is, how I cannot think of organizing the music I hear, but only be its audience. But she said that writing is the most abstract form; the other forms have con-comitant human sense organs; music has the ear, and painting the eye, sculp-ture the hands, and acting and dancing the voice and body. But writing, she said, does not have its organ. She began to cry; I'm not sure why.
—Maxine Hong Kingston

When we were young and new at teaching, a famous poet advised us to place as many artificial obstacles between the motivations of our students and their writing as we could. This seemed a curious bit of advice, even for such a famous poet, who was tall and gestured broadly in the air. He meant for us to deliberately confound our students' thinking, to make noise and get in their way.

"Don't let them think their own thoughts," he said. "It's all words anyway," we think he said.

No one argues with this principle in relation to composers, who organize notes and instruments and sound. Artists use paint and other palpable materials to create a visual, physical space. Even dancers use their bodies to create form and shape and movement. To all these media we respond emotionally as well as intellectually, but we also know that this response would escape us if the composer were careless, or the artist imprecise, or the dancer grew tired and let her body flag.

Words are confusing as a medium because they *mean* things. Expect that writing, first, is never only about what it is about, but rather what it *is*—the thing on the page, the *made*-thing.

Thus, we must train ourselves, like the dancer or musician, to give ourselves over to our material—the word, or the sentence itself, and all its material aspects, the sound and shape of it in our ear and mouth as well as on the page, its palpable body and form. We may experience bliss. For writing is an act of faith, like any other, through which, if we don't think about it too much, our meaning, paradoxi-cally, will shine through.

For this exercise, find a text you admire—a poem, a short-short story, a prose fragment from a novel you love, song lyrics. The rules are simple: replace every word in your text (excluding, to begin with and if necessary, articles and different kinds of conjunctions) with its opposite.

Ask them, the poet said, what's the opposite of *blue?* (Is it green? Is green the opposite of blue? Or red? Or not-blue? Or happy, happy, happy?)

Of *scissors?* (Paper, rock? Maybe tape. Maybe stitches, maybe sutures.)

Of *skin?*

Of *you?* That would be me; that would also be he. *That?* This. *Apple?* Eden. *Apple?* Corn. *Apple?* IBM. *Apple?* Sauce.

Is *heaven,* then, the opposite of earth? Or is it *sky,* or *moon,* or *underworld?* If I told you to pick the opposite *of a corncob,* what would you say—*that husk, any fruit, oatmeal?* This is not just a word game; it is a way of working language from the known and the familiar to the exotic and the startling, the evocative and strange, where the world is transformed again and anew in writing, again and anew.

"Also," the poet said, "tell them the poem they make of 'opposites' should make sense."

He meant that this poem made out of the opposites of everything should still be internally consistent, grammatically correct, and comprehensible. This is no small order, but it is possible.

To do so, of course, you will have to adjust your verbs to your persons. *I weep,* for example, may become *he climbs.* You will also need to be able to identify your parts of speech. Nouns substitute for other nouns, adjectives for adjectives, and so on.

Finally, you will have to give yourself permission to be surprised by what you make, and to own it, and to read it, when you're done, for unexpected meaning.

What does it *mean?* Did you *mean* that?

(How could you have? But aren't you glad you did?)

Variation 1.

Try substituting conjunctions as well, which will completely alter the logical structure of the original text. *Because,* a subordinating conjunction of causality, may become, for example, *when,* also a subordinating conjunction, but one of temporality. Or what happens to the sense of the text when *and* becomes *but* (both coordinating conjunctions)?

Variation 2.

Now try adding articles—*a, an, the*—to the kinds of words you replace. (This is more complicated than you may think.)

Variation 3.

Still working independently, but in a small group, perform your substitutions on the same text. Compare the results. How are they different? How alike? What did you learn from the other versions?

Variation 4.

With a partner or a writing group, collaborate to write a poem of opposites together. Discuss the choices you make and why you make them.

Variation 5.

Use your own text as the text you write off of. (Think of this as a translation.)

Repeat as often as you wish.

Cruise the underside of language. Work the words. Experience bliss.

(K.H.)

16 ▶ Poetry Phobia Cure-All (Not Sold In Stores)

Earlier we discussed the problem narrative anxiety (see "Narrative Anxiety Cure-All," Chapter 2), and confessed that we ourselves have our predilections and concerns. Despite years of girlhood reading (beautiful hardcover volumes with pages worn thin from my turning), I, for example, developed a late-onset case of poetry anxiety sometime in college, probably induced by the pervasive idea that poems were High Art and complex. Also, you could get them "right" or "wrong" in class. Not to mention the poets themselves, who were bohemian, black-garbed, and full of drama. Poetry held itself off, and I fell for it. The anxiety almost became a phobia.

Maybe you can understand why. Maybe poetry seems serious and difficult to you. Maybe you're afraid of being "wrong," or maybe, like me, you had a famous poet mock your work.

There are cures for what ails you, though they are sometimes bitter. One well–intended teacher suggested to me that there are two important tests for if you understand a poem: 1) if you can explicate it, in classic close-reading fashion (for which, he believed, all you needed was a good historical dictionary), and 2) if you can read it out loud.

Though I read well to myself, with eloquence and passion, and though I believe that in such moments I fully inhabit the poem, when this teacher handed me "Mont Blanc," just as with my oboe playing in high school, I opened my mouth and squawked.

Squawk, I read to the teacher, near tears. *Squawk, squawk, squawk.*

And so it happened that this teacher, who'd meant to rescue me from my ineptitudes, came instead in time to the verge of giving up, until one day, almost as if by afterthought, a throw-away comment if he'd ever made one, he said something that changed my thinking about poetry forever. He said it like maybe I was a bit dimwitted, like I should have learned it many years before. He said it with a trace of elegant ennui. "Poems are made of sentences." He said it, and then he dismissed me.

Now a sentence is a thing that you, like me, may completely understand—in which case the first section of this chapter will seem amenable to you. A sentence has its different parts and proper punctuation. It can be short or long, furrow-like or branch-like. It can declare itself absolutely, or equivocate gracefully, looping and arching, twisting and turning, a ribbon on the wind of your page.

In addition, you can tell just by looking at them, poems are made of lines, which do not, for the most part, fill up the space of the page. They only go so far, and then they stop. Lines have their own integrity, a logic all their own, governed, in many cases, by meter and form, but also by their own necessity. This is something internal, something that drives them and holds them together, not at all like plot, something poetic. A line must be a thing to contemplate, lovely on its own, but it must also work to lure you on to the next line, pulled through the poem through the urgency of where it starts and stops.

Maybe we all know this already about poems, but what my distracted teacher made clear to me that day is that much of the tension and forward movement of any poem is achieved by where and how the logic of the line interrupts the larger logic of the sentence, the way the one plays off against the other, making sound and sense.

Sound and sense, and also poetry.

This exercise is completely open-ended. It is just to write a poem. But write your poem first in whole and complete sentences, all in a single block, like prose. Remember to incorporate such standard poetic practices as the use of concrete imagery, meter and sound (assonance, dissonance, alliteration, rhyme, etc.). Make it count.

Then, when you are done, study your sentences. Identify their different parts—their subject and their predicate parts, their dependent and independent clauses parts, their prepositional phrases, their interjections, supplement and qualifiers—all, all, all that they are made of, their disparate bits and pieces, their sentence-nesses. Study them. Make them your own.

Now, reassemble them, combining every two of them together, one plus the next one, making with a kind of reverse mathematical logic, not two, but only one again. Combine your sentences, working your way all the way through the block of your poem. To do so, of course, you will have to monkey with their separate parts to make them work or sound right. You will have to combine and erase and switch around and tinker. But feel free to do so until you like the sound and feel of the whole.

Then do it again, and again, and again, until you end up with a single long sentence.

Now, here's the final poem making part: break your sentences up into lines. Do this for each of the prose blocks you've written, changing the lines as you respond to the changing logic of the longer and longer sentences. Do so in interesting ways, paying close attention to where each line breaks both itself and the sentence it is in. Make each a thing to contemplate, and end it with sufficient tension to move the reader forward to the next line. Don't let either the lines or the sentences go slack. Use correct punctuation.

Here are some prompts, if you want them, for beginning:

1. Use the word "green" fifteen times.

2. Cut a clipping from the newspaper or your favorite magazine: a) use only the words from the clipping to make your poem, or b) base your poem on what happens in the clipping.

3. Write about a place you remember, trying to recapture its essence.

4. Choose an element—air, fire, water, earth—and shape a poem that will recognizably feel like that element.

5. Write a poem in the second person and the future tense.

6. Write a poem in the form of a letter to: an old friend, someone you barely know, a lover, an ex-lover, your grandmother, someone famous, someone you just make up, yourself.

7. Write a poem in twelve-syllable lines, six lines to a stanza, three stanzas.

8. Make a list of random words collected from the dictionary, a physics text-book, your favorite novel, and use them in your poem.

9. Write a poem about the animal you would be.

10. Write a twenty-line poem in a single sentence about what you're refusing to write.

(K.H.)

Scavenger Hunt

For this exercise, you will be keeping a notebook and looking around a long time. It is designed to help you practice your attention. The rules are the same as in any scavenger hunt: Look around for the items on your list, and if you can't find them, ask someone else. In a pinch, ask your reference librarian:

The directions are simple. Find the following items as you can and record them in your notebook. Notice that there are five sections to the list. Organize your materials inside these sections. Precise notation is important. Record the source (where you found the item, and, if relevant, the circumstances of your finding). Include full bibliographic citations, complete with page numbers.

When you are done, you will use your notebook as a dictionary for writing. Begin by writing a poem composed entirely of items from your list. Or write a five part poem, structured around each of the five sections of your list. Or write a sequence of five poems, or a short-short story, or a five part story, and so on. You may use your own words to fill in between items on your list, but do so only when absolutely necessary.

See where it takes you.

You may want to make a practice of keeping such a notebook. Feel free to add to your list your own categories and sections, whatever interests you. Listen, and listen, and record.

The List.

One:

an image in a poem with the word coyote in it, or ice

five words that begin with the letter "l," including lambent

a two-part question

three possessive pronouns

seven split infinitives

seven words from a foreign language

data

a neither/nor construction

an opinion

a direct quotation

a name and place
a longitude or latitude or some other notation from a map
a measurement
an indirect quotation
a parenthetical remark
a hyphenated adjective
a participial phrase
a dangling participial phrase
three transitive verbs

Two:
three intransitive verbs
a Latin plant name
an unorthodox spelling
an awkward adverb
an allusion
something from a cookbook
seven words from page 300 of your dictionary
a symbol
another symbol
a use of the word "mud"
a slant rhyme
a single rhyme
a half rhyme
a mosaic rhyme
ten titles
a digression
several incorrect uses of a word, such as "hopefully"
five idioms
a compound word
a compound sentence
a complex sentence

Three:
a compound complex sentence
something true
something false
something intertextual

something paradoxical
something industrial
something fanciful
twelve new words you didn't know before
a pronouncement
something in the active voice
something in the passive voice
a parallel construction
a nonparallel construction
nine metaphors
five metonymies
an invocation of the alphabet
a modern parable
three musical forms
six architectural terms
twelve colors from an artist's palette

Four:
three uses of the word "cow"
twenty lines from song lyrics
five names for articles of clothing worn by the opposite sex
a concept from chemistry
a concept from biology
a concept from geology
a concept from geography
a concept from oceanography
a concept from physics
a concept from astronomy
a concept from astrology
a concept from magic
seven run-on sentences
ten lines from five of your favorite books
something from the Internet
someone else's dream
an axiom
a mathematical principle
a word beginning with each letter of the alphabet, going backward from z
seven words beginning with the letter "c," including cactus

Five:

a nursery rhyme

a haiku

six embedded clauses

three sentence fragments

an indirect object

a direct object

ten prepositional phrases, all found in poems

a list with at least ten items

something you read on a wall

something you read in the newspaper

advice someone gave you

a sports statistic

a world record

a use of the past-perfect tense

a use of the future tense

a use of the conditional tense

three subordinating conjunctions and their contexts, found in fiction

three subordinating conjunctions and their contexts, found in poems

twenty images

a natural object

(K.H.)

PART
II

Mini-
Anthology

Learning to Write

Audre Lorde

Is the alphabet responsible
for the book
in which it is written
that makes me peevish and nasty
and wish I were dumb   again?

We practiced drawing our letters
digging into the top of the desk
and old Sister Eymard
rapped our knuckles
until they bled
she was the meanest of all
and we knew she was crazy
but none of the grownups
would listen to us
until she died in a madhouse.

I am a bleak heroism of words
that refuse
to be buried alive
with the liars.

Elektra on Third Avenue

Marilyn Hacker
For Link

At six, when April chills our hands and feet
walking downtown, we stop at Clancy's Bar
or Bickford's, where the part-time hustlers are,
scoffing between the mailroom and the street.
Old pensioners appraise them while they eat,
and so do we, debating half in jest
which piece of hasty pudding we'd like best.
I know you know I think your mouth is sweet
as anything exhibited for sale,
fresh coffee cake or boys fresh out of jail,
which tender hint of incest brings me near
to ordering more coffee or more beer.
The homebound crowd provides more youth to cruise.
We nurse our cups, nudge knees, and pick and choose.

Mourning the Dying American Female Names

Hunt Hawkins

In the Altha Diner on the Florida panhandle
a stocky white-haired woman
with a plastic nameplate "Mildred"
gently turns my burger, and I fall into grief.
I remember the long, hot drives to North Carolina
to visit Aunt Alma, who put up quarts of peaches,
and my grandmother Gladys with her pieced quilts.
Many names are almost gone: Gertrude, Myrtle,
Agnes, Bernice, Hortense, Edna, Doris, and Hilda.
They were wide women, cotton-clothed, early rising.
You had to move your mouth to say their names,
and they meant strength, spear, battle, and victory.
When did women stop being Saxons and Goths?
What frog Fate turned them into Alison, Melissa,
Valerie, Natalie, Adrienne, and Lucinda,
diminished them to Wendy, Cindy, Suzy, and Vicky?
I look at these young women
and hope they are headed for the presidency,
but I fear America has other plans in mind,
that they be no longer at war
but subdued instead in amorphous corporate work,
somebody's assistant, something in a bank,
single parent with word-processing skills.
They must have been made French
so they could be cheap foreign labor.
Well, all I can say is,
Good luck to you
Kimberly, Darlene, Cheryl, Heather, and Amy.
Good luck April, Melanie, Becky, and Kelly.
I hope it goes well for you.
But for a moment let us mourn.
Now is the time to say good-bye
to Florence, Muriel, Ethel, and Thelma.
Good-bye Minnie, Ada, Bertha, and Edith.

Harlem

Langston Hughes

What happens to a dream deferred?

Does it dry up
like a raisin in the sun?
Or fester like a sore—
And then run?
Does it stink like rotten meat?
Or crust and sugar over—
like a syrupy sweet?

Maybe it just sags
like a heavy load.

Or does it explode?

712

Emily Dickinson

Because I could not stop for Death—
He kindly stopped for me—
The Carriage held but just Ourselves—
And Immortality.

We slowly drove—He knew no haste
And I had put away
My labor and my leisure too,
For His Civility—

We passed the School, where Children strove
At Recess—in the Ring—
We passed the Fields of Gazing Grain—
We passed the Setting Sun—

Or rather—He passed Us—
The Dews drew quivering and chill—
For only Gossamer, my Gown—
My Tippet—only Tulle—

We paused before a House that seemed
A Swelling of the Ground—
The Roof was scarcely visible—
The Cornice—in the Ground—

Since then—'tis Centuries—and yet
Feels shorter than the Day
I first surmised the Horses' Heads
Were toward Eternity—

Ode on a Grecian Urn

John Keats

1

Thou still unravished bride of quietness,
　Thou foster child of silence and slow time,
Sylvan historian, who canst thus express
　A flowery tale more sweetly than our rhyme:
5　What leaf-fringed legend haunts about thy shape
　　Of deities or mortals, or of both,
　　　In Tempe or the dales of Arcady?
　　What men or gods are these? What maidens loath?
What mad pursuit? What struggle to escape?
10　　　What pipes and timbrels? What wild ecstasy?

2

Heard melodies are sweet, but those unheard
　Are sweeter; therefore, ye soft pipes, play on;
Not to the sensual ear, but, more endeared,
　Pipe to the spirit ditties of no tone:
15　Fair youth, beneath the trees, thou canst not leave
　Thy song, nor ever can those trees be bare;
　　Bold Lover, never, never canst thou kiss,
　　Though winning near the goal—yet, do not grieve;
　　She cannot fade, though thou hast not thy bliss,
20　　Forever wilt thou love, and she be fair!

3

Ah, happy, happy boughs! that cannot shed
　Your leaves, nor ever bid the Spring adieu;
And, happy melodist, unwearièd,
　Forever piping songs forever new;
25　More happy love! more happy, happy love!
　Forever warm and still to be enjoyed,
　　Forever panting, and forever young;
All breathing human passion far above,
　　That leaves a heart high-sorrowful and cloyed,
30　　　A burning forehead, and a parching tongue.

4

Who are these coming to the sacrifice?
　To what green altar, O mysterious priest,
Lead'st thou that heifer lowing at the skies,
　And all her silken flanks with garlands dressed?

What little town by river or sea shore,
  Or mountain-built with peaceful citadel,
    Is emptied of this folk, this pious morn?
And, little town, thy streets forevermore
  Will silent be; and not a soul to tell
    Why thou art desolate, can e'er return.

5
O Attic shape! Fair attitude! with brede
  Of marble men and maidens overwrought,
With forest branches and the trodden weed;
  Thou, silent form, dost tease us out of thought
As doth eternity: Cold Pastoral!
  When old age shall this generation waste,
    Thou shalt remain, in midst of other woe
  Than ours, a friend to man, to whom thou say'st,
"Beauty is truth, truth beauty,"—that is all
    Ye know on earth, and all ye need to know.

Where We Live Now

Marilyn Chin

A white house, a wheelless car
In the backyard rusted

Mother drags a pail of diapers to the line
Strung between a parched elm and the garage

Janie slumps over a pot with several dents.
And cries into the rice porridge

(She doesn't like it, too bad)

A faint breeze ripples
Mother's skirt, Janie's pinafore

A dog drops a turd near the convolvulus
Another sniffs it, sneezes

Georgie shuffles forward, backward
Finally out the screen door

His radio blares Rock
But the news interjects

Boston is winning, Atlanta drums
Bad weather into our ears

(Untitled)

Peter Meinke

this is a poem to my son Peter
whom I have hurt a thousand times
whose large and vulnerable eyes
have glazed in pain at my ragings
thin wrists and fingers hung
boneless in despair, pale freckled back
bent in defeat, pillow soaked
by my failure to understand.
I have scarred through weakness
and impatience your frail confidence forever
because when I needed to strike
you were there to be hurt and because
I thought you knew
you were beautiful and fair
your bright eyes and hair
but now I see that no one knows that
about himself, but must be told
and retold until it takes hold
because I think anything can be killed
after a while, especially beauty
so I write this for life, for love, for
you, my oldest son Peter, age 10,
going on 11.

Arte Poética

Pablo Neruda

Entre sombra y espacio, entre guarniciones y doncellas,
dotado de corazón singular y sueños funestos,
precipitadamente pálido, marchito en la frente
y con luto de viudo furioso por cada día de mi vida,
ay, para cada agua invisible que bebo soñolientamente
y de todo sonido que acojo temblando,
tengo las misma sed ausente y la misma fiebre fría
un oído que nace, una angustia indirecta,
como si llegaran ladrones o fantasmas,
y en una cáscara de extensión fija y profunda,
como un camarero humillado, como una campana un poco ronca,
como un espejo viejo, como un olor de casa sola
en la que los huéspedes entran de noche perdidamente ebrios,
y hay un olor de ropa tirada al suelo, y una ausencia de flores
—posiblemente de otro modo aún menos melancólico—,
pero, la verdad, de pronto, el viento que azota mi pecho,
las noches de substancia infinita caídas en mi dormitorio,
el ruido de un día que arde con sacrificio
me piden lo profético que hay en mí, con melancolía
y un golpe de objetos que llaman sin ser respondidos
hay, y un movimiento sin tregua, y un nombre confuso.

The Art of Poetry

Between shadows and clearing, between defenses and young girls,
having inherited an original heart, and funereal imagination,
suddenly pale, something withered in my face,
in mourning like a desperate widower every day of my life,
for every drop of invisible water I drink
in my sleepy way, and for every sound I take in shivering,
I have the same chilly fever, and the same absent thirst,
an ear coming into the world, an oblique anxiety,
as though robbers were about to arrive, or ghosts,
inside a seashell with great and unchangeable depths,
like a humiliated waiter, or a bell slightly hoarse,
like an aged mirror or the smell of an empty house
where the guests come in hopelessly drunk at night,
having an odor of clothes thrown on the floor, and no flowers,
—in another sense, possibly not as sad—
still, the truth is, the wind suddenly hitting my chest,
the nights with infinite substance fallen into my bedroom,
the crackling of a day hardly able to burn,
ask from me sadly whatever I have that is prophetic,
and there are objects that knock, and are never answered,
and something always moving, and a name that does not come clear.

Translated by Robert Bly

Of Reading

Hans Ostrom

1

We receive letters of an alphabet
as if they wash ashore, lost ancient drums.
We pick them up, touch
them, stretched hide
thrumming like a bird's throat.
We turn and journey into deep
rhythms of a language.

2

I think of all the headlines
my mother has read with her sharp blue eyes.
She looks through a newspaper at History
the way a fierce bird looks at the forest.

3

My young son bounds
through my notebook till a blank page
opens like a meadow. He draws a giant spider
that has monumental legs.

4

When my father first looks
at a book, he looks it over
as if it were an occurrence
or an animal in the woods—
a deer walking through
manzanita in October.

5

Words and letters fall through the murky sky
of a computer monitor like wet snowflakes on a windless day.

6

There is a moistness to adventurous reading,
something that connects us to an astonished mud
of lore women and men of old tribes
used when they painted clothing and stone,
when they explained Night,
talked back to rain,
named the holiness of infants.

Metaphors

Sylvia Plath

I'm a riddle in nine syllables,
An elephant, a ponderous house,
A melon strolling on two tendrils
O red fruit, ivory, fine timbers!
This loaf's big with its yeasty rising
Money's new-minted in this fat purse
I'm a means, a stage, a cow in calf
I've eaten a bag of green apples.
Boarded the train there's no getting off.

25

Anonymous

I'm the world's wonder, for I make women happy
—a boon to the neighbourhood, a bane to no one,
though I may perhaps prick the one who picks me.

I am set well up, stand in a bed,
have a roughish root. Rarely (though it happens)
a churl's daughter more daring than the rest
—and lovelier!—lays hold of me,
rushes my red top, wrenches at my head,
and lays me in the larder.
                              She learns soon enough,
the curly-haired creature who clamps me so,
of my meeting with her: moist in her eye!

[onion]
[Early English Riddle]

25

Anonymous

Ic eom wunderlicu wiht,   wifum on hyhte,
neahbuendum nyt;   nængum sceþþe
burgsittendra,   nymþe bonan anum.
Staþol min is steapheah,   stonde ic on bedde,
neoþan ruh nathwær.   Neþeð hwilum
ful cyrtenu   ceorles dohtor,
modwlonc meowle,   þæt heo on mec gripeð,
ræseð mec on reodne,   reafað min heafod,
fegeð mec on fæsten.   Feleþ sona
mines gemotes,   seo þe mec nearwað,
wif wundenlocc.   Wæt bið þæt eage.

Drug Store

Karl Shapiro

> *I do remember an apothecary,*
> *And hereabouts 'a dwells*

It baffles the foreigner like an idiom,
And he is right to adopt it as a form
Less serious than the living-room or bar;
    For it disestablishes the café,
Is a collective, and on basic country.

Not that it praises hygiene and corrupts
The ice-cream parlor and the tobacconist's
Is it a center; but that the attractive symbols
    Watch over puberty and leer
Like rubber bottles waiting for sick-use.

Youth comes to jingle nickels and crack wise;
The baseball scores are his, the magazines
Devoted to lust, the jazz, the Coca-Cola,
    The lending-library of a love's latest.
He is the customer; he is heroized.

And every nook and cranny of the flesh
Is spoken to by packages with wiles.
"Buy me, buy me," they whimper and cajole;
    The hectic range of lipsticks pouts,
Revealing the wicked and the simple mouth.

With scarcely any evasion in their eye
They smoke, undress their girls, exact a stance;
But only for a moment. The clock goes round;
    Crude fellowships are made and lost;
They slump in booths like rags, not even drunk.

Excerpt from Black Mercury

Marie Silkeberg

Mother! my son called in the night.
Mother! I can't see you.

You can, my precious.
You can see my voice.

Listen to the sky now, so wildly blue,
And to black birds when they fly.

—translated by Hans Ostrom

The Children

William Carlos Williams

Once in a while
we'd find a patch
of yellow violets

not many
but blue big blue
ones in

the cemetery woods
we'd pick
bunches of them

there was a family
named Foltette
a big family

with lots of children's graves
so we'd take

bunches of violets
and place one
on each headstone

Lines written a few miles above Tintern Abbey

William Wordsworth

ON REVISITING THE BANKS OF THE WYE DURING A TOUR,

JULY 13, 1798

Five years have passed; five summers, with the length
Of five long winters! and again I hear
These waters, rolling from their mountain-springs
With a sweet inland murmur.—Once again
Do I behold these steep and lofty cliffs,
That on a wild secluded scene impress
Thoughts of more deep seclusion; and connect
The landscape with the quiet of the sky.
The day is come when I again repose
10   Here, under this dark sycamore, and view
These plots of cottage-ground, these orchard-tufts,
Which, at this season, with their unripe fruits,
Among the woods and copses lose themselves,
Nor, with their green and simple hue, disturb
The wild green landscape. Once again I see
These hedge-rows, hardly hedge-rows, little lines
Of sportive wood run wild; these pastoral farms
Green to the very door; and wreathes of smoke
Sent up, in silence, from among the trees,
20   With some uncertain notice, as might seem,
Of vagrant dwellers in the houseless woods,
Or of some hermit's cave, where by his fire
The hermit sits alone.

                    Though absent long,
These forms of beauty have not been to me,
As is a landscape to a blind man's eye:
But oft, in lonely rooms, and mid the din
Of towns and cities, I have owed to them,
In hours of weariness, sensations sweet,
Felt in the blood, and felt along the heart,
And passing even into my purer mind
With tranquil restoration:—feelings too
30   Of unremembered pleasure; such, perhaps,
As may have had no trivial influence
On that best portion of a good man's life;
His little, nameless, unremembered acts
Of kindness and of love. Nor less, I trust,
To them I may have owed another gift,

Of aspect more sublime; that blessed mood,
In which the burthen of the mystery,
In which the heavy and the weary weight
Of all this unintelligible world
Is lightened:—that serene and blessed mood,
In which the affections gently lead us on,
Until, the breath of this corporeal frame,
And even the motion of our human blood
Almost suspended, we are laid asleep
In body, and become a living soul:
While with an eye made quiet by the power
Of harmony, and the deep power of joy,
We see into the life of things.
                              If this
Be but a vain belief, yet, oh! how oft,
In darkness, and amid the many shapes
Of joyless day-light; when the fretful stir
Unprofitable, and the fever of the world,
Have hung upon the beatings of my heart,
How oft, in spirit, have I turned to thee
O sylvan Wye! Thou wanderer through the woods,
How often has my spirit turned to thee!

And now, with gleams of half-extinguished thought,
With many recognitions dim and faint,
And somewhat of a sad perplexity,
The picture of the mind revives again:
While here I stand, not only with the sense
Of present pleasure, but with pleasing thoughts
That in this moment there is life and food
For future years. And so I dare to hope
Though changed, no doubt, from what I was, when first
I came among these hills; when like a roe
I bounded o'er the mountains, by the sides
Of the deep rivers, and the lonely streams,
Wherever nature led; more like a man
Flying from something that he dreads, than one
Who sought the thing he loved. For nature then
(The coarser pleasures of my boyish days,
And their glad animal movements all gone by,)
To me was all in all.—I cannot paint
What then I was. The sounding cataract
Haunted me like a passion: the tall rock,
The mountain, and the deep and gloomy wood,
Their colours and their forms, were then to me

An appetite: a feeling and a love,
That had no need of a remoter charm,
By thought supplied, or any interest
Unborrowed from the eye.—That time is past,
And all its aching joys are now no more,
And all its dizzy raptures. Not for this
Faint I, nor mourn nor murmur: other gifts
Have followed, for such loss, I would believe,
Abundant recompence. For I have learned
90   To look on nature, not as in the hour
Of thoughtless youth, but hearing oftentimes
The still, sad music of humanity,
Nor harsh nor grating, though of ample power
To chasten and subdue. And I have felt
A presence that disturbs me with the joy
Of elevated thoughts; a sense sublime
Of something far more deeply interfused,
Whose dwelling is the light of setting suns,
And the round ocean and the living air,
100   And the blue sky, and in the mind of man,
A motion and a spirit, that impels
All thinking things, all objects of all thought,
And rolls through all things. Therefore am I still
A lover of the meadows and the woods,
And mountains; and of all that we behold
From this green earth; of all the mighty world
Of eye, and ear, both what they half-create,
And what perceive; well pleased to recognize
In nature and the language of the sense,
110   The anchor of my purest thoughts, the nurse,
The guide, the guardian of my heart, and soul
Of all my moral being.

                  Nor, perchance,
If I were not thus taught, should I the more
Suffer my genial spirits to decay:
For thou art with me, here, upon the banks
Of this fair river; thou, my dearest Friend,
My dear, dear Friend, and in thy voice I catch
The language of my former heart, and read
My former pleasures in the shooting lights
120   Of thy wild eyes. Oh! yet a little while
May I behold in thee what I was once,
My dear, dear Sister! And this prayer I make,
Knowing that Nature never did betray

The heart that loved her; 'tis her privilege,
Through all the years of this our life, to lead
From joy to joy: for she can so inform
The mind that is within us, so impress
With quietness and beauty, and so feed
With lofty thoughts, that neither evil tongues,
Rash judgments, nor the sneers of selfish men,
Nor greetings where no kindness is, nor all
The dreary intercourse of daily life,
Shall e'er prevail against us, or disturb
Our cheerful faith that all which we behold
Is full of blessings. Therefore let the moon
Shine on thee in thy solitary walk;
And let the misty mountain winds be free
To blow against thee: and, in after years,
When these wild ecstasies shall be matured
Into a sober pleasure, when thy mind
Shall be a mansion for all lovely forms,
Thy memory be as a dwelling-place
For all sweet sounds and harmonies; Oh! then,
If solitude, or fear, or pain, or grief,
Should be thy portion, with what healing thoughts
Of tender joy wilt thou remember me,
And these my exhortations! Nor, perchance,
If I should be, where I no more can hear
Thy voice, nor catch from thy wild eyes these gleams
Of past existence, wilt thou then forget
That on the banks of this delightful stream
We stood together; and that I, so long
A worshipper of Nature, hither came,
Unwearied in that service: rather say
With warmer love, oh! with far deeper zeal
Of holier love. Nor wilt thou then forget,
That after many wanderings, many years
Of absence, these steep woods and lofty cliffs,
And this green pastoral landscape, were to me
More dear, both for themselves and for thy sake.

Musée des Beaux Arts

W. H. Auden

About suffering they were never wrong,
The Old Masters: how well they understood
Its human position; how it takes place
While someone else is eating or opening a window or just walking
    dully along;
How, when the aged are reverently, passionately waiting
For the miraculous birth, there always must be
Children who did not specially want it to happen, skating
On a pond at the edge of the wood:
They never forgot
That even the dreadful martyrdom must run its course
Anyhow in a corner, some untidy spot
Where the dogs go on with their doggy life and the torturer's
    horse
Scratches its innocent behind on a tree.

In Brueghel's *Icarus,* for instance: how everything turns away
Quite leisurely from the disaster; the ploughman may
Have heard the splash, the forsaken cry,
But for him it was not an important failure; the sun shone
As it had to on the white legs disappearing into the green
Water; and the expensive delicate ship that must have seen
Something amazing, a boy falling out of the sky,
Had somewhere to get to and sailed calmly on.

Horoscope Imperatives: A 'Found' Ghazal

Wendy Bishop

for G.L.C.

It is important to realize you are looking at others through fresh eyes.
We are here to add what we can to life, not to get what we want from it.

You feel your hands are tied. You are in the right place at the right time.
It would be a grave mistake not to act. You are urged to settle your
    differences.

Continue to live according to the maxim: "We are here and it is now;
    further than that
All knowledge is moonshine." The Sun is challenged by your ruling
    planet.

Denotes joint financial arrangements, signifies a strange turn of events,
On no account should you issue an ultimatum to those in positions of
    power.

Venus, your ruler, needs to be watched like a hawk.
You would be well advised to take criticism in stride.

What occurs in an unusual manner around the 15th
Will accomplish what you have set your heart on achieving.

You do not have to compete to be noticed. July is about refusing to accept
What is second best. Finances are always a major consideration.

Planetary, July, The Sun, Pluto in Scorpio, on the 15th, rise above, you
    should,
Pay your dues, cannot fail, The Sun, your ruler, The Sun, aspected,
    imperative.

No doubt you are entitled to use others' deviousness as an excuse
Not to act. The 3rd, 12th, 15th, and 19th are likely to be days.

A word of warning: The Sun, passing over the mid-heaven point of your
    solar chart
And challenged by Uranus and Neptune. Spend a short time in a totally
    different setting.

Fortunately the Sun joins forces with Pluto and a windfall ought to save
    the day
When colleagues seem to turn against you around the 12th.

Once you have eliminated feelings of personal inadequacy, everything—
Personal and professional—should change for the better. After June.

Go Down, Moses

Anonymous

Go down, Moses,
Way down in Egyptland
Tell old Pharaoh
To let my people go.

When Israel was in Egyptland
Let my people go
Oppressed so hard they could not stand
Let my people go.

Go down, Moses,
Way down in Egyptland
Tell old Pharaoh
"Let my people go."

"Thus saith the Lord," bold Moses said.
"Let my people go;
If not I'll smite your first-born dead
Let my people go.

"No more shall they in bondage toil,
    Let my people go;
Let them come out with Egypt's spoil,
    Let my people go."

The Lord told Moses what to do
    Let my people go;
To lead the children of Israel through,
    Let my people go.

Go down, Moses,
    Way down in Egyptland,
Tell old Pharaoh,
    "Let my people go!"

My Mistress' Eyes Are Nothing Like The Sun

William Shakespeare

My mistress' eyes are nothing like the sun;
Coral is far more red than her lips' red;
If snow be white, why then her breasts are dun;
If hairs be wires, black wires grow on her head.
I have seen roses damasked red and white,
But no such roses see I in her cheeks;
And in some perfumes is there more delight
Than in the breath that from my mistress reeks.
I love to hear her speak, yet well I know
That music hath a far more pleasing sound;
I grant I never saw a goddess go:
My mistress, when she walks, treads on the ground.
    And yes, by heaven, I think my love as rare
    As any she, belied with false compare.

Design

Robert Frost

I found a dimpled spider, fat and white,
On a white heal-all, holding up a moth
Like a white piece of rigid satin cloth—
Assorted characters of death and blight
Mixed ready to begin the morning right,
Like the ingredients of a witches' broth—
A snow drop spider, a flower like a froth,
And dead wings carried like a paper kite.

What had the flower to do with being white,
The wayside blue and innocent heal-all?
What brought the kindred spider to that height,
Then steered the white moth thither in the night?
What but design of darkness to appall?—
If design govern in a thing so small.

My Daughter Considers Her Body

Floyd Skloot

She examines her hand, fingers spread wide.
Seated, she bends over her crossed legs
to search for specks or scars and cannot hide
her awe when any mark is found. She begs
me to look, twisting before her mirror,
at some tiny bruise on her hucklebone.
Barely awake, she studies creases her
arm developed as she slept. She has grown
entranced with blemish, begun to know
her body's facility for being
flawed. She does not trust its will to grow
whole again, but may learn that too, freeing
herself to accept the body's deep thirst
for risk. Learning to touch her wounds comes first.

Sonnet

Robert Pinsky

Afternoon sun on her back,
calm irregular slap
of water against a dock.

Thin pines clamber
over the hill's top—
nothing to remember,

only the same lake
that keeps making the same
sounds under her cheek

and flashing the same color.
No one to say her name,
no need, no one to praise her—

only the lake's voice, over
and over, to keep it before her.

The Windhover

Gerard Manley Hopkins

To Christ our Lord

I caught this morning morning's minion, kingdom of
daylight's dauphin, dapple-dawn-drawn Falcon, in his riding
Of the rolling level underneath him steady air, and striding
High there, how he rung upon the rein of a wimpling wing
In his ecstasy! then off, off forth on swing,
    As a skate's heel sweeps smooth on a bow-bend: the
        hurl and gliding
    Rebuffed the big wind. My heart in hiding
Stirred for a bird,—the achieve of, the mastery of the thing!

Brute beauty and valour and act, oh, air, pride, plume, here
    Buckle! AND the fire that breaks from thee then, a billion
Times told lovelier, more dangerous, O my chevalier!

    No wonder of it: sheér plód makes plow down sillion
Shine, and blue-bleak embers, ah my dear,
    Fall, gall themselves, and gash gold-vermillion.

In Praise of the Humble Comma

Pico Iyer

The gods, they say, give breath, and they take it away. But the same could be said—could it not?—of the humble comma. Add it to the present clause, and, of a sudden, the mind is, quite literally, given pause to think; take it out if you wish or forget it and the mind is deprived of a resting place. Yet still the comma gets no respect. It seems just a slip of a thing, a pedant's tick, a blip on the edge of our consciousness, a kind of printer's smudge almost. Small, we claim, is beautiful (especially in the age of the microchip). Yet what is so often used, and so rarely recalled, as the comma—unless it be breath itself?

Punctuation, one is taught, has a point: to keep up law and order. Punctuation marks are the road signs placed along the highway of our communications—to control speeds, provide directions and prevent head-on collisions. A period has the unblinking finality of a red light; the comma is a flashing yellow light that asks us only to slow down; and the semicolon is a stop sign that tells us to ease gradually to a halt, before gradually starting up again. By establishing the relations between words, punctuation establishes the relations between the people using words. That may be one reason why schoolteachers exalt it and lovers defy it ("We love each other and belong to each other let's don't ever hurt each other Nicole let's don't ever hurt each other," wrote Gary Gilmore to his girlfriend). A comma, he must have known, "separates inseparables," in the clinching words of H.W. Fowler, King of English Usage.

Punctuation, then, is a civic prop, a pillar that holds society upright. (A run-on sentence, its phrases piling up without division, is as unsightly as a sink piled high with dirty dishes.) Small wonder, then, that punctuation was one of the first proprieties of the Victorian age, the age of the corset, that the modernists threw off: the sexual revolution might be said to have begun when Joyce's Molly Bloom spilled out all her private thoughts in 36 pages of unbridled, almost unperioded and officially censored prose; and another rebellion was surely marked when E.E. Cummings first felt free to commit "God" to the lower case.

Punctuation thus becomes the signature of cultures. The hot-blooded Spaniard seems to be revealed in the passion and urgency of his doubled exclamation points and question marks ("¡*Caramba! ¿Quien sabe?*"), while the impassive Chinese traditionally added to his so-called inscrutability by omitting directions from his ideograms. The anarchy and commotion of the '60s were given voice in the exploding exclamation marks, riotous capital letters and Day-Glo italics of Tom Wolfe's spray-paint prose; and in Communist societies, where the State is absolute, the dignity—and divinity—of capital letters is reserved for Ministries, Sub-Committees and Secretariats.

Yet punctuation is something more than a culture's birthmark; it scores the music in our minds, gets our thoughts moving to the rhythm of our hearts. Punctuation is the notation in the sheet music of our words, telling us where to rest, or when to raise our voices; it acknowledges that the meaning of our discourse, as of any symphonic composition, lies not in the units but in the pauses, the pacing and the phrasing. Punctuation is the way one bats one's eyes, lowers one's voice or blushes demurely. Punctuation adjusts the tone and color and volume till the feeling comes into perfect focus, not disgust exactly, but distaste; not lust, or like, but love.

Punctuation, in short, gives us the human voice, and all the meanings that lie between the words. "You aren't young, are you?" loses its innocence when it loses the question mark. Every child knows the menace of a dropped apostrophe (the parent's "Don't do that" shifting into the more slowly enunciated "Do no do that"), and every believer, the ignominy of having his faith reduced to "faith." Add an exclamation point to "To be or not to be . . ." and the gloomy Dane has all the resolve he needs; add a comma, and the noble sobriety of "God save the Queen" becomes a cry of desperation bordering on double sacrilege.

Sometimes, of course, our markings may be simply a matter of aesthetics. Popping in a comma can be like slipping on the necklace that gives an outfit quiet elegance, or like catching the sound of running water that complements, as it completes, the silence of a Japanese landscape. When V.S. Naipaul, in his latest novel, writes, "He was a middle-aged man, with glasses," the first comma can seem a little precious. Yet it gives the description a spin, as well as a subtlety, that it otherwise lacks, and it shows that the glasses are not part of the middle-agedness, but something else.

Thus all these tiny scratches give us breadth and heft and depth. A world that has only periods is a world without inflections. It is a world without shade. It has a music without sharps and flats. It is a martial music. It has a jackboot rhythm. Words cannot bend and curve. A comma, by comparison, catches the gentle drift of the mind in thought, turning in on itself and back on itself, reversing, redoubling and returning along the course of its own sweet river music; while the semicolon brings clauses and thoughts together with all the silent discretion of a hostess arranging guests around her dinner table.

Punctuation, then, is a matter of care. Care for words, yes, but also, and more important, for what the words imply. Only a lover notices the small things: the way the afternoon light catches the nape of a neck, or how a strand of hair slips out from behind an ear, or the way a finger curls around a cup. And no one scans a letter so closely as a lover, searching for its small print, straining to hear its nuances, its gasps, its sighs and hesitations, poring over the secret messages that lie in every cadence. The difference between "Jane (whom I adore)" and "Jane, whom I adore," and the difference between them both and "Jane—whom I adore—" marks all the distance between ecstasy and heartache. "No iron can pierce the heart with such force as a period put at just the right place," in Isaac Babel's lovely words: a comma can let us hear a voice break, or a heart. Punctuation, in fact, is a labor of love. Which brings us back, in a way, to gods.

Meander

Mary Paumier Jones

I didn't know why I was so taken with the meanders of the Nova show, but I started following them to obscure corners of the library—the kinds of places you might end-up if you are, say, checking for titles by John McPhee. The more I learned about the phenomenon of the meander, the more apt it seemed as a metaphor for what happens in an essay. Throughout the writing, I was trying to call something to mind, something else that meanders, something not on the show, but important for what I am groping toward saying.

A Nova show about the forms of nature prompts me to look up "meander." Having always used the word to refer to walking, I am surprised to learn that it comes from water. Rivers and streams meander, verb, have meanders, noun. "Meander," in fact, comes from the name of a river, one in ancient Phrygia, now part of Turkey—the Maeander, now the Menderes. Change of name notwithstanding, the waters still flow from the Anatolian plateau to the Aegean Sea. A namesake, a Meander River, meanders in northern Alberta.

In what we do on foot, meandering implies an aimless wandering, with the pleasant connotation that the very aimlessness of the wander is something freely, even happily, chosen.

The meanders of water seem equally aimless, but are, it turns out, very regular in their irregularity—although if you were walking along the bank of a meandering river, you might find that hard to believe. You would head in one direction, and then curve around until you are going the opposite way, and then around again, following a path which turns upon itself and makes no sense. Could a helicopter or fairy godmother, though, raise you high enough, you would see that what seems like chaos below actually forms a regular repeating pattern of serpentine flexuosity.

The shortest distance between two points may be a straight line, but a river neither knows nor cares. It seldom flows straight for a distance of more than about ten times its width. A river erodes its banks, and the way of the world is such that one side invariably erodes faster than the other. It eventually collapses and its sediment is carried along and deposited downstream. Two curves are thus begun: the erosion point becomes the outside of one; the sediment pile, the inside of the next.

The water on the outside has to flow faster to keep up, causing more erosion, more sediment movement. The outsides get deeper, the insides shallower. At any point, the shape of the river shows its history. If other forces do not prevent, the bends over time work toward becoming perfectly elliptical. "Ellipse" comes from the Greek for "to fall short," an ellipse falling as it does short of a perfect circle.

This has all been observed in nature and shown experimentally in laboratories, and is thought by many to be sufficient explanation for meanders.

Others disagree, especially now that infra-red images from satellites show that ocean currents—which have no erodable banks—also meander. The jet stream appears to meander as well. Mathematicians have calculated that the most probable path between two points on a surface is in fact a meander. Meanders then may be the norm, not the exception. The question may be not why some rivers meander, but why every river we see does not.

•   •   •

There might be particular essays whose shape is more akin to one of the other basic natural forms—a sphere or hexagon, a spiral, say, or helix or branch—but on the whole, I think, what essays do best is meander. They fall short of the kind of circular perfection we expect of fiction or poetry. They proceed in elliptical curves, diverging, digressing.

We can float or row or swim or speed or sail along the meandering course of an essay. We can meander on foot on the river bank with the essayist. We expect only to go somewhere in the presence of someone.

Perhaps we will end up close to where we started, perhaps far away. We will not see the shape of our journey until we are done, and can look back on it whole, as it were, from the air. But we will, and very quickly, come to know the shape of our company—the mind, the sensibility, the person, with whom we are traveling. That much seems necessary to essay structure—one individual human speaking to another who wants to listen.

•   •   •

Flattened out, the thin human cortex, the gray matter of the brain, is much too large for the skull within which it must fit. The problem has been elegantly solved by intricate pleating and folding, as if the cortex were a piece of thick fabric gathered in tightly to fit. In anatomy books, we can see pictures of cross-section slices of the gathers. The shape is unmistakable, like a close-packed river shot from above, meandering within.

Primary Sources[1]

Rick Moody

Abbé, William Parker.[2] A Diary of Sketches." Concord, New Hampshire: St. Paul's School, 1976.

Bangs, Lester. "Psychotic Reactions and Carburetor Dung."[3] Edited by Greil Marcus. New York: Knopf, 1987.

Barnes, Djuna. "Interviews." Washington, D.C.: Sun & Moon, 1985.

Barrett, Syd.[4] "Golden Hair." On "The Madcap Laughs." EMI Cassette. C4–46607, 1990.

Barthes, Roland. "A Lover's Discourse."[5] Translated by Richard Howard. New York: Hill & Wang, 1978.

Bernhard, Thomas. "The Lime Works." Chicago: University of Chicago Press, 1986.

"Book of Common Prayer and Administration of the Sacraments and Other Rites and Ceremonies of the Church, According to the Use of the Protestant Episcopal Church[6] in the United States of America, The." New York: Harper & Brothers, 1944.

Borges, Jorge Luis. "Labyrinths."[7] Edited by Donald A. Yates and James E. Irby. New York: New Directions, 1964.

Breton, André. "Manifestoes of Surrealism."[8] Translated by Richard Seaver and Helen R. Lane. Ann Arbor, Michigan: University of Michigan Press (Ann Arbor Paperbacks), 1969.

Carroll, Lewis. "The Annotated Alice." Edited, with an introduction and notes, by Martin Gardner.[9] New York: Clarkson N. Potter (Bramhall House), 1960.

Carter, Angela.[10] "The Bloody Chamber and Other Adult Tales." New York: Harper & Row, 1979.

Cheever, John. "The Journals of John Cheever."[11] New York: Knopf, 1991.

———, "The Wapshot Chronicle." New York: Harper & Brothers, 1957.

Coover, Robert. "In Bed One Night & Other Brief Encounters." Providence, Rhode Island: Burning Deck, 1983.

Daniels, Les. "Marvel: Five Fabulous Decades of the World's Greatest Comics."[12] With an introduction by Stan Lee, New York: Abrams, 1991.

Danto, Arthur C. "Encounters & Reflections: Art in the Historical Present." New York: Farrar, Straus & Giroux, 1990.

"Darmok."[13] "Star Trek: *The Next Generation.*" Paramount Television, 1991.

Davis. Lydia. "Break It Down." New York: Farrar, Straus & Giroux, 1986.

De Montaigne, Michel. "The Complete Essays of Montaigne." Translated by Donald M. Frame. Stanford, California: Stanford University Press, 1958.

Derrida, Jacques. "Of Grammatology."[14] Translated by Gayatri Chakravorty Spivak. Baltimore, Maryland: Johns Hopkins Press, 1976.

Elkin, Stanley. "The Franchiser." Boston: Godine (Nonpareil Books), 1980.

"Erospri." On the Whole Earth 'Lectronic Link,[15] modem: 415 332–8410, Sausalito, California, 1985.

Feelies, The. "The Good Earth."[16] Coyote Records, TTC 8673, 1986.

Fitzgerald, F. Scott. "The Crack-Up." New York: New Directions, 1945.

Foucault, Michel. "Discipline and Punish: The Birth of the Prison." Translated by Alan Sheridan. New York: Vintage, 1979.

Gaddis, William. "The Recognitions."[17] New York: Penguin, 1986.

Genet, Jean. "The Thief's Journal." Translated by Bernard Frechtman. New York: Bantam, 1965.

Gyatso, Tenzin, the fourteenth Dali Lama of Tibet. "Freedom in Exile." New York: HarperCollins, 1990.

Hawkes, John.[18] "Second Skin." New York: New Directions, 1964.

Hawthorne, Nathaniel. "Hawthorne: Short Stories."[19] Edited by Newton Arvin. New York: Knopf, 1946.

Hogg, James. "The Private Memoirs and Confessions of a Justified Sinner." New York: Penguin, 1989.

Johnson, Denis. "Angels." New York: Vintage, 1989.

Joyce, James. "Ulysses." New York: Vintage, 1961.

Jung, C. G. "Collected Works." No. 12, Part II. "Individual Dream Symbolism in Relation to Alchemy" (1936). Translated by R. F. C. Hull. Princeton, New Jersey: Princeton University Press (Bollingen Series), 1968.

Kapuściński, Ryszard. "The Emperor." Translated by William R. Brand and Katarzyna Mroczkowska-Brand. New York: Vintage, 1989.

Lewis, James. "Index."[20] *Chicago Review* 35: I, 33–35 (Autumn, 1985).

Marcus, Greil. "Lipstick Traces: A Secret History of the Twentieth Century."[21] Cambridge, Massachusetts: Harvard University Press, 1989.

Marx, Groucho. "The Groucho Letters: Letters from and to Groucho Marx."[22] New York: Fireside, 1987.

Mitchell, Stephen. "The Gospel According to Jesus." New York: HarperCollins, 1991.

Pagels, Elaine. "The Gnostic Gospels."[23] New York: Vintage, 1989.

Paley, Grace. "Enormous Changes at the Last Minute." New York: Farrar, Straus & Giroux (Noonday Press), 1991.

Pärt, Arvo. "Tabula Rasa."[24] ECM New Series 817 764-4 (1984).

Peacock, Thomas Love. "'Headlong Hall' and Gryll Grange." Oxford: Oxford University Press, 1987.

Plato. "Great Dialogues of Plato." Translated by W.H.D. Rouse. New York: Mentor, 1956.

"Polysexuality." *Semiotext(e)*[25] 4: I (1981).

Sacks, Oliver. "Awakenings." New York: Summit, 1987.

Schulz, Bruno. "Sanatorium Under the Sign of the Hourglass."[26] Translated by Celina Wieniewska. New York: Penguin, 1979.

Sebadoh. "Sebadoh III."[27] Homestead Records, HMS 168-4, 1991.

Thomas à Kempis. "The Imitation of Christ." New York: Penguin, 1952.

Williams, William Carlos. "The Collected Poems of William Carlos Williams."[28] Volume II: 1939–62. New York: New Directions, 1988.

Zappa, Frank. With Captain Beefheart and Mothers of Invention. "Bongo Fury" (1975).[29] Barking Pumpkin Records, D4-74220, 1989.

[1]Born October 18,1961, in N.Y.C. Childhood pretty uneventful. We moved to the suburbs. I always read a lot. I did some kid stuff, but mostly I read. So this sketchy and selective bibliography—this list of some of the books I have around the house now—is really an autobiography.

[2]Art instructor at St. Paul's School when I was there (1975–79). Abbé was an older, forgetful guy when I met him. He was in his late sixties, probably. He lived alone in an apartment above the infirmary at S.P.S. His studio had burned down years before, taking a lot of his paintings, and I believe this accounted for the halo of sadness around him. He could be infectiously happy, though. His house was full of jukeboxes, dolls, and electrical toys. Games of every kind.

One time I showed him my "Sgt. Pepper" picture disk—remember those collector's gimmicks which revolutionized the LP for a few minutes in the seventies? The famous jacket art was printed on the vinyl. Abbé laughed for a good long time over that. He sat in the old armchair in my room, the one with the stuffing coming out of it, and laughed. He loved that kind of thing. He had a lot of Elvis on his jukeboxes.

[3]Lester's last published piece, in the *Voice,* appeared in my senior year of college. I moved back to N.Y.C. a little later, after six months in California, where it was too relaxed. By the time I got to New York, the East Village galleries were already disappearing. Lester was dead. The Gap had moved in on the northwest corner of St. Mark's and Second Avenue.

[4]In 1978, back at S.P.S., I took six hits of "blotter" acid and had a pretty wrenching bad trip. Eternal damnation, shame, humiliation, and an endless line of men in clown costumes chanting my name and laughing. That kind of thing. I turned myself in, confessed to a master I liked, the Reverend Alden B. Flanders. Somewhere in the middle of the five or six hours it took to talk me down, I asked him if he thought I would remember this moment for the rest of my life.

[5]"The necessity for this book is to be found in the following consideration: that the lover's discourse is today *of an extreme solitude. . . .* Once a discourse is thus . . . exiled from all gregarity, it has no recourse but to become the site, however exiguous, of an *affirmation.*"

[6]I didn't get baptized until I was fifteen. The minister, who had buried my grandparents and my uncle and performed my mother's remarriage, couldn't remember my name. Right then, the church seemed like the only thing that would get me through adolescence. I was going to get confirmed later, too, but instead I started drinking.

[7]Cf. "Eco, Umberto," and also n. 9, below.

[8]The band I played in, in college, was called Forty-five Houses. We got our name from the first Surrealist manifest: 'Q. "What is your name?' A. 'Forty-five houses.' (*Ganser syndrome,* or *beside-the-point replies.*)" Our drummer preferred women to men, but I sort of fell in love with her anyway. After we graduated, she gave me a ride on her motorcycle. It was the first time I ever rode one. I held tight around her waist.

[9]See n. 20, below.

[10]The first day of Angela's workshop in college, a guy asked her what her work was like. She said, "My work cuts like a steel blade at the base of a man's penis."

Second semester, there was a science-fiction writer in our class who sometimes slept through the proceedings—and there were only eight or nine of us there. One day I brought a copy of "Light in August" to Angela's office hours and she said, "I wish I were reading *that*"—Faulkner—"instead of *this*" (pointing to a stack of student work).

[11]As a gift for graduating from boarding school, my dad gave me a short trip to Europe. Two weeks. I was a little bit afraid of travel, though, as I still am, and in London I spent much of the time in Hyde Park, in a chair I rented for 15p a day. The sticker that served as my lease still adorns my copy of "The Stories of John Cheever," also given to me by my dad. I haven't been back to the U.K. since.

[12]We moved a lot when I was a kid. In eighth grade I had a calendar on which I marked off the days until I'd be leaving Connecticut forever. My attachments weren't too deep. I spent a lot of time with Iron Man, the Incredible Hulk, and the Avengers. I also liked self-help books and Elton John records.

[13]Picard and the crew of the Enterprise attempt to make contact with a race of aliens, the *Children of Tama,* who speak entirely in an allegorical language. Picard doesn't figure out the language until the captain of the Tamarians is already dead. A big episode for those who realize how hard communicating really is.

[14]One guy I knew in college actually threw this book out a window. Here are some excerpts from my own marginalia: "Function of art is supplementalism though devalorization of weighted side of oppositions"; Attendance as performance: more absence creates more real presence." I'm not sure what I meant, but I loved Derrida's overheated analogies: "Writing in the common sense is the dead letter, it is the carrier of death. It exhausts life. On the other hand, on the other face of the same proposition, writing in the metaphoric sense, natural, divine, and living writing, is venerated" (page 17).

[15]The WELL—as it is abbreviated—has a really good "Star Trek" conference, too. This private conference is about sex. I started messing with computers in junior high, when my grades got me out of study hall. Which was good because people used to threaten me if I didn't let them copy my homework. It was on the WELL that I learned both the address for a mail-order catalogue called Leather Toys and how to affix clothespins.

[16]My drinking got really bad in graduate school. In the mid-eighties, I was in love with a woman who was living in Paris, and I took the opportunity to get mixed up at the same time with a friend in New York. Kate, the second of these women, first played this record for me. The snap of the snare drum that begins "The Good Earth" has a real tenderness to it, for me. I was playing this record when I was really ashamed of myself and also afterward, when I was hoping for forgiveness.

[17]At the end of my drinking, when I was first living in Hoboken, I started writing my first novel, "Garden State." Later, through a chain of kindnesses, someone managed to slip a copy of it to William Gaddis, the writer I most admired, then and now. Much later, long after all this, I came to know Gaddis's son Matthew a little bit, and he said that the book had probably got covered up with papers, because that's the way his dad's desk is. But maybe there was one afternoon when it was on top of a stack.

[18]The last day of class with Jack Hawkes, we were standing out on one of those Victorian porches in Providence—a bunch of us, because there was always a crowd of people trying to get into Jack's classes (and they were usually really talented)—firing corks from champagne bottles out into the street. A couple made it halfway across. Hawkes was mumbling something about how sad it was that so many writers were so afflicted by drink. In less than a week, I was going to graduate.

[19]"Another clergyman in New England, Mr. Joseph Moody, of York, Maine, who died about eighty years since, made himself remarkable by the same eccentricity that is here related of the Reverend Mr. Hooper. In his case, however, the symbol had a different import. In early life he had accidentally killed a beloved friend; and from that day till the hour of his own death, he hid his face from men."

[20]See n. 7, above.

[21]During the period when I was finishing my first novel, I had an office job in publishing, from which I was later fired. I judged everything against the books I loved when I was a teen-ager: "The Crying of Lot 49," Beckett's "Murphy," "One Hundred Years of Solitude," etc. Besides Lester Bangs (see above), Marcus's "Lipstick Traces" was on of the few recently published books I liked. Another was "Responses: On Paul de Man's Wartime Journalism" (University of Nebraska Press).

[22]In 1987, I institutionalized myself. At that moment, Thurber and Groucho Marx and anthologies of low comedy seemed like the best that literature had to offer. I thought I was going to abandon writing—something had to give—but I didn't. I felt better later.

[23]"The accusation that the gnostics invented what they wrote contains some truth: certain gnostics openly acknowledged that they derived their *gnosis* from their own experience.... The gnostic Christians... assumed that had gone far beyond the apostles' original teaching."

[24]And Cage's book "Silence"; and "Music for Airports"; and La Monte Young's "The Second Dream of the High-Tension Line Step-down Transformer from the Four Dreams of China"; and Ezra Pound after St. Elizabeth's ; and "Be Here Now"; and Mark Rothko.

[25]The back cover of this issue consists of a newspaper photo of a man in a wedding gown slumped over on a toilet, his skin ribbed with gigantic blisters. He's really destroyed, this guy. I'd been given to believe the photo was from the *Daily News*. And since my grandfather worked for the *News* the luridness of this horror struck close. This, I learned, was an act of *pleasure*.

[26]Angela Carter assigned this book to us in sophomore year. I was taking a lot of quaaludes that spring. One night, I stayed up all night on quaaludes and wrote a story, cribbed from Bruno Schulz, about a guy who lives in a house that is *actually his grandmother*. Later, when I told Angela that I'd written the story high, she said, cryptically, "Quaaludes, the aardvark of the drug world."

[27]"All these empty urges must be satisfied."

[28]"Sick as I am/confused in the head/I mean I have/endured this April/so far/visiting friends" (pages 427–8). "Garden State" was published in the spring of 1992. I was already pretty far into my second book, "The Ice Storm." I left Hoboken for good.

[29]There was a time, when I was an adolescent, when I didn't feel like I had a dad, even though he didn't live that far away, and I saw him on Sundays. This is an admission that won't please him or the rest of my family. The way I see it, though, there has never been a problem between me and my *actual* dad. But dads make the same tentative decisions we sons make. Once, my father said to me, "I wonder if you kids would have turned out differently if I had been around to kick some ass." This was during one of those long car rides full of silences. The question didn't even apply to me, I don't think. He might have been there, he might not have. Didn't matter. I was looking elsewhere for the secrets of ethics and home.

Anomalies In Relief: Notes of a California Expatriate

Hans Ostrom

1. My Own Private Californias

As I sat down to write this essay, I heard certain skeptical readers over my shoulder ask, "California *expatriate?* How typically self-aggrandizing of a Californian—to phrase 'leaving one's home state' as expatriatism." In fact, though, the word is apt, for in the most basic terms—geologic and economic—California is a nation-state. Its land mass is huge, and its natural borders remain imposing: ocean to the west, desert-and-ocean to the south, alpine *massifs* to the east, mountains and plateaus to the north, and in the middle a valley so huge it seems divinely scooped from the crust of the earth. Its economy, I am told, is the seventh largest in the world, and while it may have its economic troubles from time to time, it doesn't really have a weakness: shipping, railroads, trucking, timber, diversified agriculture, weapons of mass destruction, commercial airplanes, an atom smasher, computers, visual media, mining, tourism, an array of manufacturing. Economically it wants for nothing. Maybe the wonder is that its economy is *only* the seventh largest in the world. At any rate, to be a native Californian and to have left is indeed to have left a real *pater* of a place, a country from which one may indeed be *ex*-ed.

Considered against images almost all people, Americans or otherwise, have of California, the place I grew up is in most ways extremely *un*-Californian. That would be Sierra City, a very small town—250 permanent residents—that probably wouldn't exist now if the Gold Rush hadn't happened; but Rush Happened, and 5,000 miners once descended—that is, ascended—on that spot, in a canyon of a river now known as the North Yuba. Unlike, say, Lincoln City, in the same county, Sierra City did not become a ghost town, probably in part because it lay on one path between the foothills and Yuba Pass, the pass the Donner Party probably would have survived.

If you look at a relief map of California, you'll see that the Sierra Nevada range, running north and south, is raked with deep canyons that run east and west, give or take a few degrees on the compass. The North Yuba is one of these. Sierra City lies 4,000 feet up into that canyon. Its economy—too grandiose a word for such a village—springs from a few retirees, some summer residents, tourists, people who take care of the state highway and the national forest, a handful of miners, and so on. It's nowhere near as etched into the mountains or as well-scrubbed as a Swiss village, but in other ways the analogy obtains.

So although, intellectually, I can craft an argument for seeing California as a kind of nation, my own private California, the one from which I'm psychically and filially expatriated, is a different kind of California indeed, one that has made me pledge allegiance to the word "anomaly".

To the extent all expatriates yearn for what is left behind, I yearn not just for a rural past but a wilderness one. Whenever I reach an acute phase of taking myself too seriously (there's not much a person can do about the chronic condition), I haul out a one-page autobiography I wrote when I was 8, for Mrs. Swafford's third-grade class at Downieville School, twelve miles down-canyon from Sierra City. (I'm still astounded, incidentally, by the bus-miles I logged in those years—24 miles a day—and by the fact that not once, knock on wood, has a bus tumbled over an embankment, plunging into the canyon below.)

In the autobiography, I dutifully report on our family pets, three hunting hounds named Jack, Jocko, and Shorty. (Shorty, poor lad, was a desperately over-sexed Redbone hound who often tried to hump my brothers' and my legs when we fed the dogs.) And then, offhandedly, I report that the family has two bobcats as well, "bobcat" being a cute name for what is essentially a species of lynx. My father had box-trapped them, and while he knew they couldn't be domesticated, he still wanted to keep them around—bottled-up ferocity, 200 proof. So he built a big cage, concrete floor and all, and kept them in there for a year or so, feeding them raw fish and raw flesh. It was a miserable existence for them. They never came out of their little houses unless you threw a fish in there; then, with truly miraculous speed, they'd leap out, grab the fish, and get back in the house—all in one tawny-gray blur of exquisitely evolved speed. No one, not even us kids, tried to name them; they were *that* wild. One summer day, my father opened the cage and came back into *our* house. From the window, we watched as the two hefty cats lounged for fifteen minutes or so in the green piece of meadow that was our yard. They stretched and rolled and preened like housecats. And for once, we were the prisoners in *our* house. They seemed drunk on sunlight. And then they were gone. Forever. A beautiful memory indeed.

In that autobiography, it's the unselfconscious matter-of-factness in my reportage that reveals my true backwoods backgroundedness. I didn't assume everyone had bobcats, but neither did I assume having them was very much out of the ordinary.

The blue diorite bluffs. The conifer forests. The robust silence of a Sierra night after snow. The miniature post office in town. How we lost all electrical power for two weeks one winter—plunked back into the 19th century. The work in carpentry and stonemasonry I did with my father. The way I learned to cook on a woodstove from my mother (the way she and my father disagreed for 50 years about how to cook on a woodstove). How the hardness of those hills wounded everyone in the family, but each in her and his particular way. The presence of the high, dry plateau of the Sierra Valley (and beyond that, all of Nevada) on the other side of those peaks. These and like elements substantially comprise the region for which I sometimes yearn. Considered against the images almost all people have of California, it is an invisible California, one that is almost impossible to explain to anyone except that rare, patient, wise person who knows how intricate and deceptive all cultures are.

After I completed my Ph.D. in English at the University of California, Davis, I took a job at a small college perched above Puget Sound in Tacoma, Washington. That was 12 years ago. Although the Sierra Nevada is, in part, what I yearn for when I yearn for California, the more important part of my expatriate experience may well be the California I carry around inside me, and therein lies a potential contradiction, which I'll try to plumb:

California made me comfortable with flux, with rootlessness, decay, fragmentation, entropy, and so forth. You might think that because I grew up in such a small town, I'd be decidedly uncomfortable with such things, which might reasonably be connected to urban life and postmodernism. While Sierra City exhibits some classic small-town attributes, however, it is in other ways as subject to flux as a port city. People come and go at a remarkable pace; the town has always been a magnet for eccentrics at both ends of the economic spectrum; and the historical connection to the Gold Rush still makes the place attractive to charming hustlers and fast-buck artists. My grandfather left Sweden and ended up a miner in those hills, working in the Keystone and Sixteen-To-One mines, the latter still operating in Allegheny. My experience in other parts of California—the Central Valley, San Francisco, Los Angeles—only contributes to this comfort with flux and flimflam surfaces of things. Put another way, I am not surprised, looking back, that I was so smitten by Venice (Italy, that is) when I first set foot there during *Carnivale* in 1981. In many ways, Venice did not need to be translated for a Sierra City boy.

In a state like Washington, and at a small, private college, this internal California makes me an inveterate outsider. For Washingtonians think of themselves as above—literally and figuratively—Californians. Just saying the word "California" is like passing a rotten onion under the nose of a Washingtonian, and to disclose that you're from California is like revealing you did a stretch in San Quentin. I've lost count of the times I've been scowled at for answering the question, "Where are you from?" honestly. Washingtonians imagine their roots are deeper and more stable, but naturally they are not thinking of the Native American culture here. They think of themselves as enclosed, as rather more homogenous than the Jigsaw State down there. When others refer to Washingtonians as "tight-assed" or smug or a tad uninteresting, the internal Californian occasionally agrees, even as other parts of my ever-in-flux Self appreciate aspects of Pacific Northwest a lot, not least of all the conifers, cousins to my beloved Sierra Nevada trees, rocking and creaking in the high winds of November.

Oddly enough, my internal California makes me more comfortable with Tacoma than Seattle. You'd think a Californian would grab onto Seattle like a life-saver, but no: for me at least, Seattle works just a little too hard at being cosmopolitan; and, tellingly, the most pretentious faculty members where I teach work just a little too hard at agreeing to see Seattle as cosmopolitan. The city and such people need each other to keep up one another's courage: "We are cosmopolitan, you and I, aren't we?" Strangely, the Seattle/Tacoma dynamic does not necessarily depend on where one lives. Some faculty members who live in Tacoma hate it but don't move. I believe this is known as self-flagellation. Some faculty members who live in Seattle are quite sanguine about Tacoma and realistic about Seattle's tendency to strain.

My internal California, however, has a soft spot for Tacoma, where my family and I live, just as it has a soft spot for Oakland over San Francisco, even though San Francisco really is what Seattle tries to be—a city with European suppleness. For Tacoma is a place where the parts of the urban solution will never quite gel. It is a hard-edged port and paper-mill city, but it also has considerable Old Money that softens those edges in ways both predictable and not. It has oddball neighborhoods that never quite fit together. Strange edifices have sprung up here: a marvelous old-style conservatory in Wright Park (and Wright Park itself contains statues of Ibsen and Schiller); a replica of the Roman Spanish Steps; a tiled dome on the Presbyterian Church that looks positively Byzantine; a high-school building that was once a hotel for robber barons, complete with gothic spires. It is also surprisingly amenable to progressives, such as a guy who started the first needle-exchange program for drug addicts in the nation, and another guy who started Safe Streets, a successful grassroots, antigang program. Tacoma will forever be an oddball city, gnawing on its own disappointments, but my internal California, as well as my external working-class background, embraces the chronic brokenness of the city and chafes at those aspects of Seattle—WASPish, tight-grinned, Eddie Bauerish—that put one on one's guard. How funny that in Spell-Check, "boorish" is recommended to replace "Bauerish."

The California I brought with me also turns me into a kind of Cassandra from time to time, though to call my seeing what's happening here "prophecy" is beyond overstatement. A favorite Washington pastime is to heap scorn on everything California does wrong: overdevelopment, squandering of water, political wild-goose chases (led by the likes of Jerry "Moonbeam" Brown and Pete "Flip" Wilson), roller-coaster real-estate rides, and so forth. And yet, seemingly every move the city councils and the state legislature make in Washington mirrors moves I've seen in California. Essentially, developers have carte blanche. The state won't adopt an income tax, so education is more underfunded each year. Like agribusiness in California, Microsoft and Boeing pretty much run the show politically, though at the moment the Christian Right is having a good run. Obviously practical urban notions like light rail go nowhere. Prime agricultural land gets gobbled up, and the state known for its constant rainfall and saturated forests is running out of water. Like Cassandra, I'd be glad to tell anyone who would listen what is quintessentially "Californian" about all this, but no one would believe me, and besides, what is quintessentially Californian about all this is actually quintessentially American. Heaping scorn on California is a symptom of denial, upon which America's greed banks, as it were. The brassy Golden State makes it easier for other states to emulate it because they can pretend not to be emulating it.

One final way in which my internal California manifests itself up here, perched between the Cascade and Olympic Ranges, is that I view the fate of California with certain cool melancholy. Lately, I have been reading a lot of historical books on Sicily and Byzantium, led there by John Julius Norwich's book on Venice. There is about California today a whiff both of splendor lost but also of cultures woven together in a marvelously intricate if overwrought tapestry. California has seen its best days. It is eating itself to death, like Elvis, that Byzantine Emperor of Rock and Roll. But unlike Elvis, it will be forced to kick at least one addiction—the addiction to defense spending, the real California Gold Rush. California, at long last, must grow up, as the United States must. Whether the maturation will kill it, kill us, is another matter. We—California, the United States, America—are at the end of one crucial phase of Empire, if not at the end of Empire itself. I watch California grow up, and mostly grow up badly, with sadness, and I'm mostly glad I'm watching it from the vantage point of Puget Sound. But neither do I want to turn my head completely, for California "is" me, in mercurial ways, and in mercurial ways I must participate in its growing up, its aging, its losing itself to gain itself. At least ritually I must participate, according to my internal California. Literally I have to participate, for what is happening to California, whether we're talking about Sacramento, San Francisco, or South Central L.A., is happening to all of us. It's an "American thing." We all have to walk that lonesome, madly overdeveloped Central Valley—together *and* by ourselves. Nobody else can walk it for us, though we shall no doubt try to hire a consultant.

2. Blessed Thickness

Not long ago, I flew from Seattle to the San Francisco Bay Area, there to meet up with a couple of graduate-school chums and spend a day or so in North Beach. I first went to San Francisco when I was 9. I was a rabid San Francisco Giants fan, and my mother, bless her heart, wanted me to see Willie Mays "in person" at least once. What a day that was, the baseball dropping out of the sky like a star into Willie's mythic glove forming the legendary basket catch. Since then I've returned to San Francisco dozens of times, rarely for more than a couple of days, occasionally for a conference but usually just to go—to walk around, to visit City Lights Books, whatever: in San Francisco, to be is to do, borrowing from Sartre.

I was struck this time by how at-home I was in this city, a city that's never and in no way been my home.

It is a city that has matured; many, many cultures have been "composted" there, creating a thickness, a rich cultural soil surprisingly rare in the United States, where cultural soils are still so stratified. —And yes, the notion of composting invites a crowd of unlovely scatological jokes.

Walking around North Beach with my friends, I felt comfortable in a way I've never felt in Tacoma or Seattle, despite the many years my wife and I (and now our son) have spent up here. I felt so comfortable that I even thought of proposing to my wife that we retire in San Francisco, some 25 years or more down the line, getting an apartment in North Beach, tottering down to the cafes each morning. I seriously doubt if we will retire there (life being what happens while you're adding to your 401-K), but the mere fact the possibility came to mind fascinated me.

As diverse as some cities and regions of the United States are, in San Francisco the diversity is so broad, the interweaving so complex, that one feels—in North Beach, at least—humanity has not just survived but thrived. D.H. Lawrence's line following the Great War: "Look, we have come through!" I wouldn't dream of overlooking the presence of homeless people, crack addicts, strip joints, and—in San Francisco at large—persistent racism and San Andreas Faults of economic inequality. Nonetheless, the palpable, workable, loamy diversity of North Beach struck me as refreshing, as authentic urbanity. Looking back these several weeks later, I realize my internal California led me to embrace North Beach as a home that never was my home. My friends and I ended up one evening at Jazz at Pearl's, no cover, two-drink minimum, a band called The Nighthawks cooking over a low flame; and I thought, cities, gardens, forests, and jazz depend upon impurity, upon a breaking-down-leading-to-recombination, upon a sweet embraceability, a blessed thickness, something Governor Pete Wilson, not to mention Tricky Pat Buchanan, wouldn't recognize if he fell over it; and he fell over it.

However (Bergman fan that I am, I must get grim), my friends and I spent part of the next day at one of the most underrated municipal museums in the U.S., Oakland's; on one floor lay a marvelous display of California's natural history, each region represented by superb little tableaus of flora and fauna. The display began with a huge relief map of the state, on the floor: You pushed a button, lights overhead came on, and a variety of transparencies appeared in rhythm—rivers, county borders, city areas, and so forth. One's first impulse is to become a child and point excitedly—"Hey, Lassen Peak's right *there!*" Then that phase quiets. You step back. The relief map ceases to be a map and becomes a more menacing analog, a representation of what postindustrial civilization does to everything. A handful of primitive peoples shrunk heads. We shrink *everything.* That is, we think everything is waiting for us to package it. A moment of Kafkaesque vertigo overtook me. This was California at my feet. The virtual had become the real, the real the virtual.

Thank God there was a wonderfully hokey yet campy, boosterish yet tongue-in-cheek exhibit in another recess of the museum: A Retrospective of the Oakland Raiders football team—the Raiders having just returned from being, well, expatriated to Los Angeles. Huge black-and-white photographs of genial, muddy thugs smashing each other's atoms. Actual Super Bowl trophies! A continuous video of "Raider action" playing on a television, with an immense pastel couch in front of it. Cult-fans like me mumbling trivia to one another. A grizzled guy with arms like a stevedore's, saying to his buddy, "You see that big painting of Yosemite out there? It was ex-*qui*-site." *California! You* are *alive!* I thought.

3. Climate, Etc., In The Marrow

My family and I lived in Sweden for six months a couple years back because I had a Fulbright Fellowship at Uppsala University. To top off six months next to the Baltic, and to render "the travel budget" a thorough-going oxymoron, we decided to spend a couple weeks next to the Mediterranean, just south of Barcelona. Standing in the warm ocean one day, baking like a fillet, watching my son engage in mud-skirmishes with Spanish kids, I thought, "I miss California."

Not that I ever got within a hundred yards of a surfboard, or anything. Still, if you peel away all the economic, political, filial, personal, and historical constructions of a "home state," you are left with something that stays in your bones, and I'm not talking about heavy metals, dioxins, or radioactivity. For me, it's that dry climate, which—leaving aside certain pockets on the coast—stretches from the high plateau bordering Oregon down to Baja. Maybe living in the Great Sponge that is the Pacific-Northwest Climate has made me obsess on the adobe spirit in my marrow; maybe not. Today, at any rate, I feel as if to be an expatriate is to be a transplanted organism, an uprooted replanted shrub, a bear trapped in Yosemite but freighted to Yellowstone. No matter how much your Self turns into other Selves, no matter how much you can't step into the same river (or ocean) twice, no matter how much work and reading and other people move you further on into oblivion, your place places you, imprints its code.

In deeper, more mysterious, and I must admit perhaps less consequential ways, then, I carry California around inside me; it flavors my expatriatism; it is one other reminder that James Baldwin, as usual, was right when he warned African-American writers and American writers in general not to be completely seduced by France or other vivid sites of expatriatism, when he said—in "Alas, Poor Richard" and other essays—essentially that home is what you carry around inside of you, what you cannot jettison and therefore deny at your peril. He was also fond of saying, as he said of living in Istanbul, that only by living in a distinctly different Elsewhere do we learn to see "home" with clarity and maturity: Yes, this notion is to some extent proverbial by now and certainly not Baldwin's original idea. But the way Baldwin acted upon and acted out the truism went beyond the proverbial, defining "expatriatism" for us in ways richer than the usual political or moveable-feast ones. Better than most, he illuminates how we travel in our native regions by traveling elsewhere, how we give the best or worst (our choice) of our native regions to new regions when we unpack, so to speak.

Homage to Baldwin, then, who understood that growing up was not staying put, nor going away, nor coming back, but all three. Baldwin understood about Harlem in the marrow, thereby giving me a way to glimpse California in my marrow, and to look at certain anomalous selves—in relief.

The Library Card

Richard Wright

One morning I arrived early at work and went into the bank lobby where the Negro porter was mopping. I stood at a counter and picked up the Memphis *Commercial Appeal* and began my free reading of the press. I came finally to the editorial page and saw an article dealing with one H.L. Mencken. I knew by the hearsay that he was the editor of the *American Mercury,* but aside from that I knew nothing about him. The article was a furious denunciation of Mencken, concluding with one, hot, short sentence: Mencken is a fool.

I wondered what on earth this Mencken had done to call down upon him the scorn of the South. The only people I had ever heard denounced in the South were Negroes, and this man was not a Negro. Then what ideas did Mencken hold that made a newspaper like the *Commercial Appeal* castigate him publicly? Undoubtedly he must be advocating ideas that the South did not like. Were there, then, people other than Negroes who criticized the South? I knew that during the Civil War the South had hated northern whites, but I had not encountered such hate during my life. Knowing no more of Mencken than I did at that moment, I felt a vague sympathy for him. Had not the South, which had assigned me the role of a non-man, cast at him its hardest words?

Now, how could I find out about this Mencken? There was a huge library near the riverfront, but I knew that Negroes were not allowed to patronize its shelves any more than they were the parks and playgrounds of the city. I had gone into the library several times to get books for the white men on the job. Which of them would now help me to get books? And how could I read them without causing concern to the white men with whom I worked? I had so far been successful in hiding my thoughts and feelings from them, but I knew that I would create hostility if I went about this business of reading in a clumsy way.

I weighed the personalities of the men on the job. There was a Don, a Jew; but I distrusted him. His position was not much better than mine and I knew that he was uneasy and insecure; he had always treated me in an offhand, bantering way that barely concealed his contempt. I was afraid to ask him to help me to get books; his frantic desire to demonstrate a racial solidarity with the whites against Negroes might make him betray me.

Then how about the boss? No, he was a Baptist and I had the suspicion that he would not be quite able to comprehend why a black boy would want to read Mencken. There were other white men on the job whose attitudes showed clearly that they were Kluxers or sympathizers, and they were out of the question.

There remained only one man whose attitude did not fit into an anti-Negro category, for I had heard the white men refer to him as a "Pope lover." He was an Irish Catholic and was hated by the white Southerners. I knew that he read books, because I had got him volumes from the library several times. Since he, too, was an object of hatred, I felt that he might refuse me but would hardly betray me. I hesitated, weighing and balancing the imponderable realities.

One morning I paused before the Catholic fellow's desk.

"I want to ask you a favor," I whispered to him.

"What is it?"

"I want to read. I can't get books from the library. I wonder if you'd let me use your card?"

He looked at me suspiciously.

"My card is full most of the time," he said.

"I see," I said and waited, posing my question silently.

"You're not trying to get me into trouble, are you, boy?" he asked, staring at me.

"Oh, no, sir."

"What book do you want?"

"A book by H.L. Mencken."

"Which one?"

"I don't know. Has he written more than one?"

"He has written several."

"I didn't know that."

"What makes you want to read Mencken?"

"Oh, I just saw his name in the newspaper," I said.

"It's good of you to want to read," he said. "But you ought to read the right things."

I said nothing. Would he want to supervise my reading?

"Let me think," he said. "I'll figure out something."

I turned from him and he called me back. He stared at me quizzically.

"Richard, don't mention this to the other white men," he said.

"I understand," I said. "I won't say a word."

A few days later he called me to him.

"I've got a card in my wife's name," he said. "Here's mine."

"Thank you, sir."

"Do you think you can manage it?"

"I'll manage fine," I said.

"If they suspect you, you'll get in trouble," he said.

"I'll write the same kind of notes to the library that you wrote when you sent me for books," I told him. "I'll sign your name."

He laughed.

"Go ahead. Let me see what you get," he said.

That afternoon I addressed myself to forging a note. Now, what were the names of books written by H.L. Mencken? I did not know any of them. I finally wrote what I thought would be a foolproof note: *Dear Madam: Will you please let this nigger boy*—I used the word "nigger" to make the librarian feel that I could not possibly be the author of the note—*have some books by H.L. Mencken?* I forged the white man's name.

I entered the library as I had always done when on errands for whites, but I felt that I would somehow slip up and betray myself. I doffed my hat, stood a respectful distance from the desk, looked as unbookish as possible, and waited for the white patrons to be taken care of. When the desk was clear of people, I still waited. The white librarian looked at me.

"What do you want, boy?"

As though I did not possess the power of speech, I stepped forward and simply handed her the forged note, not parting my lips.

"What books by Mencken does he want?" she asked.

"I don't know, ma'am," I said, avoiding her eyes.

"Who gave you this card?"

"Mr. Falk," I said.

"Where is he?"

"He's at work, at M———— Optical Company," I said. "I've been in here for him before."

"I remember," the woman said. "But he never wrote notes like this."

Oh, God, she's suspicious. Perhaps she would not let me have the books? If she had turned her back at that moment, I would have ducked out the door and never gone back. Then I thought of a bold idea.

"You can call him up, ma'am," I said, my heart pounding.

"You're not using these books, are you?" she asked pointedly.

"Oh, no, ma'am. I can't read."

"I don't know what he wants by Mencken," she said under her breath.

I knew now that I had won; she was thinking of other things and the race question had gone out of her mind. She went to the shelves. Once or twice she looked over her shoulder at me, as though se was still doubtful. Finally she came forward with books in her hand.

"I'm sending him two books," she said. "But tell Mr. Falk to come in next time, or send me the names of the books he wants. I don't know what he wants to read."

I said nothing. She stamped the card and handed me the books. Not daring to glance at them, I went out of the library, fearing that the woman would call me back for further questioning. A block away from the library I opened one of the books and read a title: *A Book of Prefaces*. I was nearing my nineteenth birthday and did not know how to pronounce the word "preface." I thumbed the pages and saw strange words and strange names. I shook my head, disappointed. I looked at the other book; it was called *Prejudices*. I knew what that word meant; I had heard it all my life. And right off I was on guard against Mencken's books. Why would a man want to call a book *Prejudices?* The word was so stained with all my memories of racial hate that I could not conceive of anybody using it for a title. Perhaps I had made a mistake about Mencken? A man who had prejudices must be wrong.

When I showed the books to Mr. Falk, he looked at me and frowned.

"That librarian might telephone you," I warned him.

"That's all right," he said. "But when you're through reading those books, I want you to tell me what you get out of them."

That night in my rented room, while letting the hot water run over my can of pork and beans in the sink, I opened *A Book of Prefaces* and began to read. I was jarred and shocked by the style, the clear, clean, sweeping sentences. Why did he write like that? And how did one write like that? I pictured the man as a raging demon, slashing with his pen, consumed with hate, denouncing everything American, extolling everything European or German, laughing at the weaknesses of people, mocking God, authority. What was this? I stood up, trying to realize what reality lay behind the meaning of the words . . . Yes, this man was fighting, fighting with words. He was using words as a weapon, using them as one would use a club. Could words be weapons? Well, yes, for here they were. Then, maybe, perhaps, I could use them as a weapon? No. It frightened me. I read on and what amazed me was not what he said, but how on earth anybody had the courage to say it.

Occasionally I glanced up to reassure myself that I was alone in the room. Who were these men about whom Mencken was talking so passionately? Who was Anatole France? Joseph Conrad? Sinclair Lewis, Sherwood Anderson, Dostoevski, George Moore, Gustave Flaubert, Maupassant, Tolstoy, Frank Harris, Mark Twain, Thomas Hardy, Arnold Bennett, Stephen Crane, Zola, Norris, Gorky, Bergson, Ibsen, Balzac, Bernard Shaw, Dumas, Poe, Thomas Mann, O. Henry, Dreiser, H.G. Wells, Gogol, T.S. Eliot, Gide, Baudelaire, Edgar Lee Masters, Stendhal, Turgenev, Huneker, Nietzsche, and scores of others? Were these men real? Did they exist or had they existed? And how did one pronounce their names?

I ran across many words whose meanings I did not know, and I either looked them up in a dictionary or, before I had a chance to do that, encountered the word in a context that made its meaning clear. But what strange world was this? I concluded the book with the conviction that I had somehow overlooked something terribly important in life. I had once tried to write, had once reveled in feeling, had let my crude imagination roam, but the impulse to dream had been slowly beaten out of me by experience. Now it surged up again and I hungered for books, new ways of looking and seeing. It was not a matter of believing or disbelieving what I read, but of feeling something new, of being affected by something that made the look of the world different.

As dawn broke I ate my pork and beans, feeling dopey, sleepy. I went to work, but the mood of the book would not die; it lingered, coloring everything I saw, heard, did. I now felt that I knew what the white men were feeling. Merely because I had read a book that had spoken of how they lived and thought, I identified myself with that book. I felt vaguely guilty. Would I, filled with bookish notions, act in a manner that would make the whites dislike me?

I forged more notes and my trips to the library became frequent. Reading grew into a passion. My first serious novel was Sinclair Lewis's *Main Street*. It made me see my boss, Mr. Gerald, and identify him as an American type. I would smile when I saw him lugging his golf bags into the office. I had always felt a vast distance separating me from the boss, and now I felt closer to him, though still distant. I felt now that I knew him, that I could feel the very limits of his narrow life. And this had happened because I had read a novel about a mythical man called George F. Babbitt.

The plots and stories in the novels did not interest me so much as the point of view revealed. I gave myself over to each novel without reserve, without trying to criticize it; it was enough for me to see and feel something different. And for me, everything was something different. Reading was like a drug, a dope. The novels created moods in which I lived for days. But I could not conquer my sense of guilt, my feeling that the white men around me knew that I was changing, that I had begun to regard them differently.

Whenever I brought a book to the job, I wrapped it in newspaper—a habit that was to persist for years in other cities and under other circumstances. But some of the white men pried into my packages when I was absent and they questioned me.

"Boy, what are you reading those books for?"

"Oh, I don't know, sir."

"That's deep stuff you're reading, boy."

"I'm just killing time, sir."

"You'll addle your brains if you don't watch out."

I read Dreiser's *Jennie Gerhardt* and *Sister Carrie* and they revived in me a vivid sense of my mother's suffering; I was overwhelmed. I grew silent, wondering about the life around me. It would have been impossible for me to have told anyone what I derived from these novels, for it was nothing less than a sense of life itself. All my life had shaped me for the realism, the naturalism, of the modern novel, and I could not read enough of them.

Steeped in new moods and ideas, I bought a ream of paper and tried to write; but nothing would come, or what did come was flat beyond telling. I discovered that more than desire and feeling were necessary to write and I dropped the idea. Yet I still wondered how it was possible to know people sufficiently to write about them? Could I ever learn about life and people? To me, with my vast ignorance, my Jim Crow station in life, it seemed a task impossible of achievement. I now knew what being a Negro meant. I could endure the hunger. I had learned to live with hate. But to feel that there were feelings denied me, that the very breath of life itself was beyond my reach, that more than anything else hurt, wounded me. I had a new hunger.

In buoying me up, reading also cast me down, made me see what was possible, what I had missed. My tension returned, new, terrible, bitter, surging, almost too great to be contained. I no longer *felt* that the world about me was hostile, killing: I *knew* it. A million times I asked myself what I could do to save myself, and there were no answers. I seemed forever condemned, ringed by walls.

I did not discuss my reading with Mr. Falk, who had lent me his library card; it would have meant talking about myself and that would have been too painful. I smiled each day, fighting desperately to maintain my old behavior, to keep my disposition seeming sunny. But some of the white men discerned that I had begun to brood.

"Wake up there, boy!" Mr. Olin said one day.

"Sir!" I answered for the lack of a better word.

"You act like you've stolen something," he said.

I laughed in the way I knew he expected me to laugh, but I resolved to be more conscious of myself, to watch my every act, to guard and hide the new knowledge that was dawning within me.

If I went north, would it be possible for me to build a new life then? But how could a man build a life upon vague, unformed yearnings? I wanted to write and I did not even know the English language. I bought English grammars and found them dull. I felt that I was getting a better sense of the language from novels than from grammars. I read hard, discarding a writer as soon as I felt that I had grasped his point of view. At night the printed page stood before my eyes in sleep.

Mrs. Moss, my landlady, asked me one Sunday morning:

"Son, what is this you keep on reading?"

"Oh, nothing. Just novels."

"What you get out of 'em?"

"I'm just killing time," I said.

"I hope you know your own mind," she said in a tone which implied that she doubted if I had a mind.

I knew of no Negroes who read the books I liked and wondered if any Negroes ever thought of them. I knew that there were Negro doctors, lawyers, newspapermen, but I never saw any of them. When I read a Negro newspaper I never caught the faintest echo of my preoccupation in its pages. I felt trapped and occasionally, for a few days, I would stop reading. But a vague hunger would come over me for books, books that opened up new avenues of feeling and seeing, and again I would forge another note to the white librarian. Again I would read and wonder as only the naive and unlettered can read and wonder, feeling that I carried a secret, criminal burden about with me each day.

That winter my mother and brother came and we set up housekeeping, buying furniture on the installment plan, being cheated and yet knowing no way to avoid it. I began to eat warm food and to my surprise found that regular meals enabled me to read faster. I may have lived through many illnesses and survived them, never suspecting that I was ill. My brother obtained a job and we began to save toward the trip north, plotting our time, setting tentative dates for departure. I told none of the white men on the job that I was planning to go north; I knew that the moment they felt I was thinking of the North they would change toward me. It would have made them feel that I did not like the life I was living, and because my life was completely conditioned by what they said or did, it would have been tantamount to challenging them.

I could calculate my chances for life in the South as a Negro fairly clearly now.

I could fight the southern whites by organizing with other Negroes, as my grandfather had done. But I knew that I could never win that way; there were many whites and there were but few blacks. They were strong and we were weak. Outright black rebellion could never win. If I fought openly I would die and I did not want to die. News of lynchings were frequent.

I could submit and live the life of a genial slave, but that was impossible. All of my life had shaped me to live by my own feelings and thoughts. I could make up to Bess and marry her and inherit the house. But that, too, would be the life of a slave; if I did that, I would crush to death something within me, and I would hate myself as much as I knew the whites already hated those who had submitted. Neither could I ever willingly present myself to be kicked, as Shorty had done. I would rather have died than do that.

I could drain off my restlessness by fighting with Shorty and Harrison. I had seen many Negroes solve the problem of being black by transferring their hatred of themselves to others with a black skin and fighting them. I would have to be cold to do that, and I was not cold and I could never be.

I could, of course, forget what I had read, thrust the whites out of my mind, forget them; and find release from anxiety and longing in sex and alcohol. But the memory of how my father had conducted himself made that course repugnant. If I did not want others to violate my life, how could I voluntarily violate it myself?

I had no hope whatever of being a professional man. Not only had I been so conditioned that I did not desire it, but the fulfillment of such an ambition was beyond my capabilities. Well-to-do Negroes lived in a world that was almost as alien to me as the world inhabited by whites.

What, then, was there? I held my life in my mind, in my consciousness each day, feeling at times that I would stumble and drop it, spill it forever. My reading had created a vast sense of distance between me and the world in which I lived and tried to make a living, and that sense of distance was increasing each day. My days and nights were one long, quiet, continuously contained dream of terror, tension, and anxiety. I wondered how long I could bear it.

My Children Explain the Big Issues

Will Baker

Feminism

I am walking up a long hill toward our water tank and pond. My daughter Montana, 23 months, has decided to accompany me. It is a very warm day, so she wears only diapers, cowboy boots, and a floral-print bonnet. At the outset I offer to carry her but she says "I walk," and then, "You don't have to hold my hand, daddy."

This is the longest walk she has taken, without assistance. I see droplets of sweat on the bridge of her nose. Just before the water tank there is a steep pitch and loose gravel on the path, so I offer again to help.

She pulls away and says, "You don't have to hold me, daddy." A moment later she slips and falls flat. A pause while she rolls into a sitting position and considers, her mouth bent down. But quickly she scrambles up and slaps at the dirty places on her knees, then looks at me sidelong with a broad grin. "See?"

Fate

I first explained to Cole that there was no advantage in dumping the sand from his sandbox onto the patio. He would have more fun bulldozing and trucking inside the two-by-twelve frame. Heavy-equipment guys stayed within the boundaries, part of their job, and the sand would be no good scattered abroad, would get mixed with dead beetles and cat poop.

Next I warned him firmly not to shovel out his patrimony, warned him twice. The third time I physically removed him from the box and underscored my point very emphatically. At this stage, he was in danger of losing important privileges. Reasonable tolerance had already been shown him and there was no further room for negotiation. There was a line in the sand. Did he understand the gravity of the situation? Between whimpers, he nodded.

The last time I lifted him by his ear, held his contorted face close to mine, and posed a furious question to him: "*Why? Why are you doing this?*"

Shaking all over with sobs of deep grief, he tried to answer.

"*Eyeadhoo.*"

"What?"

"*Eyeadhoo, eyeadhoo!*"

One more second, grinding my teeth, and the translation came to me. I had to. I had to.

Existentialism

Cole is almost three and has had a sister now for four months. All his old things have been resurrected. Crib, changing table, car sear, backpack, bassinet. There have been visitors visiting, doctors doctoring, a washer and dryer always washing and drying.

He has taken to following me around when I go to work on a tractor or pump, cut firewood, or feed the horses. We are out of the house. It doesn't matter if it is raining. In our slickers and rubber boots we stride through a strip of orchard, on our way to some small chore. I am involved with a problem of my own, fooling with a metaphor or calculating if it's time to spray for leaf curl. The rain drumming on the hood of the slicker, wet grass swooshing against the boots, I completely forget my son is there.

"Hey dad," he says suddenly, and I wake up, look down at him, and see that he is in a state of serious wonder, serious delight. "We're *alone* together, aren't we dad?"

East and West

My other daughter, Willa, is a Tibetan Buddhist nun on retreat. For three years I cannot see her. She writes me to explain subtle points of the doctrine of emptiness, or the merit in abandoning ego, serving others unselfishly.

I will write back to remind her of a party I took her to in 1970. The apartment was painted entirely in black, and candles were burning. There was loud music and a smell of incense and skunky weed. It was very crowded, some dancing and others talking and laughing. People were wearing ornaments of turquoise, bone, feather, and stained glass.

I glimpsed my six-year-old daughter, at midnight, sitting cross-legged on the floor opposite a young man with very long blond hair. He had no shoes and his shirt was only a painted rag. They were in very deep conversation, eyes locked. I did not hear what the young man had just said, but I overheard my daughter very clearly, her voice definite and assured.

"But," she was saying, "you and I are not the same person."

Consanguinity

by Jill Carpenter

I wrote the essay while working as a research writer at Utah State University at Logan. I had landed at USU at age 39. After years of teaching biology, I had retrained as a journalist, had divorced and had given up my position at Pima Community College in Tucson, where I had been for eight years. Although I dearly loved teaching at Pima, the work was part time, and USU offered a full-time job. The essay may be a good-bye to Pima, a middle-age lament, and a melding of my two selves, scientist and creative writer.

In 1990, I married a rocket scientist, and we moved to Huntsville, Alabama, where I work as a freelance writer and am a frequent contributor to The Huntsville Times. *I continue to write essays, and have completed a poetry manuscript and a collection of short stories. One essay, "My mother, the Mole," received a first place award in the 1991 competition of Alabama Pen Women. Another, "Spiderland," appeared in the inaugural issue of* Petroglyph. *I have published (as Jillyn Smith) a nonfiction book, Senses and Sensibilities (Wiley, 1989); it was one of the six finalists for the 1990 COPUS Science Book Award given by the Science Museum, London.*

When I was young, I met a coarse ruddy man named Blood who wore bib overalls. His rattly car was red with iron rust. I thought Blood an awful name. As bad as Guts. I didn't know that the word blood comes from "blut," for "blow," referring to the way blood may be brutally shed, but I was glad it wasn't my name. The prettier words sangre, sanguine, sangria refer to the blood's rich color. Name me Sanger any day.

Later, I shed blood at my loss of virginity; drops of sanguine tears signified the beginning of the heavy and heavy-hearted responsibility of sexuality and its attendant difference between the sexes. Mature, females are bloody; males are spermy, smelling of hormones and the fructose nourishment for the squiggling cells they make. Males miss the fragrant female clockwork curse of reproductive years, miss the scrubbing of rust-stained panties with cold water (quick, or it sets), the blood of miscarriage, the blood of birth, the confused splattering of menopause. They miss the constant reminder of the smell of blood, the smell of life. Perhaps that is why males have searched out blood through hunting, while females have had quite enough of it, and would rather dig anemic roots.

Last year, my menstrual blood would not cease. The doctor considered the periodicity that had become constant: "Have you been stressed in any way?" he asked. "By life," I said, "by living. But I'm in practice." "Some women's bleeding," he said, as he wrote loopy words on the prescription pad, "reacts to tiny stresses. Other women"—he ripped the sheet expertly, looked up triumphant—"are made of iron."

Synthetic hormones tamped the flow. The stream slowed. I swelled. I bought many boxes of absorbent pads. Life leaked. My blood and I were constant companions. My white dress hung forlorn, my black dress became the garb of choice. I douched, showered twice a day. But my nose told me a butcher shop was near.

As I exsanguinated, sexuality waned. I grew weary. Come in for a blood test, the doctor said. I sat in the desk, extended my left arm. The technician tied a piece of rubber tubing around my upper arm to retard venous return. The brachial vein ballooned predictably. She dabbed alcohol, produced a fat syringe. "This will sting," she said. It did. Unlike the bloodsucking parasites, the needle has not evolved a painless bite. Somewhat sadly I watched my blood, my living barometric fluid, my liquid tissue, sucked into the tube.

In two days, the nurse called. "Take iron," she said. I did.

I remembered my technician days with the salt marsh sparrows. A scientist wondered how they drink salty water without dehydrating their blood, without becoming pieces of feathered jerky. He caught them and gave them solutions of salt water to drink, then measured the saltiness of their blood. Indirectly, he measured the efficiency of their bodies to concentrate and excrete salt. I worked for him and drew the sparrows' blood. I reached inside the cage and took a bird's head between my two forefingers and wrapped my thumb around its tiny hot body. I raised and spread its wing. With sharp scissors, I snipped the vein and touched the wound with a capillary tube. The blood climbed in. I staunched the flow with styptic, returned the bird to its salty drink, took the telltale blood for study. Later, the experiment done, the scientist gone, the birds were left to me. I carried them home, a cagefull. The scarred underwings did not affect the beauty of their songs. Short-lived, however, one by one they died, and I plucked each cold limp body from the cage and buried it.

So as a teacher I was ready each semester when my students and I examined blood. I used the exercise for relevance. Teaching hospitals have a Human Subjects Office. A permit was required to collect the birds. I required no permit, I could only encourage cooperation. But group pressure helps. Is what we're doing ethical, justified? Where does human experimentation begin? What about examination of a fingernail, a piece of skin? Where does consent begin? When does a practice become invasive? Should blood donors, organ donors, human subjects be paid, should desperate people be allowed to sell their bodies? Aha. Paradoxically, an education (the students scratched their heads) contains more questions than answers.

For the examination of blood, then, I required the tacit permission of my human subjects. The fear of AIDS, I fear, may have altered feelings toward this standard laboratory test.

Great is the aversion to, yet fascination with, one's own blood. As a child I had chronic nosebleeds. I needed only to sneeze, and out came the brilliant blood. I dripped over the sink. Whence did this fluid come, and why? Was it the lubricant of gears, of the motor of my heart? Later I saw chickens beheaded, a pig butchered, a careless toad flattened by a car, a calf born and licked. Death and life. Bloody, all of them. Like me.

The sight of blood recalls pain. Red incites. And so I understood the fear and excitement of the student blood-letting. Trepidation ensued: just to get a small drop from a middle finger of the left hand. Or of the right hand, for left-handed persons. I, the teacher, was calm.

The alcohol swabs were brought forth to disinfect the fingers. The air smelled of a hospital. Students held their cleansed fingers upright, in a modified obscene gesture, while they studiously read the laboratory manual, turning pages with the opposite hand, sneaking glances at others. The title of the laboratory lesson was Blood Cells. The double O's loomed large, like eyes. They asked silently, Who will be first to draw the blood? Who will be ready?

The hermetically sealed lancets appeared. I busied myself with the stains, the microscope slides.

Will the teacher do it? Of course I would. It is easier to draw blood from another person than from oneself, although medical literature attests to the strange men who performed appendectomies and other drastic surgical procedures on themselves. I thought of the man who catheterized his own heart, as I stripped the aluminum to reveal the shiny point, as I confidently pricked my own finger, for dignity's sake, for power's sake. I was in charge. I was not queasy. Remember menstruation, remember all those nosebleeds?

Fingers differ. One was attached to a guitar player and was huge, with calluses. I knew the lancet would bend, and we'd have to try again with another, a little to the side. Another fingertip was spatulate; another pale, so pale, tapering to a point, and I doubted that it could contain anything but thin bone. Several fingertips, of course, were decorated with long fingernails, fluid catchments, some white, some painted blood-red.

A quick jab always brings forth a drop, red and shiny as a miniature bing cherry, and I am always amazed as the drop wells up, the molecules hugging each other, held together by the physical, adhesive forces that hold together a drop of water. Blood has some of the properties of sea water, but also wild properties of its own. We came from the sea, but we are more than sea. The blood is stickier, thicker, more viscous than pure water. It gets stickier as, shocked, exposed to air, it dries. We had so many things to do with the blood.

Quickly, I turned the finger, nail up, print down. I squeezed, milked the finger. Gravity helped. The drop plopped onto the glass microscope slide, plopped onto another slide, plopped onto a special paper for testing redness, thus hemoglobin, thus iron. Iron plus oxygen is red. Some was sucked—thwip, thwip, thwip—into a capillary tube for centrifuging, spinning, separating into cells. The cells—("formed elements," we call them) are heavier and fall to the bottom. On top the liquid, the yellow plasma—"straw colored," according to the manual. Even the plasma is not all water—eight point five percent is something else, created by life. My students looked at the proportion of cells to liquid to determine if they're normal: 45 percent to 55 percent. If they weren't they'd be home in bed, or in a hospital, having a transfusion.

I covered the wounded finger with the swab, with cotton, and turned my attention quickly to the blood. Spread it gracefully on a microscope slide with a second slide, I instructed. On the other, follow the instructions for staining. You'll see why. Neatly, neatly. Step by step. Avoid air bubbles when applying the thin glass cover slip, I said.

The red blood cells do not need stain. We looked at them quickly. They flow, float orange, in their liquid plasma. They are shaped like cinnamon candies, like the "belly burners" given me by a coughing microlepidopterist, like tires on rims, thick at the edges, thin in the center. The word for them is biconcave. An example, I said, of form and function. An adaptive form for their jobs—increased surface area for pickup and delivery of oxygen molecules.

Using a little iron, some amino acids, the bone marrow forms the blood cells at the rate of two million per second. You have replaced them by now, I said, with relatives, with kin. These cells are advanced—their ancestors were normal nucleated cells, but the mature children, in their decision of specialization, their occupational commitment, discarded their past, extruded their nuclei, spat out their bags of DNA, their very control centers, to make room for more of what they carry: hemoglobin.

Cells with a death wish give us life. With the nuclear extrusion comes the death sentence—no more dividing: 120 days, just 4 months, to live. During that time each biconcave cell goes on a long, long trip, around and around its world, thousands, millions of times, massing in the large veins and arteries like people on Tokyo streets, clicking together single file in the capillaries, like a roll of belly burners.

Its non-containing pigment hemoglobin snatches oxygen through the thin membrane of the lung capillaries and ignores the more numerous molecules of nitrogen gas. Oxygen is what it wants, oxygen is what it gives away to the body's cells, oxygen is what it gets more of. The cells are cycling automatons, but they see different sights, take different routes as they move through the capillary networks.

To show the students how the blood courses, I went to the pet store and bought a goldfish, a healthy one with good fins and tail. I brought it back to the laboratory in a plastic bag full of water, and let it swim free in an aquarium, until the students came in with their books and bags. Then we got out the microscopes and the thin little board with a hole in it. I wetted a paper towel, and folded it into a strip about as wide as the goldfish. I remembered the little fish net, to catch the goldfish, and I wrapped the carp quickly. Its tail stuck out. I quickly put it under the microscope, and adjusted the field of view.

The tail is thin. Light passes through. Visible were dozens of capillaries, full of red blood cells, streaming, streaming, streaming, this way in one vessel, that way in another. I told the students to look quickly; the fish's tail will get hot and dry with the light. Desiccation is the biggest threat to life. After everyone saw the blood, I unwrapped the puzzled fish like a tamale over the tank and it splashed in. We fed it a few fish flakes, gave it a rest and repeated the procedure later. I sent it home with a student who had an interest in pisciculture.

Another way: I asked the biology department to order a frog. I wrapped it in a wet towel, too, with its feet sticking out. It looked ridiculous, but it did not struggle. I spread its toes and thus the webs, the membranes between them, over the hole on the little board, which is known as a "frog board." I pinned the foot down with dissecting pins. I looked through the microscope eyepiece, focused. More red blood cells, coursing, coursing, close together but fast, like traffic moving rhythmically on the Los Angeles freeway. A little hesitation sometimes, but no jams.

The frog engineer has made the capillaries the diameter of a single cell. Frog cells, I told the students, are nucleated. The frog also gets oxygen through its wet skin. I put the frog back in the bucket of water and watched it look at me for a moment. Later a volunteer turned the frog loose in a pond, perhaps at the zoo. It may have been home-sick, but we hoped its feet healed, it caught a few insects, and died of natural causes.

Then I talked of hemoglobin. A molecule with a tail. I drew its structure on the blackboard. Hemo, the iron-containing ring, and globin, protein. Two hundred and eighty million molecules per red blood cell. Students wrote this information using their unpricked fingers. In structure, hemoglobin is very much like the green pig-ment chlorophyll of plants. An amazing thing, but not so amazing. Evidence for the interrelatedness of all life. A unifying principle. I remembered to mention the big picture. I mentioned the cyanide-based oxygen carrying pigments—the green stuff that squishes from an insect, the stuff of a lobster. Works just as well, but the stu-dents always say yuck about blood that is not sanguine.

Lastly, on the stained slides, we begin our search for other components of the blood, the less numerous components, the lovely, lovable leukocytes. They are the white blood cells that must be stained to be seen. Also cast from the bone marrow, and from tonsils, lymph nodes, the spleen. But different from the biconcave prole-tariat. These are the individuals, the wandering cells of the immune system, the war-riors, the knights, the crusaders, the wrestlers, the gobblers, the tarbabies, the cleanup crew. These are free cells, cells that are not confined to the body's vessels, but slip in and out to go where they are needed, mercenaries for the current cam-paign. Individuals, they keep us individuals; they both attack and produce an arse-nal of antibodies that ward off attack.

Years ago, one of my classmates died of cancer of the blood—leukemia. Her white blood cell production had gone awry. When too many are made, they choke the vessels. To live well, the body stays in dynamic balance, in busy equilibrium, in proportion, in moderation with all things.

We saw our first white blood cell, a neutrophil. Two-thirds of the white blood cells are neutrophils. Each neutrophil has a lobed nucleus, strung together like a hot-dog shaped balloon that has been twisted into portions. A fat place, a skinny bridge, another fat place, another skinny bridge, and on and on. Outside the nucleus, the cytoplasm is foamy. "Granular," reads the manual.

We looked again, among the teeming sameness of the red blood cells, and saw a lymphocyte. Smaller than the neutrophil, although no white blood cell is as small as a read blood cell. The telltale signs: a big, round red nucleus, surrounded by a thin rim of blue cytoplasm. A deviled egg, colored wrong. One-fifth to a quarter of the white blood cells, I noted, are lymphocytes.

We kept looking. Next we saw a monocyte, a giant cell with a giant dumbbell nucleus. Three to eight percent of the white blood cells are monocytes. Unmistakable. And the cosinophils, two to four percent, those that love the red stain. More lobed nuclei and their cytoplasm splattered with red.

Now the search began in earnest. "If you find it," we read in the laboratory manual, "notify your instructor." I looked at several slides, discarded them. Where were they, those blue-dotted cells with the pale, ethereal nuclei? Less than one per-cent of the white blood cells, they are elusive. Finally, a lonely one appeared. The instructor notified the students "Come, look, everyone," I said. "Do you see the subtle differences?"

The students looked, were engaged, as engaged as possible. I became aware of my breathing, of providing oxygen to my cells, of the blood production factories of my inner bones. I was flooded with a strange ecstasy brought on by examining bits of life. I felt an electrical frisson, a quivering depolarization of my skin, as the cells connected frogs and fish and birds and students. I'm crazy, I thought, but harmless. I have seen mitosis in a pizza, paramecia in a parsley tie. I see my love life in the cells.

With stain, the white blood cells explode with orgasmic Fourth of July color. The rarest are the most precious. I heard a soft voice in my ear, whispering, carbohydrate names: sweet stuff, honey, sugarbush. In the common, I thought, is wonder. In the rare is beauty.

I smiled sanguinely and told the students they were in the presence of beauty, that their own bodies are beautiful precious things. Two students looked up from their microscopes, startled. They were thinking that I should be an English teacher, because only English teachers find things beautiful. Science teachers are cold, and talk of facts and theories. One or two of the students probably began to worry that I would require correct spelling on the exam.

The students understood the red blood cells, but the white blood cells still looked alike to them, and would continue to look alike until they had studied them for a time. For some students, the white blood cells will look alike forever.

The students began to gather up their bags and books and disappear, slipping by ones and twos out the heavy door. When the student whose bright smile betrayed his love—for me or for biology—finally left, I erased my notes and drawings from the blackboard and wiped my hands on the sides of my laboratory coat. I am always surprised by the neatness of my script, the roundness of my circles. From the laboratory tables I picked up scattered wipes with spots of now-browned blood. The blood on the uncovered slides was dried and cracked like mud; the tiny desiccated ponds were no longer vital. I tossed the evidence of our mortality into the garbage can, picked up my own books and notes, and turned out the light. I left the back way, hanging my laboratory coat in a closet in the central laboratory, where the light was always on, where shelves were packed with charts and models and buckets of specimens, and where three brown-blooded cadavers slept in their body bags.

As I emerged into sunlight, I thought of a poetry class I took long ago. "Use strong words," my teacher said. "Darkness is a strong word. Tunnel is a strong word. Blood is a strong word."

Landscape and Dream

Nancy Krusoe

Cows

A BARN is a beautiful place where cows are milked together. Our barn has many windows facing east and west. These windows have no glass in them.

You get up early in the morning to milk cows. You pour warm white milk into heavy gray metal cans with matching metal tops that fit like a good hat, and these tops are very pretty, their shape a circle with a brim over the neck of the can.

Warm cow milk has a certain smell, a from-inside-the-body smell, the way your finger smells pulled out of your own vagina.

Women who are married to dairy farmers stand in their kitchens at their kitchen windows and stare longingly at their husbands' barns, but they don't go there. Barns are female places; they are forbidden places for women. These women stand at their kitchen windows staring at their husbands' barns because barns are beautiful female places, full of sweet-milked, happy, honey-faced cows being milked by men's hands or by machines with cups. Cows have rough-skinned teats, sometimes scraped and scratched, chapped and bleeding, which fit into these cups put on by men whose hands are not gentle.

So the wife I am talking about stands at her kitchen window facing east. She has no one to be with. Unlike the cows and the men in the barn (her husband and her son, who helps his father for a while), she is alone. I, the daughter, am in the barn, too—young enough to be there a little while longer. But I would like for the wife, my mother, to leave the farmer, to go away from the farm and the barn and this warm longing for cows.

Our barn is a cold place in winter with only the heat of cows to warm you. You stand very close to their large bodies so that you won't frost over like the windows of the kitchen where you stare, looking for your mother to see if she is watching you.

On the other side of the barn, the east side, are the hill and the lake at the bottom of the hill and the gray-brown grass that holds this hill in place in winter. Tiny slivers of ice float on the lake in winter; at dusk and during the night, and they melt each morning when the sun comes up. Our cows slide through mud to drink cold morning water, because even though they're full and ready to be milked, their mouths are saliva machines with licorice-colored tongues, thick and dark with cud and the need for water. I see them standing by the side of the lake, their knees bent a little, bracing themselves as they lean over the icy water, mud rising up their delicate sweet ankles. *Hurry, drink fast,* I say. *Hurry, hurry.*

Seeing them like this makes me want to be a cow, but which kind would I be? There are dainty, needle-brown Jerseys, big woolly Guernsey's, and the large, black-and-white spotted, famous-for-milk Holsteins. There is also the plain black cow.

When cows come to the barn to be milked, it's a happy, sloppy time of day for them, and I am there waiting. They all push in at once, rushing toward me as I stand at the far end of the barn—in case one goes wild I will stop her—and running, some of them, because their favorite food is waiting there (that delicious grainy mixture of oats and wheat and barley and who knows what else that I myself eat along with them out of cupped hands). They are running toward me, looking at me, and then abruptly turning in, one by one, each into her own place, and someone will close the stanchions around their necks for milking, because you can't have them visiting—wandering around and disturbing each other during milking—of course not. Each one has her own place, her own stanchion, and she remembers it; out of fifty or sixty stalls, each cow knows her own. How: Smell? Number of footsteps from the door to the slippery spot at the entrance to her place? Or rhythm—how many sways of the heavy stomach, the bloated udder, back and forth to the stall that is hers?

I remember how it was to be inside the barn with all those steamy, full-of-milk, black-and-white cows, with their sweet, honey-barn faces and their clover-alfalfa breath. And their beautiful straight backbones that you could rub between your fingers across the length of their bodies, a delicate spine for all that weight underneath. And light falling through the windows. I washed their udders, washed them all with the same brown cloth soaked in disinfected water, their teats covered with dirt, and sometimes I didn't get it all off they were so swollen (of course, I didn't know how it felt, not for years did I know how that felt), but they didn't mind. No words were spoken there in the barn—or if they were, they weren't between me and the men. I didn't feel it so much then—well, maybe more than I thought—but I felt the bodies of cows, dozens of them, their big, sloppy, breathy faces and sighs in the barn with me.

In the kitchen, it isn't a happy time of day: cooking breakfast, half moon, half dark. My mother stands there waiting. Anyone could come, even cows could come to her flower bed outside the kitchen window, could lie down and wait with her for the farmer—and the daughter—to return. There is nothing to stop them from coming to her, coming to her window, nothing at all.

The Farmer

Sometimes men beat their dairy cows. Sometimes they hit them with lead pipes, and the cows fall down; they slide down in their cow shit on the floor of the barn, fall down on their bones into shit puddles while the daughter is standing at the barn door staring for a very long time at the floor, at the slick running cow pee that has soaked everything the cow was standing on and is now lying in, on her bones, and she is crying.

Is the cow crying? Heaving, trying to stand up on her feet (her feet are so pretty—little hooves like tiny irons), which slip again every time he hits her.

Her head's in the stanchion, her head's trapped, but she can stand up. *Please don't get up again,* I tell her, but it makes no difference: he hits her again. I hope cows don't feel pain; I hope they don't have brains. I hope they have fires in their hearts. If they had brains, I would have to hold them and kiss them and tell my mother at the window what has gone on—not just in her garden but here in her husband's barn. I would have to tell her I hope that the next time the tractor turns over, the farmer is under it.

When a man is beating a cow, a young cow, what is he thinking? Does he think how beautiful she is, struggling to stand? Does he think how she will never stand again unless he lets her, *unless he lets her?*

I am talking about cows which sometimes aren't so beautiful to look at. They love to bathe in slushy red mud, get covered in dirt. Their brains are made of salt licks and saliva so they won't feel pain, you see what I mean? What kind of puzzle could a cow solve? Not the kind a word would solve, a kind word. That's what I mean.

I am talking about women like my mother who watch barns, waiting, because they cannot stop watching with their eyes and hearts, as if smoke will arise, as if smoke will come out of that barn, as if the men and cows will be burned, as if she can stop her daughter from being there in the barn, in the fire, as if she can hold her daughter back, can close the barn door with the power of her eyes—but this will not be enough. The mother watches her daughter move in slowly toward the barn where she will become a cow, where nothing can stop her, where the cow she becomes is the cow her father beats with a metal pipe over and over on her back, on her shoulders and her stomach, on her whole brown bony small body, and the daughter hides inside the cow's body and screams, *Stop, stop.*

But do you think he hears, or—if he hears—that he believes what has become of his daughter? What will the farmer tell his wife? What will the daughter tell her mother? Nothing. She will hear nothing about it, for remember, this is a young girl watching her father, and he's beating the cow with a pipe that's long and gray and hollow; he holds it with both his hands. The cow is young like the daughter who's watching. What can she possibly have done to deserve such a beating? Did the young cow kick the girl's father? Being young, she might not have known better, but the girl sees no blood on her father. She looks at his arms and his face and sees nothing but rage—his mouth is clamped shut and his eyes are huge and still swelling in his head. (He has taken off his glasses, and the daughter notices this: that her father isn't wearing his glasses and she can see his eyes.) He looks strange to her. He could be holding back tears, she thinks. He is holding back something, but look at all that is coming out.

The girl looks toward her house, which is across the road from the barn; she searches for her mother in the window to see if she is watching the way she sometimes does. It is too far and too dark to tell. And so the daughter looks back at the barn, at her father in the barn, this man who without his glasses has eyes she hardly knows. This young cow is called, she knows, a heifer. What else should she know?

The Kitchen

We had a chair in our kitchen that was so large I could sit in it doubled up and still have room for my brother and a tub of peas for me to shell. On my right as I sat in the chair, I could see the pasture in front of our house, out the kitchen window, where animals sometimes grazed—cows and horses. The sky was bluer here than anywhere else. Behind the pasture was a semicircle of pine trees, a screen which blocked my view of anything beyond it and formed the limits of my world.

It was on this pasture of grass that phantom men, invaders, conquerors, arose from the earth one day, riding on dusty brown horses, circling the field, riding toward our house. These horsemen wore dusty red scarves on their necks and blankets on their backs. Dirt from deep inside the earth all about them was kicked up by their horses' feet as we sat, my mother and I, inside the kitchen, waiting for them to surround us, to terrify us, to tell us what they wanted, what crimes they were going to commit. Of course, I opened the door; this was long before I began, in later dreams, to slam and lock all doors and windows against strange men. Tribesmen from deep inside the earth—what could be better? What had they come for? For me, of course. They had come to take me away, or to tell me the secrets of life—whichever, I was ready. I am sure my mother knew, could see that I was ready.

I looked at my mother and wondered what she thought about and if she loved cows the way I loved them. I am the one who watched her, and watching her was all in the world I did for years. Like her I became a cow and became a mother. I became the barn and the hill behind the barn, the lake and the water cows drink from the lake, the salt and saliva in their mouths. I became, for a while, entirely these things—nothing more. And this is not enough.

A Questionnaire for Rudolph Gordon

Jack Matthews

1) How many times was this questionnaire forwarded through the mail before it caught up with you?

2) List the various things that had occupied your mind during the morning before it arrived.

3) How many of your father's paintings have you now sold?

4) Do you sense that you are nearing the end of your "resources"?

5) Do you still dream of that little boat, nosing at the dock as if it were alive and waiting for you?

6) Did you sell the painting in which your father had put the boat?

7) This painting also showed a woman, leaning over and scooping up sand; who was the little boy she was facing?

8) Do you remember that heavy cloth bathing suit, with its straps and the heavy, scratchy wool against your skin?

9) What was your mother saying as your father painted the picture?

10) Why had you been crying?

11) Were you aware of his sitting back there, farther up the bank, painting as your mother talked to you?

12) The woman had been singing a song to calm you down; what was this song?

13) Was the woman truly your mother?

14) What if she lied to you; what if all your life she merely *pretended* to be your mother?

15) What if the man painting the picture with both of you in it (not to mention the little rowboat) was also a Pretender?

16) Why would they want to deceive you like that?

17) Why were you crying before your "mother" sang the little song to calm you down and amuse you?

18) Can you remember times when they talked to you lovingly, and you felt totally secure with them . . . only to see her eyes slip nervously to the side, to look at *him* . . . and only for him to look troubled, worried, as if they had both gotten beyond their depth?

19) Can you remember the woman saying, "No, we shouldn't have done it," and the man answering, "Anyway, it's too late now to change"?

20) The little beach cottage you stayed in was painted blood red; its porch and shutters were painted white; what was behind the little cottage?

21) Do you remember climbing this steep hill one day, and having the woman cry out in fear that you would fall and hurt yourself?

22) Can you remember the smell of the pine needles and the rough warmth of the stones as you climbed steadily upward, and then turned to look into the wind, at the bay?

23) She was smaller than you, down below; and the man was smaller, too, because they existed far beneath your feet; what did you say when they begged for you to come down?

24) Why did you say "never," instead of "no"?

25) Why were you not afraid?

26) What did you see in the bay?

27) What was the name of the great ship that lay like a shadow in the haze of the water?

28) Are you certain you cannot remember the shapes of the letters of her name, so that *now* you can read what was then only the mystery of print?

29) Why is the name of the ship unimportant?

30) Were you surprised when you looked down and saw that he had climbed so near, without your being aware?

31) Can you remember the dark expression of anger on his face as he reached out to clasp your ankle?

32) Did he hurt you, carrying you so roughly down through the rocks and pine trees to the back of the cottage?

33) What was the song you could hear so faintly from the cabin next door?

34) Was this the first phonograph you can remember ever hearing?

35) Was this the song the woman sang to you later, after you were taken down to the shore?

36) Were you crying because of the scolding you received for climbing the steep hill in back?

37) Do you remember the old smell of salt and dead fish that drifted in the air?

38) Where were your real parents?

39) Had you been kidnapped?

40) Has this thought ever occurred to you before?

41) Do you remember the toy revolver and holster you wore?

42) Do you remember the little suitcase they let you carry?

43) Do you remember the photograph of a man and woman smiling out at you in your bedroom?

44) What was written on the photograph?

45) Did the man and woman read it to you, so that you are certain it said, "From Mom and Dad with Love"?

46) Why can't you remember the faces in the photograph?

47) Was your *real* father a painter?

48) Was this man . . . *could* this man have been your real father?

49) Could the woman have been your real mother?

50) But how can you be certain they lied to you in other matters?

51) Don't we all lie to one another?

52) Isn't the lie we tell our children one expression of love?

53) Isn't it also an expression of our fear?

54) Can there be love without fear?

55) Is it possible that this man and this woman, even though they remember the specific moment you came out of *her* body, are still not certain that you are *their son?*

56) What is a father?

57) What is a mother?

58) What is a son?

59) Why have you refused to answer these questions?

60) Why have you sold so many of your father's paintings?

61) Why do you need so much money to live?

62) Why can't you find a job?

63) When did the woman die?

64) Were you there when her eyes clouded over?

65) Were you present when your father was run down by the trolley car in the city?

66) Did you know that his legs and back were terribly mutilated in the accident, and he was dead before the ambulance arrived, hemorrhaging brilliant red streams against the black asphalt of the street?

67) In your opinion, did he think of you as he was dying?

68) Did your mother think of you as she was dying?

69) Why do you think you cannot answer such questions?

70) Do you see yourself in the painting with the little boy, and the mother scooping sand up in her hand, and the rowboat nudging at the dock, like a small hungry animal desiring suck?

71) What color is the sky in the painting?

72) Why is it darker than the land?

73) Why is it darker than the water?

74) Have you sold this painting yet?

75) Is it the last of your father's paintings in your possession?

76) When you do sell it, will something break loose and drift away?

77) Will the hand be seized by a spasm, and will sand spill from it?

78) Will the child cry again, staring out upon an empty scene, while the ship fades into pale gray, leaking color out of the letters of its name?

79) Who is in the red cottage now?

80) Why do you think it is empty or torn down?

81) If your father were alive, could he reach you now and carry you back to safety?

82) Could the blood on the asphalt be thought of as your father's last and most original composition?

83) Were your father and mother as lonely as children in those last moments?

84) Would you have helped them in some way *if you could have been sure?*

85) Why do you pretend you don't know *sure of what?*

86) Have you never doubted their authenticity before?

87) Aren't there other reasons than kidnapping for stealing a child?

88) Perhaps they didn't know how you came about, and felt guilty?

89) Who can say where these things all begin?

90) Don't you understand that "these things" are the cabin, the steep hill, the boat, the sand, the man, the woman, the child?

91) Were you aware that the painting was omitted in 90?

92) If you sell it, finally, will you have enough money?

93) Don't you have the pride and the skill to make your own way in life?

94) Why does that expression remind you of him?

95) If you sell it finally, will you ever sleep again?

96) Why do you think there is no one now to sing a song to you and dry your tears and pretend to be your mother?

97) When will you stop lying in your answers?

98) Do you think even *this* would turn us away, if our hands and hearts and mouths were not packed with earth?

99) Do you truly believe that some things do not abide, beyond the habit and the way of the world?

100) Truly, this is enough for now, and somehow you must rest content with this personal questionnaire.

Love always,
Mom and Dad

How to Tell a True War Story

Tim O'Brien

THIS IS TRUE.

I had a buddy in Vietnam. His name was Bob Kiley, but everybody called him Rat.

A friend of his gets killed, so about a week later Rat sits down and writes a letter to the guy's sister. Rat tells her what a great brother she had, how together the guy was, a number one pal and comrade. A real soldier's soldier, Rat says. Then he tells a few stories to make the point, how her brother would always volunteer for stuff nobody else would volunteer for in a million years, dangerous stuff, like doing recon or going out on these really badass night patrols. Stainless steel balls, Rat tells her. The guy was a little crazy, for sure, but crazy in a good way, a real daredevil, because he liked the challenge of it, he liked testing himself, just man against gook. A great, great guy, Rat says.

Anyway, it's a terrific letter, very personal and touching. Rat almost bawls writing it. He gets all teary telling about the good times they had together, how her brother made the war seem almost fun, always raising hell and lighting up villes and bringing smoke to bear every which way. A great sense of humor, too. Like the time at this river when he went fishing with a whole damn crate of hand grenades. Probably the funniest thing in world history, Rat says, all that gore, about twenty zillion dead gook fish. Her brother, he had the right attitude. He knew how to have a good time. On Halloween, this real hot spooky night, the dude paints up his body all different colors and puts on this weird mask and hikes over to a ville and goes trick-or-treating almost stark naked, just boots and balls and an M–16. A tremendous human being, Rat says. Pretty nutso sometimes, but you could trust him with your life.

And then the letter gets very sad and serious. Rat pours his heart out. He says he loved the guy. He says the guy was his best friend in the world. They were like soul mates, he says, like twins or something, they had a whole lot in common. He tells the guy's sister he'll look her up when the war's over.

So what happens?

Rat mails the letter. He waits two months. The dumb cooze never writes back.

A true war story is never moral. It does not instruct, nor encourage virtue, nor suggest models of proper human behavior, nor restrain men from doing the things men have always done. If a story seems moral, do not believe it. If at the end of a war story you feel uplifted, or if you feel that some small bit of rectitude has been salvaged from the larger waste, then you have been made the victim of a very old and terrible lie. There is no rectitude whatsoever. There is no virtue. As a first rule of thumb, therefore, you can tell a true war story by its absolute and uncompromising allegiance to obscenity and evil. Listen to Rat Kiley. Cooze, he says. He does not say bitch. He certainly does not say woman, or girl. He says cooze. Then he spits and stares. He's nineteen years old—it's too much for him—so he looks at you with those big sad gentle killer eyes and says *cooze,* because his friend is dead, and because it's so incredibly sad and true: she never wrote back.

You can tell a true war story if it embarrasses you. If you don't care for obscenity, you don't care for the truth; if you don't care for the truth, watch how you vote. Send guys to war, they come home talking dirty.

Listen to Rat: "Jesus Christ, man, I write this beautiful fuckin' letter, I slave over it, and what happens? The dumb cooze never writes back."

The dead guy's name was Curt Lemon. What happened was, we crossed a muddy river and marched west into the mountains, and on the third day we took a break along a trail junction in deep jungle. Right away, Lemon and Rat Kiley started goofing. They didn't understand about the spookiness. They were kids; they just didn't know. A nature hike, they thought, not even a war, so they went off into the shade of some giant trees—quadruple canopy, no sunlight at all—and they were giggling and calling each other yellow mother and playing a silly game they'd invented. The game involved smoke grenades, which were harmless unless you did stupid things, and what they did was pull the pin and stand a few feet apart and play catch under the shade of those huge trees. Whoever chickened out was a yellow mother. And if nobody chickened out, the grenade would make a light popping sound and they'd be covered with smoke and they'd laugh and dance around and then do it again.

It's all exactly true.

It happened, to *me,* nearly twenty years ago, and I still remember that trail junction and those giant trees and a soft dripping sound somewhere beyond the trees. I remember the smell of moss. Up in the canopy there were tiny white blossoms, but no sunlight at all, and I remember the shadows spreading out under the trees where Curt Lemon and Rat Kiley were playing catch with smoke grenades. Mitchell Sanders sat flipping his yo-yo. Norman Bowker and Kiowa and Dave Jensen were dozing, or half dozing, and all around us were those ragged green mountains.

Except for the laughter things were quiet.

At one point, I remember, Mitchell Sanders turned and looked at me, not quite nodding, as if to warn me about something, as if he already *knew,* then after a while he rolled up his yo-yo and moved away.

It's hard to tell you what happened next.

They were just goofing. There was a noise, I suppose, which must've been the detonator, so I glanced behind me and watched Lemon step from the shade into bright sunlight. His face was suddenly brown and shining. A handsome kid, really. Sharp gray eyes, lean and narrow-waisted, and when he died it was almost beautiful, the way the sunlight came around him and lifted him up and sucked him high into a tree full of moss and vines and white blossoms.

In any war story, but especially a true one, it's difficult to separate what happened from what seemed to happen. What seems to happen becomes its own happening and has to be told that way. The angles of vision are skewed. When a booby trap explodes, you close your eyes and duck and float outside yourself. When a guy dies, like Curt Lemon, you look away and then look back for a moment and then look away again. The pictures get jumbled; you tend to miss a lot. And then afterward, when you go to tell about it, there is always that surreal seemingness, which makes the story seem untrue, but which in fact represents the hard and exact truth as it *seemed.*

•   •   •

In many cases a true war story cannot be believed. If you believe it, be skeptical. It's a question of credibility. Often the crazy stuff is true and the normal stuff isn't, because the normal stuff is necessary to make you believe the truly incredible craziness.

In other cases you can't even tell a true war story. Sometimes it's just beyond telling.

I heard this one, for example, from Mitchell Sanders. It was near dusk and we were sitting at my foxhole along a wide muddy river north of Quang Ngai. I remember how peaceful the twilight was. A deep pinkish red spilled out on the river, which moved without sound, and in the morning we would cross the river and march west into the mountains. The occasion was right for a good story.

"God's truth," Mitchell Sanders said. "A six-man patrol goes up into the mountains on a basic listening-post operation. The idea's to spend a week up there, just lie low and listen for enemy movement. They've got a radio along, so if they hear anything suspicious—anything—they're supposed to call in artillery or gunships, whatever it takes. Otherwise they keep strict field discipline. Absolute silence. They just listen."

Sanders glanced at me to make sure I had the scenario. He was playing with his yo-yo, dancing it with short, tight little strokes of the wrist.

His face was blank in the dusk.

"We're talking regulation, by-the-book LP. These six guys, they don't say boo for a solid week. They don't got tongues. *All* ears.

"Right," I said.

"Understand me?"

"Invisible."

Sanders nodded.

"Affirm," he said. "Invisible. So what happens is, these guys get themselves deep in the bush, all camouflaged up, and they lie down and wait and that's all they do, nothing else, they lie there for seven straight days and just listen. And man, I'll tell you—it's spooky. This is mountains. You don't *know* spooky till you been there. Jungle, sort of, except it's way up in the clouds and there's always this fog—like rain, except it's not raining—everything's all wet and swirly and tangled up and you can't see jack, you can't find your own pecker to piss with. Like you don't even have a body. Serious spooky. You just go with the vapors—the fog sort of takes you in . . . And the sounds, man. The sounds carry forever. You hear stuff nobody should *ever* hear."

Sanders was quiet for a second, just working the yo-yo, then he smiled at me. "So after a couple days the guys start hearing this real soft, kind of whacked-out music. Weird echoes and stuff. Like a radio or something, but it's not a radio, it's this strange gook music that comes right out of the rocks. Faraway, sort of, but right up close, too. They try to ignore it. But it's a listening post, right? So they listen. And every night they keep hearing that crazyass gook concert. All kinds of chimes and xylophones. I mean, this is wilderness—no way, it can't be real—but there it *is*, like the mountains are tuned in to Radio fucking Hanoi. Naturally they get nervous. One guy sticks Juicy Fruit in his ears. Another guy almost flips. Thing is, though, they can't report music. They can't get on the horn and call back to base and say, 'Hey, listen, we need some firepower, we got to blow away this weirdo gook rock band.' They can't do that. It wouldn't go down. So they lie there in the fog and keep their mouths shut. And what makes it extra bad, see, is the poor dudes can't horse around like normal. Can't joke it away. Can't even talk to each other except maybe in whispers, all hush-hush, and that just revs up the willies. All they do is listen."

Again there was some silence as Mitchell Sanders looked out on the river. The dark was coming on hard now, and off to the west I could see the mountains rising in silhouette, all the mysteries and unknowns.

"This next part," Sanders said quietly, "you won't believe."

"Probably not," I said.

"You won't. And you know why?" He gave me a long, tired smile. "Because it happened. Because every word is absolutely dead-on true."

Sanders made a sound in his throat, like a sigh, as if to say he didn't care if I believed him or not. But he did care. He wanted me to feel the truth, to believe by the raw force of feeling. He seemed sad, in a way.

"These six guys," he said, "they're pretty fried out by now, and one night they start hearing voices. Like at a cocktail party. That's what it sounds like, this big swank gook cocktail party somewhere out there in the fog. Music and chitchat and stuff. It's crazy, I know, but they hear the champagne corks. They hear the actual martini glasses. Real hoity-toity, all very civilized, except this isn't civilization. This is Nam.

"Anyway, the guys try to be cool. They just lie there and groove, but after a while they start hearing—you won't believe this—they hear chamber music. They hear violins and cellos. They hear this terrific mama-san soprano. Then after a while they hear gook opera and a glee club and the Haiphong Boys Choir and a barbershop quartet and all kinds of weird chanting and Buddha-Buddha stuff. And the whole time, in the background, there's still that cocktail party going on. All these different voices. Not human voices, though. Because it's the mountains. Follow me? The rock—it's *talking*. And the fog, too, and the grass and the goddamn mongooses. Everything talks. The trees talk politics, the monkeys talk religion. The whole country. Vietnam. The place talks. It talks. Understand? Nam—it truly *talks*.

"The guys can't cope. They lose it. They get on the radio and report enemy movement—a whole army, they say—and they order up the firepower. They get arty and gunships. They call in air strikes. And I'll tell you, they fuckin' crash that cocktail party. All night long, they just smoke those mountains. They make jungle juice.

They blow away trees and glee clubs and whatever else there is to blow away. Scorch time. They walk napalm up and down the ridges. They bring in the Cobras and F–4s, they use Willie Peter and HE and incendiaries. It's all fire. They make those mountains burn.

"Around dawn things finally get quiet. Like you never even *heard* quiet before. One of those real thick, real misty days—just clouds and fog, they're off in this special zone—and the mountains are absolutely dead-flat silent. Like Brigadoon—pure vapor, you know? Everything's all sucked up inside the fog. not a single sound, except they still *hear* it.

"So they pack up and start humping. They head down the mountain, back to base camp, and when they get there they don't say diddly. They don't talk. Not a word, like they're deaf and dumb. Later on this fat bird colonel comes up and asks what the hell happened out there. What'd they hear? Why all the ordnance? The man's ragged out, he gets down tight on their case. I mean, they spent six trillion dollars on firepower, and this fatass colonel wants answers, he wants to know what the fuckin' story is.

"But the guys don't say zip. They just look at him for a while, sort of funny like, sort of amazed, and the whole war is right there in that stare. It says everything you can't ever say. It says, man, you got *wax* in your ears. It says, poor bastard, you'll never know—wrong frequency—you don't *even* want to hear this. Then they salute the fucker and walk away, because certain stories you don't ever tell."

You can tell a true war story by the way it never seems to end. Not then, not ever. Not when Mitchell Sanders stood up and moved off into the dark.

It all happened.

Even now, at this instant, I remember that yo-yo. In a way, I suppose, you had to be there, you had to hear it, but I could tell how desperately Sanders wanted me to believe him, his frustration at not quite getting the details right, not quite pinning down the final and definitive truth.

And I remember sitting at my foxhole that night, watching the shadows of Quang Ngai, thinking about the coming day and how we would cross the river and march west into the mountains, all the ways I might die, all the things I did not understand.

Late in the night Mitchell Sanders touched my shoulder.

"Just came to me," he whispered. "The moral, I mean. Nobody listens. Nobody hears nothin'. Like that fatass colonel. The politicians, all the civilian types. Your girlfriend. My girlfriend. Everybody's sweet little virgin girlfriend. What they need is to go out on LP. The vapors, man. Trees and rocks—you got to *listen* to your enemy."

And then again, in the morning, Sanders came up to me. The platoon was preparing to move out, checking weapons, going through all the little rituals that preceded a day's march. Already the lead squad had crossed the river and was filing off toward the west.

"I got a confession to make," Sanders said. "Last night, man, I had to make up a few things."

"I know that."

"The glee club. There wasn't any glee club."

"Right."

"No opera."

"Forget it, I understand."

"Yeah, but listen, it's still true. Those six guys, they heard wicked sound out there. They heard sound you just plain won't believe."

Sanders pulled on his rucksack, closed his eyes for a moment, then almost smiled at me. I knew what was coming.

"All right," I said, "what's the moral?"

"Forget it."

"No, go ahead."

For a long while he was quiet, looking away, and the silence kept stretching out until it was almost embarrassing. Then he shrugged and gave me a stare that lasted all day.

"Hear that quiet, man?" he said. "That quiet—just listen. There's your moral."

In a true war story, if there's a moral at all, it's like the thread that makes the cloth. You can't tease it out. You can't extract the meaning without unraveling the deeper meaning. And in the end, really, there's nothing much to say about a true war story, except maybe "Oh."

True war stories do not generalize. They do not indulge in abstraction or analysis.

For example: War is hell. As a moral declaration the old truism seems perfectly true, and yet because it abstracts, because it generalizes, I can't believe it with my stomach. Nothing turns inside.

It comes down to gut instinct. A true war story, if truly told, makes the stomach believe.

•   •   •

This one does it for me. I've told it before—many times, many versions—but here's what actually happened.

We crossed that river and marched west into the mountains. On the third day, Curt Lemon stepped on a booby trapped 105 round. He was playing catch with Rat Kiley, laughing, and then he was dead. The trees were thick; it took nearly an hour to cut an LZ for the dustoff.

Later, higher in the mountains, we came across a baby VC water buffalo. What it was doing there I don't know—no farms or paddies—but we chased it down and got a rope around it and led it along to a deserted village where we set up for the night. After supper Rat Kiley went over and stroked its nose.

He opened up a can of C rations, pork and beans, but the baby buffalo wasn't interested.

Rat shrugged.

He stepped back and shot it through the right front knee. The animal did not make a sound. It went down hard, then got up again, and Rat took careful aim and shot off an ear. He shot it in the hindquarters and in the little hump at its back. He shot it twice in the flanks. It wasn't to kill; it was to hurt. He put the rifle muzzle up against the mouth and shot the mouth away. Nobody said much. The whole platoon stood there watching, feeling all kinds of things, but there wasn't a great deal of pity for the baby water buffalo. Curt Lemon was dead. Rat Kiley had lost his best friend in the world. Later in the week he would write a long personal letter to the guy's sister, who would not write back, but for now it was a question of pain. He shot off the tail. He shot away chunks of meat below the ribs. All around us there was the smell of smoke and filth and deep greenery, and the evening was humid and very hot. Rat went to automatic. He shot randomly, almost casually, quick little spurts in the belly and butt. Then he reloaded, squatted down, and shot it in the left front knee. Again the animal fell hard and tried to get up, but this time it couldn't quite make it. It wobbled and went down sideways. Rat shot it in the nose. He bent forward and whispered something, as if talking to a pet, then he shot it in the throat. All the while the baby buffalo was silent, or almost silent, just a light bubbling sound where the nose had been. It lay very still. Nothing moved except the eyes, which were enormous, the pupils shiny black and dumb.

Rat Kiley was crying. He tried to say something, but then cradled his rifle and went off by himself.

The rest of us stood in a ragged circle around the baby buffalo. For a time no one spoke. We had witnessed something essential, something brand-new and profound, a piece of the world so startling there was not yet a name for it.

Somebody kicked the baby buffalo.

It was still alive, though just barely, just in the eyes.

"Amazing," Dave Jensen said. "My whole life, I never seen anything like it."

"Never?"

"Not hardly. Not once."

Kiowa and Mitchell Sanders picked up the baby buffalo. They hauled it across the open square, hoisted it up, and dumped it in the village well.

Afterward, we sat waiting for Rat to get himself together.

"Amazing," Dave Jensen kept saying. "A new wrinkle. I never seen it before."

Mitchell Sanders took out his yo-yo. "Well, that's Nam," he said. "Garden of Evil. Over here, man, every sin's real fresh and original."

How do you generalize?

War is hell, but that's not the half of it, because war is also mystery and terror and adventure and courage and discovery and holiness and pity and despair and longing and love. War is nasty; war is fun. War is thrilling; war is drudgery. War makes you a man; war makes you dead.

The truths are contradictory. It can be argued, for instance, that war is grotesque. But in truth war is also beauty. For all its horror, you can't help but gape at the awful majesty of combat. You stare out at tracer rounds unwinding through the dark like brilliant red ribbons. You crouch in ambush as a cool, impassive moon rises over the nighttime paddies. You admire the fluid symmetries of troops on the move, the harmonies of sound and shape and proportion, the great sheets of metal-fire streaming down from a gunship, the illumination rounds, the white phosphorus, the purply orange glow of napalm, the rocket's red glare. It's not pretty, exactly. It's astonishing. It fills the eye. It commands you. You hate it, yes, but your eyes do not. Like a killer forest fire, like cancer under a microscope, any battle or bombing raid or artillery barrage has the aesthetic purity of absolute moral indifference—a powerful, implacable beauty—and a true war story will tell the truth about this, though the truth is ugly.

To generalize about war is like generalizing about peace. Almost everything is true. Almost nothing is true. At its core, perhaps, war is just another name for death, and yet any soldier will tell you, if he tells the truth, that proximity to death brings with it a corresponding proximity to life. After a firefight, there is always the immense pleasure of aliveness. The trees are alive. The grass, the soil—everything. All around you things are purely living, and you among them, and the aliveness makes you tremble. You feel an intense, out-of-the-skin awareness of your living self—your truest self, the human being you want to be and then become by the force of wanting it. In the midst of evil you want to be a good man. You want decency. You want justice and courtesy and human concord, things you never knew you wanted. There is a kind of largeness to it, a kind of godliness. Though it's odd, you're never more alive than when you're almost dead. You recognize what's valuable. Freshly, as if for the first time, you love what's best in yourself and in the world, all that might be lost. At the hour of dusk you sit at your foxhole and look out on a wide river turning pinkish red, and at the mountains beyond, and although in the morning you must cross the river and go into the mountains and do terrible things and maybe die, even so, you find yourself studying the fine colors on the river, you feel wonder and awe at the setting of the sun, and you are filled with a hard, aching love for how the world could be and always should be, but now is not.

Mitchell Sanders was right. For the common soldier, at least, war has the feel—the spiritual texture—of a great ghostly fog, thick and permanent. There is no clarity. Everything swirls. The old rules are no longer binding, the old truths no longer true. Right spills over into wrong. Order blends into chaos, love into hate, ugliness into beauty, law into anarchy, civility into savagery. The vapors suck you in. You can't tell where you are, or why you're there, and the only certainty is overwhelming ambiguity.

In war you lose your sense of the definite, hence your sense of truth itself, and therefore it's safe to say that in a true war story nothing is ever absolutely true.

Often in a true war story there is not even a point, or else the point doesn't hit you until twenty years later, in your sleep, and you wake up and shake your wife and start telling the story to her, except when you get to the end you've forgotten the point again. And then for a long time you lie there watching the story happen in your head. You listen to your wife's breathing. The war's over. You close your eyes. You smile and think, Christ, what's the *point?*

This one wakes me up.

In the mountains that day, I watched Lemon turn sideways. He laughed and said something to Rat Kiley. Then he took a peculiar half step, moving from shade into bright sunlight, and the booby-trapped 105 round blew him into a tree. The parts were just hanging there, so Dave Jensen and I were ordered to shinny up and peel him off. I remember the white bone of an arm. I remember pieces of skin and something wet and yellow that must've been the intestines. The gore was horrible, and stays with me. But what wakes me up twenty years later is Dave Jensen singing "Lemon Tree" as we threw down the parts.

You can tell a true war story by the questions you ask. Somebody tells a story, let's say, and afterward you ask, "Is it true?" and if the answer matters, you've got your answer.

For example, we've all heard this one. Four guys go down a trail. A grenade sails out. One guy jumps on it and takes the blast and saves his three buddies.

Is it true?

The answer matters.

You'd feel cheated if it never happened. Without the grounding reality, it's just a trite bit of puffery, pure Hollywood, untrue in the way all such stories are untrue. Yet even if it did happen—and maybe it did, anything's possible—even then you know it can't be true, because a true war story does not depend upon that kind of truth. Absolute occurrence is irrelevant. A thing may happen and be a total lie; another thing may not happen and be truer than the truth. For example: Four guys go down a trail. A grenade sails out. One guy jumps on it and takes the blast, but it's a killer grenade and everybody dies anyway. Before they die, though, one of the dead guys says, "The fuck you do *that* for?" and the jumper says, "Story of my life, man," and the other guy starts to smile but he's dead.

That's a true story that never happened.

Twenty years later, I can still see the sunlight on Lemon's face. I can see him turning, looking back at Rat Kiley, then he laughed and took that curious half step from shade into sunlight, his face suddenly brown and shining, and when his foot touched down, in that instant, he must've thought it was the sunlight that was killing him. It was not the sunlight. It was a rigged 105 round. But if I could ever get the story right, how the sun seemed to gather around him and pick him up and lift him high into a tree, if I could somehow recreate the fatal whiteness of that light, the quick glare, the obvious cause and effect, then you would believe the last thing Curt Lemon believed, which for him must've been the final truth.

Now and then, when I tell this story, someone will come up to me afterward and say she liked it. It's always a woman. Usually it's an older woman of kindly temperament and humane politics. She'll explain that as a rule she hates war stores; she can't understand why people want to wallow in all the blood and gore. But this one she liked. The poor baby buffalo, it made her sad. Sometimes, even, there are little tears. What I should do, she'll say, is put it all behind me. Find new stories to tell.

I won't say it but I'll think it.

I'll picture Rat Kiley's face, his grief, and I'll think, *You dumb cooze.*

Because she wasn't listening.

It *wasn't* a war story. It was a *love* story.

But you can't say that. All you can do is tell it one more time, patiently, adding and subtracting, making up a few things to get at the real truth. No Mitchell Sanders, you tell her. No Lemon, no Rat Kiley. No trail junction. No baby buffalo. No vines or moss or white blossoms. Beginning to end, you tell her, it's all made up. Every goddamn detail—the mountains and the river and especially that poor dumb baby buffalo. None of it happened. *None* of it. And even if it did happen, it didn't happen in the mountains, it happened in this little village on the Batangan Peninsula, and it was raining like crazy, and one night a guy named Stink Harris woke up screaming with a leech on his tongue. You can tell a true war story if you just keep on telling it.

And in the end, of course, a true war story is never about war. It's about sunlight. It's about the special way that dawn spreads out on a river when you know you must cross the river and march into the mountains and do things you are afraid to do. It's about love and memory. It's about sorrow. It's about sisters who never write back and people who never listen.

Street Map

Sheila Ortiz-Taylor

1620 Fargo Street

She is going to take her time about this. She will not be hurried. Winifred sits down at her dressing table, ties the silk flowered kimono more securely, smoothes it across her breasts. She is fragrant from her bath. The skirt from the dressing table folds about her knees: flowered chintz. She is artistic. Robert has told her this. Only Robert has known her. She picks up the polish remover, a cotton ball. The bedroom door flies open.

"You going to be ready any time soon?" says this other.

"Make me a highball," she tells the other. She feels him waiting. He might do anything. Hit her even.

She unscrews the cap from the polish remover. Looks at him. "Well?"

He turns in the doorway. He casts shadows wherever he goes. Inside this house that she hates. On this street that she hates. He has left the door open. They are eating up her space again, leaving her no air to breathe. "You come here," she yells at him, "and close this goddamn door." In the silence she waits. The sharp sound of ice trays; nothing else.

Where are they, then, she wonders, beginning to remove the old polish, those two? Creeping around the house holding hands, judging her, who was after all their mother. She tosses the used-up cotton into the trash, takes up another; then suddenly she rises, leans across the foot of the bed, swings the door shut fiercely.

Now that she is up, she stands, staring at the bed she can no longer sleep in. Robert says she is too finely made.

She sees his pale hands gathering the drapes in folds, the way he stood that day, stepping back like an artist to see if they hung just so.

Artsy fartsy, Ted had said when he was gone, when he still stood leaning out the window, watching Robert's sky blue van inching slowly up Fargo and out of sight. Could have got drapes from goddamn Sears but no she had to have custom made.

She weaves her fingers into the folds of the kimono at her neck, is standing so when this other abruptly opens the door, holds the rum and coke out to her. Holds it across the bed.

"Have they called?" she asks, taking the drink , sitting down again at the dressing table, smoothing her kimono. She sips, folds a kleenex, sets the glass on top.

"Thelma," he says, sitting on the bed.

She looks at him in the mirror. His legs are spread. He is fat, off center in the softness. Little crescents of fat ride under his eyes making him look Chinese. Robert is slender, wears black slacks, dress shirts, silk ties. Ted's cowboy shirt is open at the throat; his undershirt shows at the neck. She works on her thumb, removing the last of the polish. "What are the kids doing?"

"I dressed 'em," he says.

"They better not be getting dirty," she says, putting on foundation. "Christmas or no Christmas."

"What do you care," says her husband.

"They're a reflection," she says.

He looks at her. She is penciling on eyebrows.

"Beats the hell out of me."

"What beats the hell out of you?"

"You really want to know?" he asks. "If they're a reflection then why'd you chop her hair all funny like that? I can't even comb it, time you were done with her."

The phone rings.

"That's them again," he says, stirring to get up.

"Let it ring," she says. "Thelma knows I'm trying to get ready. I don't know why she can't give it a rest."

"They're waiting," he says.

She picks up a lipstick. It's the wrong one. "Damn," she says. Searches among the tubes.

"You've got one hell of a mouth," he says, "for a lady."

"A lot you know." She leans forward, draws two sides of a bow on her mouth, extends the line out with a brush.

He has finished his drink, gives a Chinese squint. "You done?" he asks.

"I told you I'm not ready yet."

"Drink, I mean." He rattles his ice cubes in explanation.

She looks at the sweaty glass. The color dims toward the surface, like a sunset. "You could freshen it," she says.

She never knows what he will do. Now he is standing over her, his face gone purple. "Freshen my ass," he is shouting. Two pale faces appear momentarily in the doorway, then disappear. "Wait in the car!" he yells in their direction.

It is coming now, and she had wanted just stillness, this time of her own. She had wanted to control the waiting and the time and it was slipping out of her hands, getting away from her.

"Ted, honey," she says.

"Freshen, my ass. Why can't you just answer a simple question. For once." He is pacing now, back and forth, as if the matter of answering a simple question has been oppressing him all his life. "For once." His gestures have become exaggerated, imploring. "Just this once." Now his balled fist is smacking into his left hand, making a sound as familiar as her heart.

2710 Allesandro Street

"I don't know," says my Aunt Thelma, hanging up the phone, "what could be keeping them."

I am sticking toothpicks into Mypapa's backgammon board shaped into a Chinese serpent. But I am listening too. Listening and waiting, here with all of my aunts and uncles and cousins, waiting in the warm house for presents to happen. But not until Uncle Ted and Aunt Winifred get here, the grown-ups say.

They don't live far. Only on Fargo Street. I've been there. They live on the steepest street in L.A. When you go there you think your car will just fall off backwards. Inside their house you feel that way too. Then later, when you leave, at the top of the hill you can't see anything, just space all around, until finally the hood of your car tips down and you can see where you are.

"That Winifred," says my mother.

"I just feel sorry for the children," says my Aunt Thelma, who has no children and would like some to spoil. "Especially that precious Terry Ann."

"Her hair," says my mother, shaking her head, absently stroking my hair.

"I don't know why God gives children to people who don't even deserve them, let alone want them," says my Aunt Thelma.

"Well, he won't be giving them any more," says my Uncle Earl with a yelp of laughter.

My mother and his wife look at him. He is not of their family, only married to my Aunt Thelma.

"That's right," says my Uncle Earl, "he got himself fixed after the last one."

"Fixed?" I say.

"Earl Fox!" say my aunt and my mother together.

1610 Fargo Street

He is looking at his wife in the mirror. Her top lip is bright and red with lipstick. But the bottom lip remains invisible, undefined. She is looking at him. Waiting. He feels the blood leaving his muscles. It is Christmas. His whole family is waiting on the other side of Elysian Park. "Let's go," he says.

"I'm not ready," she says. "But almost."

The telephone rings.

"It's them," he calls from the next room.

2710 Allesandro Street

My cousins and I are sitting around Mymama and Mypapa's tree watching colored oil bubbling in glass candles. We are waiting.

There is a humming behind us where the grown-ups stand. There is a story back there. The story is the one not being told to the children. The grown-ups tell the story to each other, in whispers. The children watch the bubbling tree lights, listening intently to the story not being told.

1610 Fargo Street

Winifred sits at her dressing table, having gathered time back into her hands like escaped fabric. Ted and the children are going to wait in the car until she is ready. The blank paper is in front of her. She has etched in her bottom lip. Her face is on. With her eyebrow pencil she writes across the empty sheet of paper, "I am pregnant." Then she waits, as if something more will come to her. Eventually she puts down the pencil, slides the paper away from her.

Ted's gun in her hand feels cool. She curves her fingers over the muzzle as if warming it, observes in the mirror this artistic woman whose art is in her face. Then she pulls aside the kimono, rests the muzzle against her breast, and pulls the trigger.

2710 Allesandro Street

The front door swings open. Warm air and light rush out of the house and curve around the three people standing in the brightening doorway: blank-faced Uncle Ted gripping his small son's shoulder with one big hand and with the other holding his baby girl tight against his cowboy shirt.

We are all watching from beneath the tree, cousins, not breathing, still as ornaments. My Aunt Thelma steps toward the three as deliberately as if she is in a Christmas play, and having heard at long last her cue, reaches forth empty arms to receive her long-delayed daughter.

RE/Collection

Sheila Ortiz-Taylor

The Kitchen

This woman knows the rhythm of chiles. The gas flame whuffs up, and she runs the fresh chiles quickly through the blue, feeling her nose inside crackle like the chile skins; her fingers heat but do not burn. She moves back and forth from the counter to the flame, scorching the skins, crackling them black, filling the house with the sharp smell of Mexican dirt and lizards, cooking *en un accento puro,* this woman who says she cannot speak one word of Spanish, cooking only *en la lengua,* moving with a *ritmo* that is her own. Is her mother's.

She sees her mother, pale in the casket at the old plaza church, the flames from gently moving votive candles flickering on her cheeks, her brow, her lips, her *eyes* filling from the acrid smell of the chiles as she flames the last one and spins counterclockwise the left front knob on her Tappan range.

The Patio

He lifts his nose to the breeze: *chiles relleños.* Refilled, he turns to his task, turns the tiny gold screw of the clasp for his new reed case. Clockwise, turning, easing it into place. There. Inside, the dark green velvet. He runs his thumb sideways across it. He contemplates the interior of his new reed case, moving past the importance of maintenance, the need for economy if not frugality, to the interior of the box, the interiority of it, the inside of the inside of this miniature world in which, momentarily, he looses himself. He does not know how long he stands inside his own interiority. The cosmos has eased into this reed case, measuring twelve inches square: no more. A breeze lifts the long strand under which his bald spot lies.

The Maid's Room

This room has always been called the maid's room though there has never been a maid. First the room was her grandmother's. Kind Texas grandmother, gone now. First: banished. Then: dead.

The elder daughter lies on her bed, the bed resting on the same floor boards as the bed of her grandmother. A book is open on her bed. The book lies open like a secret revealed; the book lying open over the bones of her grandmother.

Around the book transparent sheets, transparent hinges lie scattered. Inside the sheets: stamps. Stamps from foreign places, with codes and glyphs and symbols in foreign languages.

The girl picks up a crimson stamp in tweezers and places it carefully over the bones of her grandmother.

The Horseshoe

The younger daughter is pressed up against Mike Lazaroni inside his 1939 mandarin red Ford coupe. They are parked outside the girl's strange Mexican house on the curved dirt road known as the horseshoe. Somehow the red tile roof feels as if it is beneath the car. Everything feels atilt now that Mike Lazaroni has kissed the younger daughter, a wet exploratory kiss. When Mike Lazaroni leans back, a string of saliva glistens between them, then winks out like an imaginary star.

She has been kissed before. Terry Taylor never kissed her. But Howard Mackey tried to kiss her every afternoon on their way up the steep footpath from Allesandro Street School. Every afternoon she would curl her hand into a fist and strike a blow that would last only until the next day. At junior high dances the clean blond boy with no personality never tries to kiss her. Wants only to dance, her hand resting on his soft neck.

Mike Lazaroni is different. Her mother has said so. More like a man, she says. Not just because he has his own car, paid for with money earned at the Texaco gas station. It is something else, something she can smell, like odors in the gym when boys play basketball. The hot burned scent of chiles roasting.

The Kitchen

Fourteen chiles lie in an even row releasing bacon fat into the folded paper towel. Over them, she smokes a cigarette. Then runs its smoldering head under a stream of tap water, drops the wetness into the kitchen trash, rinses her hands. Four sisters, all lying in bed on the sleeping porch, smoking. Still smoking, hiding the evidence, still moving under the watchful eyes of their mother, their mother always knowing.

She laughs companionably, whistles as she whips up the eggs: My funny valentine, sweet comic valentine. Flour onto the dish and cheese—where was it?—slicing into neat rectangles with her old dull knife, the one she hides under the dishtowels from her husband. Sweet comic valentine.

The Patio

Nestled as he has been inside the green velvet, the pain surprises, hacking his chest like a dull knife. He sits down. The reed case slips from his hand, the musician who cannot breathe. If he can lie down. In his bed. He enters by the side door. Nobody sees him.

The Maid's Room

Morocco, this one says. Sumatra. Tunisia. Caracas. Belize. She studies the art, the design, the style, the words of the stamps, the wavering lines of cancellation. Por Avión, Mit Luftpost, By Air. She assembles, arranges, shapes, and fixes meaning in color, time, and place. Accomplishes movement by keeping still.

The Horseshoe

The younger daughter slams the door of Mike Lazaroni's mandarin red coupe and moves dreamily down the stairs of her Mexican house, past the cactus bed she tumbled into when she was three, past the slit in the wall saying *buzón,* down the patio steps toward the kitchen smelling of roasted chiles, where in a moment she will collide with her mother, who is saying with alarm and significance, "I can't wake your father."

She will know then—this daughter—and not know. She will know that she alone can wake him, and that she never can. She will know he is merely napping, and that he has already grown stiff, wrapped inside his prized *vicuña* skin from the Andes, that only a delicate line of saliva still connects his lip to this departing day.

A Conversation With My Father

Grace Paley

My father is eighty-six years old and in bed. His heart, that bloody motor, is equally old and will not do certain jobs anymore. It still floods his head with brainy light. But it won't let his legs carry the weight of his body around the house. Despite my metaphors, this muscle failure is not due to his old heart, he says, but to a potassium shortage. Sitting on one pillow, leaning on three, he offers last-minute advice and makes a request.

"I would like you to write a simple story just once more," he says, "the kind Maupassant wrote, or Chekhov, the kind you used to write. Just recognizable people and then write down what happened to them next."

I say, "Yes, why not? That's possible." I want to please him, though I don't remember writing that way. I *would* like to try to tell such a story, if he means the kind that begins: "There was a woman..." followed by plot, the absolute line between two points which I've always despised. Not for literary reasons, but because it takes all hope away. Everyone, real or invented, deserves the open destiny of life.

Finally I thought of a story that had been happening for a couple of years right across the street. I wrote it down, then read it aloud. "Pa," I said, "how about this? Do you mean something like this?"

Once in my time there was a woman and she had a son. They lived nicely, in a small apartment in Manhattan. This boy at about fifteen became a junkie, which is not unusual in our neighborhood. In order to maintain her close friendship with him, she became a junkie too. She said it was part of the youth culture, with which she felt very much at home. After a while, for a number of reasons, the boy gave it all up and left the city and his mother in disgust. Hopeless and alone, she grieved. We all visit her.

"O.K., Pa, that's it." I said, "an unadorned and miserable tale."

"But that's not what I mean," my father said. "You misunderstood me on purpose. You know there's a lot more to it. You know that. You left everything out. Turgenev wouldn't do that. Chekhov wouldn't do that. There are in fact Russian writers you never heard of, you don't have an inkling of, as good as anyone, who can write a plain ordinary story, who would not leave out what you have left out. I object not to facts but to people sitting in trees talking senselessly, voices from who knows where..."

"Forget that one, Pa, what have I left out now? In this one?"

"Her looks, for instance."

"Oh. Quite handsome, I think. Yes."

"Her hair?"

"Dark, with heavy braids, as though she were a girl or a foreigner."

"What were her parents like, her stock? That she became such a person. It's interesting, you know."

"From out of town. Professional people. The first to be divorced in their county. How's that? Enough?" I asked.

"With you, it's all a joke," he said. "What about the boy's father? Why didn't you mention him? Who was he? Or was the boy born out of wedlock?"

"Yes," I said. "He was born out of wedlock."

"For godsakes, doesn't anyone in your stories get married? Doesn't anyone have the time to run down to City Hall before they jump into bed?"

"No," I said. "In real life, yes. But in my stories, no."

"Why do you answer me like that?"

"Oh, Pa, this is a simple story about a smart woman who came to N.Y.C. full of interest love trust excitement very up-to-date, and about her son, what a hard time she had in this world. Married or not, it's of small consequence."

"It is of great consequence," he said.

"O.K.," I said.

"O.K. O.K. yourself," he said, "but listen. I believe you that she's good-looking, but I don't think she was so smart."

"That's true," I said. "Actually that's the trouble with stories. People start out fantastic. You think they're extraordinary, but it turns out as the work goes along, they're just average with a good education. Sometimes the other way around, the person's a kind of dumb innocent, but he outwits you and you can't even think of an ending good enough."

"What do you do then?" he asked. He had been a doctor for a couple of decades and then an artist for a couple of decades and he's still interested in details, craft, technique.

"Well, you just have to let the story lie around till some agreement can be reached between you and the stubborn hero."

"Aren't you talking silly, now?" he asked. "Start again," he said. "It so happens I'm not going out this evening. Tell the story again. See what you can do this time."

"O.K.," I said. "but it's not a five-minute job." Second attempt:

Once, across the street from us, there was a fine handsome woman, our neighbor. She had a son whom she loved because she'd known him since birth (in helpless chubby infancy, and in the wrestling, hugging ages, seven to ten, as well as earlier and later). This boy, when he fell into the fist of adolescence, became a junkie. He was not a hopeless one. He was in fact hopeful, an ideologue and successful converter. With his busy brilliance, he wrote persuasive articles for his high-school newspaper. Seeking a wider audience, using important connections, he drummed into Lower Manhattan newsstand distribution a periodical called *Oh! Golden Horse!*

In order to keep him from feeling guilty (because guilt is the stony heart of nine-tenths of all clinically diagnosed cancers in America today, she said), and because she had always believed in giving bad habits room at home where one could keep an eye on them, she too became a junkie. Her kitchen was famous for a while—a center for intellectual addicts who knew what they were doing. A few felt artistic like Coleridge and others were scientific and revolutionary like Leary. Although she was often high herself, certain good mothering reflexes remained, and she saw to it that there was lots of orange juice around and honey and milk and vitamin pills. However, she never cooked anything but chili, and that no more than once a week. She explained, when we talked to her, seriously, with neighborly concern, that it was her part in the youth culture and she would rather be with the young, it was an honor, than with her own generation.

One week, while nodding through and Antonioni film, this boy was severely jabbed by the elbow of a stern and proselytizing girl, sitting beside him. She offered immediate apricots and nuts for his sugar level, spoke to him sharply, and took him home.

She had heard of him and his work and she herself published, edited, and wrote a competitive journal called *Man Does Live by Bread Alone*. In the organic heat of her continuous presence he could not help but become interested once more in his muscles, his arteries, and nerve connections. In fact he began to love them, treasure them, praise them with funny little songs in *Man Does Live* ...

> the fingers of my flesh transcend
> my transcendental soul
> the tightness in my shoulders end
> my teeth have made me whole

To the mouth of his head (that glory of will and determination) he brought hard apples, nuts, wheat germ, and soy bean oil. He said to his old friends, From now on, I guess I'll keep my wits about me. I'm going on the natch. He said he was about to begin a spiritual deep-breathing journey. How about you too, Mom? he asked kindly.

His conversion was so radiant, splendid, that neighborhood kids his age began to say that he had never been a real addict at all, only a journalist along for the smell of the story. The mother tried several times to give up what had become without her son and his friends a lonely habit. This effort only brought it to supportable levels. The boy and his girl took their electronic mimeograph and moved to the bushy edge of another borough. They were very strict. They said they would not see her again until she had been off drugs for sixty days.

At home alone in the evening, weeping, the mother read and reread the seven issues of *Oh! Golden Horse!* They seemed to her as truthful as ever. We often crossed the street to visit and console. But if we mentioned any of our children who were at college or in the hospital or dropouts at home, she would cry out, My baby! My baby! and burst into terrible, face-scarring time-consuming tears. The End.

First my father was silent, then he said, "Number One: You have a nice sense of humor. Number Two: I see you can't tell a plain story. So don't waste time." Then he said sadly, "Number Three: I suppose that means she was alone, she was left like that, his mother. Alone. Probably sick?"

I said, "Yes."

"Poor woman. Poor girl, to be born in a time of fools, to live among fools. The end. The end. You were right to put that down. The end."

I didn't want to argue, but I had to say, "Well, it is not necessarily the end, Pa."

"Yes," he said, "what a tragedy. The end of a person."

"No, Pa," I begged him. "It doesn't have to be. She's only about forty. She could be a hundred different things in this world as time goes on. A teacher or a social worker. An ex-junkie! Sometimes it's better than having a master's in education."

"Jokes," he said. "As a writer that's your main trouble. You don't want to recognize it. Tragedy! Plain tragedy! Historical tragedy! No hope. The end."

"Oh, Pa," I said. "She could change."

"In your own life, too, you have to look it in the face." He took a couple of nitroglycerin. "Turn to five," he said, pointing to the dial on the oxygen tank. He inserted the tubes into his nostrils and breathed deep. He closed his eyes and said, "No."

I had promised the family to always let him have the last word when arguing, but in this case I had a different responsibility. That woman lives across the street. She's my knowledge and my invention. I'm sorry for her. I'm not going to leave her there in that house crying. (Actually neither would Life, which unlike me has no pity.)

Therefore: She did change. Of course her son never came home again. But right now, she's the receptionist in a storefront community clinic in the East Village. Most of the customers are young people, some old friends. The head doctor has said to her, "If we only had three people in this clinic with your experiences . . ."

"The doctor said that?" My father took the oxygen tubes out of his nostrils and said, "Jokes. Jokes again."

"No, Pa, it could really happen that way, it's a funny world nowadays."

"No," he said. "Truth first. She will slide back. A person must have character. She does not."

"No, Pa," I said. "That's it. She's got a job. Forget it. She's in that storefront working."

"How long will it be?" he asked. "Tragedy! You too. When will you look it in the face?"

Paris in '73

Grant Cogswell

I

She left him in Paris in 1973, in a Metro station that sat directly three hundred feet under the Seine, just where it curves south of the Hotel de Ville. I was six years old at the time, and I can remember that if you looked from our apartment window maybe a quarter of a mile down the street you could see the rim of the trench the river flowed in. The river always stank and always was brown, and it moved sluggishly as if just waking between its stone and concrete banks. I imagined the bottom to be hard cement too, and it was not until much later that I realized this was impossible.

The Metro station was under reconstruction, perhaps because of the river. There were holes gouged in the smooth tile, through the walls and even into the wet black dirt of the ancient riverbed itself. There were pools of water on the platform, streams dripping down from pipes, thick tile dust moistening into sludge and still more holes, and cracks, everywhere.

My mother and father were yelling at each other, at first during and over the bursts of jackhammer noise but after a while pausing angrily, waiting and looking around at the cracks in the walls before it was quiet again, and then the shouting would resume.

The French were rooting for her. She was young, tall, American, and a brunette. My father was (and still is) a stout Kansan, bald and blond-bearded, looking Bavarian and possibly violent. I was learning as we traveled that the Germans hate the French and the French hate the Germans (or anyone who looks German). So now the French stood back, commenting and jeering and watching my mother and father yell. I stood between my parents, closer to my father because it had always been that way. When I think of my teenage obesity, the places my father and I went together and where we are now, the rainy August night in Oxford when I rolled in the warm grass with a barmaid whose name I did not know, but whose mouth I explored with my own and whose birthmark I found in under five minutes, I think now of the way my mother stood at the edge of the yellow line, her arms out at her sides, with my father several feet back from the tracks, and how as the train arrived I instinctively stepped back away from the gust of wind and bumped my head on my father's belt buckle.

He turned and looked down at me and grabbed my wrist tightly. His big, red fist reminded me of the one I had seen on posters around the university that spring, posters I didn't understand the meaning of, only the rage. "Some people are angry and desperate," my father had said, "and they need to feel strong."

She hesitated a moment and they were both quiet in the rush of bodies that moved around us. Then she stepped onto the train and sat down next to a long-haired blond boy in a green fatigue jacket. The doors slid closed and we watched her run her hand over his hair, pulling one strand out and high towards the top of the window. The train moved and she dropped the hair. We watched her shift in her seat closer to him and place her hand on his smooth neck. I next saw her thirteen years later, in the Greyhound Bus terminal in Murfreesboro, North Carolina.

II

With my mother suddenly gone my father hired a German art student named Helga as a maid and sort of live-in babysitter. On the wall of her room, which had been my room before my mother left, there was a poster of Castle Neuschwanstein with big white letters along the bottom that read DEUTSCHLAND. Helga was blonde and slimly elegant like a ballet dancer. She stood with me once, looking at the poster with a glass of white wine in her hand, and said, "It does not need to *say* 'Deutschland'. It *is* Deutschland."

"It's a picture," I told her.

"You are an American," she said to me later, sauteeing her Swiss-buttered carrots, a recipe she knew by heart, "and you should be like one. It is not right that you should grow up here." She often drank at the cafes with the American students and had picked up their expressions. "You don't speak like an American. Say 'grovey'."

"Gravy," I said.

"Americans say 'grovey'. You should know that."

Under our apartment was a shop which sold gas heaters. To the left as you entered was a cafe with a big red and white striped awning and lots of outside tables. To the right was a gourmet restaurant, this one with a green awning. The restaurant gave away little lead figures of two hand-painted frogs, one mounting the other, to amuse the customers. I did not understand why two frogs would want to do this, and I asked the manager of the restaurant. The manager had one missing eye, and he left the empty socket uncovered. But he laughed at my question so hard that the blind socket began to ooze, and I ran out of the restaurant and only returned on the nights when we all ate dinner there.

After that I spent my time at the newsstand, the cafe with the red and white awning and the bench beside the big oak tree, where almost every day a man brought a guitar and an accordion and played for the coins people tossed into his velvet-lined accordion case. Sometimes, my father says, I danced and got money too. The man played songs all mad with flowery torrents of words, announcing them in a thick Scottish brogue: 'Subterranean Homesick Blues', 'Fishfly Stomp', 'Buttertown Stage', 'Blinded By the Light'. I'm starting to remember, I think, that it was the crazy lyrics of the songs as much as the notes of the guitar or accordion that made me whirl and leap like I'm told I did.

In the summer my father would get home long before it was dark, ambling slowly up the sidewalk and swinging his heavy leather briefcase. As I ate raisin cake at one of the outside tables or picked through the grate at the bottom of the oak tree for lost coins, he would cough loudly and come over to me and gather me up out of my activity and onto the stairs. Then the three of us would eat together, looking out the windows at the traffic, the afternoon light, the nuns from the seminary eating hot dogs across the street. Helga and my father would drink wine and stay at the table until long after it was finally dark and I was in my bed next to the cobwebby airshaft.

Sometimes on those nights I could hear them talking, if the wind was right, quiet and low like old, old friends, about the mountains of Germany and the plains of Kansas, and, I imagine, about my mother, and about the strange events of their lives of the kind that people talk over on warm nights with a bottle of wine between them.

I picture her telling him her idea. "I have made a film, a movie, and in it I have pictures of people in Frankfurt, and of the Black Forest and gypsies—near Heidelberg I found them—and it closes with a picture of Neuschwanstein. I want to sell it as a travel commercial." He would smile and she would continue. "It does not say 'Deutschland' in it anywhere. It shows it. That is what is important. No narrator, no one says anything."

"Subtle," he says.

"Ja, subtle."

Later he would tell her, "My aunt came back from the dead."

Helga is thinking she heard him wrong. "Back . . ."

"Back from the dead." He pulls out another cigarette but does not light it, setting it on its end and turning it over and doing the same again and again. On a night fishing in Puget Sound, my great-uncle Ray had told my father about the time he saw his dead wife. My father was seventeen. It was dusk, and that boy could not see his uncle's face clearly, but the man gestured wildly with his big, hairless hands ("Uranium prospectors' hands," he said of them) and told his story in the twilight.

My father says, "Aunt Rachel died in 1945. She was an assembly worker in the shipyard up in Seattle during the war. A riveter's gun slipped off the metal and put a rivet right through Aunt Rachel's windpipe." Uncle Ray was downtown at the bank, three days after the funeral, about to withdraw his wife's account, when he saw her face in the window of a city bus. "The bus went right by, and there she was, dead a week and staring right at him." Then he walked two blocks, found a bar and drank whisky shooters until he passed out. That night he was treated for shock at the Yesler Way Mercy Clinic.

She says, "It must have been someone who looked very much like your aunt."

"No, it was her. I don't know how, but she was. My uncle believes it, but he doesn't believe it, if you know what I mean, and so do I." My father had placed his young hands on his Uncle Ray's hairless ones and sworn to never tell anyone. But Uncle Ray had died in 1971, the winter we moved to Paris, and now he could talk about it. "It's true, it really happened, I know it did."

My father did not tell her he too watches bus windows for dead relatives as well as live ones, like sometimes his wife.

Sometime she must have told him about her uncle, this one a Gunther, who crawled into her bed one morning just before dawn when she was seven years old, "His age," she would say, looking sideways towards my bedroom. "I loved my Uncle Gunther and I trusted him, so when he said, 'I want to be with you,' I opened the covers and he crawled under." Then he began to feel her chest, looking for the ghosts of breasts that were not there yet. "It scared me very badly," she told my father. "Scared of men and of life and of everything." I see her fumbling with her wineglass and looking down, saying, "He was a molester, but it felt like . . ."

"It was rape," my father says.

After more stories they would pick up the dishes and wash them in the tiny kitchen, their laughter echoing off the tile and the sound of the wine bottle slamming down after a swig onto the counter, the cutting board, and finally into the trash, coming loud through the walls. After that they would both go to their rooms. My father would come into our room quietly, closing the door behind him. He would lay down awake for a long time, and then get up and go to the bathroom, and come back, and still be softly washing the room with his awake-breath when I fell back into sleep.

It went on this way until fall, when the days got shorter and often it was raining when my father came home at night, in the dark. Helga studied a lot then, and after dinner she would go to her room, studying math and French while I leafed through her big books and looked at the full-color prints of the Renaissance paintings. Things slowed down, were less alive, and my father and Helga were waiting. She rushed through her assignments towards spring, when she would bring her degree with her back to Frankfurt. He was waiting for word on a job he wanted with Rockwell in London. The television stayed on in the evenings until we went to bed.

When word from London finally came, just before Christmas, no one seemed to notice. At the dinner table one night my father said, "It looks like I got the job."

Helga looking down at her butter-sautéed carrots, her masterpiece, said, "That is good. You will like London."

And so, we went to London, where we lived until the summer after I first got drunk with my father and he told me that he and Helga had been in a strange kind of love.

At the airport Helga kissed me briskly on the cheek and forehead and hugged me tight, and smiling with wide wet paths on her face turned to my father.

"I have met a man," she said, grinning.

"Oh, good," said my father, and they kissed each other on the mouth, twisting themselves as if in a struggle, for what I could not tell.

"Watch out for his dentures," I said.

My father kept the job with Rockwell until twelve years later, when cancer was found in his lungs and he had to quit. He was remarried, two years after we left Helga in Paris, to a woman he had known as a child in Wichita, also separated, and burdened with a child and looking for someone to carry her into middle age.

"It was supposed to be like 'The Brady Bunch'," I told a friend much later, when I began to see what actually had happened. "We pretended for ten years or so that we had been together all along, with no acknowledgment of our differences, no attention paid to the missing parents." It didn't quite work, but it got us a long way in relative safety.

Helga graduated with her art degree, returned to Frankfurt and kept in touch for a couple of years. Her last card, which we received just before Christmas of 1976, told us she was working for an advertising agency, struggling, but would sleep on the streets before moving back in with her family. "Good for her," my father said, and pinned the card up on the bulletin board next to our Girl Scouts of America Bicentennial Calendar.

I was sixteen years old the first time I got drunk with my father. "I could have made love to Helga, but I didn't want to spoil things for you," he said. "She was beautiful, she lived in our house and she was alone. But I never slept with her. We loved each other, though. Through you, mostly."

I was never aware of this at the time, but I suppose I had it half figured out by the time he actually said it, having heard some of the things they said and having to imagine others, knowing that at some time they must have been told, it seems like the right way for things to have happened.

III

I grew up fat, lost weight, ran track in my senior year of high school, and once went into the bathroom with a pack of razorblades and a bottle of my stepmother's favorite bourbon with intentions of killing myself on the toilet, getting drunk, cutting my wrists and letting my blood flow out. All of us, my father, my stepmother, Helga, myself, seemed to be reaching for something lost, something just out of our grasp, that if found would make our lives whole again. It seems that as the years go by, sometimes we come upon times that make our pasts more our own, that, like the Talking Heads song says, give us back our names. Fiddling with our big old French radio we kept in the guest room when I was sixteen, dialing through the stations from all over Europe, I suddenly heard something familiar. It was in French, a language I had forgotten almost entirely by the time I entered junior high school. It was one of the accordion man's songs and I half-whisper-sang it, not understanding what the words meant, but remembering their sounds, and the story they told of the fisherman's drowned sons.

Also there is the more recent thing that makes me remember Paris, for the first time making me feel as if it was *me* who had been there; a month ago I took a bus to Murfreesboro, North Carolina, and I met my mother and three-year-old half-brother I did non know I had until I got off the bus. He looks like me in the dappled light that falls through the trees that grow in great stands around Murfreesboro, and there is a way her turns his head as if cautious, that makes me want to protect him from all the crazy shit the world has in store. His father is gone, on whatever device it is which pulls people from their natural obligations. It was a strange and wonderful week I spent in Murfreesboro, and I feel very different now than I ever have before. But that is a different story, and also one about a strangely physical kind of love.

Arrow Math

Katharine Haake

1. When Mount St. Helens erupted it went off with the force of 27,000 atomic bombs and tore away the entire north face of the mountain—the largest avalanche in recorded history. It was May 18, 1980, 8:32 in the morning. The mountain had been black with ash for weeks.

For a long time now I have been thinking about numbers. It comes, I suspect, from having an eight-year-old son in a progressive private school (this is, after all, LA) where math has somehow been transformed from a rigid ritual of calculation to something you can put your hands on, something bright and palpable, a box of colored cubes and sticks, the idea behind place and value, a conceptual framework. I am big these days on frameworks, any kind of structure, the smallest degree of external order by which to contain the chaos that my life, once a simple, small town life, has become—two children (both boys), my own job, a husband who, in his heart of hearts, believes in traditional gender role values, a craving for spirituality, what you feel at the ocean's edge, a river's bank or mountain's top, when you hold a round rock in your hand.

So, numbers. Mount St. Helens.

Were there ways to have predicted rather than, in retrospect, counting up your losses?

But also, narrative, for this, as you shall see, is a story, with no earthly basis in fact.

3. Twelve years later Linda stood on a flat rock high up Windy Ridge with her pre-adolescent son and watched as clouds rose from the crater that once was pure symmetry, perfect cone of the volcano, like another dream of order—earth, geometry, and balance—and surveyed the world past and present, then and now, and though not a literary type, what she thought was: is this a metaphor? What's a metaphor? A metaphor, Linda remembered from sometime in college, is an implied comparison between two things.

And then Linda started to weep.

I am reclusive by nature and don't go out much to cultural events, however vital they might be to my interests, especially not to those of a literary nature, the public performance of poets, prose readings, that sort of thing. What kind of writer does this make me, I wonder? How can you take what I have say to any kind of heart? But that is not the worst of it, for I also must confess that I find poetry more difficult and cryptic than math, which is, after all, a form of narrative, a working things out to their conclusion.

Still, from time to time I do find myself where, more typically, I would not find myself, and so it happened recently I found myself discussing a poem with its poet at a reading. He read many poems, and because I am literal-minded and somewhat slow-witted, I was not sure exactly what to say. There was one, though, at the end, the poet, David Bromige, read with Marjorie Perloff, a poem in two voices, split by a black line on the page like a fraction, which the poet, in the subsequent question/answer session described as the voice that always butts against the voice that manages to formulate a statement, any statement. Like this:

3. Linda, Linda, why are you crying?

1. In the immediate aftermath of what happened to the bulge on the side of Mount St. Helens, a bulge that had for two months been expanding five to seven feet a day—how, as if blasted by some hidden explosion, it just dropped away, in a single instant, flying completely apart—its remnants plummeted directly into Spirit Lake below, where, in the same instant, the lakebottom rose three hundred feet from its previous level and sloshed water several times that high up the surrounding slopes, a giant, churning, superheated bathtub. This was how it started, an eruption that went on for the next nine hours, spewing a vertical column of pulverized rock sixteen miles straight into the atmosphere, a black cloud pierced by lightning where ash particles collided. Much of the initial damage, though, occurred in the first few minutes—three, no more than five. Imagine concentric half circles, fanning out from the site of the eruption eighteen miles to the north, east and west in three discrete zones that would come to be called the Inner Blast Zone, the Blow-down Zone, and the Scorch Zone. Because no one had considered the possibility of the lateral blast, no one had anticipated such damage. But Mount St. Helens blew sideways, not up, a powerful reminder of the fallibility of our imaginations.

I was living in Missoula then, and I remember that when the ash came, it came not as we remember it most vividly, but as a premature and inauspicious dust. These same twelve years that separate Linda and Larry from Wyn, have brought me my two sons and their father who, in the car last summer on our way, at last, to the volcano that had once marked our lives as irrevocably as the bandannas we were forced to wear outside for a week around our faces in a public display of our human frailty, told the boys that, no, we'd never been to Mount St. Helens before, but that once, long ago, Mount St. Helens came to us.

I did not notice her that afternoon, not at any point along the way, or where we got out of the car and walked or climbed, but I imagine it must have been sometime around then that Linda finally went there too, taking Larry with her, a boy whose face in pre-adolescence has gone, like Wyn's, remote and stern, though Larry, of course, has never seen his father, never until now, I don't believe, known much about him, though certainly he must often have dreamt what it might have been like to embrace him, often longed for the flight of a baseball from his pitch, the sound of his voice in a story.

At that reading David Bromige spoke about parentheses, what happens when they do not close, how serene and seductive they can be. Even so they make their own demands, the same as the italics here before you, for they are, in their other respects, rule-bound and hierarchical, struts in a system of stabilized value, what we have learned to distinguish as primary text, and then something else, one dominent, primary, essential, the other simply not. Literally, they, these languid printer's marks, will tell you what to think, how to read, who to be. But if, again, they do not end but go on and on forever, the first quarter curve of a circle, arch of the moon, is thereby transformed from a mark that marks a closed relationship of power to one that marks instead a limpid point of departure from one form of discourse to another, from linear to contiguous logic, which if you dare to follow the imperative of movement will designate a new topography of language. For certainly a story, by any other name, is a number, a map, an act of love or faith, a pattern of tumbling equivocations, an undiscovered animal, just waiting.

How many contradictory tenets can you simultaneously hold to be true? Why is David Bromige's elegant poem structure so intractably binary, so uncompromisingly male?[1]

Or, if this were a creative writing workshop you would start asking now whose story is this anyway—Linda's? Larry's? Wyn's? David's? Mine? Could it be yours?

Then you would ask: Who is Wyn?

1. The Inner Blast Zone was demolished within three minutes—six miles of old growth forests, almost instantaneously vaporized, 500-year-old stands of cedar, Douglas fir and hemlock simply gone—poof—disappeared, and the animals, and the soil scoured down to its underlying rock, nothing left, not one living thing, not a shadow, or a breath. For another seven miles, known as the Blowdown Zone, trees were snapped off, just like that, at the base, some more than seven feet thick, not a single one left standing, or were pulled up by the roots and tossed to the ground, where, like slender matchsticks, they were combed into sworls and eddies by the subsequent volcanic winds. Beyond that, the Scorch Zone extends for another five miles, where trees were left standing but shriveled and blackened, a weirdly delicate dead forest, huge branches twisted to a desiccate lace.

8:32 in the morning.

Somewhere on nearby Coldwater Ridge, lanky Wyn Jackson had just settled down with his binoculars for another day of watching the mountain shift and grow.

1. Mount St. Helens shifts and grows.

3. What made Linda cry—the first time, not the last—was not Wyn's failure to come back that day, or the next, or the next, not even her increasing certainty that he would never come back, never be a father to the child she was carrying, never crook his arm around her neck and tell her everything would be ok, never touch her or tell her he loved her again, but when she read in the paper that the victims' bodies were so saturated with ash that inch-deep incisions dulled scalpel blades, that made her cry. She imagined Wyn's internal organs shrunken and hardened, his muscles dried

and frayed, his lungs filled with grit. She also cried to read that those who were burned survived long enough to walk several miles for help. The baby inside her flipped in terror and remorse. Linda cried for three weeks after that, and then I don't believe she ever cried again, not for thirteen years, the whole span of her child's life, Wyn's hapless progeny, and also Linda's burden, though she loved him.

The baby born in due time was a boy that she named Larry. In due time, too, they moved to LA, where Linda got a job. Larry had a look about him even then, when he was little, something distant in the eyes, a remote way of being that made people wonder of him where was he? He wasn't a bad child, but he was a sad child, and I don't know if Linda ever really tried to reach him. Linda was busy writing copy for ads for dry cleaners and dreaming of her one big break. By the time he was seven, Larry would sit reading for hours and hours, and this convinced people that he was a bright boy, like his father, with a future, as long as he refrained from any foolish act to squander it.

4. Can a boy just turned thirteen be culpable of squandering his future?

Ask me how I know them and I will tell you that I know them the way a child, learning numbers, thinks of the thousand hundreds in the same round way that he contemplates zero. Think of the zero. I have one son whose heart expands on either side of it, replete with the concept of negative/positive value as if, for him, it were a second skin. My other son, with a dreamy half smile, disappears into the vastness of the nothing itself, and though I've promised to stand there on the edge with him, forever if it comes to that, just to be there waiting when he returns, this no longer seems like such a guarantee. He's five now. When he turns eight, like his brother, how hard will I have to hold onto the edge myself to keep myself from flying after him?

I guess, in a way, what I'm saying is I don't know them at all. Larry and Linda are utterly opaque to me. I watch them the way I used to watch my algebra professor work his calculations on the board, exactly the same as I now watch the interpreters for the deaf at the school where I teach. I watch their mouths move, their hands gesticulate. What makes a language, any language, beautiful, expressive? Nouns, I'm told, are easy, but something more like syntax, inflection, what is that? I have such a strong feeling sometimes that I could save either one or the other of them, if I had any way of reaching them, but I don't. It is like Linda's fierce inability to cry. Somewhere inside all of us there is this thing—a knowledge, a regret, a desire—that we can't ever get to. I believe what drives our lives is the trying.

2. Wyn is different. Wyn I knew myself, long before Linda did, in another time and place when you could ride your bicycle from one side of town to the other without telling your mother where you were going or when you expected to return. There were days I don't believe we did expect to return but somehow expected instead to spin out there somehow and just keep on spinning. This is not nostalgia

for another time or life, for when everything had promise and even war seemed full of meaning. This is Wyn and me kissing in his closet when we're seven, catching tadpoles in the runoff back behind his house when we're nine, dancing stiffly at our eighth grade graduation, turning against Vietnam in high school (it has been that long), aloof, backpacking weeks at a time far away from any of all that, floating rivers in college and after.

One of Wyn's legs was slightly shorter than the other and he limped. This was not something he was born with but a condition that developed over time, an odd and temporary atrophying of one limb, which stiffened for awhile, stopped growing, and then turned natural again, for no apparent reason. You could feel sorry for him if, like me, you had some crazy need to rescue him from what was coming, but his leg wasn't really the problem. It was only occasionally painful and so what if he couldn't climb rocks? Rue suited Wyn. He'd get this look in his eyes and talk about Half Dome, and it was like the whole inside of me existed to engulf him, put out his sadness, his loss.

Long ago, kids used to tease him, the way kids do. I remember that they pranced, in imitation of his walk. I remember too that, one day, Wyn's face went completely white, then dark, and then he beat them up, three taunting boys at once, just like in the movies, and made them all cry uncle, cry you win.

Later I would wonder how Linda must have teased him. It was not a pretty thought, but I had it.

There was a time I believed I knew everything there was to know about Wyn, but in retrospect I must admit that, for me, everything in those days was largely comprised by such things as how, squint-eyed, he would assess a pass or lean keenly into a rapid and the way he liked a woman's neck, starting, especially, with the nape, the tiny white expanse of skin as delicate and vulnerable as a wish.

"Tell me," I once asked him, "what is it about a woman's neck."

He shrugged, knit his eyebrows, and gave me a funny little quizzical look. I know some men like the hollow, a miniature nesting place for their tongue, but Wyn wasn't like that, not predictable, not common. Perhaps it was the blue throb of a vein.

My own neck was neither long nor slender nor particularly white, but yet he stayed with me for seven years, and it was during this time that we went out together into the natural world and taught ourselves such basic facts as how to make a fire with flint and dried grass and what berries you could eat without dying. In settings like that—milky glacial green lakes, dense lacy red cedar, sweet air, thick blankets of moss and a dry bed of needles—you are quick to those your hold on the world you walked out of, you grow careless, you think less of certain outcomes, you believe you will always be happy.

> *Speaking as a novice what I'd say is that the lure of mathematics has to do not so much with the secrets of the universe as it does with the simple pleasures of order, chiefly symmetry, its most elegant expression. I have heard all about the wild side of math, but even chaos, we now know, can be predicted. Between prediction and hope lies an entire universe of uncertainty, and however much we long to anticipate the outcome, there has never been anything remotely symmetrical about the way our lives weave*

into what they are. Consider how a child's life branches out from the life of a mother's womb and then try to tell me you can hold this information up to any kind of standard or logic. This is what our lives are like. Numbers simply help us mediate the madness.

5. When the ash did come, we thought it was a thunderstorm, darkening the late spring afternoon and making prophetic what the man who would become my husband and father of my children had said earlier that day: "You'll never see these hills this green again. This is as green as they ever get."

5. What I mean, in other respects, is that I can no longer say for certain what I would do now under similar circumstances, but I do know that the child Wyn and I conceived in the mountains and aborted subsequently remains the single most profound regret of my life. It is not so much the loss of that child as it is—and I know this isn't fair—the thought of Larry somewhere out there, growing into his father's lean body, inexorable and finite.

Look, I've been reading best-sellers all summer. I know and applaud the virtues of plot, and as the possibilities proliferate there is at least a part of me that, facing them, goes mute, as if without a will, and turns with unexpected urgency to such things as equal signs, which seem so full of certainty as to have grown, in the most reassuring sense, iconic. But I don't know. Think, for example, of the nature of touch. For a woman whose body, in the act of sex, conceives another body—multiplied by two from within, and subsequently once again divided—the touching never ends, it goes on and on, first a barely perceptible flutter within her, like a kiss she's not really sure of, and then in what seems the blink of an eye, a two-year-old's fists pounding her chest in a tantrum, an eight-year-old easing his hand into hers, a man's awkward embrace on the eve of his wedding or war. For a woman, whose body, in the act of sex, conceives another body, there is no such thing as closure.
Plot models male sexual pleasure, a form, I'm told, of dominance.
For if not long before, then at last on the arc of your son's first back handspring, the equal sign snaps.
Closure is your mother's dazzling diamond brooch you cannot wear because the clasp is broken.

1. Tennis ball sized rocks flew through the gloom of the gases and ash, while three-quarters of the glaciers and snow on what remained of the mountain melted instantaneously, causing waves of mud to come boiling down the slopes, superheated slurries that sloshed the Toutle River three hundred and sixty feet out of its banks and raised its temperature to more than one hundred degrees.

1. Though the sound of the eruption was heard as far away as Canada, seven hundred miles—people reported a huge roar, a series of low seismic booms, a thunderous roll—for sixty miles in every direction an eerie hush prevailed, nothing was

heard but the thrashing of trees, snapping and falling, cracking, splintering, as the almost palpable sound waves set off by the volcanic blast itself disappeared into the heavens, arching out serenely to mark a perfect parabolic curve of silence, the scorched earth below beyond noise of the storm.

4. When Larry was eight years old he opened the front door to a Greenpeace canvasser and years later he would say that it was like a lightbulb going off in his head, the flash of recognition, total illumination. The man wore a ponytail, braided in the back, and tattered strap Birkenstock sandals. Linda was at home, but asleep, and the man told Larry he was soliciting money for whales. Larry, who had been to Sea World and sat in every Splash Zone, knew all about whales, and he emptied his coin bank for the man.

"How can I help?" he asked, desperate to detain the man until Linda woke up but hesitant to wake her, for Linda, by this time, was prone to fits of anger, unprovoked, inexplicable and violent. The man told Larry he would send some kids' material.

"I can read as well any grown-up," Larry said.

The man smiled, amused but skeptical. "Show me," he said.

Then Larry read the man's petition in a high sweet voice, with expression. When he was done, the man patted his head, and said, "When you grow up, be a warrior for the earth." Then he turned and walked away, leaving Larry choking with loss.

This was Larry, with his passions and his boyish convictions—coins, for example, the righteousness of the LA Kings and Lakers, baseball statistics, endangered animals, the disappearing ozone, and recycling, algebraic equations—and for years after that he dreamed of the man, tall, with a beatific smile. With every dream a small kernel of hatred for his mother grew and hardened in him. The lighbulb in his head was that the Greenpeace canvasser was, in fact, his father, a fact so incontrovertible in Larry's young mind that it became a guiding force in his life. All the pieces fit together. Wyn never even went to Mount St. Helens May 18, Larry knew this now, but the thing that made him so determined and remote was that whatever else he did, he would find out why, when the devastation of the mountain gave Wyn the opportunity to walk away from Linda, and from him, Wyn took it, just like that, apprenticed himself to the oceans instead, turned into a champion of whales, footloose, without earthly bonds.

I could not work an equation out for the life of me these days. You put a letter where a number is supposed to be and I go blank and panicky. As for the numbers themselves, that's why man invented calculators, but even so you have to wonder: if the father is indeed the variable—plug in the Greenpeace activist for Wyn—what will happen to this boy's bright hopes?

If it were I Wyn walked away from that day on Mount St. Helens it would be a different story, I know that. But my loss had already occurred, Linda had already replaced me, and the thing that still makes me so crazy is this whole concept of the variable. The problem is to find the value, any value, that can stand in for replacement, altering the look of the equation without changing its essential relationship, property or structure. Larry had an instinct for this, I think, but maybe that's a gender difference too, because however hard I try to get my mind around this concept I just keep stumbling over my own opposing instinct that nothing is the same as something else and that in any operation of substitution and replacement— mathematical, physical, linguistic—something must get added, something lost. If I am erased by another what becomes of who am I? It is tempting to say that in this particular case, Larry's what was added and I am what was lost, but how does this account for Linda, for Wyn?

3. The first time Linda pitched a movie she wrote down everything they said, smiling and nodding as if what they were saying was this was the best dry cleaning ad ever. Later, she could not decipher her notes. Linda spent hours and hours planning her wardrobe for success, while Larry read and read, silent and apart from her and brooding. Linda had this idea to write a script that combined *Moby Dick* and *Star Wars,* and she was so engrossed by this idea that she did not notice when Larry's leg stopped growing and, little by little, Larry started to limp.

4. Wyn met Linda on a river and Linda was a novice, not just to the ways of white water but also of Wyn. Between now and the moment on the rapid when the raft bucked and tossed her long-legged body up into the air, a sudden arc of fear, and Wyn reached out and stopped her flight, the way he would, lies Larry's whole life. You think about that. Then you think about Larry with his mother on the mountain now, that look in his eyes, something far away and hard. You think about those years, growing up in LA, the shopping malls and video arcades, dwindling library resources, gun crises in the schools. Then think about the other boys like Larry who lost their dads in Vietnam. You think about the absent fathers, the ones at the office or those who disappear from their custody arrangements, forget all about child support. There are dads who die of cancer, and dads who get shot on the streets. The world is a dangerous place. But Larry would have been half-brother to the child I did not choose and he is out there with his mother on the mountain that his father loved, it must seem to him now, more than he loved either Larry or his mother, and what it seems to me is that there must be something I could say to him, some wisdom I could offer, some memory, an icon at least.

1. Here's an icon: Before May 1980, in certain evening light, the whole flawless symmetrical cone of Mount St. Helens would reflect in Spirit Lake, mirrored postcard image, picture perfect. Wyn canoeing on the rippling ridge of glacier.

5. Here's another icon: Wyn and me, sweaty from our climb, out bodies tangled up with one another's on a flat rock by a lake. We taste salty, and where the sun hits our naked skin it glistens. This is as much as I will ever know, my whole life, of desire. Like Larry's young feeling of betrayal, my desire grows inside me, starting small and hard and then expanding to fill all the empty space.

5. In 1980, as I said, I was living in Missoula and Wyn was posted on a ridge east of Mount St. Helens with a telescope and many complex instruments of science. He would call me once a week from a town called Cowlitz before driving into Portland and Linda, and what I remember from our conversations is that we were still different then, still on the crown of the cusp. We wore wool plaid shirts and the socks I'd knit myself, though they were getting holes and Wyn couldn't even sew a button on his shirt, never mind know what to do with a darning egg and thick blunt darning needle. Also, we were guarded, having made decisions we could not retreat from, yet still torn by them, and by something, also, like fury. What, in our experience, could contain this?

Linda was the kind of woman who collected shoes and make-up and who shopped at maternity stores as soon as she knew she was pregnant. Wyn had this edge of something fated and forlorn in his voice that went away only when he talked about the mountain, turning high-pitched with excitement and conviction. The last time Wyn called me he said, "This is where history and geology collide." What I think he said next was, "I miss you," but a logging truck or some other piece of heavy equipment went by at that moment and I couldn't quite make out his words.

What I really know these days about math is a confused blend of some hazy memories from the first half of my life and what my son brings home from school, things to touch and do and make, word problems, arrow math. I suspect that I feel romantic about numbers because I was never all that good at them and also because what I've learned as a writer is, fundamentally, not to trust words. In the arrow math assignment you were supposed to take a grid of numbers and read it without value, topologically, like a map.

What you will see at once is that this does not make sense. Your son's father will most likely hit the roof. But as you try to read the arrows your son draws intently and find out where they're heading, you grow curious, as well, about what happens when you apply the reading strategies of one discourse to another. In your heart, because you are a woman, you know that language is contiguous, fluid and paradoxical, that any point along the curve of syntax represents a possible point of departure, that the obligation to make a choice among them is one you're about to reject. But watching your son with his sweet page of arrows you're thrilled to see that numbers can surprise you too, just watch them.

Think of how a child learns to count: one, two, four thousand, thirty-six-nine. Eight and eight, the child knows, makes eighty-eight, and the process of becoming a person in this culture is tied up with abandoning the purity of this logic. I don't know one way or the other about logic, but I do know that if you were to rotate the grid of this story on one axis, or shift the names among the numbers, helter skelter, everything would change, take on new meaning. If Mount St. Helens were a five instead of one, would Wyn still be alive, having fathered many sons, and contemplating, once again, an affair with me? Make Linda a zero and she disappears. Without Linda, no Larry, it's easy.

*Or what if, long ago, Wyn chose earthquakes instead, or something
old and absolute and safe, like the stratification of rock, how a canyon gets
cut, where what the wind erodes goes when it's gone?*

5. I don't believe Wyn met Linda on a river. What would Linda have been doing
on a river? This was fifteen years before adventure travel made the cover of
Newsweek, and Linda's had her nails done since she was in high school. Maybe a
video store, in the New Releases section, trying to decide about the evening's enter-
tainment which, as they discussed the possibilities, they ended up spending together.
But again, this was the seventies, before video stores, and neither Wyn nor Linda
would have gone in for disco.

A busstop, an art history class, a queue.

If there wasn't any raft, how could Linda have been bucked and Wyn save her?
Wyn would have saved her if there was a raft. What do you think: was there a raft,
and was it yellow?

*I continue to be interested here not just in a layering of narratives,
which certainly our lives are, but of, more fundamentally, the structures
that contain them. Imagine, once again, the arrow on the map. Shift it ever
so slightly and the narrative itself—Linda's ambition, Larry's detachment,
Wyn's imagination without boundaries—is completely reconfigured. Linda
learns self-sacrifice, Wyn loses his sense of direction, Larry imagines a
whole new future for himself. I believe all this is possible, even necessary,
but the arrows, as I drew them, stand exactly as I drew them, and the
problem as I see it is not how they come out, because they come out as
they come out, but how I can possibly explain this to Larry, to whom, if
not an icon, I owe an explanation, however unconvincing or bitter.*

3/4. I think that between Wyn and Linda something happened when he chose
Mount St. Helens over his other job offer, in Paris. I know that when he'd call from
the pay phone on the road he'd be full of the excitement of his calculations. I know,
too, that Linda never really took to Portland, never found a job or many friends,
never even bought a decent pair of cowboy boots, though for years in LA she's
regretted it.

This is not the kind of thing you can tell a boy like Larry, the white hot anger
that overcame his mother when his father just refused to bend his soul to hers. Wyn
turned hard and determined at the core, just like her. He was driven by the secret
the mountain was about to reveal. His purpose was so clear and absolute before
him, and because I know Wyn I know, too, that he'd have failed to put his ear to
Linda's belly, listening for his son's first heartbeat. When she would say, "Just here,
just below my navel," he would put his tongue instead to her neck and listen to the
wind outside, wonder did it portend something?

Nor can I tell Larry, who grew up, after all, in LA with his ad-writing, spike-
heeled mom, about the way that for his father, it was to have been his gift to his
mother, every river, every mountain, his whole capacity for love. Could I tell Larry

this? Could I tell him that of all the things Linda was cut out to be the wife of a geologist is not truly among them. She had tiny delicate feet and a penchant for luxuriant body oils and lotions, which, by these New Age Nineties have names like *Heaven* and *Earth*.

What can I say? Linda remains, after all, enigmatic to me, in part because as my replacement I cannot tell if it is her sameness or her difference that drew Wyn to her. And that was so long ago anyway. If we were alike, it was not in our bodies. She has the most beautiful neck and is tall, with those delicate feet. It was not even as if we were an equal exchange. I wouldn't really call what happened between Wyn and me "breaking up." When we parted it seemed simple, a matter more of destiny than of dissatisfaction, as if we were responding to our own magnetic poles. Of course what I did not know then and what it would take me many years to figure out was that it all came down to a mountain, any mountain, take your pick, and the question of ownership and power.

5. I have never had my nails done. Have you?

What David Bromige left out in his poem is the remainder, that intractable part of the fraction left over when one number does not go evenly into another. This happens more often than you would expect. We resist, like untidy numbers, the principle of easy division, because in our hearts we know with certainty that, like the bowls of ice cream we scoop out for our children, one is always bigger, one has more. To split two statements on the page by a black line like a fraction presupposes that they do go into one another, that there is balance and order and closure, that if anything at all is left over it is like the parabolic curve of silence that surrounded Mount St. Helens.[2] My problem is: 1. this is not enough voices, and 2. however hard I try to believe it is even possible, I mostly fail because I am plagued by the afterimage, the unsounded echo, the haunting regret, and the unruly remainder, the messy but necessary, and just as full of portent as any hot wind off a mountain.

3. Linda never really got her one big break, but she made a decent living, she made out. And she is enough of a mother to feel sufficiently haunted that the summer before Larry's thirteenth birthday they drove all the way to Washington to pay their respects to Larry's father. She did not expect to cry, but there it is. Linda writes good ads so she does not think like this, but if she did what she would think would be that at first Wyn replaced me with her, then he replaced her with the mountain, then the mountain replaced Wyn with—nothing. This, as much as anything, is the source of her tears, and also to a puzzle she has never quite worked out. Though all the available scientific data had indicated Wyn's position was safe, when the mountain went off sideways he ended up in the heart of the Inner Blast Zone. Linda's puzzle is *why: why Wyn, why there, why was everybody wrong, dead wrong?*

2. This is where history and geology collide.

5. I never really made it back to the mountains after Wyn, and I do believe, in other respects, this is also a story about that. Perhaps what I should tell Larry is that, with Wyn, it wasn't really Linda and it wasn't us and it wasn't even the baby, either baby, but something more primal and imperative. A woman loses her man to some addiction she has no interest in, like alcohol or gambling, and the first thing to go is the love between them. But when he turns away from her toward something she loves as well as him, something so simple as a way of walking through a forest or setting your sights at the top of the mountain, what she feels first is a betrayal so keen she has neither words nor breath to contain it, then with time she may feel fury as well.

This was our struggle, Wyn's and mine. Linda didn't care one way or another where Wyn spent, first his weekdays, then the rest of his life. To her a volcano was the same as a poker table, a nuisance at first, then, perhaps more and more, a reprieve. That Wyn intended it as his great gift to her is only a further aspect of the irony that ownership is like that. First you desire something, then it consumes you.

4. Someone should tell Larry that his father limped, like him, but that his father turned this disadvantage to advantage. By the time we finished high school all the girls found it sexy. Larry should probably know this.

5. Someone should tell me that, despite my protestations, this is more like a poem than a story, but of course I already know that.

6. This is what will happen: One day, when you are least expecting it, your eight-year-old son will come home with nine little slips of numbered paper and the assignment to arrange these slips of paper in three groups of three so that two will add up to the third. You will watch as your son plays with the slips of paper, shuffling and turning and arranging them, and you will see how profoundly he believes in the solution. Your son is happy, your husband is watching a ballgame on tv in the next room. Warm light pervades the room as your other son trundles sweetly off to sleep. Is it only you who has begun to worry that if not next week, then the week after, or the next, your son will bring home more slips of numbered paper, but some of these slips will be blank. From there to the point where letters will have come to take the place of numbers on your son's slips of paper, where one thing comes to represent another, it is a blink of the eye, and though you want to cry *hold,* cry *enough,* cry *you do not, oh you do not have to do this thing just yet,* you know the whole world stands against you and it is futile. For of course it is this very same principle that allowed the H-bomb to replace the A-bomb, raw space to replace what once was protective ozone, the perfect concept of a center to be replaced forever by its ever-shifting function. I know how wrong of me it is to want to stop this. I am like my students, who cleave to the principle of stable, finite meaning, who want things to be what they are, who believe that a rock is a rock, is a rock.

So you sit down with your son and his numbered slips of paper and, patiently, you help him work them out. It is what you do. You are his mother.

1. Now, thirteen years later, a forest is starting to grow on the ruins of Mount St. Helens, and we must believe that in time, a million years or so, another round

volcanic cone will rise where the massive crater is now, that this cone will be reflected in Spirit Lake below, ringed by stately forests, a whole new ecosystem. The Washington State Department of Game estimates that, on May 18, 1980, fifteen hundred elk, five thousand black-tailed deer, two hundred black bears, eleven thousand hares, fifteen mountain lions, three hundred bobcats, twenty-seven thousand grouse, fourteen hundred coyotes, and eleven million fish were killed, but because it was early Sunday morning, only a handful of people lost their lives. On the morning after a scattering of Northern pocket gophers emerged on the surface of the ash, pink-eyed and disoriented, but alive. Then there were insects, a few scattered flowers, the tender young thrust of a tree. For centuries, the Native Americans of the northwestern states stayed away from the peaks of the Cascade range out of fear and respect for the powerful spirits that inhabited them. What holds math, geology, and Larry together besides the knowledge that nothing ever holds, nothing, and that within this shifting universe of rock we should be grateful for any meaning we can get?

4. Even so, with Larry it still feels different, and thinking of him with his mother on that mountain is almost more than I can bear. He is only twelve, but the look in his eyes is chilling to Linda and to me he looks as ready to step off the trail into ash and pumice and keep on walking, like his father, off into that wilderness of rock, as he is to stay and listen to his mother.

He says, "What a way to go." He says, "I would have dived into the water in the lake." He says, "Like twenty-seven thousand atomic bombs. What's an atomic bomb like?"

Linda shrugs. There is no shade anywhere around and it's hot in the sun, intensely so. Her neck itches, she's tired, and she's also angry at herself for having forgotten how intolerable it once was to have gone hiking with Wyn.

He says, "Do you believe my daddy really died here?"

During all this time I have tried to imagine what I might have said to them, but looking now at Linda I am stymied by the blankness of our faces. When our bodies were new, mine and Wyn's, we traced each other on them with our tongues, spreading and touching and tasting, and maybe it was like that between him and Linda as well. But all that is so long ago now.

What I mean is that I do have some experience at what it's like to approach the zero and, face to face with both Linda and Larry after all these years, I do not know the difference anymore between a poem, an equation, and this story I made up. I made it up for Larry because, even now, nights, when I cannot sleep, what I think about is the look in Wyn's eyes when his mountain finally goes off. His last radio message was: *This is it.* (That is a poem.) And sometimes, too, I think about the look in Larry's eyes when he stands there on the mountain with his mother, and I wonder: *does something go off inside him too?* It is just a little story, and even as I say it I no longer know if I made it up for Larry to tell him something he should know, or to protect him from his father's power, which is, after all, how it is between fathers and sons.

Is this a metaphor?

A metaphor is also the rock Wyn brought back for me once—a fist-sized piece of lava, light as air—from the top of another volcano.

The pickle jar of ash I scooped up in Missoula.

What's left, Wyn's remainder, these words:

When your father was a young man a strange thing happened to him in the mountains.

Backpacking alone into a remote wilderness he came to a perfectly round lake, the milky jade color of glacial runoff around which swarms of hummingbirds dived and hovered. When he closed his eyes, he could hear the thrumming of their wings like an airy pulse.

That night your father was awakened by a loud crashing. In the darkness of his tent, he peered out through orange nylon made bright by the full moon. Nearby, where earlier he'd strung up his pack in the branches of a tree, he could just make out the shape of some huge animal, rummaging through his gear.

When the animal reared and lunged, your father could see it was a bear, and his body went cold and unfamiliar with fear. But the animal stopped short of the tent, sniffing and pawing at the ground as your father, a few inches away, imagined the rip of the bears' claw through his skin and did not move or breathe. Then the bear shook itself and began to rub its haunches against the tent, against your father's shoulder through the tent. In that moment of physical contact, your father's fear passed clean through him like a blade, and he was filled instead with a great feeling of peace that lingered long after the bear had lumbered away.

Then one autumn, years later, when he had once again hiked to a round glacial lake another strange thing happened to him.

On this occasion, your father again made camp and then went off to explore in the thin sunlight, wearing only a plaid flannel shirt. Among the nearby scrubbrush he was surprised to discover hundreds of empty hummingbird nests, and when he closed his eyes, it was as if he could hear them thrumming as he had that afternoon long before. Somewhat disturbed by this discovery, your father searched all afternoon for some way to explain it, and by the time he decided to turn back he had lost his sense of direction and could not relocate his camp.

As night began to fall, your father became alarmed that he would not survive the frigid temperatures, and he redoubled his effort to find his way back, but to no avail. It did not take long before he became aware of, first, extreme pain, and then a gradual numbing in his extremities. Truly frightened now, he felt certain he would die. When some time later he found himself back again among the hummingbird nests, he saw that they were made of soft dry moss and he stuffed his shirt with them, holding them in place with long strips of sugar pine bark.

Soon your father began to feel warm again and very sleepy, and it was in this state that the bear returned to him a second time.

Notes

[1]This, I recognize as dangerous, my earlier reference to traditional sex roles, my naming David Bromige male (what he is), for if you're male too and if you've got this far, all the way down to this footnote, any mention of gender, however ironic, may make you defensive, and why not? Speaking what is obvious entails more risk than we like to admit, for of course ideology retains its power exactly to the extent that it remains invisible. Naturally, you remember the emperor, never mind the basic issue of good taste. Now are you feeling defensive? Does your world seem tenuous, as never before? In the first place, you must trust me, for I know how, in many ways, to please you. And in the second, what turns language from description into judgment? As William Gass might say: "Are you afraid?"

Be nice.

[2]This, I might add, is a purely heterosexual form of communication. In the world at large a woman speaks, a man answers, and the line comes down between them, shutting off the further possibility of language. I do not know how men speak to each other. Even between my sons there is a quality of language I cannot quite decipher, however hard I listen to them talk. With women it is different, and though to this day I have never met Linda—she remains pure imagination—I still believe that if we had ever really talked to one another, between us we might have found some way of saving Wyn.

Excerpt from Hamlet

William Shakespeare

Act III.
Scene 1. *A room in the castle*

(*Enter* KING CLAUDIUS, QUEEN GERTRUDE, POLONIUS, OPHELIA, ROSENCRANTZ, *and*
  GUILDENSTERN.)
KING. And can you, by no drift of circumstance,
  Get from him why he puts on this confusion,
  Grating so harshly all his days of quiet
  With turbulent and dangerous lunacy?
ROSENCRANTZ. He does confess he feels himself distracted;
  But from what cause he will by no means speak.
GUILDENSTERN. Nor do we find him forward to be sounded,
  But, with a crafty madness, keeps aloof,
  When we would bring him on to some confession
  Of his true state.
QUEEN. Did he receive you well?
ROSENCRANTZ. Most like a gentleman.
GUILDENSTERN. But with much forcing of his disposition.
ROSENCRANTZ. Niggard of question; but, of our demands,
  Most free in his reply.
QUEEN. Did you assay him
  To any pastime?
ROSENCRANTZ. Madam, it so fell out, that certain players
  We o'er-raught on the way: of these we told him;
  And there did seem in him a kind of joy
  To hear of it: they are about the court.
  And, as I think, they have already order
  This night to play before him.
POLONIUS. 'Tis most true:
  And he beseeched me to entreat your majesties
  To hear and see the matter.
KING. With all my heart; and it doth much content me
  To hear him so inclined.
  Good gentlemen, give him a further edge,
  And drive his purpose on to these delights.
ROSENCRANTZ. We shall, my lord.
(*Exeunt* ROSENCRANTZ *and* GUILDENSTERN.)
KING.   Sweet Gertrude, leave us too;
  For we have closely sent for Hamlet hither,
  That he, as 'twere by accident, may here
  Affront Ophelia:
  Her father and myself, lawful espials,

Will so bestow ourselves that, seeing, unseen,
We may of their encounter frankly judge,
And gather by him, as he is behaved,
If 't be the affliction of his love or no
That thus he suffers for.
QUEEN. I shall obey you.
    And for your part, Ophelia, I do wish
    That your good beauties be the happy cause
40   Of Hamlet's wildness: so shall I hope your virtues
    Will bring him to his wonted way again,
    To both your honours.
OPHELIA. Madam, I wish it may.
(*Exit* QUEEN.)
POLONIUS. Ophelia, walk you here. Gracious, so please you,
    We will bestow ourselves. (*To* OPHELIA.) Read on this book;
    That show of such an exercise may color
    Your loneliness. We are oft to blame in this,—
    'Tis too much proved—that with devotion's visage
    And pious action we do sugar o'er
    The devil himself.
KING. (*aside*) O, 'tis too true!
50   How smart a lash that speech doth give my conscience!
    The harlot's cheek, beautied with plastering art,
    Is not more ugly to the thing that helps it
    Than is my deed to my most painted word:
    O heavy burthen!—
POLONIUS. I hear him coming: let's withdraw, my lord. (*Exeunt* KING CLAUDIUS *and*
    POLONIUS.)
(*Enter* HAMLET.)
HAMLET. To be, or not to be: that is the question,
    Whether 'tis nobler in the mind to suffer
    The slings and arrows of outrageous fortune,
    Or to take arms against a sea of troubles,
60   And by opposing end them? To die; to sleep;
    No more; and by a sleep to say we end
    The heart-ache and the thousand natural shocks
    That flesh is heir to, 'tis a consummation
    Devoutly to be wished. To die, to sleep;
    To sleep: perchance to dream; ay, there's the rub;
    For in that sleep of death what dreams may come
    When we have shuffled off this mortal coil,
    Must give us pause: there's the respect
    That makes calamity of so long life;
70   For who would bear the whips and scorns of time,
    The oppressor's wrong, the proud man's contumely,

The pangs of despised love, the law's delay,
The insolence of office and the spurns
That patient merit of the unworthy takes,
When he himself might his quietus make
With a bare bodkin? who would fardels bear,
To grunt and sweat under a weary life,
But that the dread of something after death,
The undiscovered country from whose bourn
No traveller returns, puzzles the will
And makes us rather bear those ills we have
Than fly to others that we know not of?
Thus conscience does make cowards of us all;
And thus the native hue of resolution
Is sicklied o'er with the pale cast of thought,
And enterprises of great pitch and moment
With this regard their currents turn awry,
And lose the name of action. —Soft you now!
The fair Ophelia! Nymph, in thy orisons
Be all my sins remembered.

OPHELIA. Good my lord,
How does your honour for this many a day?

HAMLET. I humbly thank you; well, well, well.

OPHELIA. My lord, I have remembrances of yours,
That I have longed long to re-deliver;
I pray you, now receive them.

HAMLET. No, not I;
I never gave you aught.

OPHELIA. My honoured lord, you know right well you did;
And, with them, words of so sweet breath composed
As made the things more rich: their perfume lost,
Take these again; for to the noble mind
Rich gifts wax poor when givers prove unkind.
There, my lord.

HAMLET. Ha, ha! are you honest?

OPHELIA. My lord!

HAMLET. Are you fair?

OPHELIA. What means your lordship?

HAMLET. That if you be honest and fair, your honesty should admit no discourse to
your beauty.

OPHELIA. Could beauty, my lord, have better commerce than with honesty?

HAMLET. Ay, truly; for the power of beauty will sooner transform honesty from
what it is to a bawd than the force of honesty can translate beauty into his
likeness: this was sometime a paradox, but now the time gives it proof. I did
love you once.

OPHELIA. Indeed, my lord, you made me believe so.

HAMLET. You should not have believed me; for virtue cannot so inoculate our old
120   stock but we shall relish of it: I loved you not.

OPHELIA. I was the more deceived.

HAMLET. Get thee to a nunnery; why wouldst thou be a breeder of sinners? I am
myself indifferent honest; but yet I could accuse me of such things that it were
better my mother had not borne me: I am very proud, revengeful, ambitious,
with more offences at my beck than I have thoughts to put them in,
imagination to give them shape, or time to act them in. What should such
fellows as I do crawling between earth and Heaven? We are arrant knaves, all;
133   believe none of us. Go thy ways to a nunnery. Where's your father?

OPHELIA. At home, my lord.

HAMLET. Let the doors be shut upon him, that he may play the fool no where but
in's own house. Farewell.

OPHELIA. O, help him, you sweet heavens!

HAMLET. If thou dost marry, I'll give thee this plague for thy dowry: be thou as
chaste as ice, as pure as snow, thou shalt not escape calumny. Get thee to a
nunnery, go; farewell. Or, if thou wilt needs marry, marry a fool; for wise men
know well enough what monsters you make of them. To a nunnery, go, and
146   quickly too. Farewell.

OPHELIA. O heavenly powers, restore him!

HAMLET. I have heard of your paintings too, well enough; God has given you one
face, and you make yourselves another; you jig, you amble, and you lisp, and
nick-name God's creatures, and make your wantonness your ignorance. Go to,
I'll no more on't; it hath made me mad. I say, we will have no more marriages;
those that are married already, all but one, shall live; the rest shall keep as they
are. To a nunnery, go.

(*Exit.*)

158 OPHELIA. O, what a noble mind is here o'erthrown!
    The courtier's, soldier's, scholar's, eye, tongue, sword;
160   The expectancy and rose of the fair state,
    The glass of fashion and the mould of form,
    The observed of all observers, quite, quite down!
    And I, of ladies most deject and wretched,
    That sucked the honey of his music vows,
    Now see that noble and most sovereign reason,
    Like sweet bells jangled, out of tune and harsh;
    That unmatched form and feature of blown youth
    Blasted with ecstasy: O, woe is me,
    To have seen what I have seen, see what I see!

(*Re-enter* KING *and* POLONIUS.)

170 KING. Love! his affections do not that way tend;
    Nor what he spake, though it lack'd form a little,
    Was not like madness. There's something in his soul,
    O'er which his melancholy sits on brood;
    And I do doubt the hatch and the disclose

Will be some danger: which for to prevent,
I have in quick determination
Thus set it down: he shall with speed to England,
For the demand of our neglected tribute:
Haply the seas and countries different
With variable objects shall expel
This something-settled matter in his heart,
Whereon his brains still beating puts him thus
From fashion of himself. What think you on't?
POLONIUS. It shall do well: but yet do I believe
The origin and commencement of his grief
Sprung from neglected love. How now, Ophelia!
You need not tell us what Lord Hamlet said;
We heard it all. My lord, do as you please;
But, if you hold it fit, after the play
Let his queen mother all alone entreat him
To show his grief: let her be round with him;
And I'll be placed, so please you, in the ear
Of all their conference. If she find him not,
To England send him, or confine him where
Your wisdom best shall think.
KING.   It shall be so:
Madness in great ones must not unwatched go.
(*Exeunt.*)

A Really Big Shoe

By Diana Marré

Introduction

AHH AHH AHH SHOE! (performer produces shoe from under a handkerchief as she mimes a big sneeze)

Oh! God, I'm allergic to these things. (twirling the shoe)

Okay! This piece is entitled, a Really Big Shoe, for several reasons.

One is because the high heel seems to me to be a perfect symbol of how society controlled women throughout the decades. I mean, think about it. This thing is so seductive. Don't you feel taller and more alluring and even . . . well . . . bitchy when you wear these? They are a very powerful object in many ways. They can even be used as weapons. I had one woman confess to me that after she couldn't wear them any more, she felt unarmed, and so she would carry a high heel in her purse when she had to ride the bus into downtown Chicago and it made her feel safer. But they also cause tremendous pain, and eventually most women have to give them up, which can be very traumatic. So that the high heel can be seen as a metaphor for that bizarre process called socialization, which is often the art of keeping those we love from damaging us.

Which brings me to the real reason why I am performing A Really Big Shoe for you today. We've all been "socialized". We all have that in common. Even though we may not get our names in the paper we're all important and we all bring some- thing to the mix we call society, positive and negative.

So I think it is important to set these characters down before we forget the peo- ple who affected us, even if the effort is sometimes painful. It may be hard to appre- ciate members of your family as characters because often they're causing you pain or embarrassment.

I'm introducing you to these characters from my past as examples. Why? Because the process has helped me examine attitudes they tried to pass on to me, and helped me realize which of these I want to keep and which I want to reject.

The first character I'm going to do for you is my sister, because she is the first person who tried to socialize me. She grew up during the Fifties. Her idols were Annette Funicello and Marilyn Monroe. She is ten years older than I am, and she was so excited when I was born she ran a fever for a week. When the news came that I was a girl, she screamed and jumped on all the furniture. My sister adored me. I think she thought I was her personal doll. I have her gestures and her vocal patterns. People can't tell us apart on the phone. She spent so much time with me that her early influence was enormous. I credit her with giving me my sense of humor, love of performance, optimism, dancing, and music. All huge gifts. But some of the messages she tried to give me were pretty . . . amazing. The first one I remem- ber clearly came when I was about three years old.

(Performer gets into a huge blond bouffant wig and becomes The Sister)

Diana, you're lucky! You're a girl! You don't have to BE ANYTHING! (Performer does song as The Sister)

Platinum Rock

Uh well I burnt my brains out doin' the platinum rock
I said I fried my brains out doin' the platinum rock
I've done so much peroxide my brain's about to pop

Uh well uh Mama don't like it she says that it's a sin
I couldn't care less because baby this look is in
I get dates with boys and go places I've never been

Uh well I flunked my math test I flunked biology too
I got no time to study gotta fix my new hairdo
If I keep on bleachin' I may flunk right out of school

Uh well uh I don't care, I love my hair
The ones who stare just envy the way I wear my platinum hair
I keep the boys in shock the way I do that platinum rock
I keep 'em all in shock the way I do that platinum rock
Take it! (12 bar instrumental solo)
It gives my brain a chill to do the peroxide chill
I'm on a chemical spill and I'm closin' in for the kill
It makes my brain feel ill
But I got my brain in shock the way I do that platinum rock

Uh well I blew my brains out on my platinum trip
My teacher hates it, my principal almost flipped
But I got my mind in shock by doin' that platinum rock
I said you know I got my mind in shock from doin' that platinum
Well you see me at the shoppin' mall, doin' the platinum shop
And you see me at the jewelry store, buyin' that platinum
flashin' that platinum rock
I said you see me at the sock hop dancin' to the platinum rock

Well, I was only fifteen, but I HAD to dye it blonde. And I knew Mother wouldn't let me, so I put some peroxide in it and then I dived into the pool. I knew the chlorine would spread it. So I came home crying with my beach hat pulled way down over my face, and when she asked me what was wrong, I took off my hat and there were these two big huge green stripes in my hair. And so I cried and cried and acted like it wasn't my fault, and it worked! She had to let me do the whole thing blonde! Father Mooney slammed me up against the wall at school and said it was a sin. I didn't even think he knew who I WAS! I could care less. The boys all love it. I knew they would. I'm gonna win a date with Troy Donahue now.

Come here, Diana. Would you unhook my skirt? You know, Diana, there must be something wrong with you, you never play dress-up. You don't know how much fun your missing. Why do you have to be outside all the time? And WHY do you spend so much time READING when you could be having fun? Here honey, why don't you let me fix your hair? Don't run away!

You know, now that I think about it, definitely the biggest and most lasting influence on my life was the first movie I ever saw. Mother took me to see it when I was only four years old but it made a huge impression on me. It was the Ballet of the Red Shoes. I totally identified with Moira Shearer in that movie, totally. I absolutely loved everything about it. I loved the color red and I loved the toe shoes, I loved the fact that the toe shoes were magical, and I just loved the whole story. True, Moira Shearer throws herself in front of a speeding train at the end, but that's not the part that got to me. What impressed me was that she HAD to dance, and I felt like I HAD to dance too. I wanted to BE Moira Shearer, I wanted to dance in the spotlight. So Mother let me start ballet the next year, when I was five. And I DID dance in the spotlight, and it WAS magical. I got better and better, and I got bigger and bigger parts, and it was fabulous, and Daddy ran the spotlight for every production.

But, after awhile, after I went on pointe, I realized that the red in the red shoes meant BLOOD. (Performer puts pink toes shoes with blood red toes, fastened to a pink ribbon, around her neck) Blood in the toe shoes. But I had this image of myself as the stoical ballerina, you know. Toughing it out backstage. And I'd just change my pads and lace up the toe shoes and get back out there. In terrible pain, but smiling all the time, never letting anybody know how much torture I was suffering. And I just did it. Hell, by then I had no choice. All anybody knew was that I was the ballerina. I had my picture in the paper all the time, you know, small town USA. So I had to do it. It was who I was.

And then I started up a dancing school in a little bitty town, riding the bus with my record player three times a week, so I had money, and I was the best dressed kid in school. So when I started wearing high heels when I was fourteen, I had no idea how much they were hurting me because my feet killed me all the time anyway. I would wake up in the middle of the night with these terrible terrible cramps in my calf muscles, and sometimes I couldn't get my heel on the floor for two hours. It was torture. But when I was out there in the spotlight, it was all worth it. And like Moira Shearer in The Red Shoes, I really believed I could be the greatest dancer in the world.

So, okay. I tried the life of a professional dancer. I danced with the Ballet Russe de Monte Carlo in New York. I danced with the San Francisco Ballet for one season. I even went on tour. And I found out that I'm just not that dedicated. Who wants to starve themselves and live like a gypsy? So I quit and got this job as a shoe model. Diana, I can make much more than I ever could as a dancer, and the best part of it is, I get to keep all the shoes! Isn't that great, Diana? I've only been doing it for two years and I already have over a hundred and fifty pairs of heels! Thanks to all those years of ballet, I have the legs for it.

Oh yeah, I'm sure Gary will make me quit when we get married. He doesn't want me to work. No, no, that's okay. I've had enough of working to last me for the rest of my life. Let him take care of me. I'll be perfectly happy to sit by the pool and paint my nails and drink Pepsi out of a champagne glass. But in the meantime, I'm having so much fun! Modeling shoes is so much easier on me than dancing. All I have to do is stand there in heels for eight hours a day, and just because I can wear a 5B and I have the legs for it, they pay me all this money and I get to keep the samples! I've already got a walk-in closet full.

So yeah, Gary did make me quit when we got married, but I had way over two hundred pairs of shoes by then, so why not? No, it didn't bother me a bit. No, no, I didn't feel guilty about it, I was ready to stay home anyway. But I think it did bother him that I could make more money at one show than he could in a whole month, and I think it bothered him too that I got so much attention from the shoe salesmen and the buyers. Him being a salesman, he knew what that was all about. But with him gone on the road all week long, I did get bored. I didn't mind so much after our daughter, Tammy, was born. She kept me company. But then after she started school, I really got bored again. I kept my tan all year round, I finally got a boob job.

Oh Diana! Don't you dare give me that Women's Lib crap! What do you know about it? You don't understand it because you never had the problem, that's all. You never even wanted those big boobs, they just got in your way. You don't know how it is, you never had to wear padded bras, you never had to subsidize Goodyear Tire and Rubber all you life. Shut up! You're just trying to scare me with all those statistics. I don't want to hear about cancer! You're just trying to make me feel guilty, just like Mother. You're getting all this crap out of those books you're always reading. Big deal. Look at me. I've never read a book cover to cover in my life and I'm doing just fine. So lay off me! Come on, pal, I really need you to be supportive of me right now. I'm having a rough time with Gary.

You know I told you we joined this Swinging Doubles group. No, it's not tennis. It's, well, it's group sex. Well, so what? For Christ sake, Diana, don't tell me you have a moral problem with it. You're a lesbian. Anyway, the point is, I finally realized what you've been trying to tell me all these years, nobody can own me. Gary is too possessive. He's so jealous of Dennis, this wonderful connection I made at Swinging Doubles, he just can't handle it. So I'm calling you to tell you we're getting a divorce. Dennis and I want to get married.

What's the matter? You don't like him? Why? Is it because of the way Dennis acted at your show? Oh Diana. Well, it was just that he was having such a great time. He loved your show! I know he stood up on his chair. I know, I know he made siren noises. I know, I know he threw limes from his drink at the actors during the curtain call. But it was just that he was so nervous about meeting you. He wanted you to know how much he liked it. Look Diana, when I tell you how he handled the situation with Tammy yesterday, I know you'll change your mind about him.

Well, Tammy came over here yesterday to move all her stuff out. She's moving into an apartment with Gary. He's hiring a housekeeper to be there with her during the week while he's out of town. Well, Diana, she's sixteen, she can drive. I mean, it's not like she's a baby. She's been a real shit to Dennis and she's been very unsupportive of me through this whole thing, so I didn't even want custody of her. When she came over to get her stuff I didn't even want to see her, so I was up in my room with the door closed watching TV, and Dennis let her in. Even after the way she's treated him, he was trying to be nice. So she gets all of her stuff out and I thought she'd left, and then she came and knocked on my door. She said, "Mother, do you have my boots? I can't find them." Well Diana, these were some boots I had paid for half of and I thought it was very selfish of her. Especially after the way she's been acting. It was the principle of the thing, you can understand that, can't you? So I said, "I don't know where they are, Tammy. If you can find them you can have them."

So do you know what she did? She went into the spare bedroom, you know, where I have my walk-in shoe closet, and she threw every single shoe I own all over the room! I mean, there must be five hundred shoes in there. It took her half an hour. I mean, the bed was completely covered and you couldn't even walk in there! It was crazy, completely crazy. Of course, she didn't find her boots because they were in the closet in the room with me. She was hysterical, completely hysterical, and I heard her slamming doors on her way out. And then, Dennis did the sweetest thing, Diana. He came up to my room and he knocked on my door and asked if he could come in and I said yes. And he came over and sat down on the bed and he put his hand on my arm and he said, "Honey, is a pair of boots really worth sacrificing your relationship with your daughter?" So I gave the boots to him and he took them down and gave them to Tammy just as she was pealing out of the driveway. Now Diana, you have to admit, that's an amazing story.

Oh Diana, I'm so depressed. I didn't know who else to call. I'm sorry to wake you up so late, but I just had to talk to somebody. I don't know what I'm going to do. Something terrible happened today. It's like a turning point in my life. I finally went to the Doctor today. I've been having a lot of trouble with my ankles for the past few months. They've been swelling a lot, and hurting. And then lately my knees have been aching. I had no idea what it was. The weather maybe, I didn't know. I kept thinking it would go away, but it didn't. It got to the point that I could barely walk. So finally I made an appointment, and today I went. He asked me a bunch of questions, he took some X-rays, he drained some fluid off my knees, and he left the room. When he came back, I could tell by the expression on his face what he was going to say. I said, "Oh no. You're going to tell me, I'm OLD!" Oh Diana, I've got bursitis in both ankles and osteo-arthritis in my knees. He said, he said I can only wear heels THREE TIMES A YEAR! That's Christmas, Easter, and ONE OFFICE PARTY! I've got over two hundred pairs of shoes I can't wear any more! Oh Diana, this means I'm old, I'm old, I know it does, I know it does. . . . .

Diana, why on earth would you want my shoe collection? They don't fit you. You're doing a show? Oh. Well, I'd give them to you but I don't have them any more. I left them in Kansas City when I left Dennis. And once again, thank God you were there to bail me out, pal. You'll never know how grateful I am. Talk about a hundred and eighty pound tumor I needed to lose. Thank God for you Diana. I might never have left him if you hadn't been there. But I left all those high heels in Kansas City. No, it's not what you think. I..I was still wearing them, after I couldn't wear them any more. The reason I left all those heels there was because Dennis wanted me to wear them, in bed. He expected it. No, I hated it! It made me feel like a whore. Well, Diana, it's not his fault. A lot of things about Dennis weren't his fault, his drinking, his ideas about women. He couldn't help it, he had this uncle who screwed him up when he was little, took him to whorehouses when he was twelve years old, taught him how to drink. And he just couldn't get into it unless I was all dressed up in the heels, platforms sometimes like the prostitutes wear, and the garter belt and the whole bit. I hated that. I said it made me feel like a whore and I told him that when I left him, that last weekend when we were together at the lake where we had a time share, and it was supposed to be such a romantic weekend. Oh yeah right. And he got drunk and embarrassed me in the restaurant as usual. And I left him at the table and walked back to the room, and I had on these red leather heels that always killed my feet, and I took them off and threw one against the wall, and it left a big red mark on that white wall, like a streak of blood, and I said, "I am never gonna wear this shit again!" And I told Dennis that, I said, "I am never gonna wear this shit again," and I asked him, "what was wrong with my naked body? Why did I have to wear all that shit? What was wrong with my naked body?"

Oh Diana, don't ask me that. I don't know. No, I never got off on it, I told you I hated it. I don't know why I did it, he just expected it of me and I didn't know any better. Hell, I don't know why women do any of the things we do, Diana. Aunt Cecile wore corsets all her life and cut off two of her toes to wear her heels. It was just the look you had to have and she just didn't question it, she just toughed it out. I don't know why I did it. I'm so humiliated I can barely admit it to you, even though I love you. I hate myself for ever allowing it to happen. I don't know what else to say, Diana. I just didn't know any better. (Performer does song, Killer Shoes)

Killer Shoes

The slipper was a dagger that plunged into my heart
seducing me with images it tore my soul apart

It spoke to me through music it sang to me in song
commanding me to dance and so I tried to dance along

It offered me a role it promised mystery and romance
I long for an identity and so I took a chance

Glamour is God
That's what they said
Wear them on stage
Wear them in bed

Suffering silently
Swallowing tears
Why did I keep it up
Year after year

Painful recollections now make me wonder why
women have for centuries bought into the lie

Flattery is powerful it's so hard to deny
truth is very hard to hear but still I have to try

Killer shoes were made for you
not for men to wear
killer shoes designed for you by
people who don't care

But you don't have to join the club because I've paid your dues
Listen to what happened to me don't wear killer shoes

Please listen to what happened to me don't wear killer shoes
walk another avenue don't wear killer shoes

(Takes off Sister Wig, bloody toes shoes from around her neck, to become Diana again)

Well, as you can see, my sister's example was ambivalent for me. Even though I got some wonderful things from her, some of her values I had to reject. Her notion of femininity: that it is smart to be dumb, that dependency on men is natural, and that the inability to wear high heels means you are totally washed up as a person, was not for me. Also her idea that being gay puts you on a moral footing with serial killers and sexual omnivores was not one that I could accept. And even though I still love her, and have tremendous sympathy for what she's been through, high fashion and homophobia are areas where we will never agree.

My mother is the next person who had a profound effect on me. And I got some wonderful things from her too. She gave me a love of travel, and literature, and an expectation of success. She encouraged me to excel academically and musically. She was my first piano teacher too. All huge gifts. Although she is physically tiny, my mother is concentrated, like nuclear waste. A little goes a long way.

(Performer puts on little old lady wig, pink linen jacket, and draws on wrist-length white gloves to become The Mother)

Suffering is not a state that comes voluntarily to us, it is a state that must be cultivated. Because we cannot get to heaven without it, it is lucky that we have to suffer for fashion. We can offer it up to the Baby Jesus. Suffering and respectability are the two things we must cultivate for salvation, no matter what temptations lie in our path. Pleasure, or hedonism, is the greatest temptation we face in our pursuit of suffering and respectability. So now I want to ask you all to join me in a hymn to anhedonia, which is the hatred of pleasure. Anhedonia is the opposite of hedonism. You will find the words to our anthem printed on your programs. Now would you all please rise and join us in singing, "Hail Anhedonia," my favorite hymn.

Hail Anhedonia

(To the tune of "All Hail The Power of Jesus' Name")
All hail the power of Anhedonia for pleasure is a sin
Obsession with the pleasure principle
Accounts for the shape we are in

All hail the power of Anhedonia for pleasure is a mortal sin
All hail the power of Anhedonia have sex just once a year
And don't enjoy it when you do
You might turn into a queer
The point of sex is reproduction and not to like it or have fun

Resist the theme of pleasure this culture tries to sell
Turn off your television set
Avoid the pain of hell
If you are used to movies and TV you'll like the bible just as well

Use moderation in all things don't run when you could walk
Chew each bite at least thirty-two times
And when your mouth's full don't talk
Sit straight act right don't play with silverware
And when your mouth is full don't talk
Amen

Well. Thank you, thank you all so much. That was just lovely. That was wonderful. I suppose I should introduce myself to you all. My maiden name was White, and Mother named me after my Aunt Rowena, but my little brother couldn't pronounce Rowena so they nicknamed me Piggy, because I was so plump as a baby. Well my little brother couldn't pronounce Piggy either so he called me BeeBee. Well, that got shortened to Bee, and it stuck. So up until I married Raymond Marré when I was twenty-five, everybody knew me as Bee White. So I used to have a little saying, I used to always say, "Be cute, be quiet, be White!"

I am blessed with a very small foot, in fact I wear a four double-A shoe, and so for years I had to order all my shoes from Cinderella Bootery of Boston. Here, I even have one of there little boxes to show you all. But they didn't really make my size, so I had to order the four B. So for years I had a little joke about that. I'd say, "Look you all, these are FOR BEE!"

I would have entered the convent when I became a convert to the Catholic faith at the age of eighteen, but my Mother wouldn't give her consent. She was a Baptist. My Daddy was Catholic, and I was fortunate to be able to attend Catholic schools and there I first met the good sisters. And now, I've finally been given the honor of being asked to be an Associate Member of the Sisters of Mercy. I am the first one to be given this honor in the whole state. Yes. Well, I feel blessed, I just feel blessed, and I thank the good Lord every day. I have a wonderful job in the gift shop out at the Catholic hospital and I get to hear daily Mass in the chapel with the sisters. I have wonderful friends, I have a wonderful car, I have a wonderful place to live. And of course, I have Jenny, my colored girl. I call her my good right arm. Yes I've had Jenny now for twenty-seven years and I don't know what I'd do without her. She's like one of the family. She can't dust, but she cleans like the black tornado. We have a little joke about that. Yes, she takes care of me all right, and I give her everything I can't use and believe me, she's grateful for anything. My children used to come along and try to throw things out of the refrigerator, like maybe a roast that smelled old, and I'd say, "Wait just a minute! Jenny can feed nine children and a husband out of that." I'm just glad I can still keep her. And of course I donate to the missions too. I have my two pet charities, one in Mississippi and one in New Orleans. And they do so much for those poor colored people. And when I take my train trips down to visit my relatives in Miami, I always stop there, and they treat me like a queen. Just like a queen. I feel like a Queen for a Day, every day!

Oh I do love the train. I love the beautiful scenery, and these nice colored boys just wait on you hand and foot. I took a train trip out to Seattle last spring to visit my daughter Diana.

Well, yes Diana, I'm happy to bring you this Cinderella shoebox, but I can't imagine why you want it. You're doing a little show? About shoes? Well how cute. It's funny you should ask me about spiked heels. Oh yes, I should say I did wear them. Heavens to Betsy, I should say I did. I was famous for my heels. Why I wore them to all the dances and I loved them. In fact, my brothers used to tease me about my high heels, they used to say, "Why Bee wouldn't be caught dead emptying the garbage without her high heels," and Daddy would add, "in the DARK!" But I always liked the open-toed shoes, not like my friend, Francie, she loves those pointy pointy toes. Oh yes she does. Why, even now, and here we are all up into our seventies, she won't give up those pointy toed shoes, oh no. She goes to see a podiatrist all the time. I don't know what he does to her, but he keeps trying to get her to give up those pointy toes and she just won't. We do get attached to them, and of course you remember how your sister kept on wearing her high heels even when she was pregnant with Tammy. Even with her hip out of place. And I could understand it because I did love my heels.

Why did I stop wearing them? Oh well, now that I think of it, it must have been because I started having my children. Yes that must have been it. Like, for instance, when I started having to carry your brother Louis around to the doctor and places, I couldn't wear them any more. Why, Louis weighed almost ten pounds when he was born and I only weighed eighty-five, so right away you could see it would be dangerous for me to try and carry him in those heels.

Yes, everything changes when you have your children. The happiest time in my life was when they were little, before they reached the age of reason. They have all been disappointments at one time or another, but Diana has been the greatest disappointment of all. I loved her so much. I had such high hopes for her. Everybody did. She was so special. She was everybody's favorite. Before she developed her . . . personality . . .

Diana Katherine! Where have you been young lady? You are filthy from top to bottom! Have you been under the house? And climbing trees? Young lady, you just march yourself right straight into that bathroom and make yourself presentable for the table. And put something on your feet! Now sit up straight, Diana. Quit playing with your silverware. Yes, these things do matter, I don't care what you think. Well, your thinking is just wrong. No, not WHAT you're thinking . . . no, no, not specifically WHAT you're thinking . . . it's just . . . it's the PROCESS..it's the IDEA that you're . . . it's the FACT that you're thinking that's wrong Diana. Yes! It's wrong. You've got to learn to stop this thinking. It's dangerous and you don't need it! What? Original? You want to be original! Why, Diana, that's the first sin of all, Original Sin. If you want to win salvation you'll stop it right this minute!

Diana, I cannot understand how anyone with your background, with your intelligence, with your education, can choose to look like a troll! You will march right straight into that bathroom and you will shave off that unsightly hair on those legs this minute young lady, or you'll wish you had! I don't care what they do in Europe, you are back in a civilized country now and you'll act accordingly. And why have you stopped wearing make-up? I understand that you were camping over there, but you've been home for three weeks. What? Oh! Oh!! Don't you dare speak to me in that tone of voice young lady! How dare you use that argument? Yes, I know. I know that animal products form the basis of most cosmetics. Yes, it's true that we spend more on lipstick in this country than we give to the missions. But Diana, what you omit when you use that moral argument, is that sometimes, wearing make-up can be an act of CHARITY!

All right young lady, come in here and sit down. I'm only going to have this discussion once. You will not go out with that boy ever again, do you hear me? He is not the class of person you should be associating with. What will people think? What will people say? He works in the kitchen at the hospital. And, he's Filipino Diana! Well, if you don't care, I do. I'll make sure you don't receive any of his phone calls, and if I find out you're seeing him behind my back, you won't go out at all.

Diana Katherine, come in here. Sit down. We have to have another little talk. That boy cannot come over here any more. I know he's your partner in the city tournament. Too bad. You'll just have to forfeit. The other boys on the tennis team are welcome over here any time, but you are not to play with him ever again. Why? Do you mean to tell me you don't know? He's black, Diana! Why, even Jenny says it's creating the wrong impression. Jenny! Jenny! Please come in here a second. See? See Diana? Even Jenny here says that boy only has one thing on his mind, isn't that right, Jenny? Thank you Jenny. You can go on back to the kitchen. See Diana, even Jenny can understand the situation. Why can't you? Well, it's up to you to tell him. I don't care how you handle it. I don't care if he has to wait out in the alley when they all come over for you, he will not step foot into this house again. And if I find out you've disobeyed me, you'll have to quit the tennis team. It's up to you.

Raymond! Go unpack the car. Just do as I say. I know you packed it in the heat of the day, I don't care. She's not going. Sit down, Diana. Young lady, you are in serious, serious trouble. Look at this. I have been intercepting your mail for the last six weeks, ever since you came home from summer school. This is a pack of filth. You have been choosing the wrong companions again. Raymond, unpack the car. She's not leaving for college tomorrow. You're not going anywhere, young lady. You are going to live right here until I can see that you're straightened out and are worthy of trust before you go anywhere. I was willing to lend you money for your education, but not now. If you think I'm going to finance your journey down the path to hell you've got another think coming young lady. Raymond, go unpack the car. Well, yes, Diana, you do have some loyal friends, people who would vouch for your character, I know that. Some of them are even my age or older, some of them are teachers and even nuns, which does show that they are people with some judgment. Some of them do love you, but they don't know you like I know you. They wouldn't love you if they were your Mother.

Well, I'm happy to be able to tell you all that my daughter Diana is finally on the right path. I admit that I was wrong about her. The low point was that awful night, after Raymond's funeral, when she got drunk in the front yard. She and Raymond were very close, certainly much closer than he and Louis were, or even he and Jeannie, and I realize she was upset. And when she saw Raymond's obituary on the front page of the paper she was so impressed by it, she said to her brother, "Oh Louis, look. Daddy's obituary is on the front page." And he said, "It must have been a slow day."

I don't think he meant any harm by it, he's just naturally so sarcastic, but she reacted strongly and I know it hurt her. So I knew she was upset, but Law! I heard her out there after midnight, drinking and carrying on so, and I woke Louis up and I said, "What is Diana doing out there in the front yard with that bottle?" And he said, "She's seldom without it." And then he looked through her luggage and he found, a marijuana cigarette! I was horrified. Drugs! In my house! And then Jeannie showed me bottles and bottles of alcohol hidden in the cabinets in Diana's bedroom. And I thought she had come home from Seattle to drink and drug her way through all of it. And then . . . and then . . . they both told me that . . . Diana was a l—, that Diana was g—, that her feelings for women had been . . . sinful . . . and I . . . I believed them.

So the next day, I told her to go. I told her that she didn't deserve a thing of her Father's and that I wanted her out of town immediately. I told her that she was in serious, serious, trouble, that she was an alcoholic and a drug addict and a . . . and a sick, sick girl. I wanted her to get on the first bus back to Tulsa and take the first plane back to Seattle, get herself into treatment, and ask for the grace of God and for forgiveness. I wasn't about to let her destroy the reputation I had built in this town. I have to live here!

Later, of course, I found out that someone she knew in high school had given her that cigarette at the cemetery. I guess he thought it would comfort her somehow, but anyway she did not bring it home with her. And then I found out that she had saved all that alcohol from her Father's office, to give to people who came up there once in awhile to have a drink. I would have just thrown it out. So, of course, none of it was true. And now I've seen the way she's living, and it's just fine, it's just wonderful, so it couldn't possibly be true, any of it. She has an apartment with a view and a dishwasher, she drives a nice car, she teaches at a brick school, so none of it is true! And I'm so relieved, and grateful, and thankful THANKFUL that she's on the right path. My conscience is clear about Diana now, and I can admit that I was wrong. And I can live in peace now, in the knowledge that I'm not a failure.

(Performer takes off wig and costume to become Diana again)

Well, as you can see, even though I got some wonderful things from her, I can't accept my mother's version of religion. I can't accept her ideas that thinking is wrong, make-up is charity, and that working class people and people of color are beneath me. And I have to disagree that being gay is a sin, or that suffering for fashion puts stars in anybody's crown. So even though I still love my mother, we disagree on these fundamental principles.

It's not hard to see the last of the women I'll do for you, my great aunt Cecile, as a character. She was so eccentric the whole town considered her a "character" long before I was born. She was a very formidable person, very tall, very rich, very independent. I got some important things from her: the notion that women could BE independent, make their own living, and not be dependent on men for their identity, that women could have their own income and run their own lives. Given the messages I was getting from my sister, this influence of my Aunt's was critical. Also, she adopted my Daddy and he obviously loved her, and that was an important factor in my feelings for her too. My Daddy's parents abandoned him when he was four years old after they divorced, and he spent four years in an orphanage before his father's sister, his aunt Cecile, came and got him and brought him up in her household. Since I loved him so much, I had to love her for rescuing him.

Aunt Cecile was the personification of high fashion. She wore whale bone corsets and killer high heels, and I later found out that she went so far as to have two of her toes amputated so she could wear the pointed toes and four inch heels. You don't want to cut off your little toes, because you lose your balance without those. We have no statistics to estimate how many female amputees blew over in a high wind before they figured this out, but we do know that it's the two toes right next to the little toes that are best to eliminate. From wearing high heels so much, Aunt Cecile's Achilles tendons became permanently shortened, so that eventually high heels were the only shoes she COULD wear. I remember her bedroom slippers. Gold lamé mules with roses embroidered on the toes.

Anyway, she used to get up in high Southern Gothic drag every afternoon to walk her dogs. You would think somebody like her would go for poodles with painted toenails, or afghan hounds or some classy dog, but no. She would go to the Pound and adopt these scruffy mongrels my sister and I called The Black Mange, and then she would feed them Kentucky Fried Chicken and Sara Lee Pound cake until they all blew up and died of cancer of the colon and rectal failure. She also drove Cadillacs, brand new every other year.

She refused to stop driving, even after she went blind at eighty. One day she hit five parked cars in a row on Grand Avenue, and then Daddy had her taken to a rest home. But she escaped from there one night after midnight by calling a cab and having him sound the horn till she could find him. She went through a fire door and set off the alarms and everything. Once she got home, she kept a handgun near her at all times and she would just open fire any time she heard things, so when she finally died at the age of ninety, they found bullet holes in all the woodwork. Obviously nobody had the nerve to try and pry her out of there again. Anyway, I'll do her theme song for you now, a little country waltz called, "Two Toes To Lose," and then I'll do a little bit of Aunt Cecile.

(Performer puts on white satin heels with red blood streaks over the amputated toes areas, long black gloves, flashy earrings and necklace, and a black, wide-brimmed hat with a red rose at the crown to become The Great Aunt)

Two Toes to Lose

I've got two toes to lose then I'll fit in my shoes
I won't have the blues any more
I can walk down the street with no pain in my feet
If I just lose those two tiny toes

I've worn corsets for years so I don't really fear amputation
If the pain in my feet can be cured by one neat mutilation
Then I'll do it and prove it can

Make my shoes fit and not hurt a bit
No matter how pointed or high
I can take heels in stride if I swallow my pride
And amputate two tiny toes

There'll be pain in my feet but it just can't compete
With the power of the pump
And the kind of control that takes over my soul
It's called fashion It's called passion for fashion it's

Hard to admit but I'll never quit
'Cause I have to wear heels with my clothes
but I'll take heels in stride when I follow my pride
And amputate two tiny toes
I'll just cut off those two tiny toes

Raymond? You and Diana just wait there on the porch for a minute, I'm changing my clothes from my walk with Blackie. Whooee! It sure is hot out there! Well, here we are. Let's all just sit out here on the screened in porch, under the fan where it's a little cooler. I need a mint julep, how about you all? Raymond? Diana? Oh, let her have some Raymond, it won't hurt her. Did you bring your guitar? Well let's have us a tune honey. Here's twenty dollars for you. My you sure are playin' that guitar so pretty. Here's another twenty dollars for you. You can rest a minute and then you can play some more. I haven't heard "Harbor Lights" or "Peg O' My Heart." My my you sure have got talent. I never would have thought you'd amount to anything, after you ate that tuna out of the cat dish on the kitchen floor, I can tell you that. Barely two years old. I'll swan you came toddlin' out here with your cheeks just bulgin' with tuna, right off the floor. And now here you are, sittin' up so pretty and playin' such pretty music. I never would have believed it. Play me another tune honey.

Raymond, here's a fifty dollar bill for another month's lessons for her. More mint julep? Oh, it won't hurt her. Here, Blackie. Have some ice cream. Yes, Blackie, you're such a good dog. Yessir, you are. Kill? Kill, you can stop now. You're a good nigger. And you're a good dog, Blackie, yes. Kill, you know it's over a hundred degrees out there. Yes, you go on around to the kitchen and get you a nice cool drink of water now. Yes, you're a good nigger, and you're gonna be drivin' a Cadillac when I die. Bless his heart, he's so simple. He really believes me when I tell him I'm gonna will him that car. Whooee!

Why'd you stop playin' honey? What do you mean, I shouldn't call him a nigger? I call him a good nigger don't I? Oh, I know. You want me to say colored. Well, let me tell you somethin' miss smarty pants. I had an Indian woman correct me right smart one time, for callin' a nigger colored. That's right. She took offense. She said to me, "Miz Cecile, I'm colored, and I'm not a nigger!" So you have to call a nigger a nigger honey. Otherwise you might hurt somebody's feelin's. Here's another twenty dollars for you honey, why don't you play us some more pretty music?

(She removes the Great Aunt costume and comes back to Diana)

Well, that's about all I can stand to do of her!

It's obvious that my Aunt Cecile's racism is what I had to reject about her. Even though I admired her independence, I hated her attitudes. I can't help but notice that she was the most physically mutilated of all these women I've presented, and also the most spiritually mutilated. I think there must be a connection there. Maybe she was such a hateful bitch because her feet were killing her all the time. We'll never know. But all three of them had high heels in common. Cruel shoes, cruel attitudes, it's taken me a long time to kick them off.

That concludes my performance, and you've been a wonderful audience! Before I open this up to questions, I'd like to end with a quote from Audre Lord.

How much of this truth can I bear to see

And still live unblinded?

How much of this pain can I use?

Suggested Reading

Reference Books

Crystal, David, ed. *The Cambridge Encyclopedia of Language.* 2nd ed. New York: Cambridge U. Press, 1997.

Hollander, John. *Rhyme's Reason: A Guide to English Verse.* New Haven: Yale U. Press, 1989.

Ousby, Ian, ed. *The Cambridge Guide to Literature in English.* 2nd. ed. Cambridge: Cambridge U. Press, 1994.

Padgett, Ron. *A Handbook of Poetic Forms.* New York: Teachers and Writers Collaborative, 1987.

Partridge, Eric. *Origins: A Short Etymological Dictionary of Modern English.* New York: Greenwich House, 1983.

Pickering, David, Alan Isaac's, and Elizabeth Martin, eds. *Brewer's Dictionary of Twentieth-Century Phrase and Fable.* New York: Houghton Mifflin, 1992.

Preminger, Alex, Frank J. Warnke, O.B. Hardison, et al., eds. *The Princeton Encyclopedia Of Poetry and Poetics.* Princeton: Princeton U. Press, 1974. Rev. 1996.

Shapiro, Karl and Robert Beum. *A Prosody Handbook.* New York: Harper and Row, 1965.

Anthologies

Bishop, Wendy, ed. *The Subject Is Writing: Essays By Teachers and Students.* 2nd ed. Portsmouth, N.H.: Boynton/Cook, 1998.

Bly, Robert. *Leaping Poetry.* Boston: Beacon Press, 1977.

Brown, Stewart, Mervyn Morris, and Gordon Rohlehr, eds. *An Anthology of Oral and Related Poetry from the Caribbean.* London: Longman, 1989.

Charters, Anne. *The Story and Its Writer: An Introduction to Short Fiction.* 3rd ed. New York: St. Martin's, 1990.

Erdoes, Richard and Alfonso Ortiz, eds. *American Indian Myths and Legends.* New York: Pantheon, 1984. [*See also numerous other titles in the Pantheon Fairy Tale and Folklore Library.*]

Ferguson, Margaret, Mary Jo Salter, and Jon Stallworthy, eds. *The Norton Anthology Of Poetry.* 4th ed. New York: Norton, 1996.

Gilbert, Sandra and Susan Gubar, eds. *The Norton Anthology of Literature by Women: The Traditions in English.* 2nd ed. New York: Norton, 1996.

Hagedorn, Jessica, ed. *Charlie Chan Is Dead: An Anthology of Asian-American Fiction.* New York: Penguin, 1993.

Ibieta, Gariella, ed. *Latin American Writers: Thirty Stories.* Boston: St. Martin's, 1993.

McMillan, Terry, ed. *Breaking Ice: An Anthology of Contemporary African-American Fiction.* New York: Penguin, 1990.

Moraga, Cherrie and Gloria Anzaldua, eds. *This Bridge Called My Back: Writing By Radical Women of Color.* New York: Kitchen Table Press, 1983.

Ochester, Ed, and Peter Oresick, eds. *The Pittsburgh Book of Contemporary American Poetry.* Pittsburgh: U. of Pittsburgh Press, 1993.

Ostrom, Hans. *Lives and Moments: An Introduction to Short Fiction.* Ft. Worth: Holt, Rinehart, and Winston, 1993.

Pack, Robert, Sydney Lea, and Jay Parini, eds. *The Bread Loaf Anthology of Contemporary American Poetry.* Middlebury: U. Presses of New England, 1985.

Reed, Ishmael, Kathryn Trueblood, and Shawn Wong, eds. *The Before Columbus Foundation Fiction Anthology: Selections from the American Book Awards, 1980–1990.* New York: Norton, 1992.

Warnock, John, ed. *Representing Reality: Readings in Literary Nonfiction.* New York: St. Martin's, 1989.

Criticism and Theory

Anderson, Chris, ed. *Literary Nonfiction: Theory, Criticism, Pedagogy.* Carbondale: Southern Illinois U. Press, 1989.

Bishop, Wendy and Hans Ostrom, eds. *Colors of a Different Horse: Rethinking Creative Writing Theory and Pedagogy.* Urbana: National Council of Teachers of English, 1994.

Booker, M. Keith. *Literary Theory and Criticism: A Practical Guide.* New York: Longman, 1996.

Chiseri-Strater, Elizabeth. *Academic Literacies: The Public and Private Discourse Of University Students.* Portsmouth, N.H.: Boynton/Cook, 1991.

Davis, Robert Con and Ronald Schleifer. *Contemporary Literary Criticism: Literary And Cultural Studies.* 3rd. ed. New York: Longman, 1994.

Eagleton, Terry. *Ideology.* New York: Longman, 1994.

Gabriel, Susan L. and Isaiah Smithson. *Gender in the Classroom: Power and Pedagogy.* Urbana: U. of Illinois Press, 1990.

Gates, Henry Louis. *The Signifying Monkey: A Theory of African-American Literary Criticism.* New York: Oxford U. Press, 1988.

Howaston, M.C., ed. *The Oxford Companion to Classical Literature.* 2nd. Ed. New York: Oxford U. Press, 1989.

Lodge, David, ed. *Modern Criticism and Theory: A Reader.* New York: Longman, 1989.

Lohafer, Susan and JoEllen Clary. *Short Story Theory at a Crossroads.* Baton Rouge: Lousiana State University Press, 1989.

Richter, David, ed. *Narrative/Theory.* New York: Longman, 1996. *[Includes glossary of Terms.]*

Tobin, Lad. *Writing Relationships: What Really Happens in the Composition Class.* Portsmouth, N.H.: Boynton/Cook, 1993.

Wellek, Rene. *A History of Modern Criticism.* 8 volumes. New Haven: Yale U. Press, 1955–92.

Books on Writing

Behn, Robin and Chase Twichell, eds. *The Practice of Poetry: Writing Exercises From Poets Who Teach.* New York: Harper Perennial, 1992.

Bellamy, Joe David. *The New Fiction: Interviews with Innovative American Writers.* Chicago: U. of Chicago Press, 1974.

Bishop, Wendy. *Released Into Language.* Urbana: National Council of Teachers of English, 1990.

Bishop, Wendy. *13 Ways of Looking for a Poem.* New York: Addison Wesley Longman: 2000.

Coltelli, Laura, ed. *Winged Words: American Indian Writers Speak.* Lincoln: U. Of Nebraska Press, 1990.

Dembo, L.S., ed. *Interviews with Contemporary Writers: Second Series, 1972–1982.* Madison: U. of Wisconsin Press, 1983.

Elbow, Peter. *Writing Without Teachers.* New York: Oxford U. Press, 1977.

Gardner, John. *The Art of Fiction: Notes on Craft for Young Writers.* New York: Knopf, 1984.

Gardner, John. *On Becoming a Novelist.* New York: Harper and Row, 1983.

Huddle, David. *The Writing Habit: Essays.* Salt Lake City: Gibbs-Smith/Peregrine Smith, 1991.

Hugo, Richard. *The Triggering Town: Lectures and Essays on Poetry and Writing.* New York: Norton, 1979.

Kirby, David. *Word Weaving: Where Poems Come From and How to Write Them.* Boston: The Writer, 1989.

Murray, Donald. *Shoptalk: Learning to Write With Writers.* Portsmouth, N.H.: Boynton/Cook, 1990.

Shelnutt, Eve. *The Writing Room: Keys to the Craft of Fiction and Poetry.* Marietta, Georgia: Longstreet Press, 1989.

Stafford, William. *Writing the Australian Crawl: View on the Writer's Vocation.* Ann Arbor: Michigan U. Press, 1978.

Stein, Gertrude. *How to Write.* New York: Dover, 1975.

Turner, Alberta. *To Make A Poem.* New York: Longman, 1982.

Willis, Meredith Sue. *Personal Fiction Writing: A Guide to Writing from Real Life for Teachers, Students, and Writers.* New York: Teachers and Writers Collaborative, 1984.

Publishing

Writer's Digest Books (Cincinnati, Ohio) annually publishes *Writer's Market, Poet's Market,* and *Fiction Writer's Market.* These volumes contain listings of small literary magazines, large-circulation magazines, and small and large publishing firms. The volumes include detailed information about the kinds of material each magazine or publisher is interested in, how open the editors are to newer writers, how to submit material for publication, and what different writers' conferences—in every region of the United States—have to offer. *The International Directory of Small Magazines and Little Presses,* also published annually, is another excellent resource, as is the *Writer's Guide to Book Editors, Publishers, and Literary Agents,* edited by Jeff Herman (Rocklin, CA: Prima Publishers, 1997). These books are widely available in bookstores and libraries.

Glossary of Selected Terms

Following is a list of terms found in *Metro*. Although many terms are often defined within the context of exercises, additional brief definitions are provided below.

Acrostic: A form of poetry. In an acrostic poem, the first letters of the lines spell out a word and sometimes even a phrase or sentence when read from top to bottom. For instance, you might write an acrostic poem in which the first letters of the lines spell out your name.

Action: In the context of fiction, the word refers to the occurrences in a story. Action may include any incident represented by the words in a story and need not concern only adventurous or violent behavior. Therefore, "action" in this context is not the same as the "action" in, for example, an "action film."

Allegory: Literature in which essential elements, such as characters, plot, setting, and situation, represent particular ideas, religious themes, or systems of values. In an allegorical poem, story, or novel, an extended parallel structure is established between the particular and the general; for instance, the figure of "Dante" in *Dante's Inferno* or of "Everyman" in *Everyman* invites comparison to "people in general" or at least "Christians in general," and the journey of such characters evokes the life-journey or spiritual journey of everyone. (Allegories, of course, are not limited to Christian cultures.) Whereas other kinds of literature may contain particular symbols, an allegory functions as an extended symbol, meant to represent an entire way of life, process of discovery, or central journey.

Alliteration: Repeated initial consonant sounds, particularly when these are stressed syllables and close to each other in a line of poetry. For example, in a poem by Mary Oliver, "Question," the following arrangement of words appears: "my horse, my hound." *Horse* and *hound* alliterate (initial stressed syllables). *My* and *my* repeat sounds exactly, obviously, and could be said to alliterate, but because they are unstressed syllables in this line of poetry, the repetition of sound is less forceful. Because the poetry of Gerard Manley Hopkins is filled with alliteration, it is an excellent "site" in which to study the technique.

Allusion: A reference that a work of literature or another kind of written text makes to other specific characters, persons, things, texts, events, and so on. Such a reference assumes a shared body of knowledge between writer and reader. For example, if a character in a story says, "I shall return," the author may be hoping that readers will recall that General Douglas McArthur said those exact words during World War II. An author who writes, "The world was all before them," is making an allusion to John Milton's *Paradise Lost*, which contains that sentence. The word should not be confused with "illusion."

Anecdote: A brief personal story, written or spoken. To describe an essay, for example, as "anecdotal" is to suggest that it is dominated by a narrative mode of rhetoric.

Antagonist: With regard to literature, the term refers to a character who is a source of trouble, destruction, or evil and who is usually in conflict with the protagonist or main character of a narrative. One simplistic expression of the antagonist/protagonist relationship is "the bad guys versus the good guys." See Nemesis and Protagonist.

Aphorism: A tersely worded nugget of wisdom or statement of principle. "What goes around, comes around" is an aphorism.

Associative: With regard to writing and reading, the word refers to a process of thinking or composing based not on a chain of reasoning but rather on "what comes to mind" intuitively.

Assonance: Repeated vowel sounds, as in "without my mount".

Autobiography: The study of one's own life, or parts thereof, presented in writing, such as a book, an essay, a diary, or a journal. An autobiography—as opposed to autobiography in general or "autobiographical writing"—chiefly refers to a book-length work by an author about his or her own life.

Blank verse: Unrhymed iambic pentameter verse; lines are counted off in five *iamb* feet (ten syllables, five accents—ta-DA) but rarely rhyme. The line, "But soft! What light through yonder window breaks?", from Shakespeare's *Romeo and Juliet,* is an example of blank verse and, implicitly, of iambic pentameter.

Caesura: A caesura is often used freely to mean a pause within a line of poetry—usually at a syntactical clause or phrase boundary. More technically, the term indicates the place a metrical break occurs, as happens in the intentional separation of strong accents within a line of Old English verse.

Canon: In the context of writing, literature, and criticism, a "canon" is an agreed-upon list of works or body of literature; however, agreement about the list or the works is often hard to achieve, fragile, or illusory.

Character: The illusion of a person, as created by the words in a story, a novel, a poem, or a play.

Cliché: An overused, unoriginal expression, idea, phrase, or theme. "Jumping from the frying pan into the fire" is an unoriginal expression, used countless times, to suggest a circumstance in which someone escapes one bad situation only to enter another one. Lack of originality and overuse make this expression an obvious cliché. See Stereotype.

Collage: In the context of visual art, a collage is a collection of images arranged in a jumbled, seemingly haphazard way, as when someone cuts out photographs from a magazine and pastes them on cardboard in a way that may at first seem chaotic. In writing, a "text-collage" is a seemingly jumbled list or arrangement of quotations, sentences, phrases, etc.

Combinatorial Play: From writer Italo Calvino, who suggested that writing is a process in which we toss words together until they make a spark that leads us down into that place in us where writing takes place, maybe the sub- or unconscious, or some other place where we have unfettered access to language.

Concrete Poetry: See Onomatopoeia.

Conflict: Drama and fiction are often said to depend on the conflict they represent. Such conflict might include a test of wills between characters, a collision in one character's life between illusion and reality, betrayal, economic or social friction between characters, violence or the threat of violence, and so on. See Crisis.

Couplet: In poetry, a two-line stanza. Often these lines are of the same "length"—containing, that is, the same number of syllables and the same pattern of meter. However, free verse can also be organized into couplets, in which case similarity of meter is not crucial. A heroic couplet is a closed couplet (finished with a period, semicolon, or other "end-stop") of rhymed iambic pentameter, most familiar as the final couplet of a Shakespearean sonnet and as the essential verse-unit in poems by Alexander Pope, such as "The Dunciad." Because rhymed couplets were often used in epic poems, which are long narrative poems containing at least one traditional hero, and in mock-epic poems such as "The Dunciad," they came to be called heroic couplets.

Creation Myth: An account of how "the world," humanity, or a specific people came to be. Stories of such original creation are part of every culture. Examples include the ancient Babylonian creation story, the Book of Genesis, and, from Native American culture, "How Coyote Got His Name."

Crisis: In the context of reading and writing fiction, the word refers to a point in a narrative when the conflict being dramatized is at its most intense—when a character, for example, is forced to make a choice, impelled to act, pushed into a significant, overwhelming, even life-changing realization. See Conflict and Epiphany.

Denouement: See Resolution.

Discursive: In the context of writing, the word refers to a kind of wandering, as in an essay that explores a topic and meanders toward conclusions about the topic, as opposed to starting with a firmly defined opinion or thesis.

Doppelgänger: German word that may be roughly translated as "the double." In the context of literature, it refers to representations of such "doubles" as split personalities, twins that share especially powerful psychic connections, or relationships that are figuratively twin-like. One of the most famous narratives of "the double" is Robert Louis Stevenson's *Dr. Jekyll and Mr. Hyde.* In this story, the extreme shift in personality is ostensibly caused by chemicals, but the narrative also contains potential symbolic features that comment on inner conflicts and psychic struggles in general.

Elegy: The term has distant roots in Greek literature but now chiefly refers to a type of poem that expresses a sustained lament—for a person that has died, for instance.

Epigraph: A sample of a published text, such as an excerpt or quoted lines of poetry, that usually appears after the title but before the body of the work.

Authors may use epigraphs to suggest one source of inspiration for, or make an oblique comment about, the work that follows.

Epiphany: In connection with fiction, the word refers to a moment in a narrative when a character experiences realization so intense that it is potentially life-changing. James Joyce is often credited with borrowing "epiphany" from its religious context and applying it to fiction, especially short fiction, and especially short fiction that concerned "the interior life"—psychological struggles, emotional upheaval, massive disillusionment.

Extended Metaphor: See Metaphor and Metaphysical Conceit.

Figurative: In the context of discussing language and literature, "figurative" refers to suggestive or metaphorical meaning a word may convey. For instance, if someone says, "I think I'll slide on over to John's house," the listener will probably realize instantly that the speaker means she or he will drive a car to John's house. Context is crucial, however. John's house may be located downhill in snowy country, and the speaker could be referring to the use of a sled, in which case the listener would take "slide" literally, not figuratively. See Metaphor.

Flashback: The word refers to when a narrative moves or "jumps" back to an earlier time, meaning that the plot proceeds out of chronological order, so that a story may begin with a scene in the "present time" of the narrative, jump back to an earlier time, then return to the "present time" with which the story began.

Focalization: With regard to fiction, the word represents a concept that complicates traditional ways of discussing point of view, and it suggests a triadic (three-way) relationship between a narrating agent (who narrates), a focalizer (who sees), and a focalized (what is seen). The five dimensions of focalization are: space, time, cognition, emotion and ideology.

Space: where the focalizer is positioned in relation to the focalized, or the narrating agent in relation to the focalizer. It is easy to see how a focalizer who sitting in the baseball stands will perceive and represent the game differently than one who has climbed a tree outside the park and is watching from high in its branches.

Time: where the focalizer is temporally positioned in relation to the focalized, or the narrating agent to either. A retrospective narrative is clearly different than one written in the present tense, and this an effect of time and focalization. It is useful to imagine time as a whole continuum, at any point on which the focalizer may look back, or forward, at what happened or will happen someday, and so may the narrating agent.

Cognition: what the focalizer can be expected to actually know about what is being focalized. If you weren't there, you can't really "know" it. The emotional and ideological components of the focalizing triad are characterized by varying degrees of consonance and dissonance among who is telling, who is seeing, and what is seen. In this sense, the narrative is strongly affected by how closely its narrating agent identifies with the feelings and beliefs of its focalizer.

Imagine, for example, different versions of an abortion story narrated by a right-to-life proponent, a supporter of "choice," and a doctor; or imagine a loss of virginity story narrated not by the girl who lost it, but by her lover or her mother, her doctor, her priest. See Point of View.

Found Poem: A poem made up almost entirely of discovered text. That is, one might find a grocery list someone has dropped on a sidewalk, and the list may seem so unusual or oddly phrased that it can be read as a poem. One might then title it and present it as a poem.

Free Verse: Beginning, it is often claimed, with Walt Whitman's poetry, writers discarded poetic conventions like set rhyme and regular meter. French poets and critics of the late nineteenth century actually coined the term (vers libre). Free verse, however, is not simply free and easy writing. Rather, it can work with rhythms of colloquial speech, concentrate on the visual shape of a poem on a page, improvise with traditional forms, draw inspiration from jazz, song, and other popular forms, and/or invent its own patterns of line and stanza. Important writers of free verse in the twentieth century include D.H. Lawrence, T.S. Eliot, William Carlos Williams, Marianne Moore, Elizabeth Bishop, Robert Creeley, Ted Hughes, Sylvia Plath, and Rita Dove, to name but a few.

Freewrite: As one might guess, to freewrite means to write freely—spontaneously and quickly. The main purpose of such writing is to generate ideas, images, and sentences without paying attention just yet to how correct or well formed the writing may be. Sometimes "freewrite" is used as a noun, meaning the product of spontaneous, rapid writing.

Genre: A synonym for "type" or "kind." In the context of literature, the word refers to different categories of literature. For example, "the novel" is a genre, and "drama" is another. Such categories can be broken down even further into "subgenres." For example, within the category of "novel" is the subgenre, "mystery novel." The terminology can get confused and confusing, however, because some critics refer to popular forms of the novel, such as science fiction and mystery novels, as "genre fiction" or "category fiction."

Ghazal: A poetic form featuring long-lined couplets, not necessarily rhymed. Generally ten to twenty-four lines in length, originally a Persian form, the ghazal traditionally develops mystical and/or romantic themes, may be monorhymed (aa, ba, ca, da) and/or include the poet's name in the last line.

Haiku: A form of poetry with roots in Shinto and Zen Buddhist spiritual traditions, the latter being a Japanese version of Buddhism, which began in India and then spread east to China and Japan. Buddhists seek enlightenment chiefly through introspection and intuition rather than through interpretation of a text or scripture. Haiku is a three-lined poem, with five, seven, and five syllables in each line, respectively. Haiku writers seek to capture a moment of perception. Haikus turn on strong natural images—using a word, called the kigo, that indicates the season—and relay intense emotions, often leading to spiritual insights. Japanese poet Matsuo Basho (1644–1694) is considered the premiere practitioner of the form. Contemporary haiku writers in English may drop the three-line stricture and/or not adhere strictly to the syllable count, in part because English and Japanese are so different.

Hermeneutics: The science of interpretation. Originally the word referred to interpreting the Bible, but it has been adopted by some literacy critics to refer to the interpretation of a wide variety of texts.

Histoire: A term from French criticism referring to the basic sequence of events in a story, events that might be summarized. The important companion term is *Recit*.

Historical Fiction: Fiction that is based on a general sense of or a record of events that actually happened. For example, Charles Dickens' novel, *A Tale of Two Cities*, is a fictional treatment of the French Revolution. Dickens combines a few facts with certain judgments, pays some attention to historical accuracy, but mostly invents characters, situations, plots, and subplots.

Homage: Deep respect. An homage is an expression of such respect—in a speech or in writing.

Hypercriticism: Refers to potentially rigid, narrow ideas about literature and other art forms. That is, some literary critics may express excessive antipathy toward popular literary forms, such as "romance" novels or science-fiction narratives.

Hypertext: A computer-assisted form of narrative that enables the reader to construct her own paths through a text. Click on hot links in the text and you can go anywhere you want. At the moment, hypertext presents itself as a radical new form of writing, but depends, for its circulation, on a highly specialized reader who not only has expertise in but also access to advanced technologies. The free and anonymous circulation of discourse widely touted by proponents of the Internet is, perhaps ironically, governed by its own new principles of limitation and exclusion. Still, it is difficult to overestimate the impact of electronic media on writing; this impact in some sense may turn out to be analogous to that of the long ago invention of the printing press.

Icon: The word denotes "image" but has taken on the connotation of "cultural symbol," so that a painting of Jesus Christ is not just a representation (image) of a man but a symbol of a complex history and cluster of religious beliefs. Nowadays, celebrities are sometimes referred to as "icons," representing attitudes, beliefs, values, and—of course—products. Some American literary critics in the 1930s, 1940s, and 1950s—among them, Cleanth Brooks and I.A. Richards—came to be known as the New Critics; they approached a work of literature as if it were a "verbal icon," an isolated construction of words, metaphors, images, allusions, and symbols, one job of the critic being to analyze the icon with a close, almost microscopic reading. See Metaphor, Sign, Symbol, and Talisman.

Implicit argument: A position or opinion that is only suggested, not plainly stated.

Inhabitation: Literally, the word means "the act of living in." In the context of writing and reading, it figuratively refers to "getting inside" a word, a form, or a genre to understand it deeply.

Inspiration: See Provocation.

Intertextuality: The word refers broadly to the ways in which a text (a poem, for example) might refer to, assimilate, or echo another text. See Allusion.

Invention: In the context of writing and rhetoric, the word refers essentially to "coming up with ideas."

Irony: A stance toward the world in language in which what is spoken or written is different (by intention or ignorance) from what the speaker or writer means. For example, one might be angry with a friend but instead of saying, "I'm angry," one says, "Thanks a lot." One would likely say the words sarcastically, sarcasm being one form of irony. In literature, a situation represented in a narrative can be ironic. For example, a character may believe he or she is exacting revenge on another character, but the vengeful act may be only self-destructive. In such a case, the narrative represents a distance between intention and consequence.

List poem: A poem with a structure that is based on the form of a list.

Literacy-biography: A nonfiction account of one's own reading habits, experiences with reading and writing, and/or material one has read.

Melodrama/Melodramatic: These terms are usually used pejoratively to describe a novel, short story, play, or film that is overly sentimental, "cheesy," trite, or predictable.

Metaphor: A figure of speech, a comparison of one thing to another. If the words "like" or "as" are used to complete the comparison, the writer has produced a different figure of speech, the simile. A conceit is a metaphor that goes beyond the equation of $X = Y$. Special terms used with a metaphor—tenor, vehicle, and ground. These come from the work of critic I.A. Richards. The tenor is considered the literal thing being referred to, the vehicle is the metaphorical (comparative term) and the ground is the relationship/similarities between the two. What sounds simple in definition here can be complicated in analytic application. In Robert Burns' line, "O my luve's like a red, red rose," "my luve" is the tenor, "a red, red rose" is the vehicle, and the ground between the two might concern beauty, youth, freshness, or fragility. As is often the case, therefore, the "ground" or connection is open to interpretation, potentially dissatisfying to readers, but also potentially ambiguous in a pleasing way. See Figurative, Metaphysical Conceit, Symbol, and Talisman.

Metaphysical conceit: John Donne, George Herbert, Andrew Marvell, and their seventeenth–century contemporaries have been termed metaphysical poets. Their metaphors were often highly intellectual, complicated, and detailed, requiring meditation by the reader to unpack the metaphor's possibilities, as in the John Donne poem "The Sun," where the lover is in mock battle with the power of the sun and claiming—because of the strength of his love—that he has, or should have, dominion over the sun. A metaphysical conceit is a particularly cerebral form of extended metaphor. See Metaphor.

Meter: Metered verse in English relies on patterns of syllables and stresses. For instance, in the word "A-choo!", there are two syllables, and in pronunciation, the second syllable, "choo," receives greater stress. All words in English receive particular syllabic stress, like par-TIC-u-lar. Poets can arrange stresses in patterns (poetic feet), and feet can be counted off: so many feet per line. The most common pattern in English verse has been iambic pentameter (da-Da-da-Da-da-Da-da-Da-da-Da) of five iambic (da-Da) feet.

Mimesis: Originally, a Greek word meaning "imitation." Aristotle used it to describe what he believed to be an important goal of poetry and, by extension, literature in general—namely, to represent, "imitate," or mirror life accurately. "Imitation" in this sense is different from imitating works of literature, such as practicing sonnet-writing by imitating one of Shakespeare's sonnets, using it as a model.

Modernism: "Modernism" (with a capital M) refers to a complex cluster of changes that literature and other arts underwent early in the twentieth century, roughly, between about 1910 and 1939. Perhaps the most condensed expression of Modernism is poet Ezra Pound's entreaty to writers, "Make it new." To simplify matters drastically, one might suggest that what Pound meant was that a new age required new forms of writing. The influence of Darwinian and Freudian thought, political upheavals such as the Bolshevic Revolution, the unprecedented horrors of World War I, and numerous other phenomena left many writers believing that previous models of the novel and poetry would not work in this "Modern" age. Contrasting specific works of Modernist literature complicates matters stupendously, however. For instance, some poems by Pound and T.S. Eliot are dense, difficult, fragmented, and highly allusive, whereas most poems by William Carlos Williams are accessible, spare, and colloquial. Similarly, James Joyce's *Ulysses,* William Faulkner's *Absalom, Absalom,* and Virginia Woolf's *Mrs. Dolloway* are extremely complicated, even daunting, narratives, whereas Ernest Hemingway's *The Sun Also Rises* is comfortably readable by comparison. What unites such widely different Modernist writers, then? First, they belong roughly to the same generation, reacting to the same cultural upheavals, and second, they all deliberately and self-consciously tried to "make it new": to experiment with style, form, subject matter, and/or attitudes and interpretations of the world—especially of contemporary events. See Postmodernism.

Narrator: With regard to stories and novels, the word refers to the effect of a "speaking" or telling voice through which the story appears to come to the reader. For example, John Updike is the author of the short story, "A & P," but the narrator is Sammy; that is, Updike created the effect of one "Sammy" telling a story in the first person ("I"). Sometimes the term "persona" is used in the place of "narrator," especially when a poem is under discussion, so that in Robert Frost's poem, "Stopping By Woods on a Snowy Evening," we might refer to a persona, distinct from Frost, who appears to be "telling" us the poem: "Whose woods these are I think I know . . . ."

Nemesis: An arch-rival.

Nostalgia: An emotion connected to a yearning for someone, something, some experience, or some state of being in the past.

Ode: A poem that celebrates, commemorates, and meditates on people or events. Originally odes were structured and written for choruses in Greek plays to sing or chant. In Pindaric odes, the chorus on stage speaks, then moves left, speaks again and moves right, and finishes with a third response. The left (strophe) and right (antistrophe) movements take the same stanza form and the final response (epode) differs. The Pindaric Ode evolved into the more meditative Horatian Ode composed in regular stanzas (having the same length, number of lines per stanza and rhyme scheme, if any rhyme is used). The Cowleyan ode is composed in free verse although it retains the lyrical and serious qualities of the ode in general.

Onomatopoeia: Describes an effect produced when poems seem to do what they are saying, when the poem imitates what it is saying. Often this is an auditory imitation—when the sound of the sea is represented by the words "salty, swishing, sliding waves," for instance. But these imitations can also be visual—when a long line echoes a discussion of the horizon or when lines are shaped to imitate the ebb and flow of a tide or to completely echo the subject of a poem, as in George Herbert's poem "Easter Wings," which appears typographically on the page in the shape of wings. Contemporary poets also embrace concrete poetry, where the typography is part of the content and the reader's apprehension of the poem. It is onomatopoeic when the dog in your poem barks "woof" as well as when you shape your poem into a dog-bone typographically or let the line talking about the dog's leash trail far out toward the right–hand margin of the page. Onomatopoeia can quickly become overly cute, or trite, but the onomatopoeic impulse can also underlie effective changes of pacing or wording in a poem.

Oxymoron: A figure of speech that joins or yokes together two seemingly contradictory or opposite things, often used ironically ("nonworking mother," for instance, or "cafeteria cuisine").

Parable: A short, relatively simple narrative designed to instruct or "teach a lesson."

Pantoum: Sixteen or more lines long, pantoums developed in Malayan literature as rhyming quatrains (abab) but developed in English as unrhymed quatrains with repeating lines: the second and fourth lines of each stanza repeat as the first and third lines of the next stanza.

Persona: See Narrator.

Plot: The specific arrangement of scenes, represented events, or increments of action that occur in a short story, a novel, or a play. One hundred writers would come up with one hundred different plots about the story of "a woman who falls in love with a vampire"—hence the distinction between "plot" and "story."

Plot-Twist: The term denotes a segment of a narrative in which the action shifts in a significant, surprising, or even shocking way. It has taken on the connotation of a predictable, overwrought, or unbelievable shift.

Poetic License: A term describing the freedom all writers, not just poets, have to play with facts or supplement them with imagination. For instance, although Charles Dickens' novel, *A Tale of Two Cities,* is based on aspects of the French Revolution, Dickens takes advantage of "poetic license" or imaginative freedom to invent characters, situations, plots, and subplots. One assumption underlying the term is that poets, writers of fiction, and playwrights, for instance, have more leeway than journalists or scientists in representing reality.

Poetry Slam: A public, competitive reading of poetry.

Point of View: With regard to fiction, there are at least two basic ways to think about point of view: 1) Whose story is it? 2) Who tells the story? In John Updike's oft-anthologized short story, "A & P," for example, Sammy is the chief character; the story is "his," chiefly because he is in the middle of the action and bears the brunt of the consequences resulting from what happens. He is also the teller of the story, the narrator, figuratively "speaking" in the first person ("I"). If Updike had chosen to use a third-person narrator, the story would still "belong" to Sammy, but Sammy would no longer be the "teller," even if the teller were to represent Sammy's thoughts. Critic Wayne Booth, in *The Rhetoric of Fiction*, provides an elaborate analysis of point of view. Structuralist and post-structuralist critics have, however, reconceived and disrupted these basic ways of thinking about point of view: See Focalization.

Postmodernism: This can be defined in relation to premodernism, that state of conviction in the natural, transparent capacity of language to reflect a shared view of reality, and Modernism, skeptical instead, in which language was turned to the purposes of art in an attempt to let the "atoms fall where they may" and reflect the subjective nature of experience. If, as critic Ortega y Gassett said, the realist (premodern) writer looks out the window to the world, and the modernist writer looks instead at the window and how the world is reflected in and through it, then the postmodern writer may be said to look at everything at once: the world outside, the glass, the frame, the window coverings, and the very process of looking. Postmodernism, often expressed as assemblage or collage, jams things together, and in so doing, calls attention not just to their convergences, but to the artificial construct by which they are produced. See Collage and Modernism.

Prose Poem: A block-shaped, (usually) paragraphed text that relies on poetic techniques of imagery, condensed language, rhythmic, repetitive, often rhymed language, and that often makes its point via metaphor, analogy or association, yet still may partake of fictional techniques like character building, plot, dialogue, and so on. Among numerous writers, American poets Karl Shapiro and Robert Bly have used this form extensively.

Protagonist: In the context of literature, the word is one very traditional way of referring to the main character of a narrative or a play. Sometimes the words "hero" or "heroine" are used similarly, but protagonists need not be heroic; they need not be brave, and they may be ordinary and flawed.

Provocation: Refers, in the context of writing, to anything that ignites one's passion and will to write. Events, ideas, exercises, any printed matter, music, arguments, and controversies are all potential sources of such provocation, which has slightly more aggressive connotations than "inspiration."

Quatrain: A poetic stanza of four lines, the most common stanza form in English poetry. Quatrains consist of four lines of verse, rhymed or unrhymed; the envelope quatrain rhyme runs abba, the couplet quatrain runs aabb, the alternating quatrain runs abab, and the monorhyme quatrain runs aaaa.

Recit: Term from French criticism used to describe the actual words on the page that convey the telling of a story. It is used in contrast to *histoire,* which refers to the general story or "story-line," as opposed to the actual execution, in words, of the story, story line, or story idea.

Resolution: The term refers to the way the specific plot of a story, novel, or play sorts out the conflict and action represented in the work. For example, the conflict and action of Herman Melville's novel, *Moby Dick,* concerns a sea captain's obsessive desire to kill the white whale. The plot "resolves" the conflict in part by having Ahab destroyed by the whale. The French term for resolution is denouement.

Rhyme: Full rhyming words have different initial consonants, similar vowel sounds, followed by similar consonant sounds. This is a complicated way of showing how moon and June rhyme—m and J are different initial consonants, oo and u are similar vowel sounds and n and ne are similar consonant sounds. In slant rhyme, the vowel sound is not exact (also called half rhyme): cloth/growth, out/mouth. Rhymes can come in one, two, and three or more syllables. Hit/sit, plastic/drastic, librarian/agrarian; three-syllable rhymes seem to move inevitably toward the humorous.

Sign: There are many kinds of semiotic systems, where meaning proceeds from the organization of meaning-making signs (sports, fashion, traffic, report cards, you name it). Here we are concerned with the linguistic sign, which consists of an arbitrary relation between a sound image, signifier—like saying the word tree—and a concept, signified—like the idea of treeness. Together, these two elements create a linguistic sign. Think, for instance, of two sides of a piece of paper; you can't have one without the other, but you can cut it up and still have the paper.

So the sign does not name or articulate a one-to-one correspondence between the signifier and the signified, but is instead: 1) arbitrary—not dependent on any prior logic— 2) relational—meaning itself exists only as a play of similarity, placement and difference between the signifier and the signified—and 3) conventional—governed by a series of agreements within community of speakers. Put another way, culturally we "agree" that tree has a relational correspondence to treeness. Thinking about signs and signifiers can be appealing, but it can also be confusing and frustrating, as all philosophizing can, partly because we are so accustomed to using language and are so busy "just using it" that pausing to ponder how words (signs) work can seem bothersome.

But for the theorist Saussure, the critical relation of language use is one of binary opposition, which enables us to say that we know what things are by what they are not. Opposition depends on principles of exchange, one thing for another—money for bread, "p" for "b." This is not to be confused with the concept of difference, which exists, on the other hand, among synonyms. Fear, dread and anxiety, for example, are different but fungible, or "in the same ballpark." Any one of these words could disappear from the language and we would not notice; but, if the concept of fear itself disappeared, what would happen to the concept of bravery? Or, the concept of, say, blueness, which we will agree on until we reach the point along the whole continuum of color where blue, in an instant, becomes not blue. For Saussure, that point of binary opposition is the critical point, for it is where meaning is made possible. For writers, especially women, the point is more problematic, for just as opposition has functioned in linguistic levels to enable meaning to take place, it has functioned at metaphysical levels to organize systems of Western thought:

god/man	law/chaos
man/woman	sun/moon
heaven/earth	light/dark
self/other	culture/nature
subject/object	good/evil
presence/absence	man/woman

and so on.

These are easily apprehended as hierarchical oppositions, in which the male pole is always privileged over the female, and for this reason, binarism—as elegant a structure as it might be, as efficient an organization—is suspect by some feminist thinkers, who envision a more fluid both/and vision as preferable to the multiple constraints of such either/or logic.

Why should we think about language in these terms at all? Shouldn't writers leave this to linguists, and ply instead the trade of their unfettered imaginations? One might say two things: 1) this kind of thinking is a critical first step toward helping us begin to understand language's slippery faultlines, its many complexities, and 2) structural linguistics provides an extremely valuable model for structural narratology (the study of the deep structures underlying stories), which is one useful system for thinking about narrative.

Sonnet: A traditional form of lyric poetry that has enjoyed widespread use in numerous languages. The eight-line octave is followed by the six-line sestet. The Italian sonnet consists of an octave rhyming abbaabba and a sestet rhyming cdcdcd. The English sonnet, which developed out of the Italian, consists of fourteen lines of iambic pentameter verse: three quatrains and a closing couplet, with the rhyme scheme of abab cdcd efef gg. William Shakespeare mastered this form, infusing it with subtle irony and elaborate word play. Poets have always adapted this structure, observing most consistently only its fourteen-line length. See Meter and Rhyme.

Speculative Fiction: Novels or short stories that take an historical event, begin with the premise, "What if this event had turned out differently?", and invent a story that dramatizes possible consequences of that premise. For example, some speculative novels begin with the premise that Germany prevailed in World War II.

Sprung Rhythm: Refers to experiments that British poet Gerard Manley Hopkins made with meter and sound in his poetry. Instead of using traditional verse-patterns of meter, Hopkins "jammed" several stressed syllables together, often creating even more powerful stresses by means of alliteration. Among his "sprung-rhythm" poems are "The Windhover" and "God's Grandeur." See Alliteration and Meter.

Stanza: A grouping of lines in a poem that forms a distinct unit. For instance, a poem might begin with three lines, followed by a distinct space, followed by three more lines, and so on. Customarily, each group of (in this case) three lines would be called a stanza. In free verse especially, stanzas do not always contain the same number of lines.

Stereotype/Stereotypical: Refers to an overly simplistic description of a person, a character, an institution, or an event. For example, we have read about (or seen in movies) a tough-talking, trench-coat-clad private detective so many times that such a character has become a stereotype, a two-dimensional representation with which we may feel we are too familiar. When writers do not provide enough specific, original detail, or when they rely on formulas of character, plot, or scene, they often produce material that readers will find stereotypical, more a product of formula than of imagination. Some, certainly not all, stereotypes may spring from bigotry, prejudice, or narrow-mindedness. See Cliché.

Supplement/Supplementarity: In the context of language and narrative, the term comes from Jacques Derrida. It suggests that when we use language, we constantly substitute one term or concept for another. In other words, in the process of making meaning, we take a linguistic sign and replace it with another, but then the original sign that we started with is slightly different—supplemented—and so we must begin the process of replacement again, with the same result. In this way, meaning is endlessly deferred, and becomes something like pure play, the thing that gives us both a kind of pleasure and an organizational structure, rather than where it was headed in the first place—a final meaning—where it might, theoretically, have stopped, except that the very thing that allows it to exist in the first place—its play—prevents it ever from stopping. For example, imagine the *Oxford English Dictionary* (OED), which publishes an annual supplement. Each year it is the definitive dictionary, containing all authorized words. Then the next year comes, and more words are added to its Supplement. Together, the OED plus its supplement continue to be the definitive dictionary, but it is no longer the same, because it has been added to. It is easy to see how this process perpetually defers a final signified—a definitive dictionary. In this case, at least according to Derrida, that's how language works.

Surrealism: A movement to free thought from reason through automatic writing, attention to dream-states, and experimentation with free associational play. French poet and editor Andre Breton was considered a main spokesperson for the movement. In 1924 he published the *Manifesto* of surrealism, and in the 1940s he came to the United States and published the magazine, *vv*. A surrealist movement in painting occurred as well. In poetry, well-known practitioners include Breton, Charles Baudelaire, Arthur Rimbaud, Steven Malarme, Fredrico Garcia Lorca, and later Pablo Neruda, Robert Bly, John Ashbery, and

James Tate. In his book, *Leaping Poetry*, Robert Bly includes surrealistic poems from several countries and also speculates about differences between French surrealism and surrealism in Spanish and Latin American poetry. Works by artists Salvador Dali, Juan Miro, and Rene Magrette are representative of the breadth of surrealist painting.

Suspense: In the context of fiction and other narratives, the word refers to an effect of uncertainty created by the story. A classic example of suspense occurs in mystery or crime fiction when, in the story, someone has been murdered but the narrative has not yet revealed the murderer. The identity of the murderer is held in suspense. Virtually all narratives depend upon some kind of suspense or delay. When the delay seems excessive, readers often get bored, literally tired of waiting. When the delay seems insufficient, readers may respond by saying that the author seemed to "give the story away": to reveal too much too soon. When we are reading quickly, with the sense that the delay is pleasurable but that we would like to know, soon, how a narrative or a segment therein is going to turn out, then the suspense or delay is probably operating as the writer intended it to.

Syllabic Verse: Line length in syllabic poems is fixed by syllable count—say ten per line—or in a shaped pattern, as the 5, 7, 5, syllable pattern that signals a Western haiku. British poet Robert Bridges worked extensively in syllabic verse. See Haiku.

Symbol: Something that stands for something else, as when a flag stands for a nation. In the context of literature or writing, a symbol is an image, character, object, or place (for example) that represents something else or something more. For instance, fall leaves may be described so as to symbolize the passing of time or even death. Also, cultural symbols, such as the Christian cross or a Native American eagle-feather, may be "imported" into a work of literature, given a specific narrative, dramatic, or poetic function, one that may even be ironic. See Figurative, Metaphor, and Talisman.

Synecdoche: One part standing for the whole—sunbeams, for example, standing for the heat and force of the sun, or an individual for a group.

Syntax: The specific arrangement of words, especially in a sentence, clause, or phrase. The syntax of the sentence, "I like you very much," is unsurprising and conventional. "Very much I like you," although it contains precisely the same words, is jarring because we are not used to seeing these words in this relationship to one another.

Talisman: An object that people, such as the owner of the object, believe to have power beyond its functional use. For example, someone may believe that his or her key-chain is "lucky," in which case the key-chain has become a talisman, more than a metal holder of keys. See Metaphor and Symbol.

Tanka (Also called waka or uta): A traditional Japanese poem that is rendered in English in five lines of 5, 7, 5, 7, 7 syllables, respectively. Historically, tankas were combined with prose, linked together, and/or published to include exchanges of verse between poets. Subjects vary but often center on travel, love, and the seasons. As with haiku, in Japan today there are regular tanka competitions and a continuing appreciation of this form.

Tercet: Three line stanzas. When all three lines of rhyme, tercets become triplets. When the rhyme patterns interlock, like this—aba, bcb, cdc (linking stanzas)—the tercet turns into terza rima. See Rhyme.

Terzanelle: A nineteen line poem divided into six stanzas—five interlocking triplets and a quatrain. Of French and Italian origin, it adapts terza rima to the villanelle form by the use of a repeton: A1BA2, bCB, cDC, dED, eFE, fA1 (or F) F (or A1) A2 (A1 and A2 are refrains; BCDEF are repetons).

Thing Poem: A poem of which "the subject is an object"—an inanimate object such as a tool or a building—but also perhaps an animate object, such as an animal or insect. The poem might represent the object in a careful, closely observed way, as William Carlos Williams' "The Red Wheel Barrow" does. Or it might focus on the object but then use it as a vehicle to meditate on ideas or emotions, as John Keats' "Ode on a Grecian Urn" does. Other thing poems express free associations/impressions that spring from observation. Poems of this sort are sometimes surrealistic: Robert Bly's "The Dead Seal" and "The Dried Sturgeon" are good examples, as are many poems by Charles Simic, including "The Stone."

Triggering Subject: In Richard Hugo's book, *The Triggering Town,* the term "triggering subject" refers to that source within the writer that makes her want to write. All writers have one, Hugo says, and for him it was a small town in the American West that has seen better days and is in decline. It is a potentially useful metaphor because it works to demystify classic theories of the muse, however much it still defers to certain received ideas of inspiration. But Hugo further maintains that every writer has as well an idiosyncratic, highly personal sense of language, and that learning how to write is a process of transferring allegiance from the triggering subject to personal language, what marks each writer's writing as her own.

Truism: A widely accepted concept, belief, or idea.

Villanelle: A nineteenth-line poem divided into six stanzas—five tercets and one quatrain turning on two rhymes and built on two refrains: A1bA2, abA1, abA2, abA1, abA2, and abA1A2 (A1 and A2 are refrains).

Writers' Workbook: A space for writing anything, really, for the literal collecting and collaging of the writer's observations, way of thinking, mind. What is overheard or imagined, snatches of language and thought. Also, for doodling and drawing, for lodging tiny bits of detritus from life. Some writers keep a tiny notebook they carry everywhere with them. Here they write things down on the fly.

Acknowledgments

Alexander, Michael. "Appendix B: Suggested Solutions to the Riddles" from *The Earliest English Poems,* translated by Michael Alexander (Penguin Classics 1966, Third edition 1191) copyrights © Michael Alexander, 1966, 1977, 1991. Reproduced by permission of Penguin Books Ltd.

Alexander, Michael. From *The Earliest English Poems,* translated by Michael Alexander (Penguin Classics 1966, Third edition 1191) copyrights © Michael Alexander, 1966, 1977, 1991. Reprinted by permission of Penguin Books Ltd.

Alexander, Michael. "Riddle No 25" from *The Earliest English Poems,* translated by Michael Alexander (Penguin Classics 1966, Third edition 1191) copyrights © Michael Alexander, 1966, 1977, 1991. Reprinted by permission of Penguin Books Ltd.

Alexander, Michael. "Riddle No 25" from *The Earliest English Poems,* translated by Michael Alexander (Penguin Classics 1966, Third edition 1191) copyrights © Michael Alexander, 1966, 1977, 1991. Reproduced by permission of Penguin Books Ltd.

Auden, W. H. "Musée des Beaux Arts" from *W. H. Auden: Collected Poems* by W. H. Auden, edited by Edward Mendelson. Copyright © 1940 and renewed 1968 by W. H. Auden. Reprinted by permission of Random House, Inc.

Baker, Will. "End Note" by Will Baker, teacher, writer, farmer.

Baker, Will. "My Children Explain the Big Issues" by Will Baker. Copyright © 1993 by Will Baker. From *Whole Earth Review,* Summer, 1993. Reprinted by permission of the author.

Bishop, Wendy. "Horoscope Imperatives" by Wendy Bishop was first published in *The Ohio Poetry Review* 2.1 (Spring/Summer 1995). Reprinted by permission of the author.

Bloomfield, Lisa/Katharine Haake, map/index, 1995, Iris ink jet prints, 22" × 30" each panel. Reprinted by permission.

Carpenter, Jill. "Consanguinity" by Jill Carpenter from *Creative Nonfiction,* Vol. 1, issue 1. Copyright © 1993 by Creative Nonfiction. Reprinted by permission of the publisher.

Chin, Marilyn. "Where We Live Now" by Marilyn Chin. Copyright © 1987 by Marilyn Chin. First appeared in *Dwarf Bamboo,* 1987, The Greenfield Review Press, Greenfield Center, NY 12833. Reprinted by permission of the publishers.

Cogswell, Grant. "Paris in '73" by Grant Cogswell as appeared in *Northridge Review,* Spring, 1988. Reprinted by permission of the author.

Cook, Devan. "Jazz, Fried Okra Afternoon" by Devan Cook. Reprinted by permission of the author.

Cullen, Countee. "Black Magdalens" by Countee Cullen. Reprinted by permission of GRM Associates, Inc., agents for the Estate of Ida M. Cullen. From the book *Color* by Countee Cullen. Copyright © 1925 by Harper & Brothers; copyright renewed 1953 by Ida M. Cullen.

Frost, Robert. "Design" from *The Poetry of Robert Frost,* edited by Edward Connery Lathem. Copyright © 1969 by Henry Holt and Co., copyright 1936 by Robert Frost,©1964 by Lesley Frost Ballantine. Reprinted by permission of Henry Holt and Company, LLC.

Haake, Katharine. "Arrow Math" by Katharine Haake. First published in *Michigan Quarterly Review.* © 1995 by Katharine Haake. Reprinted by permission of the author.

Hacker, Marilyn. "Fourteen" by Marilyn Hacker in *Assumptions.* Reprinted by permission of Frances Collin Literary Agent. Copyright © 1985 by Marilyn Hacker.

Hawkins, Hunt. "Mourning the Dying American Female Names" is from *The Domestic Life,* by Hunt Hawkins, © 1994. Reprinted by permission of the University of Pittsburgh Press.

Hughes, Langston. "Harlem (2)" from *Collected Poems* by Langston Hughes. Copyright © 1994 by the Estate of Langston Hughes. Reprinted by permission of Alfred A. Knopf, a Division of Random House, Inc.

Iyer, Pico. "In Praise of the Humble Comma" by Pico Iyer as appeared in *Time Magazine,* 6/13/88. Copyright © 1988 Time Inc. Reprinted by permission.

Jones, Mary Paumier. "Meander" by Mary Paumier Jones from *Creative Nonfiction,* Vol. 1, issue 1. Copyright © 1993 by Creative Nonfiction. Reprinted by permission of the publisher.

Krusoe, Nancy. "Landscape and Dream" by Nancy Krusoe. First published in *The Georgia Review.* Copyright © 1993 by Nancy Krusoe. Reprinted by permission of the author.

Kumin, Maxine. "Appetite," from *Selected Poems 1960–1990* by Maxine Kumin. Copyright © 1998 by Maxine Kumin. New York: W. W. Norton & Company, Inc.

Lee, Chang-rae. From "Coming Home Again." This article originally appeared in *The New Yorker,* October 16, 1995. Reprinted by permission of International Creative Management, Inc. Copyright © 1995.

Lee, Li-Young. "Eating Together" copyright © 1986 by Li-Young Lee. Reprinted from *Rose,* by Li-Young Lee with the permission of BOA Editions, Ltd.

Lorde, Audre. "Learning To Write", from *Our Dead Behind Us* by Audre Lorde. Copyright © 1986 by Audre Lorde. Used by permission of W. W. Norton & Company, Inc.

Marré, Diana. "A Really Big Shoe" by Diana Marré Copyright © 1990 by Diana Marré Reprinted with permission of the author.

Matthews, Jack. "A Questionnaire for Rudolph Gordon" by Jack Matthews. First published in *The Malahat Review,* #39, July, 1976. Reprinted by permission of the author.

Meinke, Peter. "this is a poem to my son peter" from *The Night Train and the Golden Bird,* by Peter Meinke, © 1977. Reprinted by permission of the University of Pittsburgh Press.

Moody, Rick. "Primary Sources" from *The Ring of Brightest Angels Around* by Rick Moody. Copyright © 1995 by Rick Moody. By permission of Little, Brown and Company (Inc.).

Nasrin, Taslima. "Character" by Taslima Nasrin, translated from the Bengali by Carolyne Wright and Farida Sarkar. This article originally appeared in *The New Yorker,* August 22–29, 1994.

Neruda, Pablo. "Arte Poética" by Pablo Neruda. Reprinted from *Neruda and Vallejo: Selected Poems,* edited by Robert Bly, Beacon Press, Boston, 1971, 1993. Copyright © 1993 Robert Bly. Reprinted with his permission.

Neruda, Pablo. "The Art of Poetry" by Pablo Neruda. Reprinted from *Neruda and Vallejo: Selected Poems,* edited by Robert Bly, Beacon Press, Boston, 1971, 1993. Copyright © 1993 Robert Bly. Reprinted with his permission.

O'Brien, Tim. "How to Tell a True War Story" from *The Things They Carried.* Copyright © 1990 by Tim O'Brien. Reprinted by permission of Houghton Mifflin Co./Seymour Lawrence. All rights reserved.

Ostrom, Hans. "Anomalies in Relief: Notes of a California Expatriate" by Hans Ostrom. Copyright © 1999 by Hans Ostrom. Reprinted by permission of the author.

Ostrom, Hans. "Of Reading" by Hans Ostrom. Copyright © 1999 by Hans Ostrom. Reprinted by permission of the author.

Paley, Grace. Reprinted by permission of Farrar, Straus and Giroux, LLC. "A Conversation with My Father" from *The Collected Stories* by Grace Paley. Copyright © 1994 by Grace Paley.

Pinsky, Robert. "Sonnet" from *The Want Bone* by Robert Pinsky. Copyright © 1991 by Robert Pinsky. Reprinted by permission of HarperCollins Publishers, Inc.

Plath, Sylvia. From "Metaphors" from *Crossing the Water* by Sylvia Plath. Copyright © 1960 by Ted Hughes. Copyright Renewed. Reprinted by permission of HarperCollins Publishers, Inc. and Faber & Faber Ltd.

Shapiro, Karl. "Drug Store" by Karl Shapiro. © Karl Shapiro, *Collected Poems 1940–1978,* by permission of Wieser & Wieser, Inc, New York, New York.

Silkeberg, Marie. From *Black Mercury* by Marie Silkeberg, Akustik Alhambra. Stockholm: Bonniers, 1994. Translated from the Swedish by Hans Ostrom. Copyright © 1999 by Hans Ostrom. Reprinted by permission of Hans Ostrom.

Skloot, Floyd. "My Daughter Considers Her Body" by Floyd Skloot. First appeared in *Southern Poetry Review* (Fall 1979). Reprinited by permission of Southern Poetry Review.

Taylor, Sheila Ortiz. "Re/Collection" from *Imaginary Parents,* University of New Mexico Press. Copyright © 1996 by Sheila Ortiz Taylor. Reprinted by permission of the publisher.

Taylor, Sheila Ortiz. "Street Map" from *Imaginary Parents,* University of New Mexico Press. Copyright © 1996 by Sheila Ortiz Taylor. Reprinted by permission of the publisher.

Turkle, Ann. From "Cheetos" by Ann Turkle. Reprinted by permission of the author.

Williams, William Carlos. "The Children" by William Carlos Williams, from *Collected Poems 1939–1962,* Volume II, copyright © 1962 by William Carlos Williams. Reprinted by permission of New Directions Publishing Corp.

Williams, William Carlos. "This is Just to Say" by William Carlos Williams, from *Collected Poems: 1909-1939, Volume I,* copyright © 1938 by New Directions Publishing Corp. Reprinted by permission of New Directions Publishing Corp.

Wright, Richard. "The Library Card" from *Black Boy* by Richard Wright. Copyright, 1937, 1942, 1944, 1945 by Richard Wright. Copyright renewed 1973 by Ellen Wright. Reprinted by permission of HarperCollins Publishers, Inc.

Index

Note: Titles of poems, essays, book-chapters, and short stories appear in quotation marks. Titles of books—such as autobiographies, works of criticism, and novels—appear in italics, as do titles of plays, works of cinema, and magazines. For works that are reprinted completely in *Metro*, a number in **bold** print indicates the page on which the work begins. Numbers not in bold type indicate pages on which a work is mentioned, cited, and/or excerpted.